Practices and Principles

Practices and Principles

APPROACHES TO ETHICAL

AND LEGAL JUDGMENT

MARK TUNICK

PRINCETON UNIVERSITY PRESS

PRINCETON NEW JERSEY

Library of Congress Cataloging-in-Publication Data

Tunick, Mark.
Practices and Principles : approaches to ethical and legal
judgment / Mark Tunick.
p. cm.
Includes bibliographical references and index.
ISBN 0-691-01560-0 (cloth : alk. paper)
1. Sociological jurisprudence.   2. Law and ethics.   3. Kant,
Immanuel, 1724–1804.   4. Hegel, Georg Wilhelm Friedrich, 1770–1831.
I. Title.
K370.T86   1998   340'.112—dc21   97-29599   cip

This book has been composed in Berkeley Book Modified

Princeton University Press books are printed on acid-free paper and meet the guidelines for
permanence and durability of the Committee on Production Guidelines for Book
Longevity of the Council on Library Resources

http://pup.princeton.edu

Printed in the United States of America

1 2 3 4 5 6 7 8 9 10

FOR SARAH AND RACHEL TUNICK

CONTENTS

Practices and Principles

Introduction

THE PROBLEM

There are many things we would like to do or have but can't. Sometimes what holds us back is want of ability, time, money, or other resources. Salieri wanted Mozart's fame but couldn't earn it. Roghozhin wanted Nastasya Filippovna, but there are some things his money couldn't buy. Other times we have the power to satisfy our inclinations, but something else holds us back: the idea that doing what we would like is morally wrong or socially inappropriate. There are times when doing what we would like is to fail to discharge an obligation or fulfill a duty we have, is to act badly. For some of us, that is a sufficient constraint, as powerful a hindrance to fulfilling our desire as physical incapacity. For others, the idea that doing something is unethical, or is to act badly, in itself is not a powerful deterrent, and becomes one only when a formidable sanction is attached, a sanction such as legal punishment or the loss of our friends' respect or trust.

I am concerned in this book with these ethical and legal constraints. There are many questions to be asked about them: How do they arise? How do we distinguish those that are justified from those that are unjustified and coercive impositions by those with power? Is it rational to be deterred by judgments that are not backed by force of law or threat of social sanction? While these questions are all important, this book focuses on still another: How do we decide what ethics and the law require? As we shall see, it is often not clear what is required to be moral or, where actions come under the purview of the law, what the law requires.

Within a society that shares moral traditions and social practices, there may be disagreement about what these traditions and practices require. Members of my society are brought up learning the practice of promising. But suppose I make a promise to you that you don't really care if I keep; or I make a promise to someone who has since died: am I obligated to keep it? Many of us disagree about the answer, even though we were taught the same practice. Members of my society value privacy, and our Constitution expresses this value by prohibiting the government from invading our privacy with unreasonable, warrantless searches.[1] Yet members of my society, including the judges and Supreme Court justices charged with interpreting the Constitution, disagree about what counts as a reasonable search and therefore about what the right of privacy entails. A majority of justices

---

[1] "The right of the people to be secure in their persons, houses, papers, and effects, against unreasonable searches and seizures, shall not be violated, and no Warrants shall issue, but upon probable cause, supported by Oath or affirmation, and particularly describing the place to be searched, and the persons or things to be seized" (U.S. Constitution, Amendment IV).

have declared that warrantless searches of garbage left for curbside pickup or of a person's backyard greenhouse from a helicopter hovering overhead do not violate reasonable expectations of privacy; yet vigorous dissents, as well as surveys by social scientists and commentaries by legal scholars, show that this understanding of reasonableness is sharply contested.[2]

We find disagreement about what ethics and the law require not only among members of societies with shared traditions and practices, but between members of different societies. For example, the Romans and Greeks commonly exposed freeborn infants, leaving them in the open either to die or to be taken in by strangers. While other societies, ours included, find this practice repulsive, the Greeks and the Romans thought it odd that Egyptians, Germans, and Jews raised all their children rather than exposing some.[3]

Still another sort of disagreement, of increasing importance given the increasing cultural diversity of our society, is the disagreement about what ethics and law require among members of the same society who come from different ethnic and cultural backgrounds—disagreement among people who live in the same territory, are subject to the same laws, and may even be fellow citizens, but who have different traditions and practices. For example, Fumiko Kimura, a Japanese mother living in California, recently attempted *oyako-shinju*, or parent-child suicide, to rid herself of shame on learning that her husband had supported a mistress. While she herself did not die, her two children drowned in the attempt. The Japanese community had petitioned to apply Japanese law, arguing a defense of cultural difference. The mother, it was argued, should be tried not by the standards and law of the United States but by the standards she was raised to live by. If the point of punishment is to mete out just deserts, the argument went, there would be no point punishing her with the full force of the law. She was not acting with malice or even acting badly. Rather, she was behaving properly according to the standards of her own culture. The argument has some force, yet is also troubling—the ambivalence we may feel was apparent in the eventual judgment. The Japanese community sought involuntary manslaughter charges and probation. Kimura was eventually convicted of voluntary manslaughter, which can bring a maximum of thirteen years in prison, but was sentenced only to one year in jail and five years probation and was ordered to undergo psychiatric treatment.[4] We may feel that drowning one's children is simply wrong and that

---

[2] See *California v. Greenwood,* 486 US 35 (1988)—garbage search upheld, 6–2 decision; *Florida v. Riley,* 488 US 445 (1989)—helicopter search upheld, 5–4 decision; and the discussion in chapter five.

[3] Philippe Ariès and Georges Duby, eds., *A History of Private Life* (Cambridge: Belknap Press, Harvard University, 1987), 1:9.

[4] See *People v. Kimura,* A-091133, Superior Court of Los Angeles; reported in *National Law Journal,* Aug. 5, 1985, 1; Nov. 4, 1985; and Apr. 27, 1989. Kimura's defense counsel cast his appeal in terms of temporary insanity, relying not on a free-standing cultural defense but on existing American definitions of psychiatric defenses; but appeal was made to how "the roots of her Japanese culture" directed Kimura's behavior. See Holly Maguigan, "Cultural Evidence and Male Violence: Are Feminist and Multiculturalist Reformers on a Collision Course in Criminal Courts?" *New York University Law Review* 70 (1995): 68; and "Comment: A Place for Consideration of Culture in the American Criminal Justice

the fact that some people engage in this practice does not justify it. We may feel there are principles by which we can criticize such objectionable practices. Yet there is also force in the argument that people live by different codes and standards, and that it would be unfair to judge them by standards not their own. In *Ex Parte Crow Dog,* the defendant sought a writ of habeus corpus after having been charged with the murder of a fellow Native American. The defendant argued that he should not be tried by federal law and in a "white man's court," and the Supreme Court was sympathetic. Justice Matthews wrote:

> [The law, here,] is sought to be extended over aliens and strangers; over the members of a community separated by race, by tradition, by the instincts of a free though savage life, from the authority and power which seeks to impose upon them the restraints of an external and unknown code, and to subject them to the responsibilities of civil conduct, according to rules and penalties of which they could have no previous warning; which judges them by a standard made by others and not for them, which takes no account of the conditions which should except them from its exactions, and makes no allowances for their inability to understand it. It tries them, not by their peers, nor by the customs of their people, nor the law of the land, but by superiors of a different race, according to the law of a social state of which they have an imperfect conception, and which is opposed to the traditions of their history, to the habits of their lives, to the strongest prejudices of their savage nature; one which measures the red man's revenge by the maxims of the white man's morality.[5]

There is great force in this argument, yet it is also deeply troubling. Are we completely to excuse behavior unacceptable to us because it is accepted elsewhere? Congress did not think so and responded to *Ex Parte Crow Dog* with new legislation to avoid future jurisdictional loopholes.[6] In later cases the Supreme Court has been less tolerant of evidence concerning cultural difference. In *U.S. v. Reynolds,* the Court upheld a law prohibiting polygamy in the territories even though polygamy is an accepted practice of the Mormons.[7] Chief Justice Waite offered an argument just as compelling as Justice Matthews's:

> Laws are made for the government of actions, and while they cannot interfere with mere religious belief and opinions, they may with practices. Suppose one believed that human sacrifices were a necessary part of religious worship, would it be seriously contended that the civil government under which he lived could not interfere to prevent a sacrifice? Or if a wife religiously believed it was her duty to burn herself upon the funeral pile of her dead husband . . . ?

System: Japanese Law and the Kimura Case," *Detroit College of Law Journal of International Law and Practice* 4 (1995): 515: "Oyako-shinju rarely results in harsh penalties in the event the parent survives. Mitigation articles in the [Japanese] Penal Code are usually employed by the courts so that the survivor receives either a short prison term or probation."

[5] 109 US 556 (1883), at 571.

[6] 23 Stats 362, 385, Sec. 9, Mar. 3, 1885. Discussed in Lawrence Friedman, *Crime and Punishment in American History* (New York: Basic Books, 1993), 98.

[7] 98 US 145 (1878).

If we believed this, then in effect we "permit every citizen to become a law unto himself."[8]

Recent court cases in the United States have been divided between tolerance for and rejection of cultural evidence, some taking the position of Justice Matthews, others, that of Chief Justice Waite. In one case a Chinese immigrant was given five years probation for the beating death of his wife in New York. The husband had learned she was sleeping with another man and hit her eight times over the head with a hammer. The sentence imposed on the husband relied on evidence that in his culture a wife's adultery brings great shame. The sentence was the lightest allowed for the reduced charge of second-degree manslaughter.[9] However, about ten years ago in Los Angeles, Vietnamese men were prosecuted for beating their wives even though this was accepted practice in their culture. Cultural evidence failed to pursuade the courts, and the result has been that word of the enforcement of American law has spread among the Vietnamese community, and the beatings seemed to subside.[10] In this case at least it was possible for nonnatives to understand the law and adapt to it though it was, in Justice Matthews's words, "opposed to the traditions of their history, to the habits of their lives, to the strongest prejudices of their savage nature."

Faced with disagreement about what ethics and law require of us, where are we to turn? Justice Matthews and those sympathetic to the defense of cultural difference would turn to our traditions, habits, prejudices, and practices. Apart from the problem that a person might adhere to conflicting practices and belong to conflicting traditions, and that disagreement can arise even from within a practice or coherent set of traditions, this position is open to the criticism, ringing through Chief Justice Waite's decision, that certain practices and traditions are objectionable and should not be anyone's guide to ethical or legal conduct. *What force do the existence of practices, customs, and traditions have when we make ethical and legal judgments?* That is the central problem taken up in this book.

PRACTICES AND PRINCIPLES

In François Truffaut's film *The Wild Child* (L'enfant sauvage), a young boy, later named Victor, is discovered living like an animal in the forest. It is 1798 France. The boy is taken in by Jean-Marc-Gaspart Itard, a doctor at the National Institute for the Deaf and Dumb in Paris. Itard wants to civilize Victor. During the course of his efforts, he conducts an experiment, what he calls an "abominable test": by treating Victor unjustly, he will see if Victor experiences a universal sense of justice. Itard had been teaching Victor to fetch objects after pointing to the corresponding words written on a blackboard. If Victor fetched the wrong object, he would be punished by being put in a closet, a treatment Victor greatly disliked. If Victor fetched the correct object, he would be rewarded. Itard's experiment would be to put Victor in the closet after he fetched the correct object. Itard

---

[8] 98 US at 166.
[9] *National Law Journal*, April 17, 1989, 3.
[10] Ibid.

wants to see if Victor would rebel upon being punished without reason. After Victor fetches the correct object, Itard drags him toward the closet. Victor is confused at first, and then indeed rebels, physically resisting Itard, even biting him. The experiment was a success. Itard remarks afterward that this was "irrefutable evidence that the sentiment of what is just and unjust is in Victor"—he has been lifted from a savage to a moral being. Itard concludes that Victor understands a universal sense of justice, one that distinguishes humans from beasts.

But is this obvious? Itard assumes that Victor's response rests on an understanding that he has suffered the injustice of being punished for no reason; presumably *any* civilized human being would regard such arbitrary punishment as an injustice. Yet perhaps Victor's response was not outrage at an injustice but surprise or uncertainty at the undermining, not of a universal principle of justice, but of an expectation established by a pattern of behavior between Itard and him. Was the wrong that Victor experienced the violation of a universal principle of justice (that punishment must be for some reason), or rather, the frustration of an expectation arising from a practice that had developed between Victor and Itard, the breaking of a rule of their little game?

This incident from Truffaut's *The Wild Child* brings us back to our problem: how do we decide what ethics and the law require? Itard seems to believe there are universal principles of right conduct, principles we could use to criticize practices human beings should universally regard as objectionable—we might think of practices such as *oyako-shinju,* infant exposure, or wife-beating, although what Itard has in mind is a practice of undeserved punishment. While Itard's reading of Victor's reaction is plausible, one purpose of this book is to pursue a line of argument underlying the other reading: that the wrong that Victor experienced was not the wrong of violating a universal principle, but the wrong of frustrating expectations that emerged from a shared practice.

I call this book *Practices and Principles* because it examines two approaches, not necessarily mutually exclusive, to the problem of determining what ethics and the law require. A principle approach looks for (perhaps transcultural) standards or principles (of perhaps universal human validity), which we can use to criticize local conceptions of right or proper conduct. A practice approach looks to shared understandings that are reflected in social practices, cultural norms, and traditions.[11] These approaches provide us with two ways of confronting a choice with ethical or legal implications.

William Godwin, in his *Enquiry Concerning Political Justice* (1798), presents us with one such choice: "I have promised to bestow a sum of money upon some good and respectable purpose. In the interval between the promise and my fulfilling it, a greater and nobler purpose offers itself, and calls with an imperious voice for my cooperation. Which ought I to prefer?"[12] Having been taught that we must keep our promises, for many of us the answer seems clear: Godwin must bestow the money as originally promised. But, as we shall see, not everyone agrees with

[11] The practice-principle dichotomy does not necessarily correspond to a particular-universal dichotomy: principles needn't be universal, just as norms needn't be limited to a single culture.

[12] William Godwin, *An Enquiry Concerning Political Justice* (New York: Alfred Knopf, 1926), vol. 1, bk. 3, chap. 3.

this answer, Godwin included. Even if we do agree that Godwin must keep his promise, we can still ask *why* he should—simply because this is what we were taught, in which case those living in a society whose members don't promise might be warranted in thinking he needn't keep his promise? Or does the obligation to keep a promise arise, not because doing so is a cultural requirement for those brought up with the practice of promising, but because failing to keep a promise violates a valid moral principle that does not depend on our having the practice of promising?

Godwin's concern is whether there is a general obligation to keep promises. The law of contracts is concerned with which specific promises must be kept. For example, suppose I agreed to buy your cow for a certain sum, motivated by the reasonable belief that the cow would provide me milk, but it turns out the cow is barren. Am I morally bound to fulfill my part of the bargain by paying you the agreed upon sum? Or suppose a contractor builds a house for me but fails to use the type of pipe I specified in our contract. Even though the pipe actually used is of the same quality as the type I specified, may I withhold payment until the contractor tears down the walls and replaces the pipe with the right type? Am I morally obligated in either case to fulfill the contract? As these are contractual disputes, coming under the purview of the law, a judge will resolve these issues by drawing on the law of contract. But as we shall see, in these and many other contract cases, it is far from clear how a judge should decide what one's legal obligation is. Where shall the judge turn to find the answer?

Finally, consider the problem arising in U.S. constitutional law of whether a government search without warrant is unreasonable and therefore proscribed by the Fourth Amendment. The Court answers this question by determining whether the warrantless search violates an expectation of privacy that society regards as reasonable. This requires the Court to decide what expectations of privacy society regards as reasonable. As we have seen, what is reasonable to the majority of the Court is not reasonable to everyone. How do we decide whether an expectation of privacy is or isn't reasonable?

Some philosophers and theorists believe that we should resolve questions about promissory obligations by appealing simply to the rules of the practice of promising, and that we should resolve questions about contractual obligation by turning to the existing law of contract. They would respond to Godwin's question about promises by noting that to make a promise is to invoke a social practice that requires us to keep our word even though doing so becomes inconvenient. The point of the practice of promising, they would argue, is to rule out as illegitimate the sort of prudential calculation Godwin's "greater and nobler purpose" tempts us to make. Others, failing to see how we could, or why we should, appeal to existing rules and practices to determine what we ought to do, or to explain how obligations arise, determine what we should do in particular cases by turning instead to principles of right or rational conduct, principles that may or may not conform with existing law or practice. This is the position Godwin himself takes with respect to promises. In answering his own question "which ought I to prefer?" Godwin responds, "That which best deserves my preference. A promise can make no alteration in the case." In deciding what action to take, Godwin does not feel bound by the existence of a social practice of promising, or of a shared understanding that promises must be kept; instead he invokes a principle that one should do what yields the greater good.[13]

This debate about promises is an instance of a wider debate among political and legal theorists. On the one hand are those who believe there are abstract principles of right conduct—that is, principles with which we can make judgments without reference to the rules, purposes, or other features of practices— principles that are valid or have weight independent of the existence of social practices, and that we can and should use to establish, reform, criticize, or explain the features of social practices. On the other hand are those who believe that to answer the question of where our duty or obligation lies or what action is morally proper, we must turn to existing practices and their rules, and that if any principles guide us, they are principles already implicit or immanent in our practices. The former adhere to what I shall call a *principle conception,* the latter, to what I shall call a *practice conception.*

Those who decide what our obligations and duties are by turning to social practice must respond to the obvious challenge that our practices can be irrational, unreasonable, or thoroughly evil. We have already encountered some examples of troubling practices, and there are many others. But it seems unnecessary to chalk up a list of evil practices to show that deference to practice is an inadequate theoretical position. It seems sufficient just to note that the fact that we do something is not as strong a reason (if it is any reason at all) for doing it, as that there are principled reasons for doing it. Some moral philosophers believe it is wrong to kill animals for food or scientific experiments because it is wrong to cause pain or suffering, and animals can suffer. They believe this despite the fact that we do exploit animals in these ways.[14] We needn't agree with them that killing animals for food is wrong to agree that the fact that we do exploit animals in this way does not justify this practice. The fact that I eat meat (or keep promises or expect privacy in my phone conversation) is not itself a reason for me to encourage, require, or expect you to eat meat (or keep promises or expect privacy in *your* phone conversations).

In this book I reject uncritical deference to social practice. Our practices may be objectionable, even thoroughly evil, and there must be standards for determining this. However, in contrast to some strands of liberal thought, I shall argue that the fact that there are principles we can use to criticize practices does not mean we can ignore social practice. This book attempts to show the important role social practices have in determining what ethics and the law require, even if we are committed, as I think we should be, to principled criticism.

Some theorists who adhere strictly to a principle conception seem to deny any role to existing practices in ethical and legal judging. For Immanuel Kant, "we cannot do morality a worse service than by seeking to derive it from examples."[15]

---

[13] Ibid.

[14] See Colin McGinn, *Moral Literacy or How to Do the Right Thing* (Indianapolis: Hackett, 1992).

[15] Immanuel Kant, *Groundwork of the Metaphysic of Morals,* trans. H. J. Paton (New York: Harper

Thomas Paine, responding to Edmund Burke's praise of longstanding traditions, writes that "government by precedent, without any regard to the principle of the precedent, is one of the vilest systems that can be set up." For Paine, "it must be from the justness of their principles, and the interest which a nation feels therein" that laws derive their support.[16] Thomas Scanlon echoes Kant in arguing that the obligation to keep promises derives from general principles and not from practice: "When promises give rise to clear obligations, these can be accounted for on the basis of general moral principles that do not refer to the existence of social practice."[17]

There is great force in this position. Why do something simply because it happens to be our practice? How can the existence of a practice be a ground of judgment? Surely if we think it right to keep a promise, it is because there are good reasons for doing so, reasons independent of the fact that the practice of promising requires us to keep promises. The force of a principle conception is all the greater when we think of all the repugnant practices that have existed or of how many practices arose only because of the physical domination of a powerful class. Who could defend compliance with such practices simply on the ground that these practices exist?

While acknowledging the importance of principled criticism, I do not agree that social practice can be ignored in ethical and legal deliberations. I shall point to the limitations of an ethical or legal theory relying solely on principles that make no reference to social practice. One limitation with such a theory is that the principles it invokes may be too general to account for our ethical intuitions or to provide persuasive judgments about right conduct. Some moral philosophers, for example, appeal to the principle that it is wrong deliberately to cause damage or pain or death to someone else.[18] This principle, however, is too general to accord with many judgments upon which most of us would agree. Sometimes a person inflicts pain on another, yet this falls within the bounds of acceptable behavior: a critic writes a harsh review of an author; or a woman fails to return a man's love. There are societal norms for when we can reasonably chastise or inflict pain on others for which the general moral principle fails to account. We might refine the moral principle to account for these exceptions, but in doing so we no longer are appealing to principles that do not refer to existing social practice; rather, we are articulating a principle to account for social practice. Suppose we are thinking about when behavior counts as sexual harassment. For example, you are a male employer and are attracted to one of your female employees whose prospects for advancement hinge on your professional evaluation of her work. Is it appropriate for you to ask her out on a date? To give her a hug? We might appeal to a principle that it is wrong for someone with power over another person to act in a

and Row, 1964), 408 (page reference is to the Royal Prussian Academy edition, included in Paton's edition).

[16] Thomas Paine, *Rights of Man* (New York: Doubleday, 1989), 432, 435.

[17] Thomas Scanlon, "Promises and Practices," *Philosophy and Public Affairs* 19, no. 3 (summer 1990): 220.

[18] See McGinn, *Moral Literacy,* 40–41.

way that is offensive to a reasonable person. But to apply this principle, we need, among other things, some standard of when it is reasonable to regard actions as offensive. Is it reasonable to be offended by being asked out on a date? How do we decide? In some contexts it is normal to touch or hug others, and it would be unreasonable to be offended by such action; yet in other contexts such conduct is offensive. It seems to me that to interpret the standard of reasonableness that our ethical principle invokes, we must appeal to social practice, norms, or shared understandings. While defending principled deliberation in ethics and law, I shall argue that in important instances of ethical and legal deliberation we cannot rely solely on principles to the exclusion of social practice. One reason is that practices set up expectations that are often the basis for our judgments of whether conduct is reasonable or proper.

Some word should be said about what is meant by *social practice*. I often use it interchangeably with other terms, such as *custom, convention, institution, law, tradition, shared understanding,* and *norm,* without concerning myself with the differences between each of these. They all refer to standards of human behavior recognized within a community or communities; they all are part of what Kant refers to as "anthropology," to which he thinks we need not appeal in deciding what morality requires. Sometimes "practice" refers to rule-governed activity, but practices need not be defined by rules.[19] Some practices, such as playing chess, have explicit rules that tell us what is and isn't appropriate. Moving one's pawn from one end of the board to the other in one turn isn't appropriate, since it violates the rule for moving pawns. But not all practices have determinate rules. "Practice" can refer more broadly to a way of doing things that is not defined by rules. To consult practice in this broader sense isn't to consult a discrete practice with identifiable rules; it is to consult our ethical life, or "what is done."

We might say an individual has her very own practice, but we probably would not call this a *social* practice. Two people might develop a practice just between themselves—as did Itard and Victor—and we might call this a social practice, or we might choose to call a social practice only a practice recognized by a larger group or community. Deciding whether an activity is best described as a practice, norm, tradition, or convention, whether a social practice can exist only among two people or must be shared by a larger group, and other such definitional issues is not essential to the central argument of this book.[20] That argument concerns the Kantian claim that we cannot derive morality from anthropology.[21] Kant's principled approach denies any essential role in determining what moral-

[19] See chapter three, pp. 87–88. Ludwig Wittgenstein implies that practice can refer to activity that is not determined by rules: "Not only rules, but also examples are needed for establishing a practice. Our rules leave loop-holes open, and the practice has to speak for itself" (*On Certainty,* trans. Denis Paul and G. E. M. Anscombe [New York: Harper and Row, 1969], par. 139).

[20] Sometimes the distinction between shared understandings, laws, practices, and so forth is important: a law might not reflect a shared understanding, or even what practice is; see, for example, chapter six, footnote 22, on the Enrollment and Conscription Act of 1863. We *do* need to attend to these differences when we are debating what social practice (broadly understood) actually is.

[21] Kant takes this unbending position in several passages, see the first two sections of chapter two.

ity requires to past or present examples of human conduct. According to the Kantian approach, the fact that something is recognized as right has no bearing on whether it is right, and this is the case if it is recognized as right by two people, a group of people, an entire nation, or by all societies ever; or whether the recognition takes the form of an institution, law, custom, convention, shared understanding, or norm.

BUILDING ON KANT AND HEGEL

The debate between the two approaches—practice conception and principle conception—appears in many contexts: it occurs between Kant and Hegel, Burke and Paine, act-utilitarians and rule-utilitarians, as well as between contemporary liberals and communitarians. It is a focus of dispute among theorists of contract law and among moral philosophers writing on promises. It is implicit in the debate among jurists concerning the reasonableness of expectations of privacy, an issue central to the interpretation of the Fourth Amendment and tort law. It is expressed in debates about what actions should be punished, what sentence is appropriate for a given crime, and what counts as sexual harassment. And it is central to the dispute between cultural relativists, who believe judgments of right and wrong are relative to the norms and practices of one's culture, and universalists, who insist that what's right and wrong is not contingent on provincial standards but is established by universal standards, standards that are valid for all human beings. I believe all these debates are points of departure for a coherent intellectual journey. My motivation for undertaking this journey is a concern with practical problems, such as whether and in what circumstances we should keep our promises and contracts, or whether the government's use of forward-looking infrared devices to detect marijuana cultivation violates reasonable expectations of privacy, or what constitutes sexual harassment, or what effect we should give the defense of cultural difference in criminal cases. In the rest of this book I shall discuss the debate as it occurs between Kant and Hegel, among moral philosophers thinking about promissory obligation, and among legal theorists and jurists thinking about contracts and the law of search and seizure. While the general question of whether in determining what ethics and the law require we should appeal to transcultural principles, or to social practice, is very abstract, I believe pursuing this question can help us think more clearly about the concrete and practical problems that initially spark the impulse to theorize.

There are many ways to approach the issues I take up. Moral philosophers, jurisprudentialists, and sociologists all could consult a vast literature within their respective disciplines and employ their own distinct methods and styles of argument. I am a theorist of politics, trained in political theory. Teaching courses on obligations, punishment, privacy, constitutional law, and the history of political thought has led me to see important connections between political theory, moral philosophy, and the law, and one purpose of this book is to show these connections by relating the debate between Kant and Hegel and debates about promises, contracts, and reasonable expectations of privacy to the two approaches to theory I have outlined. Because my purpose in this book is to consider the role social practice plays in ethical and legal judging, there are many aspects of the particular debates, between Kant and Hegel and concerning promises, contracts, and privacy that I cannot explore. I make no claim to resolving all the deep philosophical and legal controversies I address. By turning to these particular debates we can see how a deeper issue is at stake in each of them: what force do the existence of practices, customs and traditions have in ethical and legal judging? This deeper issue is central to two broader debates, between cultural relativists and universalists, and between communitarians and liberals (with cultural relativists and communitarians pointing to the importance of social practice and tending to ignore the role of principles, and universalists and liberals emphasizing the importance of principles and tending to ignore the role of social practice). One hope is that showing how this deeper issue is central to the Kant-Hegel debate and the debates about promises, contracts, and privacy will help clarify these particular debates. Another hope is that linking the broader debates between relativists and universalists and between communitarians and liberals to the particular controversies about promises, contracts, and privacy will show precisely what is at stake *practically* in the broader debates, which tend to be argued about at a highly abstract level. My final hope is that the discussion of particular controversies, in which I shall point to the role played in ethical and legal judging both by principles that transcend provincial practices *and* by culturally variant norms will suggest that the proper resolution to the relativism-universalism debate and to one version of the communitarian-liberal debate is to avoid a choice between one or the other side.

It should by now be clear that in setting up the general problem as a confrontation between practice and principles, I do *not* mean to suggest that we must choose between the two. Where there is no ethical community, no shared practices or understandings, we have little but principles to which we can appeal. But where there are shared practices and understandings, at times we need to appeal to them. The practices, norms, and understandings that we share may influence not only which principles we shall want to appeal to, but also how we interpret and apply principles. While vindicating a practice conception and a political theory that emphasizes the role our political identity and the ethical practices and understandings we share with fellow citizens plays in ethical deliberation, the argument does not imply that we cannot or should not criticize our social practices.

The argument that in deciding what morality or the law requires we should neither assume a position of uncritical deference to nor completely ignore our social practices should not be surprising or controversial. Indeed, one might think that while some theorists emphasize principles more and some pay attention to practices more, no past or present theorist would disagree that good moral and legal theory requires attention to both principles and practices. Yet some leading theorists do explicitly claim that in deciding what is right we need not or should not appeal to convention or practice. The idea that right and wrong are not a matter of fashion or convention and the idea that we can always subject our practices and customs to critical scrutiny to ensure that they are justified are deeply felt and intuitively appealing. But they are mistaken. That social practice must come into play in ethical and legal judgment may be a truism to some, but it is a truism of which we sometimes need reminding. Even enthusiastic rationalists who insist that we can always detach ourselves from our practices and customs in order to question and replace them should acknowledge this truism despite their declarations to the contrary. In this way the book can be seen as an example of the Socratic elenchus: getting those who hold to a particular proposition—in our case the proposition that moral or legal judgment properly involves the application of principles that do not refer to the existence of social practice—to see that they also hold other views inconsistent with that proposition, so that they come to doubt that proposition. The argument I advance about the important role of social practice has yet to be won. But this book has more interesting and challenging aims than merely showing that practice is important—that claim is too vague to be of much use. Liberal, rationalist, enlightenment, and universalist thinkers may well acknowledge the need to pay attention to culturally variant practices, but their proclaimed sensitivity means little unless they specify how practice is important, and in what sense we should or must recognize the claims of those who defend practices and traditions against the piercing light of reason. One important aim of this book, then, is to show to those who already are willing to admit that we must be attentive to both practice and principle precisely how social practices and principles interact when we make ethical and legal judgment, to show *how* practice is important. When we understand some of the complex ways in which practices and principles interact, we will be able to show to the unbounded rationalists for whom everything is subject to principled scrutiny that sometimes uncritical deference to practice is appropriate and justified, that everything is not always "up for grabs." We will also see that whether someone has acted reasonably, morally, or legally may depend on that person's cultural background or political identity.

I explain and defend my position by turning to cases of ethical and legal judging, showing how any adequate account relies on principles that themselves are constrained by practice. I see no better way of establishing that social practices constrain our application of principles and of explaining precisely *how* the interaction of practice and principles work, than by illustrating their interaction in particular instances of ethical and legal judging. Most of this book is therefore dedicated to three case studies. Before presenting the case studies of chapters three through five, though, we shall turn to the competing views of Kant and Hegel in chapter two. Their debate provides some historical and intellectual roots for the ensuing discussion of practices and principles. On Kant's view, we decide what we morally ought to do without making any reference to what we do; rather, we apply the categorical imperative, which is valid universally, for all rational beings. It, and not social practices, determines what morality requires. I argue that while Kant explicitly claims to derive moral imperatives (such as that we must keep our promises) from principles without referring to the existence of social practices, he does not succeed—he implicitly and necessarily presupposes practice. On Hegel's view, we determine what we ought to do or where our obligation lies not by applying some abstract principle, such as the categorical imperative, but by turning to social practices, to our ethical life (*Sittlichkeit*). Hegel does not advocate blind deference to existing practices. He insists that we have good reasons for our practices—practices must be *rational*. But for Hegel, rationality is not an abstract principle that does not appeal to social practice. For Kant, we ought to conform with a valid moral principle even if it is not generally adhered to or recognized. For Hegel, moral judgments must be rooted in actual agreement, as expressed in our sharing social practices. Nowhere in the writing of moral philosophers do we find so forceful an exponent as Kant of the view that in deciding what is morally right we must appeal to rational principles unconstrained by "anthropology"; and nowhere do we find so forceful a critic of Kant's principle conception as Hegel. Chapter two is foundational, treating a historically important discussion of issues relevant to contemporary ethical controversies, and serves as our introduction to the practice-principle debate.

Chapter three marks a move toward concreteness and specificity, being the first case study of an ethical or legal issue. I choose the first case, promises, in part because it has already been referred to in chapter two's discussion of Kant's position, in part because it is perhaps the most important and paradigmatic case of moral obligation, and because the discussion of promises sets the stage for chapter four's discussion of contracts, which lets me extend my argument about practices and principles to the distinct topic of legal as opposed to moral obligations.

Some theorists, adhering to a practice conception, argue that we have to keep our promises because that is what uttering the promise means. There is a social practice of promising, the meaning (and rule) of which dictates that we must keep our promise. Other philosophers appeal to an abstract principle that seems not to depend on the existence of a social practice of promising to justify an obligation to keep promises. I shall argue, however, that there are important senses in which such a principle cannot be applied without reference to social practice, where by practice I refer not just to discrete, rule-bound practices but to social practice in general, to what we mean in saying "that is our way." For example, Neil MacCormick sees the obligation to keep a promise as an instance of a more general obligation that arises when we knowingly induce reliance in another to their detriment, and has us decide whether we have an obligation by applying a principle of reliance. But to apply this principle, we need to know when it is reasonable to rely on someone's word. I might make utterances to you that make you think I will provide financial support to you for life, and as a result you quit your job; but it isn't always reasonable for you to rely on my utterances in this way. Whether reliance is reasonable turns on social practice.

Chapter four complements chapter three by discussing promises in a legal context. Many issues in contract law are variations on the issues concerning promises, the primary difference being that the former concern legal as opposed to moral obligations. Chapter four deepens the argument as it stands in chapter three. Where chapter three primarily addresses the abstract question of whether obligations exist absent shared social practices and whether there are what I call natural wrongs, chapter four further concretizes the argument by showing the ways appeals to practice and to principles combine in thinking about particular examples of promises.

With contract law we are concerned with the question, which promises should the state legally enforce? Particular questions that arise include: Should the state enforce gratuitous promises (promises without "consideration")? Should the courts enforce contracts made under duress, and if not, how do we distinguish duress from other sorts of persuasion? Is there an obligation to bargain in good faith? Does it extend to an obligation to disclose information about a transaction, such as that the house I am trying to sell to you has termites in hard-to-find places? Those adopting a principle conception attempt to resolve contract law issues by appealing to abstract principles. The leading principles pointed to are economic efficiency, fairness, and Charles Fried's "promise principle." I shall argue that as in the case of promises, in contract law applications of a principle may require us to appeal to social practices; but also, which principle a judge chooses to apply to resolve contractual disputes may depend on social practices and norms. In *Holcomb v. Zinke,* the court ruled against a seller who failed to disclose defects to the buyer.[22] In doing so the court rejected the principle of buyer beware—that one should be held accountable for that to which one agrees regardless of the substance of the agreement. The court argued that this ancient caveat emptor rule, which "may have had some merit in the agrarian society," is "no longer an expression of American mores." The rejected principle accords with the practices of an agrarian society but not with the practices of our more techno-logically advanced and complex society.

Chapter five turns to constitutional law and the problem of how we are to interpret the Fourth Amendment's proscription against unreasonable searches and seizures. The Court prohibits warrantless searches that violate expectations of privacy society regards as reasonable. How do we decide what counts? The answer necessarily turns on social practice and will vary among societies and throughout history. Expectations of privacy are shaped by a community's sense of space (itself influenced by architecture and family structure), desire or need for intimacy, need to control crime, acceptance of new technologies, and other cul-turally variant factors.

However, it won't do simply to defer to practice to determine whether an expectation of privacy is reasonable. Existing practices of exposure may be unac-ceptable to us, or, in the case where exposure is achieved by new technologies, there may be no settled practice. A state may implement surveillance practices that take hold so effectively that people no longer expect privacy where once they had it, but this does not mean it would be unreasonable still to have an expecta-tion of privacy. I therefore defend a principle to distinguish reasonable and un-reasonable expectations of privacy, what I call "the mischance principle." It holds that where exposure is intentionally undertaken to reveal what could not be

[22] 365 NW 2d 507 (ND, 1985).

accidentally discovered by otherwise legitimate means there is a reasonable expectation of privacy against that exposure. But the mischance principle is not an abstract or universal principle; application of it requires appealing to culturally variant practices of normal inquiry that determine what is subject to chance observation.

Chapter five extends the argument about the role of social practices in ethical and legal judging. In the discussion of promises we shall see that the reasonableness of keeping at least certain promises probably varies little among different societies; there are significant variations among societies regarding whether an expectation of privacy is reasonable, so chapter five presents an important contrasting case. In addition, the discussion of privacy lets us see other specific ways in which practices shape expectations by showing how family structure, architecture, technology, as well as ideology influence expectations of privacy.

Obviously the book's argument could have been made with chapters on different ethical and legal issues. One rationale for my selection of examples, beyond what was said above, is that it engages us with three distinct discourses—moral philosophy, civil law, and constitutional law. This lets us see how the complex relation of practice and principle arises in a variety of areas. One purpose of the book is to show connections among different disciplines, to get moral philosophers and legal and constitutional theorists to see how issues they face have parallels in other disciplines and have historical roots in Kant and Hegel. I believe that thinking about the Kant-Hegel debate can help us with contemporary ethical and legal controversies, and these latter controversies let us see what is at stake in the Kant-Hegel debate. Because of its interdisciplinary nature, this book does not presuppose much familiarity with any of the particular topics it takes up, so that, for example, constitutional scholars unfamiliar with Kant and Hegel should easily follow the discussion in chapter two, while Hegel scholars unfamiliar with U.S. constitutional law should easily follow the argument in chapter five.

As I have already indicated, it is *not* my purpose in chapter two to settle the Kant-Hegel debate, nor in chapter three to decide which of the various principles best resolves questions about promises nor in chapter four to defend one particular approach to contract law as the best. Each of these controversies is too complex to be resolved here. My purpose in these chapters, rather, is to show how practices and principles each play a role in an adequate approach to ethics and the law. Chapter five is different in one respect. There I take pains to develop my own principle to resolve issues in privacy law. While there already were outstanding accounts of principled approaches to promises and contract law, when turning to privacy law I came across few convincing accounts of principles that could help us decide whether an expectation of privacy is reasonable. In chapter five I have some interest in defending the mischance principle. But that is not my only interest. The point of chapter five is primarily to provide an account of the importance of culturally variant practices and norms even for someone committed to principled criticism.

My argument throughout the book has implications for the debate in contemporary political theory between cultural relativists and universalists and between liberals and communitarians, and in the final chapter I explore some of these implications.

Some of the most stimulating and insightful comments and criticisms from which I benefitted in researching and writing this book were received in the classroom. In closing this introduction I would like to express my gratitude to the remarkable Stanford students who partipated in my undergraduate courses on promises, privacy, and modern political theory, and particularly to Eric Beer-bohm, Emily Chang, Deborah Kun, Howard Loo, Alyze Lowen, Ari Richter, and Jason Weintraub. I also want to thank Jeremy Buchman, Maki Arakawa, and Lorri Elder for their research assistance; and the readers for Princeton University Press for their helpful suggestions. Lastly, for the several years during which I was immersed in the texts of Kant and Hegel, in contract and Fourth Amendment case law, philosophy journal articles, and social science research, I was able, despite the demands of my undertaking, to lead something approaching a balanced life thanks to the friendship of a group of unusually good souls. To Jay Boniface, Sarah Claus, Henry Dinsdale, Robert Fisher, Chris Wheeler, as well as to Beth, Carlos, Dan and Andy, Eric, Geoff, Jim, Joan, Jochen, Philippe, Rick, Roy, Virginia, and the rest of the II Fornaio morning ride, I'd like to express here what a sometimes reserved disposition, and the difficulty of saying much of *any-thing* while struggling to hang in until the fire station sprint, has kept me from saying often enough: your friendship during these years has meant a great deal to me.

Kant versus Hegel

FOR IMMANUEL KANT, the answer to the question of how I ought to act is not found by turning to society's norms of appropriate behavior or to the rules of practices. There are passages in which Kant suggests in no uncertain terms that anthropological facts about human behavior, or about the conventions and practices from which the empiricist might distill codes of right conduct, are entirely irrelevant to the question of how I ought to act. The answer to that question is found, for Kant, by applying "reason."

> Nothing can protect us against a complete falling away from our Ideas of duty, or can preserve in the soul a grounded reverence for its law, except the clear conviction that even if there never have been actions springing from such pure sources, the question at issue here is not whether this or that has happened; that, on the contrary, reason by itself and independently of all appearances commands what ought to happen; that consequently actions of which the world has perhaps hitherto given no example— actions whose practicability might well be doubted by those who rest everything on experience—are nevertheless commanded unrelentingly by reason.[1]

For Kant, ethics is not an empirical science. Statements of duties are not generalizations of expectations about how one should conduct oneself that have arisen in the course of human affairs. The duties of friendship, for example, are not based on norms of behavior among friends that have developed over time. Rather, the moral imperative that we be loyal to friends is required, "although up to now there may have existed no loyal friend," inasmuch as "this duty, prior to all experience, is contained as duty in general in the Idea of a reason which determines the will by a priori grounds."[2] Morality, for Kant, is an a priori or deductive science. "In practical philosophy we are not concerned with accepting reasons for what *happens,* but with accepting laws of what *ought to happen,* even if it never does happen."[3] For Kant, "we cannot do morality a worse service than by seeking to derive it from examples."[4]

In the passage about loyal friends, Kant insists that we must be loyal to friends to be moral even if there has never been an example of a loyal friend. Kant seems committed to the view also that in determining what we must do to *be* a loyal

---

[1] Immanuel Kant, *Groundwork of the Metaphysic of Morals,* trans. by H. J. Paton (New York: Harper and Row, 1964), 408. Page references are to the edition issued by the Royal Prussian Academy in Berlin, included in the margins of Paton's edition.

[2] Ibid.

[3] Ibid., 426–27.

[4] Ibid., 408. Also, 411: "Morality cannot be abstracted from any empirical, and therefore merely contingent, knowledge."

friend we cannot rely solely on practices of friendship. For Kant we cannot consult "anthropology," or studies of how humans do behave or have behaved in the past, to determine how we ought to act, in part because empirical evidence, or, in the language of recent philosophy, a brute fact, cannot in itself entail evaluative judgments.[5] We cannot infer from the fact that people keep their promises, or even that they believe they ought to keep their promises, that anyone ought to keep a promise. To justify that moral judgment, it is not enough to point to facts in the world. The ways in which people behave, or have behaved in the past, may serve as examples for how we think we should behave, but, on Kant's view, we cannot be sure that we are right to follow these examples unless reason shows them to accord with what morality requires. Nor would it be sufficient to consult existing conceptions of the ideal of loyalty to determine what we must do to be a loyal friend, unless reason shows these conceptions to be valid:

> Every example of [morality] presented to me must first itself be judged by moral principles in order to decide if it is fit to serve as an original example—that is, as a model: it can in no way supply the prime source for the concept of morality . . . Imitation has no place in morality, and examples serve us only for encouragement—that is, they set beyond doubt the practicability of what the law commands; they make perceptible what the practical law expresses more generally; but they can never entitle us to set aside their true original, which resides in reason, and to model ourselves upon examples.[6]

Kant, then, adheres to what in chapter one we called a principle conception of ethics.[7]

G. W. F. Hegel's philosophy is in many respects a reaction to and criticism of Kant. Hegel's political philosophy, which takes up the questions what is right, and what our duties and obligations are, rejects Kant's position that ethics are nonempirical, a priori, and divorced from anthropology. Hegel understands Kant to decide what is right by applying a concept of right that does not refer to the existence of social practices, by applying purely abstract principles. For Hegel, this approach, also taken by liberals who believe that pure principles can determine the best constitution, is naive: it

> is based on the separation which reflection and understanding make between the concept and its reality. Holding to an abstract and hence untrue concept they [liberals] do not grasp the idea; or—which comes to the same thing insofar as the content, though not the form is concerned—they have no concrete view of a people and a state.[8]

As we shall see, in Hegel's view we determine what is right, or what our duties and obligations are, by turning not to abstract principles, but to the rules and

---

[5] See Kant, *Metaphysics of Morals*, trans. Mary Gregor (Cambridge: Cambridge University Press, 1991), 217. Hereafter *MM*. Numbers refer to pages in the Prussian Academy of Sciences edition, included in the margins of Gregor's translation.

[6] Kant, *Groundwork*, 408–9.

[7] While Kant believes *morality* is divorced from anthropology, he thinks law is a sphere distinct from morality and Kant's legal as opposed to moral theory does make reference to social practices. See discussion below.

[8] G. W. F. Hegel, *Reason in History*, trans. Robert Hartman (Indianapolis: Bobbs-Merrill, 1953), 58–59.

concrete principles of our existing ethical life, including the laws of the state. Hegel does not reject appeals to principles; but he thinks the principles we have to guide us necessarily are immanent in or otherwise make reference to our existing practices. For Kant, practice should be built upon principles that are valid prior to or independent of our having any practices, while for Hegel guiding principles are derivative of social practices—the practice is prior to the principle. For Kant, the rationale of rules allowing civil society to flourish "cannot be discovered empirically but can be derived only through reason a priori," whereas for Hegel, "the philosopher can know the truth about [a society] only a posteriori and not a priori."9

In this chapter we begin our exploration of the role practices and principles play in ethical deliberation by turning to the competing approaches of Kant and Hegel. Kant touts abstract principles as the only rational source of moral judgment; Hegel criticizes appeals to abstract principles, instead pointing to standards of judgment that are immanent in or otherwise make reference to the practices of a shared ethical life. The purpose here is not to defend either philosophy. That would involve a lengthy, critical discussion of the complexities of and deep philosophical assumptions underlying each theory that cannot be undertaken here. Rather, the purpose in turning to the Kant-Hegel debate is to see how it presents us with two approaches to ethics—one rejecting the role of existing social practices and norms in determining what we ought to do, the other seeing their role as essential; and, by drawing on some of the difficulties with each theorist's position, to point out some of the strengths and weaknesses of these approaches.

KANT'S PRINCIPLE CONCEPTION

In his *Metaphysics of Morals* (1797) and *Groundwork of the Metaphysic of Morals* (1785), Kant takes up these questions: What is our duty? What ought we to do? What would a pure, moral will will? Much is at stake for Kant in finding definitive answers to these questions. Without a metaphysics of morals, he writes, we would have "no certain moral principles to guide judgment or to discipline the mind in observance of duty, the precepts of which must be given a priori by pure reason."10

A metaphysics of morals is a science of ethics, which Kant characterizes as the science of freedom.11 The science of ethics uncovers laws of absolute necessity,

---

9 Howard Williams, "Politics and Philosophy in Kant and Hegel," in *Hegel's Critique of Kant*, ed. Stephen Priest (Oxford: Clarendon Press, 1987), 199. Williams adds that "to know how the citizens of a society ought to act the philosopher need do no more, in Hegel's view, then look closely at that society and the rules that govern it" (200). Elsewhere I argue that for Hegel to "look closely at" involves not passive description but creative and critical philosophical interpretation. (See Mark Tunick, *Hegel's Political Philosophy* [Princeton: Princeton University Press, 1992].) Williams implies that it involves only the former: "Hegel does not see philosophy as playing the same reforming and improving role that Kant advocates for it. The theme of Hegel's political philosophy is, on the contrary, resignation before the facts of the present" (201).

10 MM, 217.

11 Kant, *Groundwork*, 387.

laws dictated by pure reason, valid for all rational beings.[12] It tells us what a moral will wills. How can a science that uncovers laws of necessity be a science of freedom? For Kant only the pure moral will acting for the sake of duty and not out of any empirical inducement is free. Freedom, here, means autonomy. To act from some motive or inducement is to depend on empirical things beyond my control, is to be subject to the realm of contingency or chance. This is no longer to be autonomous, is to be unfree. For Kant, to be free is "to be independent of determination by causes in the sensible world."[13] To be free we must be independent not only of interested motives but also of the will of others: "only I myself can make something my end. . . . Another can indeed coerce me to do something that is not my end, but not to make this my end."[14] On Kant's view, we are free (in the moral sense Kant has in mind) only when we act upon laws that neither are imposed on us by other agents nor depend for their successful realization on circumstances beyond our control. An example of a law the realization of which hinges on circumstances beyond our control is a law enforcing the principle of utility, that would require us to act in such a way that we increase the aggregate of pleasure in our society. Since we can never be sure that the consequences of our actions will have the effect required by this law, Kant would say we would be unfree living according to it.

In Kant's view, we are free by obeying only those laws we impose on ourselves.[15] But the authority of the laws we are free in obeying derives not from our consenting to them but from reason. That I consent to a law does not make the law right. Moral laws are valid not because we think they are valid or agree to them but because they really are, objectively, valid. By willing these laws, we are free under them despite their necessity.

The law Kant uncovers, the principle for free, moral action, is the categorical imperative. When we act in accordance with it, our will is autonomous, unconditioned by interested motives, and hence free. The categorical imperative sets up a standard for action that is unconcerned with the benefits we might reap from the action. Kant says the "sublimity" of the categorical imperative lies in the "freedom from dependence on interested motives."[16] On Kant's view we would not be free if we willed according to a hypothetical imperative, which commands us to do a thing for its consequences.

[12] Ibid., 389.

[13] Ibid., 452.

[14] *MM*, 381.

[15] Here I refer to moral laws. Kant argues that we are bound to obey even the laws of a dictator, as doing so is preferable to living in an anarchic state of nature, but he would not say we are morally free obeying these laws. Kant sharply separates morality from law, and moral laws from what he calls "pragmatic laws," or laws enacted by government and enforced by legal punishment. He recognizes a pragmatic need for government and laws that coerce us into respecting the rights of others, though he would deny that an individual who obeys a law from fear of punishment is morally free. For discussion of Kant's separation of morality and law and references to relevant passages in Kant's texts where this distinction is made, see Mark Tunick, "Is Kant a Retributivist?" *History of Political Thought* 17, no. 1 (spring 1996): 62–66.

[16] Kant, *Groundwork,* 439.

Hypothetical imperatives declare a possible action to be practically necessary as a means to the attainment of something else that one wills (or that one may will). A categorical imperative would be one which represented an action as objectively necessary in itself apart from its relation to a further end.[17]

If we follow a hypothetical imperative—as when we decide to keep a promise because we believe doing so will lead the promisee to lavish rewards on us in the future—we might fail to achieve our objective, since we live in the world of contingency. Our will can be frustrated. But for Kant, whether one acts well cannot hinge on circumstances beyond one's control:

In morals the proper worth of an absolutely good will, a worth elevated above all price, lies precisely in this—that the principle of action is free from all influence by contingent grounds, the only kind that experience can supply.[18]

Only by willing according to a categorical imperative will we never be frustrated by contingencies. Kant thus rejects theories that commend actions insofar as they yield happiness: "If eudaemonism (the principle of happiness) is set up as the basic principle instead of eleutheronomy (the principle of the freedom of internal laws), the result is the euthanasia (easy death) of all morals."[19] For Kant, morality is concerned with the good of an action "let the consequences be what they may."[20] A good will is good in itself not for what it accomplishes. Its value is independent of its usefulness. Its usefulness doesn't commend it. Accordingly, in Kant's view, to be moral our actions must not only conform with the moral law of pure reason, but be done for the sake of the moral law, for the sake of duty, and not for the beneficial consequences that might (or might not) result by so acting. To help others because this gives one inner pleasure is not to act morally.

Kantian morality requires we act for the sake of duty and not for consequentialist reasons—only then are we free. But what precisely must we will to will our duty and be free, in Kant's view? In determining the *content* of morality, Kant has us turn not to social practices and norms but to the categorical imperative. Understanding Kant's principle conception requires knowing precisely what the categorical imperative is and what it requires us to do. Kant gives it various formulations. In one version called the Formula of Universal Law (FUL), the categorical imperative holds that "I ought never to act except in such a way that I can also will that my maxim should become a universal law."[21] To see what this means, we must first know what Kant means by a "maxim." In an often cited footnote to the *Groundwork*, Kant defines "maxim" as "a subjective principle of action" or "a principle on which the subject *acts*." It may or may not conform with a "law," which is objectively valid for every rational being. Laws are principles on which one ought to act; maxims are principles on which a subject actually acts.[22]

---

[17] Ibid., 414.
[18] Ibid., 426.
[19] MM, 378.
[20] Kant, *Groundwork*, 416.
[21] Ibid., 402.
[22] Ibid., 421 n.

Maxims need to be tested to see whether they are valid. According to the FUL, we test a subject's maxim by the standard of "bare conformity to universal law,"[23] a test that does not make reference to the possible benefits of acting upon the maxim.[24]

To illustrate how concrete moral directives can be generated from the FUL, Kant gives an example concerning promises, the subject of our next chapter:

> Suppose I seek [t]o learn in the quickest way and yet unerringly how to solve the problem "Does a lying promise accord with duty?" I have then to ask myself "Should I really be content that my maxim (the maxim of getting out of a difficulty by a false promise) would hold as a universal law (one valid both for myself and others)? And could I really say to myself that every one may make a false promise if he finds himself in a difficulty from which he can extricate himself in no other way?" I then become aware at once that I can indeed will to lie, but I can by no means will a universal law of lying; for by such a law there could properly be no promises at all, since it would be futile to profess a will for future action to others who would not believe my profession or who, if they did so over-hastily, would pay me back in like coin; and consequently my maxim, as soon as it was made a universal law, would be bound to annul itself.[25]

Kant here illustrates how we determine what we ought to do. We begin with a maxim or a rule we lay down for ourselves and test it by asking whether we could will that this rule become a universal law.

Kant claims generally that in deciding what morality requires, reference is to be made neither to existing social practices (to anthropology) nor to the consequences of the action. If we ought to keep our promises, in Kant's view, it should not be because there is a social practice that requires us to nor because keeping our promises will benefit us. If future benefits were the only reason to keep my promise to you, then in deciding whether to carry out my promise—which, let us assume, I'd rather not do since doing so is burdensome—I should have to think about whether you will reciprocate. Suppose you leave the country tomorrow for good? Or are ungrateful? I would also have to consider whether my reputation would suffer if I break my promise. Would anyone find out, anyone whose trust I would not want to lose? Is the probable damage to my reputation of not keeping my promise greater than the loss to me of carrying out my promise? Once I start down this road of moral calculation, I can never be certain about the right thing to do. The moral propriety of my action would depend on things unpredictable and outside my control, such as whether you remain in the country or spread word of my unreliability. But, in Kant's view, morality must not rest on such

---

[23] Ibid., 402.

[24] Ibid., 416: "[The categorical imperative] is concerned, not with the matter of the action and its presumed results, but with its form and with the principle from which it follows." It is somewhat puzzling of Kant to say that the categorical imperative is concerned only with the "form" of an action, rather than with its "matter." Kant does think that the categorical imperative leads to particular commands, such as that we ought to keep our promises and ought not to lie or steal. As we shall see later in this chapter, it is precisely the idea that the categorical imperative is concerned only with "form," that it is merely formal, that Hegel seizes on in criticizing Kantian morality as empty.

[25] Ibid., 403.

uncertain grounds. We must keep our promises simply because the categorical imperative requires us to. The demands of morality are dictated not by practice nor by utility but by an application of the universalizability test. We may wonder, though, whether in the passage above Kant indeed derives a specific moral command—that it is wrong to make a false promise—without appealing to consequentialist reasons and without presupposing the rules of a social practice of promising. Is Kant really able to determine what ethics requires without doing what he says we must not do?

Kant seems to be falling back on the sort of consequentialist reasoning he elsewhere rejects when he says that if I make false promises, and everyone else does as well, then no one would be able to make promises. This seems to base the obligation to keep a promise on the consequentialist argument that if I didn't keep my promises, and other people followed my example, eventually no one could rely on promises and a useful social practice would dissolve. The argument appears to be that we should keep our promises because we want to be able to benefit from the practice in the future. Kant would resist this interpretation of his argument. Kant wants to say not that false promises are wrong because if accepted they would lead to the destruction of a useful practice—though this might be true—but, rather, that a maxim of making a false promise "would be bound to annul itself." Promising requires that the promisee believes the promisor intends to do what she promises, and Kant's argument is that in a world where everyone lived by the maxim that one should make false promises, it would be impossible to make a promise, true or false, for no promisor could ever induce in a promisee the requisite belief about their intention. The point, for Kant, is logical and not empirical: it is not that false promises would likely lead to widespread distrust of promises and we would regret that, but that the very idea of making a false promise is incoherent.[26]

A maxim urging false promises yields a contradiction in conception when universalized, just as does a maxim urging deceit. As Onora O'Neill notes:

> A maxim of deceit can readily be seen as one that we cannot even conceive as universally adopted. The project of deceit requires a world with sufficient trust for deceivers to get others to believe them; the results of universal deception would be a world in which such trust is lacking, and the deceiver's project is impossible.[27]

The problem with my making a false promise is not that it leads to the destruction of the practice of promising—if it were, then making a false promise that was never found out would not undermine the practice and would not therefore be wrong, while in fact for Kant it is wrong; rather, it is that if the maxim that I may make a false promise ever were to become a universal law "there would not be *and would never have been* any promises."[28] False promises are ruled out by the categorical impera-

---

[26] This is not to say that Kant thinks false promises are logically impossible—they surely are not, for they occur all the time.

[27] Onora O'Neill, "Universal Laws and Ends-in-Themselves," *Monist* 72, no. 3 (July 1989): 347.

[28] J. Kemp, "Kant's Examples of the Categorical Imperative," in *Kant: A Collection of Critical Essays,* ed. Robert Paul Wolff (Garden City, N.Y.: Doubleday, 1967), 252–53. While I find Kemp's formula-

tive's requirement that the maxims by which we act be universalizable, that we not be an exception to rules by which everyone could be willing to live.

One reason I suspect Kant resists the consequentialist argument for keeping promises is that it is parasitic on the practice: the consequentialist argument (that making a false promise would undermine a useful practice) presumes there already is an existing practice of promising, yet Kant claims that moral commands do not depend on the existence of social practices. Even if we accept that Kant's argument can plausibly be construed in a way that distinguishes it from the consequentialist argument that derives the obligation to keep promises from the need to comply with rules to avoid the contagion of rule-breaking that could lead to the ultimate destruction of the useful practice to which the rules belong,[29] the question still remains whether Kant derives the demand to keep promises without presupposing a social practice that requires promises to be kept. If there never had been in the history of humankind a society with the practice of promising or its equivalent—a practice that subjects to social condemnation or other sanctions people who disappoint expectations they create in others upon which these others may rely—would Kant, in deciding what we ought to do, still be able to conclude that one ought to keep promises? Given his insistence that anthropology, or present and past examples of human behavior, is irrelevant to moral inquiry, he surely should. For Kant the fact that a society morally sanctions certain acts does not make these acts wrong: if they are wrong, it is because reason, and not social norms and practices, dictates that they are wrong. Kant suggests that the existence of a social practice has no bearing whatsoever on what really is morally right and wrong. Yet, I shall argue, his own example of promises casts doubt on this.

The categorical imperative reveals false promises to be logically incoherent. To be able to promise, one must induce the belief in the promisee that one will carry out one's promise so that the promisee can rely on the expectation created by the promise. To make a false promise is to undermine the very requirement needed to make promises or induce reliance. In the next chapter, I shall consider whether it is possible to induce the requisite reliance absent a shared social practice, or, rather, whether promisees reasonably rely on promises only because there is a social practice that creates the expectation that the promisor will do what she says. If the latter is the case, false promises are wrong only because there is a social practice creating the sort of expectations that the false promisor undermines. But in this chapter I shall consider another way in which Kant presupposes the existence of social norms in his promising example. To see this argument, we must turn to another of Kant's formulations of the categorical imperative.

---

tion here helpful, it does not dispel suspicions that Kant's argument is ultimately consequentialist. For we can ask why we should care if there never had been the practice of promising, and the most plausible answer to that question would appeal to the benefits of the practice.

[29] Another consequentialist argument for keeping promises is that if I make a false promise, my reputation will be tarnished, no one will trust me, and this will be to my future disadvantage. Kant would also reject this argument as an account of why we must keep promises. He does not even consider it in the passage cited above.

Kant's FUL is supposed to show that a false promise is logically contradictory; such a promise violates conditions presupposing its very possibility. The moral conclusion that it is wrong to make false promises or to deceive results from the requirement that we should act in such a way that the maxim guiding our act could be a universal law. Underlying the FUL is an idea of human equality that demands we not be an exception to rules by which everyone could be willing to live. This idea, implicit in the FUL, becomes explicit in another formulation Kant gives the categorical imperative, the Formula of the End-In-Itself (FEI): "Act in such a way that you always treat humanity whether in your own person or in the person of any other never simply as a means but always at the same time as an end."[30] Kant says the two formulations are of "precisely the same law."[31] Onora O'Neill has given an important account of this equivalence, and turning to it lets us better see the basis of Kant's claim that one must keep promises.

O'Neill's account hinges on this point: the FUL requires that we refrain from adopting plans not to which others in fact do not consent but to which others *could* not consent.[32] It demands that "we reason only on principles that others *can* (not *will* or *would*) act on."[33] Maxims that violate the duties Kant's categorical imperative determines we have fail the universalizability test if "the means required for all to adopt and act on the maxim might be incompatible with the results of all adopting and acting on the maxim."[34] This would occur if adopting the maxim would undercut the agency of those whose consent must at least be possible. O'Neill explains by discussing the example of a maxim urging murder or assault:

> Both instrumental and brute violence undercut the agency of those whom they victimize. It is not merely that victims do not *in fact* will the maxims of their destroyers and coercers: they are deliberately made unable to do so or unable to do so for some period of time. A test that demands action only on maxims that all can adopt will require that action not be based on maxims of victimizing.[35]

To be applied, then, the FUL requires of maxims that they not victimize agents, so that it is *possible* for everyone to will the maxim to be tested. Any maxim that commends an action that would undercut another's agency is ruled out.[36] This

[30] Kant, *Groundwork*, 429.

[31] Ibid., 436.

[32] Onora O'Neill, "Reason and Politics in the Kantian Enterprise," in *Kant's Political Philosophy*, ed. Howard Williams (Chicago: University of Chicago Press, 1992), 73–74: Reason demands that we "refrain from adopting plans that others cannot adopt." Also, O'Neill, "Universal Laws," 353.

[33] O'Neill, "Reason and Politics," 76. This idea of what it means to be moral is similar in some respects to contemporary accounts of what it means to be reasonable. John Rawls (*Political Liberalism* [New York: Columbia University Press, 1993]) says that being reasonable means being willing to govern one's conduct by principles from which you and others can reason in common; to be reasonable is to cooperate on terms all can accept (49–50). See also Thomas Scanlon, "Contractualism and Utilitarianism," in *Utilitarianism and Beyond*, ed. Amartya Sen and Bernard Williams (New York: Cambridge University Press, 1982).

[34] O'Neill, "Universal Laws," 347.

[35] Ibid.

[36] Ibid., 348.

requirement, for O'Neill, amounts to the same requirement expressed by the FEI. Both the FUL and the FEI require that our actions not "disable" agents from adopting our maxims. "Any set of maxims that could be universally adopted among a set of interacting finite beings who are capable of agency is a set of maxims which secures and does not destroy the agency of those whose interaction it constrains."[37] Violating the FEI by treating an agent as a means preempts their willing and denies them what is required by the FUL: "the *possibility* of collaboration, consent—or dissent. It is not merely that we may act in ways to which they *do not* consent; we act on maxims to which they *could not* consent."[38]

While O'Neill's account convincingly equates the two formulations of the categorical imperative and seems to provide a way to derive from it concrete moral commands—we cannot act in a way that undercuts human agency—there is a problem with it that points to a general difficulty with Kantian morality, which Hegel's criticism will suggest as well. The problem is this: if I break a promise or lie to you, or even hit you over the head for no reason, I do not really disable you from being able either to consent to or dissent from my action. Murder and assault that incapacitates one's mental faculties seem the only obvious cases where a victim is denied this possibility. In developing her argument, O'Neill relies on a passage in the *Groundwork* where Kant writes, "The man whom I seek to use for my own purposes by such a (false) promise cannot possibly agree with my way of behaving to him and so cannot himself share the end of the action."[39] O'Neill takes the *cannots* here to mean the victim of the false promise is *precluded* from consenting because of incapacity upon being a victim. "The false promisor," she writes, "the deceiver, the coercer, the rapist *guarantee* that their victims cannot act on the maxims they act on."[40] But this is an unnatural reading of Kant's passage. "Cannot" here more plausibly means "surely would not," not, "is unable to." It is hard to see how being the victim of a false promise disables me in the way O'Neill must assume it does if her account is to succeed.

The categorical imperative demands that everyone could consent to a maxim that one might adopt; it requires that an action not undercut the agency of anyone else, so that it remains possible for everyone to consent to the maxim. On O'Neill's account, this is to say that actions must respect persons as ends in themselves. This requirement is supposed naturally to lead to concrete moral commands, including the command that we keep our promises, or not lie. One commentator, for example, writes that

> Hegel's charge that Kant imports the content of his examples from institutions legitimated elsewhere may be sustained in other cases, but not here (regarding promises), where form and content are united in the principle of treating all persons as ends in themselves. Promise-keeping is a necessary instantiation of that principle.[41]

---

[37] Ibid., 356.

[38] Ibid., 353.

[39] Kant, *Groundwork,* 429; cited in O'Neill, "Universal Laws," 353.

[40] O'Neill, "Universal Laws," 353.

[41] Timothy O'Hagan, "On Hegel's Critique of Kant's Moral and Political Philosophy," in *Hegel's Critique of Kant,* ed. Stephen Priest (Oxford: Clarendon Press, 1987), 145.

Promise-keeping is supposed to be necessary in light of the FEI: the person who makes a false promise "is intending to make use of another man *merely as a means* to an end which he does not share."[42]

But why does breaking a promise *count* as treating someone merely as a means? Why should we regard making a false promise as victimizing an agent? My making a false promise to you hardly incapacitates you from consenting to my action, as O'Neill supposes. It does victimize you, violate you, fail to give you the respect you are owed. But suppose it is a violation, is failing to give what is owed, only because a social practice has arisen from which we get our idea of what is owed. Kant is committed to rejecting this supposition, inasmuch as he insists ethics is a priori, that it does not make reference to existing practice. Yet Kant gives no alternative account of *why* making a false promise violates human agency. Kant might think this is just intuitively obvious. But absent further argument, there is no reason to see the wrong of a false promise as an affront to universal reason, rather than as a frustration of an expectation arising from a social practice; just as, absent further argument, there is no reason to prefer Itard's interpretation of Victor's outrage at being punished for no reason as arising from a sense in Victor that universal justice has been violated to one that sees Victor's outrage as simply frustration of an expectation that arose because a practice had been established between him and Itard.[43]

Kant intends the categorical imperative to be an abstract principle, a principle that leads us to moral judgments without referring to norms or social practices. Kant explicitly, repeatedly, and emphatically takes the position that social practice cannot be a source of authority for a moral will, and that the requirements of morality are not determined by convention or practice. There are, however, several passages in Kant's *Metaphysics of Morals* in which he does appeal to conventional understandings. For example, he suggests that a duelist who kills a fellow soldier and a "dishonored" mother who kills her illegitimate infant should not be capitally punished for their offenses as are other murderers because both acts are motivated by a feeling of honor. Given that public opinion regards a soldier who backs away from a humiliating affront as a coward, and a woman who brings a child into the world outside of marriage as a disgrace, Kant argues, we cannot expect legislators to proscribe actions the soldier or mother would take to avoid this shame. Kant writes: "Here penal justice finds itself very much in a quandary. Either it must declare by law that the concept of honor (which is here no illusion) counts for nothing and so punish with death, or else it must remove from the crime the capital punishment appropriate to it, and so be either cruel or indulgent."[44] In appealing to conventional attitudes toward illegitimacy and cowardice in determining *penal law,* however, Kant is not contradicting his view that *morality* is determined without appeal to practice or convention, for in Kant's view morality and law are distinct spheres subject to different approaches. In consider-

---

[42] Ibid.

[43] See my discussion of Trouffaut's *The Wild Child* in chapter one above.

[44] *MM,* 336–37.

ing what the law requires Kant thinks it is appropriate to consider consequences, but he thinks that is inappropriate when considering what morality requires.[45] Kant's moral theory eschews appeals to social norms and practices in part because it is deontological. If morality is to be categorical and not hypothetical, then the determination of what morality requires cannot depend on practice-imposed sanctions or rewards. Since Kant believes legal as opposed to moral theory is pragmatic and consequentialist, it is perfectly consistent for him to appeal to social practices and conventions in his legal theory, or "doctrine of right," while at the same time maintaining that morality is divorced from anthropology.

There is reason to think that Kant does not succeed in establishing an entirely nonempirical, a priori account, at least of why promises must be kept. Hegel believes the Kantian project of developing a nonempirical, a priori morality, a morality based purely on abstract principles, is misguided. Now we shall turn to Hegel's objections.

HEGEL'S CRITICISM OF KANT'S PRINCIPLE CONCEPTION

In the last section, some doubt was cast on Kant's claim that the obligation to keep promises derives from pure reason without any reference to social practices. In this section we turn to Hegel's own expression of this doubt. Hegel points to a limitation of principle conceptions such as Kant's, and offers a very different account of morality, one that insists that in deciding what we ought to do we turn to our social practices. Yet, as we shall see, a practice conception raises its own difficulties. Turning to Hegel's will let us explore some of them.

Hegel agrees with Kant that ethical constraints that prevent us occasionally from satisfying our natural inclinations do not make us unfree; he agrees with Kant that we are free in doing our duty. He says that developing this idea is Kant's great contribution:

> I should do my duty for its own sake, and it is in the true sense my own objectivity that I bring to fulfillment in doing so. In doing my duty, I am with myself [bei mir selbst] and free. The merit and exalted viewpoint of Kant's moral philosophy are that it has emphasized the significance of duty.[46]

But Hegel disagrees with Kant's approach to determining the content of duty.

On Kant's view, any action is right "if it can coexist with everyone's freedom in accordance with a universal law, or if on its maxim the freedom of choice of each can coexist with everyone's freedom in accordance with a universal law."[47]

---

[45] See Mark Tunick, "Is Kant a Retributivist?" *History of Political Thought* 17, no. 1 (spring 1996): 60–78.

[46] G. W. F. Hegel, *Elements of the Philosophy of Right*, trans. H. B. Nisbet (Cambridge: Cambridge University Press, 1991), par. 133Z. Hereafter cited as *PR*, with reference to paragraph numbers, remarks (R), and additions (Z).

[47] *MM*, 230; cf. Kant, *Groundwork*, 402.

Hegel's response is that this merely formal criterion for right lacks content and is empty. For Hegel, we determine what is right not by applying a formula such as the categorical imperative but by turning to the ethical life of our community. In his early *Natural Law* essay, Hegel says of Kant's categorical imperative that it pronounces right by completely abstracting from all content of the will, for in Kant's view, "to introduce a content is to establish a heteronomy of choice." But Hegel thinks this abstraction, this appeal to pure reason that avoids reference to existing social practices and norms, deflects us from "what is precisely of interest," namely, "to know *what* right and duty are."[48] In Hegel's view to know this we must turn to the laws and practices of our ethical life.[49] In the following sections, we shall deal with Hegel's own account of how we determine what is right. In this section we shall focus on Hegel's criticism of Kant's principle conception.

In Paragraph 135 of the *Philosophy of Right*, Hegel refers to the categorical imperative obliquely and in his notorious jargon as a principle of "abstract universality, whose determination is *identity without content* or the abstractly *positive*, i.e. the indeterminate." In the remark to this paragraph, Hegel clarifies his criticism of Kant's moral philosophy. Kant's failure is "to cling on to a merely moral point of view without making the transition to the concept of ethics." From Kant's point of view,

> no immanent theory of duties is possible. One may indeed bring in material *from outside* and thereby arrive at *particular* duties, but it is impossible to make the transition to the determination of particular duties from the [categorical imperative's] determination of duty as *absence of contradiction*, as *formal correspondence with itself*, which is no different from the specification of *abstract indeterminacy*; and even if such a particular content for action is taken into consideration, there is no criterion within that principle for deciding whether or not this content is a duty. On the contrary, it is possible to justify any wrong or immoral mode of action by this means.[50]

Hegel understands the categorical imperative to impose on moral maxims a requirement of mere "absence of contradiction." While he doesn't explain very well just how he thinks this standard of noncontradiction is supposed to work, he might have understood it in the following way. In Kant's view, it is contradictory to express support for the institution of private property and then to steal, since

[48] G. W. F. Hegel, *Natural Law: The Scientific Way of Treating Natural Law, Its Place in Moral Philosophy, and Its Relation to the Positive Sciences of Law,* trans. T. M. Knox (1802–3; Philadelphia: University of Pennsylvania Press, 1975), 436, hereafter *Natural Law*. Numbers refer to pages in vol. 4 of Hegel's *Werke,* ed. H. Büchner and O. Pöggeler (Hamburg, 1968), included in Knox's edition.

[49] *PR*, 135; Hegel, *Lectures on the History of Philosophy,* trans. E. S. Haldane (London: Kegan Paul, 1892), 3:460–61. For further discussion of Hegel's criticism of Kantian morality as "empty," see Charles Taylor, *Hegel* (Cambridge: Cambridge University Press, 1975), 370–72, 376; Allen Wood, *Hegel's Ethical Thought* (Cambridge: Cambridge University Press, 1990), 154–58, which is critical of Hegel's understanding of Kant's argument; Mark Tunick, *Hegel's Political Philosophy*; and Tunick, "Are There Natural Rights?—Hegel's Break with Kant," in *Hegel on the Modern World,* ed. Ardis B. Collins (Albany: SUNY Press, 1994).

[50] *PR*, 135 Rem.

by stealing one would undermine an institution one otherwise wants to maintain. Theft is ruled out because it is an expression of a maxim supporting "no property" that contradicts a principle the thief also supports, that property should be respected. We might suppose that the thief supports the latter principle from the fact that the thief would object to anyone stealing his own property, even the things he himself stole from others, in which case the thief's own will is inconsistent. Stealing therefore is ruled out by the categorical imperative's requirement of non contradiction.

Consider again the example of a thief, only this time a thoroughly consistent thief. This person doesn't respect property at all, and when his own is stolen, he just shrugs his shoulders, perhaps smiles in appreciation of the cunning of the thief who stole from him, and recovers his losses by stealing yet again. This thief's maxim is simply "steal when it suits you." As we shall see shortly, Hegel seems to think that Kant's categorical imperative would endorse this maxim, and since the maxim is clearly unacceptable, this shows the categorical imperative to be defective. The categorical imperative cannot recommend consistent respect of property as against consistent thievery without presupposing the need for property, without sneaking in a norm that property be respected.

The Kantian might respond that the point is not whether the thief acts consistently or not; whether the thief really endorses private property and in stealing acts in contradiction with his own genuine will or just believes there is no reason to respect property rights is beside the point. What matters is that stealing requires there to be property, yet were we to universalize the maxim that one may steal, there could be no property. There is a logical contradiction in the very act of stealing. But, Hegel would argue, this still does not show that stealing is wrong or that we should have the institution of private property. It shows only that if we want property as an institution, then we cannot regard stealing as right.

Hegel agrees that it is wrong to steal property, but he does not think that we find the proper account of why it is wrong in Kant's moral philosophy. The standard of "absence of contradiction" is too weak:

> The fact that *no property* is present is in itself no more contradictory than is the non-existence of this or that individual people, family, etc., or the complete *absence of human life*. But if it is already established and presupposed that property and human life should exist and be respected, then it is a contradiction to commit theft or murder; a contradiction must be a contradiction with something, that is, with a content which is already fundamentally present as an established principle. . . . But if a duty is to be willed merely as a duty and not because of its content, it is a *formal identity* which necessarily excludes every content and determination.[51]

The categorical imperative tells us only that if we have property we must not steal, or that if we have promises we must keep them, but it does not tell us whether or why we should have property as opposed to not-property or promises as opposed to not-promises:

[51] PR, 135 Rem. Cf. PR, 135Z; and *Natural Law*, 437.

If the specification of property in general be posited, then we can construct the tautological statement: property is property and nothing else. And this tautological production is the legislation of this practical reason; property, if property is, must be property.
But if we posit the opposite thing, negation of property, then the legislation of this same
practical reason produces the tautology: non-property is non-property. If property is
not to be, then whatever claims to be property must be cancelled. But the aim is precisely to prove that property must be; the sole thing at issue is what lies outside the
capacity of this practical legislation of pure reason [the categorical imperative], namely
to decide which of the opposed specific things must be lawful.[52]

Indeed, we might say that the categorical imperative doesn't even "tell us" that if
there is property we must not steal: it only reminds us of this; all it can do is insist
we abide by those rules of practices upon which the maintenance of the practice
depends.

In Hegel's view, there already are established principles present that determine
how we ought to act. We find them when we turn to ethical life, when we make
"the transition to the concept of ethics" and turn for moral guidance not to a
formal principle of non-contradiction but to principles immanent in our shared
understandings and practices. Without appealing to these immanent (as opposed
to abstract) principles, we could just as easily say "not-property" is acceptable.
That is Hegel's criticism of Kant's categorical imperative as empty.

Kant surely does not think the categorical imperative justifies not-property just
as easily as property, or that it justifies a consistent policy of murder, although it
has been understood to do just that, and not only by Hegel.[53] It is easy to see how
murder, or perhaps even deceit, is ruled out by the FEI, for these actions make us
unable to consent to one's maxims. But, as I've argued, stealing from me or making
a false promise to me does not obviously incapacitate me to that extent. False
promises or theft violate the FEI only because we regard them as victimizing; but
the categorical imperative cannot itself tell us why we should regard them as
victimizing. It may seem natural to think that having one's property stolen or being
the recipient of a false promise is to be a victim, is to be treated improperly merely
as a means; but it seems natural only because we have expectations that our
property be respected, that promises be kept, and we have these expectations
because we have been brought up with and share certain social practices. One
could imagine a society without private property where there was no expectation of
exclusive possession, or a society without promising where there was no expectation that one would keep one's word. In such a society, what to us would look like
theft or a false promise would not be regarded as victimizing. Of course there are
good reasons for wanting the practice of promising or the institution of private
property, reasons that might justify regarding false promises and theft as wrongs;
but the categorical imperative does not itself point to any of these reasons.

[52] *Natural Law* 437; cf. *PR*, 135Z: "The criterion that there should be no contradiction is nonproductive—for where there is nothing, there can be no contradiction either."
[53] John Stuart Mill, in chapter 1 of *On Utilitarianism*, says that Kant's categorical imperative justifies "the most outrageously immoral rules of conduct."

I have suggested a way to understand Hegel's argument that the categorical imperative cannot make particular determinations of duty without bringing in matter from the outside: it is only by reference to the expectations that arise from social practice that we have a conception of what counts as treating a human being as a means, of what counts as violating the categorical imperative. Absent such external reference, which Kant claims is unnecessary and even destructive of morality, then the categorical imperative could justify the respect of property just as well as its thoroughgoing repudiation.[54]

In rejecting Kant's claim to develop an a priori, nonempirical moral theory, Hegel puts in its place a theory that insists we appeal to the social practices of our ethical life in determining what ethics and the law require. As we shall see in the following sections, this position has difficulties of its own.

HEGEL ON THE IMPORTANCE OF SOCIAL PRACTICE

Hegel poses the question "what is duty?" in paragraph 134 of *Philosophy of Right* (hereafter *PR*). In paragraph 136 he raises the possibility that the answer to this question is given by "conscience": "conscience knows itself as thought, and that this thought of mine is my sole source of obligation." But there is a problem with appealing to conscience as the standard for determining duty; as a "rule for a mode of conduct," it is not "rational, absolutely valid, and universal."[55] Conscience is a subjective standard (*PR* 137). Hegel does think it essential in the modern world that the source of right come from within: "Conscience represents an exalted point of view, a point of view of the modern world, which has for the first time attained this consciousness, this descent into the self."[56] But conscience can dissolve into any subjective feelings at all, and such feelings are not the basis of right and obligation. In his *Lectures on the Philosophy of Religion*, Hegel asks, "Is then something true or legitimate because it is in my feeling? Is feeling the verification, or must the content be just, true, or ethical in and for itself? These days we often find the former contention advanced." Hegel takes his stand against this view:

> We have means enough in our consciousness for evaluating this contention. In our consciousness we know very well that, in order to know that a content is of the right kind, we must look about for grounds of decision other than those of feeling. For it is true that every content is capable of being in feeling: religion, right, ethics, crime,

---

[54] O'Hagan interprets the FEI as ruling out some of the very property relations Kant suggests it supports: "[The FEI] can be used as a powerful critical tool for excluding forms of property which would reduce persons to the status of means to others' ends." He suggests the categorical imperative "excludes capitalist property relations" ("On Hegel's Critique," 144–45). O'Hagan adds that the "never simply . . . but always at the same time" proviso of the FEI leaves a "loophole through which the 'right Kantian' can escape." That the categorical imperative can be interpreted both as justifying *and* excluding private property is precisely Hegel's point.

[55] *PR*, 137 Rem.

[56] *PR*, 137 Rem.

passions. Each content has a place in feeling. If feeling is the justifying element, then the distinction between good and evil comes to naught, for evil with all its shadings and qualifications is in feeling just as much as the good. Everything evil, all crime, base passions, hatred and wrath, it all has its root in feeling. The murderer feels that he must do what he does.[57]

Hegel, like Kant, believes we can be right or wrong about many moral issues and seeks an objective standard of ethics.

Hegel does not deny the importance of conscience. Like Kant, Hegel believes that if we are to be free obeying the moral law, then that law must not be externally imposed—it must come from within. Conscience is a source of moral guidance, but only insofar as it conforms with objective standards. What conscience dictates must be justified. Conscience must be what Hegel calls "true conscience," and true conscience comes only in ethical life.[58] The practices and institutions of ethical life provide the standards for right conduct, and only when our conscience— our subjective standards for action—accord with these objective standards do we act rightly, do we do our duty.

In Hegel's view, the objective standards of right are found in laws (by which I shall also refer to practices and institutions). They inhere in an "ethical substance," which no single person makes.[59] To violate these laws is to violate our very substance. Hegel speaks of the ethical substance, or the "objective ethical order," as "an object over against the subject," an "absolute authority and power infinitely more firmly established than the being of nature," but an object that is not "alien to the subject.[60] On the contrary, [the individual's] spirit bears witness to [the ethical order] as to its own essence."[61] The individual stands related to the laws of the ethical substance as to "the substance of his own being."[62]

The idea Hegel is trying to convey in these passages is that we have been socialized by the laws of our community to such an extent that our membership in this community is essential to our identity—were we brought up with other practices, we would be a different person, have a different identity. Hegel's concept of an ethical substance relies on some obscuring metaphors that Hegel doesn't explicate in precise terms; nevertheless, the following claims seem clear: we have our conception of right because we have been brought up with certain practices. Had we lived in a different ethical community with substantially different practices, we would have a different conception of right. Moreover, the laws and practices that shape us existed prior to our developing our notion of right; it

---

[57] Hegel, *Lectures on the Philosophy of Religion,* ed. Peter C. Hodgson (Berkeley: University of California Press, 1988), 144–45.

[58] *PR,* 137 and Rem.

[59] Cf. *PR,* 273 Rem, end.

[60] *PR,* 144, 146.

[61] *PR,* 147.

[62] *PR,* 148. See in general *PR,* 144–56. For further discussion see Mark Tunick, *Hegel's Political Philosophy,* chap. 4; Charles Taylor, *Hegel,* chap. 14; and Allen Wood, *Hegel's Ethical Thought,* pp. 196–97, 243–46.

is wrong to think that we have an idea of right that we then use to construct practices conforming with the idea.

Hegel rejects the view that laws are constructed according to abstract principles or a notion of right that we have prior to the development of these laws. Laws are right prior to a particular individual's willing the existence of or consenting to them. Statutory laws against theft merely formalize our already existing practice of respecting the property of our fellow citizens. The practice is prior to the positing of it in law. In Hegel's view, we are first born into an ethical community; as children, he writes, we are "suckled at the breast of universal ethical life."[63] We are brought up just to practice, and only later do we come to agree with the reasons for the practice. This is why Hegel speaks of our ethical substance as our "ground and goal."[64] It is our ground in the sense that it shapes us; we have our ideas of right, our values, our identity, as a result of having been brought up with the practices of our ethical life, practices that we found already there, that none of us actually instituted. It is our goal in the sense that we are free complying with the demands of ethical life only when we come to see the reasons for them, to see their rationality.[65]

Of course all laws have an origin, were at some point enacted. Hegel speaks of the maker as the "founder," a figure that has taken on mythical proportions:

> Laws are the ground or scaffold of a people, they belong to the oldest memories—they are ascribed to gods and heroes. . . . Lawgivers have a lasting influence. . . . [They] are eternally honoured, and are present in our daily life. But the grounding of these laws are often said to be older than these men, they are said to be eternal, or divine. [One thinks of] Antigone. In this way they *appear* as natural laws, something unchanging.[66]

But the myth of the founder, like the myth of the social contract, is an after-the-fact rationalization of the emergence of norms no assignable individuals ever make.[67] Hegel acknowledges the Solons and Numas: "Famous but few are the names of the lawgivers"; but he says that their accomplishment was essentially to "collect" the laws—they codified what already was practiced.[68]

Hegel's approach in answering the question "what is our duty?" differs fundamentally from Kant's. While Kant insists that something is right only if it complies with an abstract principle, and that the existence of social norms and prac-

---

[63] *Natural Law*, p. 115.

[64] Hegel, *Phenomenology of Spirit*, trans. A. V. Miller (Oxford: Oxford University Press, 1977), par. 439: "Spirit, being the substance and the universal . . . is the unmoved solid ground and starting point for the action of all, and it is their purpose and goal." Cf. *Phenomenology*, pars. 348, 439–40, 680, 801. Cf. *PR*, 142: "Self-consciousness has in the ethical realm its absolute foundation and the end which actuates its effort"; *PR*, 143, the "totality of the Idea" is the will's "foundation and content."

[65] For an extensive discussion of how in Hegel's view we are free obeying laws only when we come to see their rationality, see Tunick, *Hegel's Political Philosophy*, chap. 3.

[66] *Vorlesungen über Rechtsphilosophie*, ed. Karl-Heinz Ilting(Stuttgart: Friedrich Fromann, 1974), 4:918. Translations from the lecture notes are my own.

[67] Hegel regards social contract theory not only as historically false but as philosophically objectionable. See *PR*, 29 Rem, 75 Rem, 100 Rem, 258 Rem, 281 Rem.

[68] *Vorlesungen*, ed. Ilting, 4:918.

tices that characterize how many of us do act has no bearing on how we ought to act, for Hegel how we ought to act necessarily is dictated by how we do act. To know what ethics demands, we must turn to our ethical life. There we find laws that reflect the spirit of our age. They have shaped us and express values that we have internalized, so that conforming with these laws has become our second nature.[69] Taken together, they constitute our substance, our identity. To violate them is to violate ourselves, to act against our own implicit will.

The problem with Hegel's account, as it has been explained so far, is that it offers little justification for adhering to the norms and practices with which we have been brought up apart from the fact that they are familiar to us and are readily known. He turns to them in part because they are "objective," unlike feelings, convictions, or Kantian moral principles, all of which he takes to be subjective. But does the fact that practices and laws provide objective standards mean that they are right? What if our practices are *bad*? What if they oppress, exploit, emiserate? Must we still say they are right, as it were by definition, or because we have been shaped so deeply by them? Are there no critical standards by which we can assess *whether* our practices are right, or which among them are and which aren't right, in Hegel's view?

Hegel believes there are.[70] He determines what ethics requires by turning to the practices of ethical life with which we have been brought up. But he doesn't think the fact that these practices exist in itself justifies them. The reason Hegel thinks we have for regarding private property as right, for example, is not simply that it is an existing institution, but that by having private property each member of our ethical community is able to recognize and be mediated with each other, and Hegel regards this mediation process as a necessary step in our realizing our implicit freedom.[71] Hegel arrives at this rationale or justification of private property because he is committed to finding a justification for an existing institution that seems to him central to the modern world. But it is important to him that the existing institution can be justified by appealing to a reason beyond its mere existence. So while Hegel and Kant take divergent positions in the practice-principle debate, it would be incorrect to characterize this difference simply as: Kant appeals to principles not practice; Hegel appeals to practice not principles. For Hegel *does* see the need for principled justification or criticism of practices.

Hegel, like Kant, is a rationalist. He would be no more tolerant than Jeremy Bentham of the Burkean conservative who asks us to settle with what we are used to simply because it is what we are used to. (Bentham considers such a person as

---

[69] PR, 151. On Hegel's idea of laws being our "second nature," see also Hegel, *Philosophie des Rechts: Die Vorlesung von 1819/20*, ed. Dieter Henrich (Frankfurt: Suhrkamp Verlag, 1983), 124, 210; Wood, *Hegel's Ethical Thought*, 198; and Tunick, *Hegel's Political Philosophy*, 32, 53–54, 73, 95.

[70] This is a point that apparently has not been recognized by several commentators. See, for example, footnote 9, above; Sean Sayers, "The Actual is the Rational," in *Hegel and Modern Philosophy*, ed. David Lamb (London: Croom Helm, 1987); Sidney Hook, "Hegel Rehabilitated?" *Encounter* 24 (January 1965): 53–58; and Ossip Flechtheim, *Hegels Strafrechtstheorie* (Berlin: Duncker und Humblot, 1975). For reference to other commentators who read Hegel as uncritical, and for criticism of this interpretation, see Tunick, *Hegel's Political Philosophy*, 152–67.

[71] PR, 72.

"labouring under a general and incurable imbecility.")[72] In Hegel's view, the content of ethics and the law arises largely from custom, is handed down to us, but what justifies this content and explains why we are not unfree in doing our duty is not the fact of its existence. We are obligated to comply with the demands of our ethical life only if that ethical life is rational: "Whatever is to achieve recognition today no longer achieves it by force, and only to a small extent through habit and custom, but mainly through insight and reasons (*Einsicht und Gründe*)."[73] The state is based on reasons and principles, and we must know this. If we do not, then our obligations are based merely "on authority."[74] For Hegel, "legitimacy comes from rational principles grounding law, not from tradition or custom."[75] Hegel thinks there are, and must be, reasons that ethics and the law have the content they do. That something happens to be what we do is not itself a sufficient reason for doing it.

While Hegel thinks ethical judgments should be principled, the principles that ground these judgments must be of the right sort—they must not be "abstract." Abstract principles are principles with which we can make judgments without reference to the rules, purposes, or other features of practices. When teachers grade essays on the basis of grammatical correctness, coherence, or the amount of evidence used to support the argument of the essay, they are appealing to principles that make reference to the practice of assigning essays, principles that are not abstract. These principles, such as that coherence merits a good grade, make reference to a particular practice, and are inapplicable in other contexts, such as judging moral guilt or deciding when to punish legally, whether to keep a promise or what level of taxation to impose. Abstract principles can be used to make all sorts of judgments precisely because they do not depend on features of particular practices. Kant's categorical imperative is an abstract principle.

One problem Hegel sees with at least some abstract principles is that they are indeterminate. Hegel is critical of Kant because Kant, in determining what our moral duties are, refuses to appeal to what is done, instead proposing what Hegel understands to be a formal principle of consistency, the categorical imperative, that, Hegel argues, is unable to determine the content of our moral obligations.

Another problem Hegel sees with abstract principles is that they do not alone motivate us to perform our duties or obligations. For Hegel, what often motivates us is not knowledge that our duty conforms with principles—abstract or otherwise—but, rather, a feeling such as love for the object of our duty. Hegel says Kant's categorical imperative lacks concreteness, because to live by it we

---

[72] Jeremy Bentham, *Book of Fallacies*, in Bowring, ed., *Works* (Edinburgh: William Tait, 1838), 8:392–93. See also Justice Holmes, "The Path of the Law," *Harvard Law Review* 10 (1897): 469: "It is revolting to have no better reason for a rule of law than that it was laid down in the time of Henry IV. It is still more revolting if the grounds upon which it was laid down have vanished long since, and the rule simply persists from blind imitation of the past" (cited in Justice Blackmun's dissent in *Bowers v. Hardwick*, 478 US at 199 [1986]).

[73] *PR*, 316Z, p. 353, modified translation.

[74] *PR*, 270 Rem, p. 299.

[75] Hegel, *Philosophy of History*, in G.W.F. Hegel, *Werke in zwanzig Bänden*, ed. Eva Moldenhauer and Karl Michel (Frankfurt am Main: Suhrkamp Verlag, 1986), 12:417.

need not know anything particular about ourselves or those to whom we have obligations. In this respect, Hegel notes, the categorical imperative is similar to the Christian abstract conception of duty. In his lectures and own marginal comments to the *Philosophy of Right*, Hegel criticizes the Christian prescription of universal love. Hegel writes that "universal human love" is "universal" but "empty," for "human beings are concrete individuals";[76] and in his lectures he asks: "How can I demand the welfare of the Chinese? . . . The Bible is more rational in saying love thy neighbor as yourself, i.e. the people with whom you come into relation."[77] Hegel's point here is that we have obligations and other commitments and are disposed to make good on them, not because of some abstract principle but because we already are involved in concrete relations that do require us and make us want to act in certain ways. This understanding of our interest in being moral contrasts sharply with Kant's. For Kant, "all respect for a person is properly only respect for the law of which the person provides an example. . . . All so-called moral interest consists solely in respect for the law."[78] But for Hegel, ethics is "implanted in the child in the form of feeling."[79] We are motivated to be moral not out of respect for an abstract, universal principle but because we care about and feel for the people with whom we come into relation. We are brought up with the practices, laws, and institutions that determine what our obligations are. Acting in accordance with their demands has become second nature to us, is what we have come really to will.

Hegel, as we've seen, does not think that practices or institutions are justified because we have strong feelings for them. Their legitimacy comes from "rational principles." While Hegel generally opposes abstract principles,[80] he does not reject appeals to principles. What other sorts of principles are there? Sometimes Hegel appeals to principles that are immanent in discrete practices or institutions, such as marriage (PR 168), private property (PR 41, 46Z), hereditary monarchy (PR 279, 280), or legal punishment (PR 99 Rem.). Here a principle is a formulation of the purpose of the practice or institution. For example, by turning to features of legal punishment we might conclude that the purpose of punishment is to mete out just deserts, and this purpose becomes a principle of punishment, used to determine whether we should punish in a particular case.[81] A principle of just deserts might justify an insanity defense, insofar as we think punishing someone for violating the law when that person was incapable of conforming with the law would be to give that person what they don't deserve; it could also be used to

---

[76] Hegel, *Werke*, 7:238, corresponding to *PR*, 126.

[77] Hegel, *Vorlesungen*, 4:338, lines 16–22. Cf. *PR*, 280, p. 218: "Love, the ethical moment in marriage, is, as love, a feeling for actual individuals in the present, not for an abstraction."

[78] Kant, *Groundwork*, 402 n. 14 (last five lines).

[79] *PR*, 175Z, p. 213.

[80] But not always. For example, he is sympathetic to principles of equality and of human rights to property, insofar as they are used to criticize feudal privileges. However, as we shall see, he opposes using the principle of equality as a basis of wealth distribution.

[81] For further discussion of immanent criticism of the practice of legal punishment, including discussion of its limitations, see Mark Tunick, *Punishment: Theory and Practice* (Berkeley: University of California Press, 1992).

criticize aspects of existing practice, as when, for example, we invoke a sentence grossly disproportionate to the offense. Such immanent principles are not abstract, for they presuppose a practice. But they do not help us to justify or criticize practices as a whole. Appealing to a principle immanent in the practice of punishment to tell us how we should punish won't satisfy someone who doesn't think we should punish people at all.

There is another principle to which Hegel appeals and that serves as his standard for justifying practices as a whole (as opposed to actions within practices)— the principle of *rationality*. In Hegel's view, we should appeal to the practices of ethical life in determining what ethics and the law require not merely because they exist, but because and insofar as these practices are rational.

Hegel's Principle of Rationality

Unfortunately Hegel does not clearly lay out what he means by rationality, and sometimes what he says is confusing. In one passage Hegel says that to be rational is to accord with "recognized principles," suggesting that something is rational if it conforms with an abstract principle (*PR* 270, p. 291). But Hegel implicitly distinguishes principles of the right sort from abstract principles: "Predicates, principles, and the like get us nowhere in assessing the state, which must be apprehended as an organism" (*PR* 269Z, p. 290). Something is rational, for Hegel, not if it conforms to abstract principles, but if it can be apprehended in a certain way.

While Hegel does not expressly state his criteria of rationality, from his texts I think we can single out three conditions, all of which he thinks must obtain for a practice to be rational. A practice is rational, and commands our commitment, if it is part of a system of ethical life that is (1) coherent, (2) functional and enduring, and (3) if we are "at home" in this system of ethical life.

Ethical life as a whole is rational in part if it is a coherent system: "The fact that the ethical sphere is the *system* of these determinations of the Idea constitutes its *rationality*."[82] A particular practice or law is rational if it is part of a system that we can understand to be a coherent whole, our ethical substance.[83] Hegel praises Montesquieu for understanding that particular laws or practices "should not be considered in isolation and in the abstract, but rather as a dependent moment within *one* totality, in the context of all the other determinations that constitute the character of a nation and age; within this context they gain their genuine significance, and hence also their justification."[84] Practices or laws are rational in part if they are integral parts of a system, cohering with the other practices and institutions of ethical life. A rational practice is closely interwoven with other

---

[82] *PR*, 145, p. 190. Cf. *PR*, 3 Rem; *PR*, 261 Rem, p. 283: "The part should be considered only with reference to the whole"; and *PR*, 211Z, p. 243: "Right . . . must be a system in itself." Cf. Michael Hardimon, "The Project of Reconciliation: Hegel's Social Philosophy," *Philosophy and Public Affairs* 21, no. 2 (spring 1992): 168: Hegel seeks to show that "the family, civil society, and the state formed a single coherent, intelligible system that promoted both individuality and community."

[83] That practices cohere does not mean that there will be no conflicts of duties—see *PR*, 127–28.

[84] *PR*, 3 Rem, p. 29.

practices so that to change one would require changing others. They all hang together as part of a coherent system. According to this criterion, we can say that in a modern state a practice of allowing theft would be irrational for it would undermine the institution of private property, which itself is interwoven with other practices, such as entering into contracts and working for wages so that one can come to acquire family capital. If property were not secure, many of our other practices would not be secure.

Hegel is not offering merely a coherence theory, however. Our practices, laws, and institutions are rational not merely so long as they cohere with other practices, laws, and institutions that we share. They must promote our values; they must promote our capacity to realize our potential as free human beings; they must provide an enduring home that develops and reflects what we call the "character of a nation." In short, they must satisfy the other two criteria of rationality.

Hegel characterizes the modern state or ethical substance as "a fixed and *enduring* determinacy."[85] A practice is rational if it is an integral part of an enduring system. To be enduring, the system of laws, practices and institutions must be functional. In discussing proposals for absolute equality of property, Hegel notes how such a system would not last very long since the more diligent would soon acquire more, and he concludes, "But if something is impracticable, it ought not to be put into practice either."[86] Institutions that conform with abstract principles such as equality may be appealing in theory, but for Hegel one test for whether an institution is rational is that it is a well-functioning part of an enduring system of ethical life. Functionality is a criterion of rationality.[87]

The third of Hegel's criterion for rationality is that the system of ethical life of which a rational practice is an integral part, not just endures but is our home. "Only the will that obeys the laws is free, for it obeys itself and is at home [*bei sich selbst*] and free."[88] This idea of "being at home," which for Hegel is the same as being "free," is central to Hegel's political philosophy, and I have discussed it at length elsewhere.[89] What I want to emphasize here is that while "being at home in" might strike us as an extremely subjective criterion for rationality, Hegel does not intend it to be. As recent commentators have emphasized, there are objective conditions for being at home: my basic needs and welfare must be met; and the practices and laws of my ethical life must reflect the character of my people—its values must express my values.[90] The obligations that arise from rational social institutions and laws are obligations to people with whom we identify, to whom we feel a special bond and sense of commitment. These feelings and bonds arise in part because we are brought up and educated to share in the same practices.

---

[85] *PR*, 270Z, p. 302, my emphasis; cf. *PR*, 272, p. 305. Also, *PR*, preface, p. 11, on "enduring."

[86] *PR*, 49Z, p. 80.

[87] Cf. Steven B. Smith, *Hegel's Critique of Liberalism: Rights in Context* (Chicago: University of Chicago Press, 1989), 225.

[88] Hegel, *Werke*, 12:57.

[89] Tunick, *Hegel's Political Philosophy*, chaps. 3, 6.

[90] Hardimon, "Project of Reconciliation," 183, 185.

Private property, contracts, marriage, the administration of justice, military service, etc. are rational institutions and practices, in Hegel's view, not merely because they are interdependent but because they perform a bond-creating function that preserves the system of ethical life and gets its members to be at home in it. To be at home, I must have my interests expressed and have the opportunity to cultivate my capacity for ethical commitments, which requires that I be recognized by others as a free being. Hegel's purpose in *Philosophy of Right* is to show how the practices and institutions of the modern state realize these objectives; that they do so is what makes them rational.[91] Slavery is not rational, in Hegel's view, for the slave is denied recognition by others and the ability to develop the other capacities needed to be at home. Hegel argues that it is through the institutions of property, contracts, marriage, and other institutions of the modern state that we are able to feel and see that we are at home, and states lacking these or functionally equivalent institutions are not rational.[92]

When Hegel argues that we come to know what ethics and the law require by turning to our existing laws, he is not claiming that, by definition, every existing law is right or that existing laws are right because they exist. Hegel insists that laws are right only if they are rational, and so he appeals to principles and not just to social practice. But unlike for Kant, for Hegel the principles to which we must appeal are not abstract.

I am not here defending Hegel's principle of rationality. Some of us may feel it is no less subjective than is Kant's categorical imperative in Hegel's eyes, and I have doubts that the principle could ever be articulated precisely enough to be of much practical use to those dealing with the sorts of particular ethical and legal issues with which the rest of this book is occupied—it is simply too general a principle.[93] What I think is important to emphasize, though, is that Hegel takes a theoretical position that recognizes the importance both of social practice and of principles.

Hegel is not an antirationalist, blindly deferring to existing practices. He appeals to principles but to principles that refer to the existence of practices. His

---

[91] For a more detailed account of how Hegel claims to show that the institutions of the modern state are necessary for the realization of our freedom, see Mark Tunick, "Hegel's Nonfoundationalism: A Phenomenological Account of the Structure of *Philosophy of Right*," *History of Philosophy Quarterly* 11 (1994): 317–38.

[92] I believe Hegel is committed to saying that other institutions that served the same function as private property, marriage, etc., of providing the means for our recognition by others and of developing our capacity for ethical commitments, would be rational; in other words, I do not think Hegel is committed to the specific institutions he discusses in *Philosophy of Right* merely because they arose in history. Had other institutions developed instead but which also provided a home (as Hegel understands this term), Hegel would have defended them too, so long as they also were coherent parts of an enduring system of ethical life.

[93] In *Hegel's Political Philosophy*, I argue that *Philosophy of Right* is relevant in thinking about practical controversies such as legal punishment. I find of most practical benefit not Hegel's principle of rationality, but his accounts of the principles immanent in many of our practices, such as punishment, property, contract law. See also Mark Tunick, "Hegel's Justification of Hereditary Monarchy," *History of Political Thought* 12 (1991): 481–496, for another example of how Hegel appeals to immanent principles.

principle of rationality asks not "What practices would conform with the principle?" but rather "Are these practices coherent and functional, and are we at home and free in them?" Precisely because Hegel appeals to principles, he is not committed to blind adherence to practices. His position is that we are bound to do what ethical life requires, *if* that ethical life is rational.[94] But he does not think we can use principles to build practices from scratch. That is utopian. For Hegel, philosophy is

> comprehension of the present and the actual, not the setting up of a world beyond which exists God knows where—or rather, of which we can very well say that we know where it exists, namely in the errors of a one-sided and empty ratiocination.[95]

The theorist has to start with the materials at hand and is constrained by the practices and traditions that exist and have developed in history. For Kant, moral philosophy must be divorced from anthropology; for Hegel they are intricately connected.

IMPLICATIONS

We have seen how Kant and Hegel take different approaches to ethics. In this section we consider a few implications of each sort of approach.

Universalism versus Relativism

In Kant's view no reference to social practice is needed to determine what morality requires. What is morally right does not depend on the culture to which I belong or the historical period in which I live.[96] Morality, in Kant's view, is universal, is the same not only for all humans but for all rational beings,[97] Hegel disagrees. In Hegel's view, what is right is determined by one's ethical life, which consists of a set of coherent practices that may differ from the practices of another society. In Hegel's state they consisted of practices such as acquiring and alienating property, promising and contracting, marriage rituals, legal punishment, marriage, raising children, working in civil society, and fighting in wars.[98] This

---

[94] This suggests that Hegel should allow for the possibility of justified disobedience. Elsewhere I argue that he does. See Mark Tunick, *Hegel's Political Philosophy* (Princeton: Princeton University Press, 1992), 116–20 ; and Mark Tunick, "Hegel on Justified Disobedience," forthcoming in *Political Theory*.

[95] PR, preface, p. 20.

[96] In the last line of his "On a Supposed Right to Lie," Kant notes that principles bear that name solely on account of their "universality." This essay originally appeared in September 1799 in *Berlinische Blätter* and appears in *Grounding for the Metaphysics of Morals,* trans. James Ellington (Indianapolis: Hackett, 1993), 63–68.

[97] Kant, *Groundwork,* 408: "the moral law is of such widespread significance that it must hold not merely for men but for all rational beings generally."

[98] Cf. Sibyl A. Schwarzenbach, "Rawls, Hegel, and Communitarianism," *Political Theory* 19, no. 4 (November 1991): 556.

set of practices reflects a coherent set of principles and values, a moral background, shared by its participants. To share in these practices is to share in an often unstated set of understandings about the world, a set of understandings that will be different for different peoples living with different sets of practices. Hegel, then, implies that morality will be not universal with respect to all human beings, but specific to an ethical community.[99] The dispute between Kant and Hegel regarding the importance of social practice in moral judgment becomes a dispute about whether morality is universal or culturally relative.

Consider the moral obligation to keep a promise. In Kant's view, the obligation is not contingent on the existence of a practice of promising or even on a shared understanding that promises must be kept; rather, the obligation is dictated by reason and holds universally. While this view that promising is universal is widely held, there is an opposing view that holds that promissory obligations presuppose a certain background of knowledge that not all societies share.[100] For example, Fred Korn and Shulamit R. Decktor Korn claim to have found a society without promising.[101] They note how a U.S. Peace Corps volunteer, teaching in Tonga, complained to a Tongan teacher that there are no textbooks for teaching English to Tongans. The Tongan teacher replied, "Don't worry. I have such books and I'll see you get them." The American took this as a promise; yet the books never came and he concluded that Tongans don't keep their promises. But this conclusion, the Korns argue, is inappropriate, for the Tongan utterance "*is not regarded* as creating an obligation." "The speaker may or may not do as he says he will, but if he doesn't no Tongan will think ill of him." The point of the Tongan utterance, to Tongans, is to "express solidarity and concern"; merely to express sympathy or a wish that one *could* help is too weak, "for this is something anyone might say." But the utterance does not imply, to Tongans, an intention to perform the act. The Korns explain that the Tongan concept of the future is incompatible with our notion of promising. For them, the future is "indefinite and uncertain"; "saying that one will do something in the future leaves it understood that things may turn out differently." Consequently, there is no reliance on the utterance.[102] To the American, it was odd that a Tongan would utter what appears to be a promise without implying an intention to perform; but given the Tongan background of moral understandings and their concept of the future, the utterance

[99] When Hegel refers to ethical life as "universal" or as reflecting "universal rationality," he generally does not mean universal to all human beings; rather, he refers to standards shared "universally" by members of an ethical substance, which he means to contrast with particular standards of individuals; or to standards to which human beings in the modern, rational state adhere.

[100] The view that promising is universal is suggested by H. L. A. Hart, *Concept of Law* (Oxford: Clarendon Press, 1961), 188–95; Hannah Arendt, *The Human Condition* (Chicago: University of Chicago Press, 1958), 213–16; Hanna Pitkin, *Wittgenstein and Justice* (Berkeley: University of California Press, 1972), 227; and Alexander Sesonske, *Value and Obligation* (New York: Oxford University Press, 1964), 80–81; as noted in Fred Korn and Shulamit R. Decktor Korn, "Where People Don't Promise," *Ethics* 93, no. 3 (April 1983): 445.

[101] Korn and Korn, "Where People Don't Promise," 445: On the Tonga Islands "there is no institution of promising."

[102] Ibid., 447–49.

makes perfect sense: "saying but not doing does not jeopardize the relationship; on the contrary, it is a means of preserving it."[103] The Korns' account relies on an appreciation of how the existence of a discrete practice depends on a background of knowledge shared by participants in the ethical life of the society,[104] and it is this idea of a background of knowledge or understandings about the world that is central to Hegel's philosophy of right.

Hegel's position has relativist implications in that he thinks conceptions of right presuppose shared understandings that are particular to systems of ethical life, to ethical communities.[105] Though he insists that practices be rational, his standard of rationality appears to require acceptance of any coherent system of practices that works, shapes us, and in which all of its members are at home. If the criteria of rationality are met by practices—and he does not think they are met by slavery, Athenian democracy, or feudal property law, none of which endured and none of which provided the means for *all* to be recognized by others and to be at home—then there is nothing more to be said; the practices are right.[106] This is troubling for we might think it possible to identify with and be at home in practices yet those practices are wrong. In rejecting abstract principles, Hegel seems to leave no room for this possibility.

But we should not be too quick to pigeonhole Hegel as a relativist. His political theory resists easy categorizations. At times Hegel does appeal to standards that are not necessarily immanent in practices and which could be used to criticize even a set of coherent practices. In criticizing slavery, Athenian democracy, and feudal property law for failing to provide the means by which all human beings of these societies would be recognized by others and obtain a consciousness of their implicit freedom, Hegel appeals to a principle that *all* human beings should be at home in their world, should find their place, and he uses this idea to criticize states prior to the French Revolution, which did not recognize this universal right of man. Presumably Hegel would regard as irrational any society in which recognition was not regarded as important. He sees recognition and the satisfaction

---

[103] Ibid., 450.

[104] It is precisely the idea that practices fit together as a coherent system that points to what seems unconvincing in the Korns' account. The Korns note that there are other obligations among the Tongans, including marriage and familial obligations, status and friendship obligations, and most importantly for our discussion, legal contracts. It is hard to see how the Tongans can have legal contracts and property to alienate through contracts but not promissory obligations. If promissory obligations make no sense given the Tongan practice-background, we might wonder how they can have contractual obligations; and if they do have contractual obligations—if the practice of contracting makes sense to them—we might have doubts about the Korns' claim that the Tongans do not promise.

[105] Hegel isn't clear about what the boundaries of an ethical community are. At times he suggests that the ethical life of the modern state he discusses in *Philosophy of Right* is an amalgam of practices and institutions from the leading European nation-states. I discuss this issue in detail in "Political Identity and the Ties that Bind: Hegel's Practice Conception" (unpublished manuscript).

[106] It is not merely the collapse of ancient Greece that established its irrationality, but also the fact that Greek practices did not provide the means for all its members to be, or even feel, at home. There are other reasons Hegel gives as well for why Greek society was not rational; see Tunick, *Hegel's Political Philosophy*, 81–84, 164.

and freedom to which it leads as essential to being human, and is committed to
the principle that all human beings are entitled to this recognition.[107]

Kant's commitment to abstract and universal principles that make no reference
to the existence of social practices places him squarely in the camp of universalists. Hegel's recognition of the importance of the practices making up our ethical
life, in contrast, has relativist implications. But Hegel's texts allow for both relativist and universalist readings. Hegel is a universalist in some ways, a relativist in
others. He rejects Kant's claim that morality is distinct from anthropology, and he
emphasizes the importance culturally and historically variant practices have in
determining what is right. In doing so he does not advocate uncritical deference
to existing practices. While the principles he invokes to evaluate existing practices are immanent in these practices, Hegel believes the practices of ethical life
from which critical principles derive serve a universal objective—the realization
of freedom. It is tempting to conclude from the fact that there are both relativist
and universalist strands in his thought that Hegel's theory is incoherent. But I
think we should resist seeing appeals to both relativist and universalist ideas as
necessarily inconsistent. In chapter six, when we turn to the contemporary
relativism-universalism debate, I shall argue that there is a partial truth to both
sides, and this will become more apparent once we appreciate the complicated
ways in which practices and principles interact.

Political Identity and the Ties that Bind

Kant's universalism goes hand in hand with his denial of the role of culturally
variant practices in determining the content of morality. For Kant, moral codes
do not depend on one's political identity. One implication of Kant's universalist
moral theory and commitment to a principle conception is that, in his view, there
is little that binds people of particular communities—political identity isn't very
important at all. For Hegel, in contrast, one's political identity largely determines
one's morality, one's conception of right.

The disagreement between Hegel and Kant about the role of shared practices in
determining what is right reflects their very different accounts of the ties that bind
members of a political community. For Kant a community shares a general will
that confirms that which is right a priori and by reason.[108] For Hegel, too, a
community shares a general will, but the character of this general will is very
different. For Kant, what unites individuals in a general or common will is that
these individuals "can come into practical relations with one another."[109] That
there is a general will is a postulate derived a priori from reason, for the general
will presupposes only that individuals come into contact with one another in

---

[107] For a more detailed discussion of the extent to which Hegel is a relativist, a discussion that
brings into this controversy Hegel's conception of historical development, see Tunick, "Hegel's
Nonfoundationalism."

[108] See MM, 255–57.

[109] MM, 263.

ways that affect each others' rights, which they will do given the spherical shape of the earth.[110] A state consists in a group of people whose members "cannot avoid interacting."[111] Eventually Kant thinks that "since the earth's surface is not unlimited but closed," we will come to interact with all human beings and the right of nations will lead "inevitably" to a cosmopolitan Right.[112] But for Hegel, the general will is particular and universal; it is an ethical substance. And for Hegel, we say that practices are right not by an a priori determination of reason that is confirmed by reflection but because they are shared by people who make up an ethical substance, so that where for Kant violating right is to act contradictorily and against reason, for Hegel it is to commit an act of self-contradiction.

Kant takes the position, sometimes seen as the defining feature of classical liberal theory, that ties to community are less important than ties to the species, that all humans, no matter their political identity, are essentially the same. While Hegel does not deny that all human beings are worthy of respect just because they are human beings, he takes a position in contrast to Kant's, a position that might be seen as a defining feature of communitarian political thought, namely, that shared practices and understandings are ties that bind and a basis for a shared identity.

One way practices play this role, in Hegel's view, is by establishing common interests; people benefit from having certain practices and consequently have a common interest in their maintenance.[113] In addition, through institutions and practices, activity becomes habitualized, becomes "second nature" for members, what they are used to (Gewohnheit), and this provides a basis for a shared identity.[114] Through practices and institutions, a shared disposition (Gesinnung) is instilled that binds members of an ethical substance.[115] Practices both engender

[110] MM, 338, 311; cf. 263.

[111] MM, 312.

[112] MM, 311.

[113] See Hegel, Encyclopedia, vol. 3, par. 515; also, in his early essay, "German Constitution," Hegel says that a state presupposes a sense of a common interest or good, and it is just this sense that was lacking in Germany then (Hegel, German Constitution, 106). In the Philosophy of History, Hegel speaks, with regret, of Germany after the Peace of Westphalia as a "constituted anarchy," built on "the principle of private right that the privilege of all the constituent parts . . . to act for themselves contrarily to the interest of the whole . . . is guaranteed and secured by the most inviolable sanctions"(436). Hegel praises Frederick II of Prussia because he "comprehended the general object of the state"—Hegel says he was the first sovereign "who kept the general interest of the state steadily in view, ceasing to pay any respect to particular interests when they stood in the way of the commonweal"(441). In this work Hegel also says India lacks an ethical life (Sittlichkeit) because there is no sense of commonality; duties are based on caste not on membership in society as a whole (148)—Sibree translates Sittlichkeit here as "morality" and not "ethical life," thereby deflecting attention from this important passage.

[114] PR, 268.

[115] Cf. Charles Taylor, Hegel (Cambridge: Cambridge University Press, 1975), 382. Hegel says dispositions themselves are too subjective a bond—we "require a mechanism, too"(Vorlesungen, 1:326, lines 17–26; corresponding to PR, 267). Dispositions and sentiments of patriotism themselves arise from institutions and practices (ibid., 4:641, lines 17–19). Hegel adds that while the state needs an ethical disposition on the part of its members, it cannot demand it as a duty, or punish those who lack it (ibid., 3:735, line 32; 3:736, line 13).

and presuppose commonly held judgments about what is appropriate or right—the sharing of these judgments (such as that it is normally wrong not to keep one's promises) helps define and maintain a moral community. In the concluding chapter we shall return to the topic of political identity and the ties that bind when we apply what has been said about practices and principles to the contemporary "liberal"-"communitarian" debate.

KANT OR HEGEL: PRINCIPLES WITHOUT PRACTICE OR PRINCIPLES IMMANENT IN PRACTICE?

For Hegel, morality and political identity are inseparable. For Kant they are utterly divorced. Kant goes out of his way to insist that in determining what is morally right we need not appeal to social norms or practices. If something is right, it is so not because it is what we do or have done in the past but because it accords with principles that are valid for all rational beings, regardless of time or place. Hegel does not disagree with the idea that to justify our actions it is not sufficient to show how they are simply required by existing practices: when we need to justify those practices, we must do more than point to the fact that these practices exist. The practices must be shown to accord with some standard of rationality. So it's wrong to characterize the dispute between Kant and Hegel as follows: Kant sides with principles alone, while Hegel sides with practices alone. Hegel and Kant agree that morality must invoke principles. But for Hegel, the principles that guide the moral person are immanent in her ethical life. Hegel recognizes a crucial role for social practice in ethical judging. Kant does not.

Kant seems right that the reason it is wrong to break a promise is not that doing so violates a social practice. But his claim that the demand to keep promises exists even absent a social practice is hard to accept. I have suggested that Kant's argument for why it is wrong to break promises—that doing so treats humans as means—itself assumes that we regard false promises as victimizing the promisee, and arguably we regard it as so only because we share the practice of promising and various background understandings.

In the *Natural Law* essay, Hegel says that Kant's categorical imperative is "superfluous."[116] But Hegel surely cannot mean that applying rational principles is superfluous in deciding what we should do, as he himself sees the need for this. Hegel's point of disagreement with Kant concerns the need to appeal to empirical matters, to existing practices, to what is done. The dispute between Kant and Hegel is a dispute over the relevance of existing practice in determining what morality requires. If we see the Kant-Hegel debate as a debate between principled criticism and blind deference to traditions and existing practices, then it would be hard not to side with Kant against Hegel. But I have argued that this is not how

[116] "The sole thing at issue is what lies outside the capacity of this practical legislation of pure reason, namely to decide which of the opposed specific things must be lawful. But pure reason demands that this shall have been done beforehand, and that one of the opposed specific things shall be presupposed, and only then can pure reason perform its now superfluous legislation" (437).

the debate should be characterized. Hegel is just as much the rationalist as Kant. Both Kant and Hegel rightly appreciate the need for principled criticism. Kant goes astray, however, in insisting that moral principles need make no reference to social practice. In the rest of the book I shall argue both for principled criticism and for sensitivity to culturally variant norms and practices. At the end of the book, it is my hope, we shall agree that Hegel makes the better case in their real debate, which concerns the relevance of existing practice in determining what ethics requires, insofar as he recognizes the importance our social practices and shared understandings have when we choose and apply principles.

CHAPTER THREE

Promises

THE PROBLEM

John Locke believed the obligation to keep promises existed in a state of nature.

> The promises and bargains for truck, &c. between [t]wo men in the desert island . . .; or between a Swiss and an Indian, in the woods of America, are binding to them, though they are perfectly in a state of nature in reference to one another: for truth and keeping of faith belongs to men, as men, and not as members of society.[1]

Differences in language might prevent the Swiss and the Indian from actually using the word *promise* or its equivalent to create an obligation. But Locke's point is that a promissory obligation could arise between them even though they do not share a social practice of promising, or the word *promise*. The obligation is natural not conventional. Locke believed that the obligation binds all human beings, regardless of their political or cultural identity. In Locke's view, the obligation to keep promises is natural and universal to the species.

Locke attributed other obligations or duties to a state of nature that seem clearly to be conventional, most notably the duty to respect the rights of private property.[2] But many theorists have shared his view that the obligation to keep promises is natural and holds regardless of one's cultural or political roots. Grotius, for example, characterized the obligation to keep promises as natural, a dictate of reason:

> God himself, who can be limited by no established rules of law, would act contrary to his own nature, if he did not perform his promises. From whence it follows that the obligations to perform promises spring from the nature of that unchangeable justice, which is an attribute of God, and common to all who bear his image, in the use of reason.[3]

In chapter two we saw that Kant also claims that the obligation to keep promises does not depend on the existence of a social practice; for Kant, the obligation arises from the categorical imperative and exists for all rational beings. Recently, several moral philosophers have echoed Kant, arguing that creating promissory obligations does not require a social practice. F. S. McNeilly argues that a pair of

---

[1] John Locke, *Second Treatise of Government* (Indianapolis: Hackett, 1980), chap. 2, para. 14.

[2] Ibid., chap. 5, para. 25, on property existing prior to any express compact.

[3] Hugo Grotius, *The Rights of War and Peace*, trans. A. C. Campbell (Washington, D.C.: M. Walter Dunne, 1901), sec. 11:4 (p. 134). At one point, though, Grotius says that natural means "nothing more than what is received by general custom," or what is "the general practice among some nations," or what is "customary and habitual" (12:25, p. 159).

promisors could exist within a society "in which there is no general practice of promising of any kind."[4] R. S. Downie writes that there is a "natural" moral obligation to carry out one's firm intentions.[5] Neil MacCormick argues, "It is quite unnecessary in the explanation of promising and of the obligation to keep promises to invoke the concept of a power-conferring rule enshrined in a social practice."[6] Thomas Scanlon writes that "when promises give rise to clear obligations, these can be accounted for on the basis of general moral principles that do not refer to the existence of social practices."[7]

However, others disagree with Locke's claim. They insist that the obligation to keep promises exists only if there is an antecedent social practice; the obligation is conventional not natural. A classic account of this view is given by David Hume: "A man, unacquainted with society, could never enter into any engagements with another, even tho' they could perceive each other's thoughts by intuition." "Fidelity is no natural virtue," writes Hume, and "promises have no force, antecedent to human conventions."[8] Among recent moral and legal philosophers, H. L. A. Hart takes a similar position. He argues not only that promising requires prior accepted procedures for promising but that the obligation to keep promises arises from these prior procedures. He begins by noting, "If no such procedures exist, promising is logically impossible, just as saluting would be logically impossible if there were no accepted conventions specifying the gestures of formal recognition within a military group."[9] This in itself is not a fatal objection to Locke's position. While it casts doubt on Locke's suggestion that what we call a promise could be made in a state of nature even between people of different societies with different languages, we can read Locke's passage to mean that the obligations which those with the social practice of promising *call* promissory obligations can arise in a state of nature even if they wouldn't be characterized as promissory. That saying the words *I promise* will only be promising given the existence of the practice does not mean that what we call promissory obligations depend on a social practice of promising.[10] It may be that A can undertake an obligation to do something for B by promising only if A and B share in a moral community, language game, or social practice. But it may also be the case that A

---

[4] F. S. McNeilly, "Promises De-Moralized," *Philosophical Review* 81 (1972): 75.

[5] R. S. Downie, "Three Accounts of Promising," *Philosophical Quarterly* 35, no. 140 (July 1985): 267–68.

[6] Neil MacCormick, "Voluntary Obligations and Normative Powers I," *Proceedings of the Aristotelian Society* 46 (1972), supp., p. 61.

[7] Thomas Scanlon, "Promises and Practices," *Philosophy and Public Affairs* 19, no. 3 (summer 1990): 220.

[8] David Hume, *A Treatise of Human Nature,* ed. L. A. Selby-Bigge, 2d ed. (Oxford: Oxford University Press, 1978): 516, 519.

[9] H. L. A. Hart, "Legal and Moral Obligation," in A. I. Melden, ed. *Essays in Moral Philosophy* (Seattle: University of Washington Press, 1958), 101.

[10] That the words *I promise* will only be promising given the existence of a practice is noted by John Rawls in his "Two Concepts of Rules," *Philosophical Review* 64 (1955): 30. Cf. A. I. Melden, "On Promising," 64–65: "the promise utterance has no use except in the context in which the parties concerned are members of or constitute a moral community and, in this sense, are in agreement."

can undertake an obligation *of the same kind* as the promissory obligation without invoking a practice. The obligation arising when one says "I promise" may be just one particular instance of a more general class of obligations that exist naturally. The conditions that arise when one utters "I promise" can arise without appealing to the conventional device of uttering those words, and we might speak of the existence of those conditions as the existence of a promissory obligation even if they exist in a world without that conventional device. As we shall see, that is precisely Scanlon's position, and is consistent with what Locke says. But Hart rejects even this position. For Hart, it's not just that saying "I promise" won't be promising without a preexisting social practice or set of procedures, but that one does not have an obligation even when one undertakes actions that are functionally equivalent to uttering "I promise" unless one invokes an obligation-conferring practice: "The obligation springs not from the nature of the promised action but from the use of the procedure."[11] In Hart's view, no obligation can arise between the Swiss and Indian in the woods of America, not simply because they don't speak the same language (for, as Locke might note, there are other ways they could communicate the idea of an obligation), but because they don't share in an obligation-conferring practice. Without the procedure or practice, the obligation would not arise.

Other theorists, seemingly rejecting Locke's approach and, like Hume and Hart, seeing promissory obligations as based on social practice or convention, explain the obligation to keep promises by pointing to some prior agreement. In 1949 H. A. Prichard initiated a wave of philosophical discussions of promising that consider the conditions needed for a promissory obligation to arise. Prichard argues that to make a promise already presupposes "the thought of obligation."[12] Prichard does not say explicitly that promises presuppose a rule-governed practice, but he argues that they do presuppose that each party believes that the other has certain obligations and will do what it thinks it is bound to.[13] We acquire this belief only by experience, "by finding that [one] has frequently carried out other acts he thought duties because he thought them duties."[14] This is a decidedly anti-Kantian position, for it holds that an obligation arises only when there already is a pattern of behavior giving rise to an expectation. For Kant, obligations do not depend on how humans behave or have behaved in the past.

Promises, argues Prichard, presuppose a previous agreement but not an ordinary agreement:

> Promising to do this or that action . . . can only exist among individuals between whom there has already been something which looks at first like an agreement to keep agree-

---

[11] Hart, "Legal and Moral Obligation," 102.

[12] H. A. Prichard, *Moral Obligation* (Oxford: Oxford University Press, 1949), 174.

[13] Ibid., 174: "[It seems clear] that promises can only be made between members of a group of men—which need not consist of more than two—each of whom believes, and in acting to some extent relies on the belief, that the others are beings who not only think they have certain obligations but are likely to do what they think themselves bound to do."

[14] Ibid.

ments, but is really an agreement not to use certain noises except in a certain way, the agreement nevertheless being one which, unlike ordinary agreements, does not require the use of language.[15]

Prichard did not clarify the sort of agreement promising presupposes, but he seems to refer not to a Kantian hypothetical agreement but to an actual agreement based on experience—to a practice, understood as a pattern of behavior that motivates and gives rise to expectations. Other moral philosophers agreed with Prichard that promising presupposes a prior agreement, and tried to make clearer the nature of the agreement. D. W. Hamlyn argued that Prichard's point that promissory obligations presuppose a prior agreement is "in danger of an infinite regress," for we may always ask why I am bound to this prior agreement.[16] Hamlyn's way out of the regress is to see the agreement that promises presuppose as "a normal background of social institutions"—a concept on which Hamlyn unfortunately does not elaborate.[17] G. E. M. Anscombe sees the previous agreement as a "language game," which we learn along with "the practices of reason."[18] Other theorists identified the background agreement without which there would be no promissory obligations as a particular social practice or institution. For Hanna Pitkin, "the making of particular promises or contracts presupposes the social institution of promising or contracts."[19] Phillips and Mounce see this practice as alone providing the reason for a promisor to do what was promised:

> Within the practice of promise keeping one has a reason for saying that a man ought to perform an action if he has undertaken to do so; within that practice this is what constitutes a reason for such a judgment. But one has not decided oneself that this should count as a reason. What is to count as a reason or justification is determined by the practice of promise keeping to which one may belong, but which has not been brought into being by one's decision. It is only from within such a practice that one can speak at all of making a moral judgment or decision.[20]

Both John Searle and John Rawls argue along the same line, that when one makes a promise one has an obligation to keep it because one invokes a practice. They imply that absent the social practice, there would be no promissory obligations. We shall discuss Rawls's position when we discuss utilitarian accounts of promising later in this chapter. For Searle, promising is a speech act, a "conven-

---

[15] Ibid., 179.

[16] D. W. Hamlyn, "The Obligation to Keep a Promise," *Proceedings of the Aristotelian Society* 62 (1961–1962): 180.

[17] Ibid., 185.

[18] G. E. M. Anscombe, *Ethics, Religion and Politics,* vol. 3 of *Collected Papers* (Minneapolis: University of Minnesota Press, 1969), 16, 102. Cf. Marcel Mauss, *The Gift,* trans. W. D. Halls (London: Routledge, 1990), 12, 38: to understand the obligation of gift-giving among the Maori, one needs to see it as a "phenomenon of social structure" incorporating juridical, religious, economic, and aesthetic subsystems.

[19] Hanna Pitkin, "Obligation and Consent II," *American Political Science Review* 60 (March 1966): 46.

[20] D. Z. Phillips and H. O. Mounce, *Moral Practices* (New York: Shocken Books, 1970), 12.

tional act" that means undertaking an obligation. That one ought to keep one's promises is a fact "whose existence presupposes certain institutions."[21] For Searle, that one has an obligation and ought to keep one's promise is an "institutional fact."[22]

It should by now be clear that this debate about promises presents us with an instance of the general debate with which this book is concerned. In deciding what ethics and the law require, must we turn to existing practices and their rules or, rather, can we turn to moral principles, principles of reason, principles that do not refer to the existence of practices—what we might call abstract principles? Such principles might generate obligations, or dictate that certain actions are wrong, for all human beings, regardless of their social background. We might call such principles natural principles, and the wrongs they point to natural wrongs. In the law a distinction is made between crimes that are *malum in se* and those that are *malum prohibitum*. Crimes of the former sort are intrinsic wrongs; crimes of the latter sort are wrongs only because the legislature says they are wrongs. A natural wrong is the moral analogue of a *malum in se* crime. Is the wrong of breaking a promise a natural wrong? In this chapter we consider the debate between practice and principle conceptions by turning to Locke and Hume's disagreement about promises. When it is morally wrong for me to break a promise to you, is it wrong because breaking a promise is forbidden by the social practice of promising? Or is it wrong, rather, because breaking a promise violates a moral principle from which my obligation arises and would arise even were there no practice of promising or other social practices or conventions shared between us?

SCANLON'S EXAMPLE

In answering this question, I shall begin with an example, similar to Locke's example of the Swiss and Indian in the woods of America but more provocative and detailed. The example is Thomas Scanlon's and goes like this:

> Suppose I am stranded in a strange land. In an attempt to get myself something to eat, I make a spear. I am not very good at using it, however, and when I hurl it at a deer it goes wide of the mark and sails across a narrow but fast-running river. As I stand there gazing forlornly at my spear, lodged on the opposite bank, a boomerang comes sailing across and lands near me. Soon a strange person appears on the opposite bank, picks up

---

[21] John Searle, "How to Derive 'Ought' from 'Is,'" in *The Is-Ought Question*, ed. W. D. Hudson (New York: St. Martin's Press, 1969), 126, 121–22, 130.

[22] For criticism of Searle's derivation of a moral ought from an institutional fact, see, for example, R. M. Hare, "The Promising Game," in *The Is-Ought Question*, ed. Hudson; J. R. Cameron, "Ought and Institutional Obligation," *Philosophy* 46, no. 178 (October 1971): 324, 330: institutions don't in themselves create moral imperatives or prescriptions, only requirements; J. C. Smith, *Legal Obligation* (London: Athlone Press, 1976), 80; E. M. Zemach, "Ought, Is, and a Game Called 'Promise,'" *Philosophical Quarterly* 21, no. 82 (January 1971): 62–63: Searle fails to show any moral obligation to keep promises, for we have no obligation to adopt the institution.

my spear, and looks around in a puzzled way, evidently searching for the boomerang. It now occurs to me that I might regain my spear without getting wet by getting this person to believe that if he throws my spear across the river I will return his boomerang. Suppose that I am successful in this: I get him to form this belief; he returns the spear; and I walk off into the woods with it, leaving the boomerang where it fell.[23]

Is what I have done wrong?

Apparently the stranger and I share no social practices. We made certain gestures to each other that resulted in his throwing me my spear, but the gestures make no reference to any established practice between us, since so far as we know there are none. If each of our communities did have a practice of promising, then even though we did not know of the other community's practice, we might say that we shared in the practice when we exchanged gestures. We might have shared expectations because we each happened to live in societies that practiced promising, if each society did indeed practice promising and if the practice in each society allowed that gestures of the sort made between me and the stranger can substitute for the actual words *I promise*. (We *can* make promises without actually saying the words.)[24] Scanlon does not discuss this possibility, and instead seems to assume that no promise was made, but that something *like* a promise was made. It seems that with his example he wants us to imagine that the

---

[23] Scanlon, "Promises and Practices," 201.

[24] Oswald Hanfling argues that saying the words *I promise* is not a necessary condition for promising: "Suppose that A, having said 'I'll meet you,' and knowing that B is counting on him, fails to turn up. B could properly complain that A had 'broken the promise.' It would be absurd for A to try to answer this complaint by saying "But don't you remember? I only said I would meet you; I didn't actually promise." See his "Promises, Games and Institutions," *Proceedings of the Aristotelian Society* 75 (1974–1975): 16. Cf. David Hillel Ruben, "Tacit Promising," *Ethics* 83, no. 1 (October 1972): 71–79: two friends are in the habit of meeting at 5 P.M. for a drink—they've done this without exception for years. Is failing to appear a violation of an obligation? Yes: "By not appearing, the first friend had broken a tacit promise" (73). Durrant also argues that other gestures or locutions can do the job of "I promise" (R. G. Durrant, "Promising," *Australasian Journal of Philosophy* 41 [1963]: 46). Sidgwick says promises refer not only to words, but to "all signs and even tacit understandings not expressly signified in any way. . . . The promisor is bound to perform what both he and the promisee understood to be undertaken" (Henry Sidgwick, *The Methods of Ethics*, 7th ed. [Indianapolis: Hackett, 1981], 304).

However, the words *I promise* are sometimes important, for they distinguish promises from statements of intention or resolutions in which the speaker does not intend to undertake an obligation. Recall Hanfling's example, above. We may indeed side with A, or at least think that while A should apologize, he did no wrong, precisely because creating an expectation is not necessarily promising—see H. A. Prichard, "The Obligation to Keep a Promise," in his *Moral Obligation* (Oxford: Oxford University Press, 1949), 170–71; and J. L. Austin, *Philosophical Papers* (Oxford: Oxford University Press, 1961), 68: "When I say I fully intend to, I do so for my part . . . but if I say I promise, you are entitled to act on it."

We may disagree also with Ruben's discussion, above. We might think the appropriate response to the friend who fails to show up at 5 P.M. is not to accuse her or him of committing a moral wrong or of being unreliable but rather, to be worried and concerned, precisely because the jump from the creation of an expectation to a promise was never made. Our judgment may depend on the extent of "detrimental reliance" on the expectation; for example, if I knew my friend traveled great distances at considerable expense to meet me at 5 P.M., and I simply did not show up, and didn't inform my friend I would not be there, then we might judge me more harshly then if there were no detrimental reliance.

stranger knows nothing about the practice of promising or at least that this may be the case, and that if what I have done is wrong, it is wrong for some reason other than that I have violated a shared social practice. Scanlon, who believes what I have done in the example is indeed wrong, developed the example to make two points: that the wrong involved does not depend on the existence of a social practice[25] and that the wrong of breaking a promise is the same sort of wrong.[26]

Does Scanlon's case present us with an instance of a natural wrong? Does the example vindicate the principle conception, which claims there are (perhaps transcultural or universal) standards or reasons for determining right conduct, standards that do not depend upon social conventions or practices? In the following sections we shall examine Scanlon's example in light of some of the leading principle conceptions of promising, including Scanlon's. I shall argue that while there are principles that persuasively account for why we should think I acted badly in Scanlon's example, the judgment that I acted badly nevertheless presupposes social practices—I shall argue that in this case, at least, there is no natural wrong. While the wrong of promise-breaking is better explained by appealing to a moral principle than to the fact that a practice-rule was violated, which moral principles we use and how we apply them to determine what ethics requires depends on our social practices and norms.

Before turning, in the next section, to principle conceptions of promising that could account for why I acted wrongly in the example, I want first to consider whether we should necessarily agree that I acted wrongly. Consider two scenarios in which the strange man on the other side of the river does not judge my action to be wrong.

1. He believes that we were playing a game: I tossed the spear farther than he tossed the boomerang, or I exhibited the straighter stick, and so I win; he is somewhat surprised that I did not walk away with my prize, and he might have wondered at the strange gestures I made prior to his tossing over the spear, but he does not think I committed a moral wrong.

2. The strange man is well aware that I made the equivalent of a lying promise, but rather than judge me as having wronged him, he praises my cleverness.

In each of these cases, at least someone has good reason to think what I did was not wrong. Scenario 1, however, does not undermine Scanlon's position, for it lacks the requisite conditions that make what I did wrong in Scanlon's example—the scenario changes the example. The example requires that I get the stranger to form a certain belief, but this fails to occur in scenario 1. Scenario 2

---

[25] Scanlon, "Promises and Practices," 201: "Intuitively, what I have done in this example is no less wrong than it would have been if I had promised the stranger that I would return his boomerang if he threw back my spear. Yet nothing like a social practice of agreement-making is presupposed in the example."

[26] Ibid.:"It may seem that what I have done could not be the same kind of wrong as that involved in breaking a promise. I believe that it is the same kind of wrong."

does pose a challenge to Scanlon's position, a challenge we shall return to in the final section.

While not everyone would agree that I have wronged the strange man by walking away without trying to return his boomerang, Scanlon's judgment seems reasonable enough, and in the next section I proceed on the assumption that Scanlon is correct, that I have wronged the man.

The question then becomes, what reason have we to think that I have wronged him? Scanlon, who assumes there is no shared social practice between us to provide the reason, searches for some moral principle to provide the reason. In section three I shall consider some leading prospects: Neil MacCormick's principle of reliance; the principle of utility; and Scanlon's principles of unjustified manipulation and of fidelity.[27] Of each of these principles we shall ask four questions:

1. Does the principle explain the wrong involved in Scanlon's example?

1a. If it does, does it do so without appealing to social practice, that is, does it show the wrong is a natural wrong?

2. Is the wrong of breaking a promise best explained as a violation of the principle?

2a. Does the principle explain the wrong of breaking a promise without appealing to social practice, that is, does it show the wrong of breaking a promise is a natural wrong?

Given the focus of this book, our primary concern is with questions 1a and 2a. It is not my aim to resolve fully question 2, though discussion of the various principle conceptions of promising naturally leads us to consider some of their merits and limitations. As resolving the question of which principle approach is best is peripheral to our concern with the role of social practices in ethical and legal judging, and with whether there are natural wrongs, I shall use sub-headings to distinguish discussion of questions 1a and 2a from the discussion of question 2.

Before proceeding, though, some words should be said about the formulation of the second question. There may be different reasons it is wrong to break a particular promise: breaking it causes harm to the promisee; breaking it reveals a malicious deception on the part of the promisor; breaking it violates a social practice. Different wrongs may be involved in one and the same broken promise. Whether a particular wrong is involved depends on the facts of the case. (Did the promisee rely on the promise to his detriment? Did the promisor maliciously deceive?) A single principle can't possibly explain the wrong of breaking every promise unless there is some essential feature to all promises. I tend to doubt that there is. To me one of the most sensible statements about promises was written by Hanna Pitkin. Considering the question of why promises obligate, Pitkin paraphrases Wittgenstein: "There are a hundred reasons, there is no reason. There is no absolute, deductive answer to the question."[28] By asking whether a given principle "best explains" the wrong of breaking a promise, I mean to ask not

---

[27] I do not discuss Kant's categorical imperative here. Kant's account of promising was discussed extensively in chapter two.

[28] Pitkin, "Obligation and Consent II," 47.

whether it accounts for every instance of promise breaking but whether it offers the most convincing interpretation of the reaction we have in general to those who break promises, abstracting away features of particular promises that seem less central to promises in general. I think we can ask this without being essentialists. As Wittgenstein indicates with his idea of "family resemblances," there can be important features of a concept (such as promising) without it having essential criteria.

PRINCIPLE CONCEPTIONS OF PROMISING

MacCormick's Reliance Principle

Neil MacCormick argues that an obligation to keep a promise can arise even absent the existence of a rule-based social practice of promising. "It is not necessary to suppose that promisors either intend to invoke, or to be taken as invoking, any particular moral, social, or legal rules in making promises."[29] Even when we do invoke the rule-defined practice of promising, the wrong of breaking the promise is explained by pointing not simply to the fact that the rules of a practice were violated, but to "good reasons why promise breaking should be regarded as wrongful."[30]

For MacCormick, the obligation arises whenever the conditions set forth by an obligation principle are satisfied. According to this obligation principle, if the following conditions obtain, that

A. You rely on me doing x;
B. You would suffer if I did not do x; and
C. I knowingly or intentionally induced you to rely on my doing x;

then I have an obligation to do x, or at least to take action to prevent your suffering any harm by relying on my doing x.[31] I shall call MacCormick's principle "principle R," R for reliance. Promising is one conventional means of satisfying the conditions set forth in principle R, though not all promises satisfy these conditions, and the conditions can be satisfied in other ways besides saying "I promise."

Principle R and Scanlon's Example

Does Principle R explain the wrong involved in Scanlon's example? It can do so only if my behavior in Scanlon's example satisfies its conditions. I got the strange man to form a belief that if he returned my spear I would return his boomerang, and he does return the spear. Condition A is met as the man relied on a belief I instilled in him. For condition B to be satisfied, the strange man must have suf-

---

[29] MacCormick, "Voluntary Obligations and Normative Powers I," supp., p. 63.
[30] Ibid., 62.
[31] Ibid., 68.

fered by my not returning his boomerang.[32] It isn't obvious that he has. Perhaps he is out a spear he might have kept but for my actions. But he wasn't entitled to the spear, at least according to my society's rules about property, and even if his society had different rules, he might not have wanted it. By walking away without returning his boomerang he must cross the river to retrieve it, which he would have had to do had I not been around in the first place. My behavior caused no additional suffering in this respect. Apart from the possible suffering incurred from the loss of a spear that wasn't even his to keep, he suffered the effort of throwing the spear across the river needlessly. These losses seem trivial, hardly the basis for saying I wronged him. If we take condition B of principle R to base the obligation not to violate principle R on the more general obligation not to harm others unjustifiably, then principle R doesn't seem to apply because it seems unconvincing to say I *harmed* the strange man.

The strange man might have suffered in one other way, however. He seems to have opened himself up to me with a gesture of cooperation—I imagine him smiling broadly as he tosses the spear to his new friend. And then I disappoint him. His smile, I imagine, disappears, replaced by an expression of dismay, of having been used, and perhaps of anger. Perhaps he has lost a little faith in humanity as well. This is a sort of suffering. It is the suffering of being wronged.

Principle R can establish that the man has been wronged only if its conditions have been met. Condition B, that the man suffers by my actions, can only be persuasively satisfied if we presuppose what we are supposed to use principle R to establish—that the man has been wronged. If we do presuppose this, then we have established that the man has been wronged by some means other than applying principle R. Principle R, then, does not itself explain the wrong involved in Scanlon's example.[33]

Principle R as an Account of the Wrong of Promise-breaking

While MacCormick's principle of reliance doesn't explain this wrong, we still might think it does explain the wrong of breaking a promise. But while the principle of reliance does point to an important reason that it is wrong to break many promises, I want to suggest that the wrong of breaking a promise is not best explained as a violation of that principle. My reasoning is two-fold. First, we can distinguish the class of promises giving rise to clear obligations from the class of actions inducing detrimental reliance by noting instances of the former class that do not belong to the latter. If not all broken promises that we regard as moral wrongs are violations of principle R, we can't say principle R characterizes a more general class of wrongs to which the wrong of breaking a promise belongs. Second, where the circumstances of a promise do satisfy the conditions set forth

[32] I leave aside the possibility that I don't know how to throw a boomerang—after all, it's a boomerang—and the question of whether I wrong him if I try but fail to return it.

[33] I therefore do not consider whether the principle shows the wrong is a natural wrong (question 1a, above).

in principle R, the principle doesn't adequately characterize or capture the wrong of breaking the promise.

Of course not all utterances of "I promise" satisfy the conditions of principle R. Promises made within a play do not induce reliance. Promises to do bodily injury—threats—also fail to satisfy the conditions, since it is not true that the promisee would suffer if the promisor did not do what was promised. But such promises do not give rise to moral obligations, and failing to keep such promises is not wrong.[34] So while these examples show that not all broken promises are violations of principle R, they do not show that the wrong of breaking a promise is distinct from the wrong of violating principle R. MacCormick might say these promises do not give rise to obligations precisely *because* they do not satisfy the conditions of principle R.

Are there promises that *do* give rise to clear obligations it is wrong not to fulfill but that do not satisfy the conditions set forth in principle R? Some moral philosophers suggest that *all* promises bind, whether they are relied upon or not, or whether or not the promisee even wants the promise to be kept.[35] This seems too extreme, for it is hard to see why anyone should have a moral obligation to keep a pointless promise.[36] But that it may not be wrong or blameworthy to break pointless promises does not mean the reliance principle explains the wrong of breaking promises. Promises can have a point even though they are not relied upon. Thomas Scanlon makes this clear with another of his examples. Harold asks a friend of his to promise not to reveal a dark secret from Harold's past that would greatly embarrass Harold. There is no reciprocation or "consideration" for the promise—it is unilateral; and there is no reliance, since Harold can't do anything

---

[34] Durrant argues that saying "I promise" in a play isn't really promising, in "Promising," 46–47. Vera Peetz distinguishes promises from threats, and notes that threats create no obligation, in "Promises and Threats," *Mind* 86 (1977): 580. Cf. John Searle, *Speech Acts* (Cambridge: Cambridge University Press, 1969): 58: to be a promise, the hearer must prefer the promisor doing A to not doing A, and the promisor must believe the hearer would prefer his doing A to not doing A. Cf. Páll Ardal, "And That's a Promise," *Philosophy Quarterly* 18, no. 72 (July 1968): 229: "I promise I'll get you for this" is a threat and nobody would think we are obligated to carry out threats. Cf. C. K. Grant, "Promises," *Mind* 58 (July 1949): 362: the promisee must want or desire the action promised.

[35] For example, Rawls and Pitkin; others suggest, if not that all promises bind, at least that even unrelied upon promises must be kept—see Joseph Raz, "Voluntary Obligations and Normative Powers II," *Proceedings of the Aristotelian Society,* supp., vol. 46 (1972): 101; and A. I. Melden, "On Promising," *Mind* 65, no. 257 (June 1956): 50: the obligation to keep a promise does not depend on reliance upon it, because if it did my obligation would depend on what another person does, which Melden does not think is the case. Melden's criticism of the reliance principle might be avoided if condition B of principle R held instead that "it is reasonably foreseeable that you *could* suffer if I did not do x."

[36] See Jan Narveson, "Promising, Expecting, and Utility," *Canadian Journal of Philosophy* 1, no. 2 (December 1971): 219–20: if the promisee would not be disappointed, and did not rely on my promise, it is indifferent whether I keep it. Cf. G. J. Warnock, *The Object of Morality* (London: Methuen, 1971), 113: "Is it in any way culpable, then, not to keep a promise that there is, as it may turn out, no point in one's keeping? I do not really see how one could sensibly hold that this is culpable." Warnock adds, though, that we would *admire* "even wholly pointless fidelity to undertakings"(113). Pitkin, Rawls, Searle, Durrant, and others would maintain that such promises must normally be kept because that is what promising means.

if his friend breaks the promise and tells. Harold is not "relying on [the promise] to plan his life." Yet, Scanlon argues, there is an obligation. Sometimes we want assurance but not just so we can rely on it.[37] The example points to a class of promises upon which there is no reliance, but which generate obligations it is wrong or culpable not to fulfill. Another class of promises arguably generates such obligations even though there may be no detrimental reliance: promises made to someone who has since died. Grant argues that "no one believes" there no longer is an obligation in this case and that the fact that we must keep even these promises shows the promissory obligation is not based on a wider principle requiring that we not disappoint others.[38]

Clearly I am more culpable when breaking my promise results in serious harm to the promisee as a result of detrimental reliance on the promise, than when breaking my promise results in mere inconvenience, or than in breaking a pointless promise. Some promises it is irresponsible, reckless and cruel not to keep. The extent of the wrong of breaking a promise, like the extent of the wrong of lying, depends on the promise or lie. Suppose I promise to deliver ten gallons of paint to you next Monday in return for payment at the market price. I fail to deliver, breaking a promise, but this is of no matter to you since you can get the same paint at the same price from a store next door. There was no detrimental reliance upon my promise. The wrong I committed may seem almost trivial, though I think I should have delivered the paint. If I had promised to deliver, not ten gallons of paint, but wiring that meets certain standards of flame-resistance, and I break my promise by delivering a lower quality wire that is unsafe to use, I have committed not just the wrong of breaking a promise; I have other obligations and duties as well, and failure to provide the proper, safe materials violates some of those. But while different wrongs may be involved in one and the same broken promise, there is a distinct wrong I have committed apart from the wrong of causing harm or inducing detrimental reliance. It is a wrong for which I might pay the penalty of not being trusted again.[39]

Not all promises that give rise to clear obligations satisfy the reliance principle. But we may think there is another problem with the reliance principle besides its failing to account for the fact that certain promises that are not relied upon generate moral obligations. The argument I want to suggest here is that principle R fails to capture the moral response uniquely appropriate to promise-breakers, even to those who break relied-upon promises.

Consider the following example: Jack and Jill have been friends for a while. One evening their friendship takes a romantic turn, and it keeps on this course.

---

[37] Scanlon, "Promises and Practices," 207–8.

[38] Grant, "Promises," 366. But everyone does *not* agree that "deathbed" promises obligate the promisor once the promisee dies. See Russell Hardin, *Morality within the Limits of Reason* (Chicago: University of Chicago Press, 1988), 64–65. Páll Ardal suggests there is no point in keeping such promises and suggests that we feel strongly that we ought to keep them because we have been morally educated to keep promises ("And That's a Promise," 236–37).

[39] Cf. Hume, *Treatise of Human Nature*, 522: promising expresses a willingness to undertake an obligation and be subject "to the penalty of never being trusted again in case of failure."

Having overcome their moral doubts, they openly discuss having sex. Neither is prepared for the commitment entailed in having a baby, so each agrees that they will not have sex with the other unless adequate precautions are taken to prevent pregnancy. Consider now the following three cases:

1. *The promise:* Jill promises to take a birth control pill every day and intends to keep her promise (the pill is only effective if taken every day). But occasionally she forgets and misses a day or two, even as the two have sex.

2. *The lie:* Jill says she has taken a birth control pill for several years now and that she has never gotten pregnant, and that she intends to continue taking the pill. She says this with the intention of alleviating Jack's concerns. In fact she did not take the pill ever, nor does she now, and the two have sex.

3. *Inducing reliance without a promise:* Jill says she has taken a birth control pill regularly for several years now for medical reasons and that she has never gotten pregnant, and that she intends to continue taking the pill. She says this with the intention of alleviating Jack's concerns. In fact she had taken the pill for several years, but she was not always careful about taking it every day, nor is she now; she occasionally misses a few days. She takes no special precautions following their discussion, and on one occasion forgets to take the pill twice in two days before the two have sex.

In case 1 a promise is made, an obligation created, and a wrong committed by Jill. The wrong is that of breaking a promise. It is not the wrong of lying, for Jill simply forgot to take the pill.[40] But by promising, she had a responsibility not to forget; she had an obligation to take measures to ensure she would not forget, and, at the very least, to warn her partner that she is not certain if she had taken the pill every day. Had she not promised, Jack could have avoided the risk entailed in having sex or taken other precautions, and now he can rightly blame her for breaking her promise.

In case 2 no promise is made. The wrong involved looks like the wrong of violating principle R. But the wrong can be characterized in other terms as well.

[40] G. J. Warnock in *Object of Morality* argues that the wrong of breaking a promise is the wrong of not telling the truth. Why ought I to keep my promise? "I ought to do it just because I *said I would*"(101). "If I offer *as true* an affirmation about my future conduct, then I will have spoken falsely not *merely* if I do not now intend so to act, but *also* if in future I do not in fact act accordingly; so therefore I *must* act, if I am not *to have* spoken falsely"(108). "I cannot, of course, non-culpably, just change my mind; for to do that is simply to make my utterance false"(109). "The nature of the obligation invoked" in promising is "the requirement of veracity"(109). The position has been convincingly criticized. Sidgwick notes that we aren't bound to make our actions correspond with our assertions—for example, if I assert an intention to give up alcohol, but I don't, I'm not untrustworthy or immoral; but I am if I promised to abstain. For Sidgwick, the duty of promise-keeping is the duty to conform not to our assertions but "to expectations that I have intentionally raised in others" (*Methods of Ethics*, 303–04). See also Don Locke, "The Object of Morality, and the Obligation to Keep a Promise," *Canadian Journal of Philosophy* 2, no. 1 (September 1972): 141: "The basic moral value [in promising] is not veracity . . . but something to do with co-operation and mutual trust." P. S. Atiyah notes that courts distinguish between a lie and a breach of promise. Telling a lie isn't usually actionable, and when it is, it is only where deceit causes harm (*Promises, Morals, and Law* [Oxford: Oxford University Press, 1981], 105).

Jill has been not merely irresponsible or forgetful but deceitful. The wrong involved in case 2 is not the wrong of breaking a promise, but the distinct wrong of lying, which, though not always, at least in this case seems a greater wrong.

In case 3 no promise is made. The wrong involved is that of violating principle R. Is it the same wrong that Jill commits in case 1?

Let us pursue case 3 further. Suppose that Jill gets pregnant and now must confront Jack with the news. She explains how she did not lie, and did not intend to get pregnant, but that she simply forgot to take the pill a few times. What response is appropriate from Jack? Consider the following three possibilities:

i. "But you promised! How can I ever trust you again?"

ii. "You lied to me. That was cruel, and I want nothing more to do with you."

iii. "You knew I agreed to have sex with you on the condition that you took the pill. How can I ever rely on you again?"

Cases 1 and 3 *are* very close. In both cases we may feel Jill had an obligation to at least warn Jack that she may have missed a day. But they aren't exactly the same. Reply i is an inappropriate response given the situation described in case 3. Jill never promised. She made statements about her past practice, suggesting that she would continue this practice and that it would provide protection. If Jack accused her of breaking her promise, she might respond, "But I never promised." Perhaps this response would seem disingenuous. It might seem the response more to be expected were Jill a liar now gloating over her successful deception. If Jill regretted forgetting to take the pill, she might be unwilling to defend herself in this way. Still, she might respond:

"I regret what happened. But you can't put all the blame on me. I never *promised* anything, and it was foolish of you simply to assume it was up to me alone to take the pill. You should have asked if I had taken the pill, and not simply assumed I had. You might have taken other precautions just in case."

Here Jill suggests that Jack's reliance was unreasonable. If she *had* promised, it would have been more reasonable for Jack simply to assume she had taken the pill.[41] By promising, rather than just indicating her past and present practice, she would have provided additional assurance. Were he given that assurance, he might even have felt awkward asking her each time before the two had sex if she had indeed taken the pill, awkward because asking this might have suggested to her that he did not think her promises meant much. But Jill did not promise, and so Jack should have taken extra precautions. This is not to say Jill did no wrong; but the wrong she did in case 3 was not the wrong of breaking a promise. It was the wrong of violating principle R, which, in this case, seems to me to be a distinct and slightly less culpable wrong. Reply iii seems best to capture the appropriate response for Jack to make, though we might want to say that in

---

[41] If this seems unconvincing, imagine that in case 1 the exchange went like this: Jill: "I promise to take the pill every day." Jack: "OK, but this is important. Are you sure you will take it every day?" Jill: "I said I promise. You needn't worry, really." Jack: "But even missing one day is no good; you must really make certain." Jill: "Look, I said I *promise*! Stop doubting me!"

making it he is unduly self-righteous for being unwilling to take on some of the responsibility himself.

My breaking a promise says something about my character, and what it says is different from what is said about my character when I violate principle R. When I make a promise that gives rise to a clear obligation and then break it, this says to you that you cannot trust me.[42] That is not necessarily implied when I violate principle R in other ways than by breaking a promise. Sometimes inducing detrimental reliance and then failing to do what I indicated I would do shows that I am irresponsible or negligent—this, perhaps, is the appropriate judgment of Jill in case 3. But it might indicate that I am clever and cunning. It might sometimes indicate that you cannot trust me, if I was in a position where I had your trust. But merely satisfying the conditions of principle R does not in itself put me in a position of trust. Promising does.

Case 3 is so close to case 1 because it wouldn't be inappropriate for Jack to say of Jill in case 3 that he cannot trust her, even though there was no promise. The concepts of relying on and trusting may overlap here. Jill may be in a position of trust because of their friendship. There are clearer cases where principle R is satisfied and x is not done, yet the appropriate response is not "I cannot trust you." Jane wants Dave to go to a party. He dreads going, so in order to get him to go, she tells him she'll probably be there too. Principle R is satisfied, but Jane has no obligation to go, even though Dave will suffer being there without her. We can't say she is untrustworthy because she doesn't go. Or consider an example MacCormick uses in arguing for his reliance principle: Jones is swimming at a beach at the foot of a cliff. The tide suddenly rises fast and only if he makes a desperate dash can he reach safety. MacDonald is on the cliff holding stout rope, sees Jones's predicament, and lowers the rope. Jones sees and waits for the rope, losing time, so that he can no longer reach safety otherwise than by climbing up MacDonald's rope.[43] If Jones then releases the rope, thereby frustrating Mac-Donald's reliance, he wrongs MacDonald. The wrong can be accounted for by principle R. But in violating principle R Jones has not necessarily shown himself to be an untrustworthy person; rather, he has shown himself to be a reckless and mean-spirited fiend. The wrong MacDonald commits seems best characterized as the wrong of causing harm to another, not the wrong of breaking a promise.

Principle R and Social Practice

Even if we agree the principle of reliance does not adequately explain the wrong of breaking promises, we still might regard it as a valid principle that can help us determine what ethics or the law require. It does, after all, seem wrong to violate principle R. MacCormick claims that the wrong of violating principle R is a natu-

---

[42] There are cases where we don't think breaking a promise is wrong or reveals that the promisor is untrustworthy: for example, coerced promises, extremely improvident promises, impossible promises, immoral promises, or promises in which the promisee releases the promisor. Such promises don't give rise to clear obligations.

[43] MacCormick, "Voluntary Obligations and Normative Powers I," 67.

ral wrong, a wrong independent of the existence of a social practice. While principle R does not explain the wrong of breaking a promise upon which there is no reliance, and, I have suggested, fails to capture what is distinctly wrong about promise-breaking, it does provide a convincing account of why breaking certain promises—promises upon which the promisee had relied and where this reliance leads to suffering—are especially wrong. But MacCormick has succeeded in showing that a natural wrong is involved in the breaking of such promises only if principle R characterizes this wrong without presuming the existence of shared conventions or practices. Does it?

Let's begin with what I think Hume's answer would be. For Hume, there is no obligation to conform with principle R, or any of the more refined variations other moral philosophers discuss, until a convention arises that includes sanctions in some form, such as moral disapproval. Unless there is a practice of promising, and therefore a shared judgment that it is wrong to break a promise, it is, in Hume's view, not wrong to break a promise, even if doing so violates principle R. Suppose I knowingly induce reliance in you that I will help push oars to propel our boat, and then I don't lift a finger to help you; Hume suggests that until a convention arises we cannot say I've acted wrongly.[44]

Hume might agree that it is useful to conform with principle R, or with some modified version that could better account for the wrong of making false promises. He might say that even before the practice of promising arises, it would be a bad thing to violate such a principle—doing so would not promote the public interest. But I think it is Hume's argument that we cannot say it is *wrong* to violate the principle until the practice of promising has been established. We ought to hold to this principle, but we aren't obligated to prior to its establishment by human convention: "A promise would not be intelligible, before human conventions had established it . . . even if it were intelligible, it would not be attended with any moral obligation."[45]

It takes time for a shared judgment to arise that it is wrong to break promises. The judgment will necessarily arise, Hume thinks, because the practice of promising is in the interest of society.[46] This judgment, which, once the practice is established, becomes the moral sanction of the practice, acquires force only after "repeated experiences" of cooperation and transgression.[47] But in Hume's view, we must wait for this process to play out before we can say an obligation exists to keep promises.

Hume's argument loses much of its force if we relax our understanding of the word *obligation*. In Hume's view, as it has been laid out above, an obligation is by definition institutional, or presupposes a convention. There *can* be no natural obligations, where the necessity of the "can" is grammatical. A. J. Simmons distinguishes obligations and duties that are natural from those that are positional: "Natural duties are moral requirements, while a positional duty need be no more

[44] David Hume, *Treatise of Human Nature,* 490.
[45] Ibid., 516.
[46] Ibid., 519.
[47] Ibid., 490.

than the consequence of an established 'requiring rule' in any institutional setting."[48] Hume is saying that obligations must necessarily be positional, or make reference to conventions. In Hume's view, principles may tell us what we ought to do but can't tell us what our obligations are, for obligations by definition make reference to social institutions or practices. There is some sentiment for distinguishing obligation statements from ought statements in this way.[49] But doing so unduly restricts our actual use of the word *obligation,* which we do invoke in situations where we are not making reference to institutions or a rule-governed practice. It is not ungrammatical to speak of an obligation that is not positional.

It is difficult to see how an obligation that is merely positional or institutional has any moral force.[50] That an institution or rule requires me to do something isn't a moral reason for doing it. MacCormick claims to have found in principle R a moral reason for acting. Stopping at Hume's criticism—that while MacCormick may have found such a ground, until a convention arises we could not say it is the ground for an "obligation" it is wrong or culpable not to fulfill— would not settle our question of whether there are natural principles that determine what ethics requires. We might have good reason to think there are no natural obligations, or that we cannot say one acts badly unless the act flouts a convention or social practice. But we should not forego consideration of those reasons because of a cramped understanding of the meaning of *obligation.* To use H. L. A. Hart's phrase, this would be putting a "definitional stop" to an important substantive issue.[51]

I therefore want to pursue a further criticism of the view that MacCormick has found a natural principle. The criticism is that *to apply* principle R convincingly, we need some appeal to social practice.

A moral obligation does not always arise whenever the conditions set forth by principle R obtain. Intentionally or knowingly getting you to rely on my doing something, and then not doing it, is not always a wrong. For it is not always *reasonable* for you to rely on me. There are situations where I induce you to rely on my doing x, and you do so rely, and I do not do x, and you suffer as a result, but the appropriate response is to say, not that I am obligated to do x, or even

---

[48] A. J. Simmons, *Moral Principles and Political Obligation* (Princeton: Princeton University Press, 1979), 13–14; cf. 7–9.

[49] On the distinction between *ought* and *obligation,* see Richard Brandt, "The Concepts of Obligation and Duty," *Mind* 73 (1964): 391; Stanley Cavell, *Must We Mean What We Say?* (New York: Charles Scribner's Sons, 1969), 28; Richard K. Dagger, "What Is Political Obligation," *American Political Science Review* 71, no. 1 (1977): 86–87; Carole Pateman, *The Problem of Political Obligation* (Berkeley: University of California Press, 1985), 28; Richard E. Flathman, *Political Obligation* (New York: Atheneum, 1972), 34–39; James Mish'alani, "'Duty,' 'Obligation' and 'Ought,'" *Analysis* 30, no. 2 (December 1969): 39; J. C. Smith, *Legal Obligation* (London: Athlone Press, 1976), 47–48.

[50] Simmons argues that "if a positional duty is binding on us, it is because there are grounds for a moral requirement to perform that positional duty which are independent of the position and the scheme which defines it" (*Moral Principles and Political Obligation,* 21). Cf. p. 26: "no positional duty is a moral requirement." Cf. Cameron, "Ought and Institutional Obligation."

[51] H. L. A. Hart, "Prolegomenon to the Principles of Punishment," *Proceedings of the Aristotelian Society* (1959–60); reprinted in *Theories of Punishment,* ed. Stanley Grupp (Bloomington: Indiana University Press, 1971).

that I ought to do x, but rather, that your reliance was unreasonable. Consider two examples:

1. The fake punt: I coach a football team now setting up to punt on fourth down. Believing my team will punt, our opponent sends out its punt-return squad. But instead of punting, we fake the punt and run for a first down. By setting up to punt, I knew the other team would relax their defense, making it easier to get the first down. I knowingly induced reliance, the other team did in fact rely and suffered as a consequence of that reliance. But despite having satisfied the conditions set forth by principle R, I am not obligated to have my team actually punt, to warn the other team that we won't really be punting, or to compensate the opposition for their suffering once our fake punt succeeds. The opposing team's reliance is unreasonable.

2. Low-price Lou: Lou owns a store and sets the lowest prices in town, hoping to attract loyal customers. You come to rely on Lou's having the lowest prices and no longer shop around for better bargains. Lou knows you rely on his having the lowest prices and occasionally reminds you that he does. He then learns of a new store that opens and sets even lower prices than his. Is Lou obligated to continue to maintain the lowest prices or to tell you about the lower prices at the new store? Of course if he still told you that he offered the lowest prices in town after the new store appeared, he would be lying, and that would be wrong. But is it wrong of Lou to let you continually rely on a belief he instilled in you in the past, a belief now false? No. Your reliance is unreasonable.

Some appeal to practice is necessary to determine whether reliance is reasonable.[52] In the above examples, we must know something about football or retail sales to determine whether or to what extent a moral obligation exists. Promising is one conventional means of indicating that reliance is reasonable. The existence of the conventional device of promising is a useful way of delimiting the obligations defined by principle R. If I could've promised but didn't, instead only declaring an intention, then the fact that I did not promise may suggest that relying on my declaration is unreasonable. MacCormick seems not to allow that reliance may be unreasonable. For him what matters is whether you in fact rely upon my representations about future conduct or present fact, and whether I induced this reliance.[53]

We might need to appeal to practice not only to judge whether an action inducing reliance generates a moral obligation—which it might not do if society would not regard the reliance as reasonable; but also to judge whether an action can be said to conform with principle R in the first place. Principle R requires that I *knowingly or intentionally* induced you to rely on my doing something. Merely creating an expectation in you that you rely on to your detriment does not itself mean I act badly if I fail to satisfy this expectation. Suppose you accuse me of

[52] In saying reliance is "reasonable," I mean that a judgment of moral condemnation would be appropriate if the act relied upon were not undertaken. It might be rational or prudent to rely, yet unreasonable.

[53] "Voluntary Obligations and Normative Powers I," 66.

inducing you to rely on my doing x, and you suffer when I do not do x, but I deny both intending to assure you that I would do x and knowing that you would be so assured. By denying that my action satisfies condition C of principle R, I seek to deflect blame and avoid the consequences of an adverse moral judgment. With respect to Scanlon's example, I might deny that I intended to get the strange man on the other side of the river to believe I would return his boomerang if he threw me my spear. I either did or did not have the requisite intent or knowledge, and whether I acted wrongly is contingent on the fact of the matter. But sometimes we want to make a moral judgment though we lack access to these facts. If others need to decide whether I acted wrongly, and I deny having satisfied condition C, it is still possible to decide whether I acted wrongly. If I said the words *I promise,* I cannot later deny the intention to induce reliance. My use of these words implies that intent. The basis for determining when it is unreasonable to disavow the requisite state of mind is sometimes determined by appeal to social practice, as when the words *I promise* are used.[54]

Sometimes it is unreasonable to disavow the requisite state of mind regardless of the social practices with which the actor might be familiar. MacCormick shows this with his Jones and MacDonald example. MacCormick argues that MacDonald has an obligation to help Jones in the scenario and does a wrong otherwise, because Jones has relied on MacDonald to his own detriment.[55] MacCormick says that even if MacDonald did not intend or know that Jones would rely on his apparent rescue offer, MacDonald "ought to have realized that Jones would make [this] supposition."[56] There are reasons why MacDonald might not know what he "ought to have realized"—perhaps he suffers from mental incapacity. But MacCormick's point is that MacDonald has an obligation that does not depend on MacDonald belonging "to a society which recognizes some practice or institution."[57] MacCormick suggests that being from a different society would *not* be a reason, at least not an *acceptable* reason. Whether it would is precisely the question we need to answer to decide whether we should recognize a natural wrong in this instance.

A Kantian would say MacDonald has failed to respect Jones as an end, has made him unable to consent to the maxim upon which MacDonald acts. Such victimization is ruled out by the categorical imperative, which requires that I act in such a way that I can will that my maxim should become a universal law. In chapter two I suggested that the notion that making a false promise to Jones victimizes him and is therefore ruled out by the categorical imperative is a notion parasitic on the practice of promising. We have this idea of victimizing only because we have the practice and the expectation that promises are to be kept. The idea that causing Jones's *death* victimizes him is not similarly parasitic on a

[54] Cf. Raz, "Voluntary Obligations and Normative Powers II," 100: "It is clear that social convention may nonetheless determine what acts can reasonably be taken to express an intention to undertake an obligation and confer a right."

[55] MacCormick, "Voluntary Obligations and Normative Powers I," 68.

[56] Ibid.

[57] Ibid., 68.

practice or convention—death does make one unable to consent to maxims. For this reason we might think that MacCormick's principle of reliance points to a natural wrong in this case, though it is better characterized not as the wrong of breaking a promise, but as the wrong of causing gratuitous, serious harm to another. A harm principle, of which the principle of reliance might be regarded as one version, holds that it is wrong unjustifiably to cause harm to another. As such, the principle may apply in all societies, and may look like a natural principle pointing to natural wrongs. But two points must be considered before accepting this conclusion. Even if some version of a harm principle were shared by all societies, universal principles aren't necessarily natural principles. Universal principles may derive from social practices minimal features of which are common to the practices of virtually all human societies. Second, the harm principle that may apply everywhere is a very thin principle. The thick principle we need to apply in particular cases will vary among societies.[58] There are some examples which all human beings might agree are violations of the harm principle and therefore wrongs (*malum in se* crimes). But what counts as harming or as causing harm varies among societies. For example, the judgment that invading someone's privacy harms them presupposes consequences of the invasion that are foreseeable only in societies in which there was an expectation of privacy and privacy is valued. So, too, whether reliance is reasonable varies among societies. For example, P.S. Atiyah notes that the judgment that it is wrong to break a promise because the promisee was harmed by the promisor itself supposes that the promisee was harmed *by* the promisor. But this "is not a factual statement; it is an ascription of moral responsibility" that itself needs justification. In justifying it, some "prior principle of obligation" is presupposed. Atiyah notes that we could imagine a society where a person relying on a promise is regarded as a fool, for example England before the late eighteenth century.[59] That society apparently would not have regarded reliance on (at least commercial) promises as reasonable. In chapter six we shall return to this idea of thin, universal principles that must be made thick to provide guidance on particular issues and that in becoming thick are constrained by culturally variant social practices.

Utilitarianism

Utilitarianism refers to a range of theories that claim to determine what ethics and the law require. We cannot possibly consider all the important versions. I shall focus on the classical utilitarianism of Jeremy Bentham, though we shall have occasion to consider in some detail R. M. Hare's two-level utilitarianism, and John Rawls's rule-utilitarianism. I choose Rawls because he has an extensive discussion of promises; while Hare's approach is in some ways similar to Rawls's, it gives voice to a strand of utilitarianism—act-utilitarianism—that Rawls rejects.

---

[58] I borrow the terms "thin" and "thick" as well as the idea of thin and thick principles from Michael Walzer, *Thick and Thin* (Notre Dame, Ind.: University of Notre Dame Press, 1994), a work I discuss in chapter six.

[59] Atiyah, *Promises, Morals, and Law,* 64–65.

Bentham conceived of utilitarianism as a universally valid principle by which we could determine whether a practice or law was justified. Rather than defer to the authority of tradition, rather than worship "dead men's bones," we should use "reasoning deduced (if the subject be of a practical nature) from the consideration of the end in view," and make judgments based "on the completest evidence that the nature of each case may admit."[60] For Bentham, we should "draw from the principle of general utility the justificative reason of everything that is susceptible of justification." Utility is "alone the true standard and measure of right and wrong."[61]

For Bentham, the principle of utility is the ground of all moral actions; it is a principle that lacks any further ground, and is not to be questioned: "Systems which attempt to question it deal in sounds instead of sense, in caprice instead of reason, in darkness instead of light."[62] Our privileged guide is

> that principle which approves or disapproves of every action whatsoever, according to the tendency which it appears to have to augment or diminish the happiness of the party whose interest is in question.[63]

Utilitarianism and Scanlon's Example

Does Bentham's principle of utility explain the wrong involved in Scanlon's example? A utilitarian calculation that considered my interests, and weighed the costs and benefits to me of walking away without trying to return the strange person's boomerang would probably conclude that I have acted wrongly.[64] By doing this I likely promote ill will and lose out on all future benefits that might have resulted from mutual cooperation between myself and my people on the one hand, and, on the other hand, the strange man, his people, and anyone the strange man might tell. The benefit to me is that I needn't attempt to return his boomerang, which might not be a trivial benefit if I am not very good at throwing boomerangs. (The benefit is not that I acquire a boomerang, since in Scanlon's example I walk away, leaving it where it lies.) In light of these considerations, probably the utilitarian calculation favors the attempt and would justify a moral sanction for failing to try.

Suppose, however, that I knew there would never be future encounters between members of my society and members of the stranger's society and no word of the incident would ever get around. In this case, a utilitarian calculating my interest or the interests of my community might conclude that what I have done is not wrong.[65] But not necessarily. If we imagine ourselves in the example walk-

---

[60] Bentham, *Book of Fallacies*, in *Works*, 8:392, 8:401.

[61] Ibid., 8:401.

[62] Jeremy Bentham, *Principles of Morals and Legislation*, chap. 1, secs. 12, 11.

[63] Ibid., chap. 1, sec. 2.

[64] Application of the utilitarian principle may depend on whose interest we take to be in question: Mine? My society's? The strange man's? Humankind's? It may also depend on how we interpret the relevant party's interest. I might give a different interpretation than does the strange man.

[65] Not all versions of utilitarianism would necessarily allow this move. R. M. Hare (*Moral Thinking: Its Levels, Method and Point* [Oxford: Oxford University Press, 1981]) offers a utilitarian theory that

ing away, the boomerang left lying on the ground and the stranger left wondering on the other bank of the river, we may feel a pang of guilt. The utilitarian might use this pang of guilt as data to include in the calculation of the net benefit of walking away, and it might tip the scale. But if the utilitarian concludes that my or my society's utility would increase by my walking away, which is possible if we assume no future encounters between me or my people and the strange man and his people and no word gets out about my behavior, then the utilitarian might criticize this pang of guilt as irrational—why feel guilty for promoting the good?

Suppose also that the strange man's response to my action is not disdain but respect, or that upon returning home to my people I brag about what I've done and receive accolades and praise. Should the utilitarian take such responses as data to input into the utility function? Or could the utilitarian criticize such responses as irrational? To know how to apply the principle of utility, we need to know whether to regard such "pangs of guilt" or societal responses of praise and blame as already given preferences to enter into the utility function, or as themselves to be justified or criticized by the principle of utility. Must the utilitarian presume social practices engendering such pangs of guilt or societal responses, or is her or his task, rather, to decide what social practices should be without presuming any? Is the principle of utility a natural principle that can account for the wrong in Scanlon's example without appealing to social practice?

The Principle of Utility and Social Practice: I

The best source we have for Bentham's answer is his essay "Of the Influence of Time and Place in Matters of Legislation."[66] There Bentham argues that it is proper to give the effect of justification, exemption, extenuation, or aggravation to cultural grounds.[67] All laws everywhere and always ought to be founded upon the principle of utility.[68] "Thus far at least, human nature may be pronounced to be everywhere the same."[69] But application of the principle of utility will depend on mutable features of culture and geography. Variations must be allowed in laws to account for cultural and geographical differences between peoples.

One sort of adjustment needs to be made to account for how the foreseeability of harm from certain actions varies among countries. "Stripping a man stark naked, might cause death in Siberia, in circumstances in which it would be only

---

incorporates a universalizability requirement: "It is a misuse of the word 'ought' to say 'You ought, but I can conceive of another (identical) situation . . . except that the corresponding person 'ought not'"(10). "In answering [what I ought to do], I am prescribing universally; I must, in order to answer it rationally, rationally prefer that the answer should be agreed on whatever role I play in the resulting sequence of events"(215—note that Hare uses "rational" here in the way Rawls and Scanlon use "reasonable," see chapter two, note 33, above). This might imply that a rational moral judgment must not depend on whether I encounter the people again as long as there is the chance that others in my situation could.

[66] In Bentham, *Works*, ed. Bowring, part 1.
[67] Ibid., 174.
[68] Ibid., 193.
[69] Ibid., 172.

play in the East Indies."[70] In countries that are nurseries of plague, it might be an offense to enter a port.[71] Firing a pistol may be allowed in a field in England but not in the Swiss Alps, where doing so can trigger an avalanche.[72] Bentham refers to such reasons as "physical" grounds for variation in laws, and says these grounds are "insurmountable."[73]

Another reason laws may vary in different places is that notions of culpability differ. Bentham notes that killing a Hallachore who touches a man of a superior tribe isn't regarded as blameworthy.[74] Lending money at 6 percent is regarded as usury in England but not in Bengal, where one may lend at up to 12 percent without facing legal sanctions.[75] What counts as harmful, and therefore whether we regard someone as culpable, can vary by country.

This second class of reasons for variations in law are not physical but moral grounds and are not "insurmountable."[76] These reasons are rooted in perhaps unjustified custom, and Bentham sometimes implies that the utilitarian legislator is *not* simply to take preferences arising from these customs as brute data for the utilitarian calculation. If a custom motivated people to do what is against their interests, Bentham at times suggests that we should use the principle of utility to criticize the custom, or moral ground. In several passages Bentham suggests that a people may be *misguided* in their beliefs that they are happier with a certain law or practice, and that a legislator can invoke the principle of utility to criticize it. He praises Peter the Great for passing a law obliging Russians to cut off their beards and to wear clothes short like Europeans. Bentham says this was justified on the supposition that Peter the Great tried to make his people more European and thus more happy.[77] Bentham argues as well that even though countries regard usury as wrong, the principle of utility dictates that usury should not be a crime. Bentham defends the principle that "no man of ripe years and of sound mind, acting freely, and with his eyes open, ought to be hindered, with a view to his advantage, from making such bargain, in the way of obtaining money, as he thinks fit."[78] Bentham is critical also of the practice among the Hallachore of killing a man who touches a member of a superior tribe. But he adds:

---

[70] Ibid., 173.

[71] Ibid., 174.

[72] Ibid., 175.

[73] Ibid., 177. In his comparison of stripping a man in Siberia as opposed to the East Indies, Bentham relies partly on a physical ground (the cold of Siberia) but also on his other sort of ground for variation. To say that in the East Indies stripping a man may be "only play" is to point to a moral, not a physical, ground for leniency.

[74] Ibid., 174.

[75] Ibid., 176.

[76] Ibid., 177.

[77] Ibid., 183. Bentham's equating of being more European with being happier is perhaps an unfortunate example for those wanting to use Bentham's arguments to support a universalist position, since Bentham, here, seems to rely less on reason than on prejudice.

[78] Bentham, *Defense of Usury*, in *Works*, ed. Bowring, 9:3. Bentham assumes that no individual would make a worse judgment than a legislator: "no simplicity, short of absolute idiotism, can cause the individual to make a more groundless judgment, than the legislator"(8). "[The borrower] knew that, even in his own judgment, the engagement was a beneficial one to himself, or he would not have

A prejudice so strong, though altogether unjust and ferocious, would require great forbearance on the part of the legislator; it would require art to soften and to combat it. But it would be better to yield to it altogether for a time, than uselessly to compromise his authority, and expose his laws to hatred.[79]

To appease dissatisfaction upon changing custom-rooted law, Bentham recommends compensation in money or honor, and in general, that the legislator adopt a "gentle means" of change. "Example, instruction, and exhortation should precede or follow, or if possible, stand in the place of law."[80]

In these passages Bentham does not defer to given preferences in calculating the utility of a law or action. However, such preferences, shaped by custom, must be taken into account:

Prejudice and the blindest custom must be humoured; but they need not be the sole arbiters and guides. He who attacks prejudice wantonly and without necessity, and he who suffers himself to be led blindfold a slave to it, equally miss the line of reason.[81]

When reason shows us change is for the good, we should change: "The welfare of all must not be sacrificed to the obstinacy of a few, nor the happiness of ages to the quiet of a day."[82] But where the evil of the remedy is greater than the evil of the disease we should "humour" prejudice and custom. Someday it may be easier to bring change.[83]

While habit has some force for Bentham,[84] often he implies that though we may believe we are happy with our habits and practices, we may be wrong, and would be happier with different ones. But he does not always take this view. While Bentham is critical of customs that motivate us to do what is against our interests, at times he implies that our interest is simply what promotes our given preferences, and if we prefer having a particular custom, then the utilitarian can only input this preference into the utility function used to calculate what best furthers our pleasure. In an important passage from "Influence of Time and Place," Bentham respects an Indian woman's belief that she will "find her ac-

---

entered into it" (10). Bentham's faith in the individual over the legislator may seem odd given his discussion in "Influence of Time and Place" of Peter the Great.

[79] Bentham, "Influence of Time and Place," 174.

[80] Ibid., 181–82.

[81] Ibid., 180.

[82] Ibid., 182. Bentham then criticizes Hindoo "Decoits" who are permitted by Hindoo custom to rob and murder (182).

[83] Ibid., 178.

[84] See also Bentham's *Book of Fallacies*: "*Provisional* adherence to existing establishments is grounded on considerations much more rational than a reliance on the wisdom of our ancestors. Though the *opinions* of our ancestors are as such of little value, their *practice* is not the less worth attending to; that is, in so far as their practice forms part of our own experience" (*Works*, 8:400–401). In the *Anarchical Fallacies* Bentham says contracts have binding force from "the habit of enforcing contracts" (*Works*, 8:502). But see *Pannomial Fragments* (*Works*, 9:219): "Habit is the result of a system of conduct of which the commencement is lost in the abyss of time," and which leads to a "disposition of obedience." Bentham is trying to mark out a "line of reason" regarding deference to habit—recall the quote referenced in note 81 above.

count" through self-immolation, so long as her preference is genuine and not coerced:

> In India, the wife often resolved to burn herself upon the death of her husband; if the acts were altogether voluntary, and she were persuaded she could find her account in it, it might be represented as tyrannical to oppose her; but such permission should not be granted till after she had undergone an examination and the fact of her consent were indubitably ascertained.[85]

So long as we are certain her action is voluntarily undertaken, Bentham, here, is unwilling to say the woman has misguided beliefs or false consciousness; rather, she is being a good utilitarian. If a woman had always been taught that her place was in the home, that pursuing a professional career was improper, and that what really mattered was selflessly serving her husband and children, and came wholeheartedly to believe that this was the only path to true happiness, Bentham, at times, suggests that we cannot say that she ought to lead her life differently; we can't say she is not truly happy, even though we may feel she could be far happier in a society providing her the opportunity to pursue a profession and in which she would share domestic work with her husband.

The evidence, then, is ambiguous about whether Bentham thinks the preferences people have for certain customs are to be uncritically entered as data in a utilitarian calculation, or whether they ever are to be regarded as erroneous, as false motivations that get people to do what is against their (true) interests.[86] Consequently Bentham offers no clear answer to the question of how the utilitarian is to respond to 'pangs of guilt', or to the possibility that walking away without returning the boomerang in Scanlon's example were regarded in my society not as culpable but as meriting praise.

Bentham thinks that the principle of utility, when applicable, is the only rational guide for all people everywhere. He is aware that its application will vary among peoples and yield variations in law. He notes, for example, that killing appears to be *malum in se,* a natural wrong, but adds that laws against murder declare all sorts of exceptions and defenses, so that ultimately the distinction between *malum in se* and *malum prohibitum* is hard to draw.[87] The principle of utility, like MacCormick's reliance principle, is in some sense universally valid. But how it is applied in particular cases will often depend on culturally variant norms and practices. Sometimes Bentham suggests that there are natural preferences humans should have, and if they form preferences connected with certain practices that are contrary to these natural preferences, a rational legislator should gently change these practices. But sometimes he suggests otherwise, acknowledging that laws will vary because what leads to happiness in one place may not lead to happiness in another, or because what is regarded as yielding

---

[85] Bentham, "Influence of Time and Place," 181.

[86] That Bentham leaves open the possibility of both interpretations is one example of what Hanna Pitkin has characterized as a "slipperiness" in Bentham's work. See her "Slippery Bentham," *Political Theory* 18, no. 1 (1990): 104–31.

[87] Bentham, "Influence of Time and Place," 192–93.

happiness in one place may not be so regarded in another. This is sometimes due simply to the fact that people socialized by different practices come to have different preferences.

There is another way the existence of a social practice constrains the operation of the principle of utility. Some practices establish rewards for compliance or sanctions for noncompliance. An individual deciding what to do on utilitarian grounds, living in a society with such a practice, will need to take into account this possibility of rewards or sanctions, while someone in a society without such a practice would not. Bentham thinks promising is such a practice; by turning to his account of promising we can see another way in which the existence of a social practice can play a crucial role in a utilitarian determination of what ethics requires.

Utilitarian Accounts of the Wrong of Promise-breaking

In chapter one we were presented with William Godwin's problem:

> I have promised to bestow a sum of money upon some good and respectable purpose. In the interval between the promise and my fulfilling it, a greater and nobler purpose offers itself, and calls with an imperious voice for my cooperation. Which ought I to prefer?[88]

Godwin, a utilitarian, responds: "That which best deserves my preference. A promise can make no alteration in the case." In deciding what action to take, Godwin does not feel bound by the existence of a social practice of promising, or of a shared understanding that promises must be kept; instead he invokes a principle that one should do what yields the greater good.[89] Godwin does not consider in his calculation that in not carrying out what one promised one would be violating the rule of a social practice and that this could have certain consequences that might effect a calculation of what yields the greater good. In saying a promise "can make no alteration," he implies that there are no such consequences. Godwin therefore is unable to explain why we often think it wrong to break promises that are inconvenient to keep. Bentham can.

For Bentham, the fact that a promise was made must be taken into account in deciding what the promisor ought to do:

> Men are not always held by the particular utility of a certain engagement; but in the case in which the engagement becomes burthensome to one of the parties, they are still held by the general utility of engagements—by the confidence that each enlightened man wishes to have placed in his word, that he may be considered as trustworthy, and enjoy the advantages attached to probity and esteem.[90]

---

[88] William Godwin, *An Enquiry Concerning Political Justice* (New York: Alfred Knopf, 1926), vol. 1, bk. 3, chap. 3.

[89] Ibid.

[90] Bentham, *Principles of Morals and Legislation*, chap. 2, "Objections Answered." The passage continues: "It is not the engagement which constitutes the obligation by itself . . . . It is the utility of the

A society will establish the practice of promising, and sanctions for violating its rules, because doing so is advantageous. Once the practice exists, an individual deciding whether to keep a promise must take into account the probable mischief of disobeying the rules of the practice and suffering the penalty.[91] Breaking a promise might give us a bad reputation, and cause us to suffer in the future. That it can have this effect presupposes the sanction-imposing practice.[92] This consideration will in most cases tip the scale and call on us to do what we promised. Bentham does not discuss which promises, if any, the principle of utility would justify breaking. Presumably there are occasions where the benefit of breaking a promise exceeds the costs that would result, including the cost of the sanction imposed by the social practice.

This is a question taken up explicitly by John Rawls in his rule-utilitarian defense of promise-keeping. Rawls argues that a promise presupposes a rule-governed practice of promising. When we promise, we are "inside" this practice, and once inside we are not free to conduct an all-things-considered utilitarian calculation of whether we should keep our particular promise, which is the calculation an act-utilitarian would make. Rather, on Rawls's view, we must keep our promise, since that is what it means to promise:

> If a person is engaged in a practice, and if he is asked why *he* does what *he* does, or if he is asked to defend what he does, then his explanation, or defense, lies in referring the questioner to the practice. He cannot say of *his* action, if it is an action specified by a practice, that he does it rather than some other because he thinks it is best on the whole. . . . One doesn't so much justify one's particular action as explain, or show, that it is in accordance with the practice.[93]

---

contract which gives it force." This might be taken to mean the utility of the particular promise creates the obligation to keep it. But this reading would undermine the earlier part of the passage, which implies that the utility of keeping promises *in general* has greater force than the "particular utility of a certain engagement." In another passage, from *Fragment on Government,* Bentham asks, "Suppose the constant and universal effect of an observance of promises were to produce *mischief,* would it *then* be men's *duty* to observe them?"(*Works,* vol. 1, sec. 45) Bentham's answer is no (vol. 1, sec. 46). His argument is not that if keeping a particular promise produced mischief one needn't keep it, but that if keeping promises generally produced mischief, one needn't keep promises—we shouldn't have the practice.

[91] Bentham, *Fragment on Government,* in *Works,* vol. 1, sec. 42: "For what *reason* is it, that men *ought* to keep their promises? . . . that it is for the *advantage* of society they should keep them; and if they do not, that as far as *punishment* will go, they should be *made* to keep them."

[92] Cf. Michael H. Robins, "The Primacy of Promising," *Mind* 85 (1976): 326 and note: "Any assignable sense of rational interest in keeping promises (against one's inclinations) is invariably tied to avoiding a bad reputation, etc. which is parasitic upon the very practice it is supposed to motivate."

[93] John Rawls, "Two Concepts of Rules," 27. Joseph Raz, "Reasons for Action, Decisions and Norms," in *Practical Reasoning,* ed. Joseph Raz (Oxford: Oxford University Press, 1978), gives an important account of promising that also is premised on the notion that if I promise to do x, I exclude balancing all reasons for doing or not doing x. Raz presents the "intuitive model" of practical reasoning as holding that "it is always the case that one ought, all things considered, to do whatever one ought to do on the balance of reasons"(130). Raz modifies this account by noting there are times when we have reason *not* to act on the balance of reasons, when we have "exclusionary reasons." A promise is an exclusionary reason, a "reason for performing the act [the agent] decided to perform and for

From within a practice, such as promising, a practitioner can justify her act *only* by appealing to the rules of the practice.[94] Bentham takes a different position. For Bentham, the fact that I promised in itself is no reason to keep the promise:

> Some other principle, it is manifest, must be resorted to, than that of the *intrinsic* obligation of promises upon those who make them. Now this *other* principle . . . , what other can it be than the principle of utility?[95]

For Bentham, the sanctions imposed by the practice of promising must be taken into account for a rational decision to be made. Bentham, unlike Rawls, thinks that in deciding whether to keep a particular promise we *should* weigh the benefits and burdens of doing so, and not simply rely on the practice-rule that promises are to be kept.

While Rawls disagrees, saying that we are not free to disobey the rules of a practice once we are "inside" the practice, he does *not* argue that we must blindly defer to whatever practices we have.[96] We can ask whether we should want our rule-governed practices, and we answer this by appealing to the principle of utility.[97] But once we commit to the practice for utilitarian reasons, we are bound by its rules.[98] In the case of promising, the rule of the practice is said to specify

---

disregarding further reasons and arguments"(134). A promise is in some ways like a decision, where we "put an end to deliberation" (135). Where Rawls defers to the constitutive rules of the practice of promising to determine one's obligations, though, Raz does not seem committed to the view that the fact that promising is a practice requires us to treat promises as valid exclusionary reasons. In one passage addressing the role of social practice in moral deliberation Raz writes, "There is no doubt that the existence of some practices is a reason for action." "But not all rules are of this nature. Many moral rules are usually claimed to be of universal validity regardless of whether they are practised or not"(139).

[94] Rawls, "Two Concepts of Rules," 27: "When the challenge is to the particular action defined by the practice, there is nothing one can do but refer to the rules." Cf. Rawls, *A Theory of Justice* (Cambridge: Harvard University Press, 1971), 344. Cf. Hanna Pitkin, "Obligation and Consent II," 48: to the promisor who asks "but why am *I* obliged—why can't I be an exception?" all we can say is "that is how . . . promises work."

[95] Bentham, *Fragment on Government*, in *Works*, vol. 1, secs. 47–48.

[96] Rawls, "Two Concepts of Rules," 32: "It might seem that I am saying that for each person the social practices of his society provide the standard of justification for his actions; therefore let each person abide by them and his conduct will be justified. This interpretation is entirely wrong. The point I have been making is rather a logical point. . . . It is simply that where a form of action is specified by a practice there is no justification possible of the particular action of a particular person save by reference to the practice . . . There is no inference whatsoever to be drawn with respect to whether or not one should accept the practices of one's society." Cf. Hanna Pitkin, *Wittgenstein and Justice*, 226–27: we can still question the social institution; and R. G. Durrant, "Promising," 55: "The general question, 'Has one a moral obligation to keep one's promises?' is absurd. The whole point of promising is that there should be such an obligation. . . . On the other hand, the question whether we should have the institution of promising, and how, whether on utilitarian grounds or otherwise, it is to be justified, is perfectly proper."

[97] Rawls, "Two Concepts of Rules," 24: "rules . . . are themselves the subject of the utilitarian principle."

[98] In later works, Rawls offers a different argument, characterizing the obligation to keep promises as an obligation of fairness. In *A Theory of Justice* (Cambridge: Harvard University Press, 1971) Rawls writes: "We are not to gain from the cooperative labors of others without doing our fair share"(111–

that we must normally keep our promises. Absent the practice there would be no obligation.

In Rawls's view, we must keep a promise even when doing so is onerous and counter to utility, unless the consequences of keeping it are "extremely severe."[99] This has led to the criticism that Rawls's rule-utilitarianism is not really utilitarian, for it uncritically defers to the rules of social practices.[100] R. M. Hare developed another account of utilitarianism that, like Rawls's, acknowledges the importance of practice-rules such as the rule that one must keep one's promises, but which avoids the criticism made of Rawls by refusing to insist that we are bound by rules when an application of the principle of utility to our particular case dictates that we should not adhere to them.

Hare distinguishes two levels of moral thinking: critical, and intuitive. Critical thinkers arrive at "correct answers" to moral questions.[101] They do so by an omniscient act-utilitarian calculation that takes into account the interests of all relevant parties.

> No judgment will be acceptable to [the critical thinker] which does not do the best, all in all, for all the parties. Thus the logical apparatus of universal prescriptivism . . . will

---

12; cf. pp. 342–43). "All obligations arise in this way"(112). Cf. John Rawls, "Legal Obligation and the Duty of Fair Play," in *Law and Philosophy,* ed. Sidney Hook (New York: New York University Press, 1964), 3–18. Cf. Thomas Scanlon, "Promises and Practices," 199–200: for Rawls, the reason it's wrong to break a promise isn't *just* that the practice says so, but that one has voluntarily benefitted from the practice and so is obligated to abide by its rules, out of fairness—it's wrong to be a free rider.

In these later works, the obligation is no longer "conceptual"—if one invokes the practice by promising, one must promise, because that is what promising means—but is based on fairness, or the obligation "to be a good sport." The *content* of the obligation is defined by the institution or practice "the rules of which specify what it is that one is required to do" (Rawls, *Theory of Justice,* 113). For criticism of this mixture of arguments, see Pateman, *Problem of Political Obligation,* 120.

[99] Rawls, "Two Concepts of Rules," 17: "Various defenses for not keeping one's promise are allowed, but among them there isn't the one that, on general utilitarian grounds, the promisor (truly) thought his action best on the whole, even though there may be the defense that the consequences of keeping one's promise would have been extremely severe."

[100] Warnock criticizes rule-utilitarianism as in effect not a moral philosophy, for in morality "there should occur the constantly repeated attempt to achieve the best judgment on the full concrete merits of each individual case" (*Object of Morality,* 67). See also Flathman, *Political Obligation,* 204. H. J. McCloskey argues that rule-utilitarianism can't account for why there should not be exceptions to rules where the exceptions wouldn't damage the institution, in his " 'Two Concepts of Rules'—A Note," *Philosophical Quarterly* 22 (October 1972): 89, reprinted in *Contemporary Utilitarianism,* ed. Michael Bayles (Gloucester: Peter Smith, 1978), 124. Another of McCloskey's several criticisms is that rule-utilitarianism leads to relativism: "To point to the practice is not to give a valid moral reason for holding another man in slavery"(p. 133). McCloskey also mentions the "Nazi rule in practice relating to treatment of Jews" (135). This latter criticism seems misplaced, ignoring how rule-utilitarianism is still utilitarian, insisting that the practices that guide us are themselves justified—see Rawls, "Two Concepts of Rules," 32.

[101] Hare thinks there are correct answers to moral questions, see *Moral Thinking,* 5–7, 16–17, 32; "archangels," who are perfect critical thinkers, "will all say the same thing, [on] all questions on which moral argument is possible"(46).

lead us in critical thinking (without relying on any substantial moral intuitions) to make judgments which are the same as a careful act-utilitarian would make.[102]

We use critical thinking to select prima facie principles and resolve conflicts between them.[103] One example of a prima facie principle is that promises should be kept.

We cannot always be critical thinkers. We need useful practical guides, educative tools that instill moral dispositions. At the intuitive level of moral thinking, we rely on these dispositions, and on prima facie principles that are ultimately justified by critical thinking.[104] But it is inevitable that we shall have to break our intuitive-level rules from time to time. Prima-facie principles are of use in moral education and character-formation because they are "to a certain degree simple and general." But precisely because they are simple and general, "we shall encounter cases . . . in which to obey them . . . would run counter to the prescriptions of an angelic moral thinking."[105] In these cases, prima-facie principles can be overridden.[106] These principles, like the constitutive rules of practices, are useful practical guides. But unlike intuitionists, Hare thinks our dispositions to act on these intuitive principles are subject to "critical thought when that is appropriate and safe."[107] While we may on occasion need to override these principles, most of the time they are reliable guides to right action: "It is possible to go on holding them while allowing that in particular cases one may break them."[108]

Hare considers a promise I make to my children to take them on a picnic, where keeping it means I must severely disappoint a friend. "In such a conflict between intuitions, it is time to call in reason."[109] Hare says there is a correct answer to what I ought to do at the critical level—I ought not to disappoint my friend.[110] In breaking the promise, I may feel regret—the force of "I ought to keep my promise" remains with me at the intuitive level. But if an act-utilitarian calculation shows that the promise should be broken, I ought to break it.[111] Rawls would have me keep the promise, or perhaps have me ask my children to release me from it (since that is allowed by the practice)—unless the disappoint-

---

[102] Ibid., pp. 42–43. cf. R. M. Hare, "Ethical Theory and Utilitarianism," in *Utilitarianism and Beyond,* ed. Amartya Sen and Bernard Williams (Cambridge: Cambridge University Press, 1982), 31, 35.

[103] *Moral Thinking,* 45.

[104] Ibid., 36.

[105] Ibid.

[106] Ibid., 35.

[107] Ibid., 39; cf. 40.

[108] Ibid., 59.

[109] Ibid., 32.

[110] Ibid., 27.

[111] As we've seen, there is also a Kantian element in Hare's account of promising. In his "The Promising Game" (in *The Is-Ought Question,* ed. W. D. Hudson [New York: St. Martin's Press, 1969], 156), Hare argues that in deciding whether one ought to keep one's promise, we ask "whether [one] can subscribe to the principle [that one ought to] when applied to all cases." See also footnote 65, above.

ment of the friend would be so great that the consequences of keeping the promise would be "extremely severe," which seems unlikely.

There are some advantages as well as some shortcomings of utilitarian explanations of the wrong involved in promise-breaking. In some of its versions, utilitarianism avoids some of the problems MacCormick's principle of reliance had. Mac-
Cormick's principle could not explain the wrong of breaking promises that are
not relied on and cause no harm. Rawls's and Bentham's versions of utilitarianism
can. If such a promise was very burdensome to keep, we might think breaking it
is *not* wrong; Godwin or Hare's version could explain why it is not wrong. Bentham's and Rawls's theories might, as well, but it is hard to be sure: Bentham
seems to leave open the possibility that breaking some promises is justified but
says little about which; Rawls says we needn't keep promises if the consequences
of doing so are extremely severe but says nothing about what counts.[112]

MacCormick's principle of reliance was inadequate also because, I argued, it
fails to capture the moral response uniquely appropriate to promise-breakers,
that they have shown themselves to be untrustworthy. Bentham, Hare, and Rawls
all point to how having a practice of promising, or a prima facie moral principle
requiring the keeping of promises, is useful. For Rawls and Bentham, the wrong
in breaking a promise is the wrong of violating a rule of a useful practice. For
Hare it is the wrong of not doing what is best on the whole.[113] While these are all
helpful explanations of the wrong, I think they are not as rich an account of the
wrong as the one we shall see Scanlon gives and that they, like MacCormick's, fail
to capture the moral response normally appropriate to promise-breakers. It is not
that the promise-breaker has violated a rule, or has failed to do what promotes
social utility, but that he has let the promisee down and can't be trusted. Even if
the utilitarian accounts do explain the wrong of promise-breaking to our satisfaction, the question that is our primary concern in this book remains: whether they
do so without appealing to social practice.

The Principle of Utility and Social Practice: II

Both Rawls and Bentham clearly rely on the existence of a practice in explaining
the wrong of promise-breaking. For Rawls, the principle of utility explains the
wrong of breaking a promise, but indirectly: breaking a promise violates a social
practice that itself is justified on utilitarian grounds. For Bentham, the principle
of utility directly explains the wrong of breaking a promise, but the existence of a
social practice is crucial in applying the principle. For Bentham the practice creates a sanction that an individual must weigh in deciding whether to do what was

---

[112] Which version of utilitarianism we should prefer might depend on whether we think we ought
to keep such promises; alternatively, whether we think we ought to might depend on which theory
we prefer.

[113] I prefer Hare's account because it seems right that it is not morally wrong to break certain
promises, such as unrelied-on burdensome promises. While I would feel regret breaking even these
promises, Hare's theory accounts for this reaction. However, it is not silly to think it is wrong to break
such promises, and for those who do, Hare's account may be less satisfying than Rawls's.

promised; for Rawls, the individual is not free to do a utilitarian calculation—if I promised, I must keep my promise, for this is what promising means. Bentham's utilitarianism leaves open the possibility that what we call a promissory obligation it would be blameworthy not to fulfill could arise even absent a practice, in cases where the principle of utility supports fulfilling this obligation regardless of the existence of a sanction. But on Rawls's account, a social practice is necessary for an obligation to arise. In "Two Concepts of Rules," the obligation arises as a point of logic. In Rawls's later work, the obligation is explained by the principle of fairness. In both versions the obligation depends on the existence of a social practice. In the Locke-Hume controversy, Rawls clearly sides with Hume.

Does Hare's account explain the obligation to keep a promise without appeal to a social practice? That may depend on which of Hare's two levels of moral thinking we are at. When we are at the intuitive level thinking about whether morality requires us to keep a promise, our judgment is shaped by the disposition to keep promises, a disposition that has been instilled in us, and which is continually reinforced by social sanctions for breaking promises. Working at the intuitive level, Hare's account would, I think, take into consideration how promise-breaking engenders practice-instilled responses of reprobation, though in *Moral Thinking* Hare does not himself discuss at any length the connection between prima facie principles and dispositions on the one hand, and social practice on the other.

While at the intuitive level of moral thinking judgments of promise-breakers may well rely on social practice, Hare suggests that reliance on practice-instilled dispositions and sanctions engendering regret at promise-breaking would *not* be determinative, perhaps would not be important at all, at the critical level of moral thinking: the regret of violating a prima facie moral principle such as that we must keep our promises would not weigh in the angelic critical thinker's calculation. This becomes clear when Hare writes that a good man might fail to do the right act. In other words, if the regret a good man would feel in going against his moral dispositions and prima facie principles, and in earning the reputation of being untrustworthy, governed his decision, the good man would on occasion fail to do what is morally correct. This suggests that a critical thinker, who seeks to do what is correct, would not weigh this regret in the calculation.[114] It might seem, then, that while Hare's intuitive moral thinker does rely on social practice, his critical thinker does not. Since Hare ultimately advocates critical thinking to decide what ethics requires, this would mean that on Hare's approach no reference to social practice is required in deciding whether we must keep promises. But I do not think that this is the right conclusion to draw.

We saw that for Bentham custom and tradition cannot be ignored in deciding

---

[114] Hare, *Moral Thinking*, 135. Hare's discussion here is not about promises; he might think it more than regretful that one earns a reputation of untrustworthiness, but he doesn't discuss this. In "Ethical Theory and Utilitarianism," Hare suggests that it is *rational* to fulfill the prima facie obligation to keep promises and keep a deathbed promise, even if doing so might not be morally right in a rare case (37–38, 33).

what we ought to do. Hare's critical moral thinker, too, while rejecting *the authority of* custom and practice, cannot ignore their existence. The existence of a practice with sanctions and rewards bears even on the critical thinker's deliberations. It is a social fact that must be taken into account. The critical thinker might think it unjustified to have the practice and the sanctions and rewards that go along with it; but once sanctions and rewards *do* come into play, they cannot be ignored in a rational calculation of what to do. Rawls, we saw, also argues that we are not free to ignore practice-rules once we are "inside" the practice. While we are free to ask whether we should have the practice, until we convince society to abolish the practice, we must take into account the fact that it exists; for Rawls we do this by adhering to its rules; for the act utilitarian we do this by taking into account the rewards and sanctions the practice imposes. Hare's critical thinker also appeals to social practices when taking preferences into account in deciding what is right; these preferences must to some extent be taken as given, and social practices and upbringing play a role in the development of these preferences.

That the critical thinker presupposes social practices and shared understandings when applying the principle of utility is apparent when we turn to Hare's discussion of maternal loyalty. The issue he takes up is whether mothers should be required to treat their own children the same as others, or rather, whether it is justified to favor one's own offspring, to have for them special ties of affection and loyalty. Hare defends such loyalty and special treatment, arguing that it can withstand the critical scrutiny of the act-utilitarian:

> If mothers had the propensity to care equally for all the children in the world, it is unlikely that children would be as well provided for even as they are. The dilution of the responsibility would weaken it out of existence.[115]

This judgment presupposes acceptance of a number of practices and preferences. One can imagine a society in which children were raised communally, in a way that avoids the overwhelming coordination problems that would result were no particular person responsible for a given child's needs.[116] In such a society, maternal favoritism might even be destructive. But in our society, with our family structure, it is easiest and best to divide the labor of providing for children in the way we do. Once we set up this division of labor, feelings are likely to develop further, giving a mother an even greater disposition to do more for her own children. Hare reaches the proper conclusion, but only by presupposing certain practices, dispositions, and already-given preferences.

Hare at times acknowledges the importance of empirical facts in critical thinking. He says that "in the selection of principles for use in this world of ours, facts

---

[115] Hare, *Moral Thinking*, 137.

[116] The suggestion is not fantastic. In the early sixteenth century in England relations within the nuclear family, including those between parents and children, were not much closer than those with neighbors or friends. Wet nurses played an important role in caring for infants of the wealthy. See Lawrence Stone, *Family, Sex, and Marriage in England 1500–1800* (London: Weidenfeld and Nicolson, 1977), 105–14.

about the world and the people in it are relevant."[117] He notes that "what prima facie intuitive principles of substantial justice are the best for a particular society to adopt will vary according to the circumstances of that society. These will include the propensities of its members." He adds, though, "but of course it may well be right to seek to change social attitudes, if change would be for the best."[118] Like Bentham, Hare is aware that existing practices constrain the application of rational principles; also like Bentham, he suggests that these practices are subject to principled criticism; but like Bentham, he does not explore precisely to what extent preference-shaping practices are up for grabs, or, rather, are to be taken as given. When Hare speaks for the angelic moral thinker, the consummate rationalist, he suggests everything is subject to principled criticism, that social norms and practices are all up for grabs, and that thought seems wrong, even though the commitment to principled criticism seems right.

SCANLON'S PRINCIPLES M AND F

Scanlon's Principles Applied to Scanlon's Example

Thomas Scanlon, like MacCormick, Bentham, and Hare, takes the position that in justifying certain moral judgments it will not do merely to appeal to the existence of practice-rules. Rather, to justify the judgment that an action is wrong is to give a principled reason why it is wrong, and not merely to show that it is regarded as wrong by custom, or proscribed by existing rules:

> If a convention or social practice is taken to consist in the fact that people accept certain rules or norms and typically act in accordance with them, then we need a mediating moral principle to explain how such practices can be morally binding and generate specific obligations.[119]

A practice can be only a "nonmoral source of motivation."[120]

Scanlon believes that my walking away with the spear without returning the boomerang is wrong, and that it is wrong not because I have violated the rules of a social practice; there is nothing like a social practice of agreement-making presupposed in the example, and even if there were, that would not explain why it is wrong. For Scanlon, the wrong is explained as a violation of a general moral principle that does not refer to the existence of a social practice. He calls it principle M, a principle proscribing unjustified manipulation. It states:

> In the absence of special justification, it is not permissible for one person, A, in order to get another person, B, to do some act, x (which A wants B to do and which B is morally free to do or not do but would otherwise not do) to lead B to expect that if he or she

[117] Ibid., 5; cf. 157.
[118] Ibid., 159.
[119] Scanlon, "Promises and Practices," 222.
[120] Ibid., 213.

does x then A will do y (which B wants but believes that A will otherwise not do) when in fact A has no intention of doing y if B does x, and A can reasonably foresee that B will suffer significant loss if he or she does x and A does not do y.[121]

Does principle M explain the wrong involved in Scanlon's example?

Principle M is similar to MacCormick's principle R, although the former requires not actual but foreseeable reliance. As it is stated above, principle M runs into the same difficulty accounting for the wrong in the example that MacCormick's principle encountered. For the principle to apply, it must be foreseeable that the strange man on the other side of the river would suffer "significant loss." But he is not much worse off for my not trying to return his boomerang. Had I made no gestures, he would still be without his boomerang. He is only out one spear, which was not even his. If we modified principle M by dropping its last clause, which requires that A foresee that B will suffer "significant loss," the principle could characterize the wrong involved. The wrong is very much like the wrong of deception.[122]

Scanlon's (Modified) Principle M and Social Practice

Does this modified version of principle M explain the wrong involved in Scanlon's example without appeal to social practice, and therefore show it to be a natural wrong?

If principle M applies to the example, this means that the strange man forms certain beliefs; that he possesses a boomerang that he wants back; that he returns the spear (as opposed to attacks me with it). The man can "return" the spear and want back his boomerang only if he understands something like our concept of property. He has to have the idea that someone can be entitled to a thing even if it is not in his immediate possession. This itself may require the concept of having one's will in a thing.[123] The idea of property presupposed is very rudimentary— it is not the same idea as private (as opposed to communal) property, and needn't presuppose social institutions unique to capitalist societies. It is so rudimentary that it would be odd to encounter a human being without it. If the strange man was unfamiliar with this idea, and in fact was not "returning" the spear but playing some game, or attacking me, then principle M (or the modified version) would not apply, for its conditions would not be satisfied. The principle can only be applied among people capable of forming the necessary expectations in each other, and this may occur only if certain concepts or practices are shared. But also, agreeing that violating principle M is wrong may also depend on our sharing

---

122 Scanlon suggests that the wrong in his example can easily be taken for the wrong of deception (cf. Ibid., 203). For this reason he thinks principle M fails fully to capture the wrong of promise-breaking. As we shall see, he develops another principle, principle F, to capture that wrong.

123 See G. W. F. Hegel, *Philosophy of Right*, ed. Allen Wood (Cambridge: Cambridge University Press, 1991), Pars. 41–58.

social practices as well as understandings. For it may be that the strange man, rather than blame me, praises my cleverness.[124]

Scanlon's Explanation of the Wrong of Promise-breaking

Scanlon notes that breaking a promise is one way of violating principle M, but it is not the only way, as the example involving the spear and boomerang illustrates. Nor are all instances of promise-breaking violations of principle M. Principle M requires an intention to deceive, but not all-promise breakers make lying promises. Scanlon formulates another principle, principle F (for fidelity), that more fully captures the promissory obligation. It states:

> If (1) A voluntarily and intentionally leads B to expect that A will do x (unless B consents to A's not doing x); (2) A knows that B wants to be assured of this; (3) A acts with the aim of providing this assurance, and has good reasons to believe that he or she has done so; (4) B knows that A has the belief and intentions just described; (5) A intends for B to know this, and knows that B does know it; and (6) B knows that A has this knowledge and intent; then, in the absence of some special justification, A must do x unless B consents to x's not being done.[125]

Principle F is rather more complicated than MacCormick's principle R. Precisely because of its complexity it is able to avoid some of the difficulties MacCormick's principle was unable to overcome. While principle R could not account for the obligation to keep promises that lack detrimental reliance, such as the promise Harold's friend has an obligation to keep, principle F can. And while violating principle R does not necessarily evoke the response that seems uniquely appropriate for the promise-breaker, that he can't be trusted, violating principle F does.

Scanlon's Principle F and Social Practice

Principle F seems to capture well the wrong unique to promise-breaking. But does it do this simply because it is the practice of promising under another name?[126] Does the family of moral principles Scanlon articulates explain the wrong of promise-breaking without appealing to social practice, or are his principles simply explicit formulations or elucidations of existing practice, accounts of the principles immanent in the practice of promising and necessarily presupposing the practice?[127] Are these principles natural principles pointing to natural wrongs?

---

[124] We might think that even though this might be the response engendered in someone with his social background, he ought not to think that way. For further discussion of this point, see chapter 3, "Conclusion," below.

[125] Scanlon, "Promises and Practices," 208.

[126] Scanlon insists that it is not (Ibid., 210).

[127] Scanlon also articulates two other related principles, along with principles M and F. Principle D (for due care) holds that "one must exercise due care not to lead others to form reasonable but false expectations about what one will do when there is reason to believe that they would suffer significant loss as a result of relying on those expectations"(204). Principle L (for loss prevention), holds that "if

In deciding this, it is important to distinguish two claims regarding the relation of principles to practice. One claim is that the reason it is wrong to do a particular action such as breaking a promise is *not* that the action violates a practice-rule, or demand of a practice, but that it violates a moral principle; if it is wrong to break a rule of a practice, some reason must be given apart from the fact that a rule was broken. This argument is sometimes advanced with respect to the obligation to obey law. The claim is that if it is wrong to break a particular law, say by trespassing, it is wrong only because trespassing is a bad thing, and not because in trespassing one breaks the law. A second and distinct claim is that we can explain why actions (such as breaking a promise) are wrong by appealing to natural principles, that is, to principles that do not presuppose the existence of social practices or shared understandings—the second claim is that there are natural wrongs.

Scanlon makes *both* claims. He claims that the wrong of breaking a promise can (and must) be explained by a reason other than simply the fact that a practice-rule was violated:

> When I say "I promise to help you if you help me", the reason I suggest to you that I will have for helping is just my awareness of the fact that not to return your help would, under the circumstances, be wrong: not just forbidden by some social practice, but morally wrong.[128]

He also makes the distinct claim that the wrong of breaking a promise can be explained without appealing to social practice. In Scanlon's view,

> the wrong of breaking a promise and the wrong of making a lying promise are instances of a more general family of moral wrongs which are concerned not with social practices but rather with what we owe to other people when we have led them to form expectations about our future conduct.
>
> When promises give rise to clear obligations, these can be accounted for on the basis of general moral principles that do not refer to the existence of social practices.[129]

The first claim I take to be correct: the fact that in not keeping a promise we are breaking a rule of the practice itself doesn't explain why we should regard violating the rule as acting badly, and the practice as *morally* binding.[130] If I promise to pick Jack up at the airport tomorrow night, and this means I can't go to an

---

one has intentionally or negligently led someone to expect that one will follow a certain course of action x, and one has reason to believe that that person will suffer significant loss as a result of this expectation if one does not follow x, then one must take reasonable steps to prevent that loss"(204).

[128] Ibid., 200. Cf. 222, on the need for a mediating moral principle.

[129] Ibid., 211, 220.

[130] Hanna Pitkin, drawing on the work of Stanley Cavell, implies that the practice is not *morally* binding: To say we ought to keep our promises suggests that "we are acting well when we do fulfill. But we aren't normally, neither well nor ill" (*Wittgenstein and Justice*, 230; citing Stanley Cavell, *Must We Mean What We Say?* [New York: Charles Scribner's Sons, 1969], 30). It is more convincing to say one doesn't act well in keeping promises than it is to say one doesn't act badly in breaking a promise. I take it as evident that a moral wrong is usually involved, that it usually is appropriate morally to blame one who unjustifiably breaks a promise.

engagement with Jill, and Jill asks me to explain why I must pick Jack up, it may suffice just to say, "because I promised." If she asks why the fact that I promised Jack means I must miss the engagement, I could explain that this is what it means to promise, and that may be a satisfactory reason. But if Jill continues to press me, asking why I should regard myself as morally bound to comply with the rules of the practice, then it won't do simply to say that this is what the practice requires. That answer isn't likely to satisfy Jill.

The second claim, that moral principles explain the wrong of promise-breaking without reference to social practice, or that the principles are not concerned with social practice, demands closer examination.

One objection to this second claim is that Scanlon knows what principle F holds only because he already knows that it is wrong to break a promise, just as he is able to formulate principle M only because he already knows it is wrong to make a lying promise. Scanlon's method is to test principle F against his intuitions about whether an obligation arises in particular examples. He presents examples where his intuition tells him an obligation does exist, and examples where it tells him there is no obligation, and develops a principle to capture the features of the situations in which obligations do arise. As this principle accords with his intuitions, he concludes that it is reasonable to adhere to the principle.[131] While the purpose of developing a moral principle is to use it to criticize some of our intuitions or to guide us when we have no clear intuitions, we choose the principle in the first place because it makes sense of many of our intuitions. Scanlon developed principles M and F to account for certain moral intuitions, but, the objection goes, Scanlon has these intuitions only because he has been brought up in a society with the practice of promising. The principles *are* concerned with social practice in that they are immanent in the practice of promising—the principles we invoke are chosen because they best accord with the intuitions we have as a result of sharing certain practices and norms.

Scanlon denies that he is appealing to a social practice in deciding what ethics requires:

> When, for example, I try to determine whether a promise to do x obligates a person to do x even at the cost of y—it seems to me that I am engaging in moral reflection, not in an inquiry into what the accepted rules of our social practice of agreement-making are.[132]

But if the moral reflection involved in developing principle F consists in fitting the principle to intuitions we have because we share certain practices, then Scanlon is wrong to see moral reflection as *excluding* inquiry into what our social practices require.

Scanlon's claim that in moral reflection he is not involved with inquiry into social practice is unpersuasive because there are other ways to consult a social

---

[131] Scanlon, "Promises and Practices,": 201 ("intuitively"); 203 ("it is entirely reasonable for us . . ."); 204 ("Its validity consists just in the fact that one can reasonably . . ."); 208–9 ("have reason to," "reasonable for"); 217.

[132] Ibid., 215.

practice than by inquiring into its rules. Scanlon thinks that in explaining promising he *must* be consulting a moral principle, not the rules of a practice, because
there are very few rules to turn to when we need to determine the limits of
promissory obligations.[133] The "printed form" provided by the practice of promising "appears to be nearly blank."[134] We therefore need principles.

Scanlon assumes that consulting a practice necessarily is consulting rules.[135] But
knowing how to engage in some practices is more involved than that. Many practices lack rules in the strict sense. Some practices—especially games or contests—
have clear rules, but many do not, for example, gift-giving, dating, lecturing, grade-
giving, courtesy, and promising. Lacking rules or clearly acknowledged standards,
we might justify an action we take within the practice by arguing that it was
consistent with our understanding of the point of the practice.[136] Arguably this is
what Scanlon himself does. In the case of promising, in consulting the practice we
may find conflicting views. We who practice promising disagree about what it
requires.[137] One source we have to consult is the law of contracts, but it is not the
only source, perhaps not even the best, since other considerations enter when we
consider which promises the state should legally enforce. My point is that the
practice view of promising Scanlon criticizes, the "preprinted lease form where one
just fills in the blanks," is a straw man.[138]

There are hard cases in which social practice is indeterminate. But it doesn't
follow from the fact that social practices are sometimes indeterminate that they
play no role at all in moral reasoning. Scanlon's principle F is itself indeterminate,

---

[133] Ibid., 215 n. 3. Oswald Hanfling, in his fascinating article exploring the connection between
promising and games, rejects the view that promising is a game, in part because there aren't really
rules of promising as there are rules of games or legal institutions. He notes it's unclear how one
consults the rules of promising. "What, after all, *are* the 'rules' of promising?"—"there seems to be just
one basic rule—to do what one promised" ("Promises, Games and Institutions," *Proceedings of the
Aristotelian Society* 75 [1974–1975]: 23–24).

[134] Scanlon, "Promises and Practices," 216.

[135] We saw that John Rawls similarly argues that a practice is by definition stipulated by rules
("Two Concepts of Rules," 24—"rules define a practice"). Yet Rawls acknowledges that "practice" is an
"involved concept" and likely has "border-line cases" (29). He notes that there are different sorts of
rules: "rules of practices" (rules in the strict sense), and maxims and "rules of thumb"(29). But he
implies that "rules of thumb" don't belong to practices, since practices, by definition, have "rules in
the strict sense."

[136] This idea is discussed in chapter two. With respect to the practice of punishment, see Mark
Tunick, *Punishment: Theory and Practice* (Berkeley: University of California Press, 1992). With respect
to promises, see Páll Ardal, "And That's a Promise": Ardal uses his account of the purpose of
promising—to provide assurance to the promisee—to argue that where the promisee no longer cares
about the assurance, there is no obligation (235).

[137] This is a point Jan Narveson makes in "Promising, Expecting, and Utility," 209. See also Henry
Sidgwick, *Methods of Ethics*: there is no clear consensus concerning, for example, coerced promises,
promises with conflicting prior obligations, improvident promises: "the *consensus* seems to become
evanescent, and the common moral perceptions of thoughtful persons fall into obscurity and disagreement"(311; cf. p. 309). See also Rawls, "Two Concepts of Rules," 30–31: "The rules defining
promising are not codified," and "it is likely that there is considerable variation in the way people
understand the practice."

[138] Scanlon uses the "lease form" metaphor ("Promises and Practices," 214).

having as one of its provisions the "special justification" loophole. Consider the following deathbed promise: John promises his grandfather, whose death is immanent, that after the funeral he will toss the grandfather's expensive diamond ring into the ocean. The grandfather believes doing this will put an end to a curse that will otherwise afflict John. John makes this promise to appease the grandfather, who would not otherwise rest in peace. The conditions of principle F are all satisfied, but it is far from clear whether John must actually toss the ring. It might not be wrong according to the principle if the "special justification" clause comes into play. Should it? This may well depend upon whether in our society people regard it as ever reasonable not to fulfill deathbed promises. This seems to depend not on abstract moral reflection alone but, in part, on our attitudes about the respect owed to the wishes of those now dead. How do other people in our society act upon making deathbed promises? Which deathbed promises do they keep, and which do they not keep? If John were morally conscientious and deliberated carefully about his decision regarding the ring, it seems to me he would seek answers to such questions; in doing so he *would* be inquiring into social practice.

Scanlon and the Kant-Hegel Debate

I've argued that one role social practices play in moral reflection is as a source of intuitions that ground the moral principles we develop. Scanlon, however, could reply that even if social practices played this role, the fact that we may derive a principle from a practice or set of practices need not mean the principle derives its *moral authority* from the practices. Scanlon could argue that the principle still would have weight even were our practices to change or disappear. So long as it is reasonable to consent to the moral principle—so long as it is a good principle—how we arrived at it or whether people agree to it is beside the point. Scanlon indeed seems to take this position when he writes that "[the principle's] validity does not depend on its being generally recognized or adhered to."[139]

Accepting Scanlon's position is in effect to side with Kant against Hegel. Kant, it will be recalled, held that "actions of which the world has perhaps hitherto given no example . . . are nevertheless commanded unrelentingly by reason."[140] The ways in which people behave or have behaved in the past may serve as examples for how we think we should behave, but, in Kant's view, we cannot be sure that we are right to follow these examples unless reason shows them to accord with what morality requires: "Every example of [morality] presented to me must first itself be judged by moral principles in order to decide if it is fit to serve as an original example—that is, as a model: it can in no way supply the prime source for the concept of morality."[141] Hegel criticizes Kant for invoking a speculative *ought* that is not rooted in actual agreement. In Hegel's view, speculative *oughts* don't create expectations and obligations; there are lots of things a

---

[139] Ibid., 210.
[140] Kant, *Groundwork*, 408. Kant's position is discussed in chapter 2.
[141] Ibid., 408–9.

philosopher might think we ought to agree to as reasonable; but we are justified in making moral judgments only if they are rooted in actual agreement, as expressed in our practices and institutions.

If principle F was never adhered to, or not generally recognized, would violating it still be wrong? If we arrive at it because it once did accord with our practices, and our practices then change, would it still be valid? Would it be valid for societies with very different practices?

The earth still is round and orbits the sun even if everybody we ask says it stands still and is square. But must John keep his deathbed promise if everybody he asks says no? If in his society people normally do not keep such promises? That is not certain at all. This is not to say that we decide what is right by taking a vote; or that practices which a society accepts, or recognizes as valid, are right because they are accepted or recognized as valid. But Scanlon needn't take the position that social practices play no role in moral reflection just to avoid the position that morality is a matter only of convention, or of consensus. Hegel rejects the position that morality is determined by vote or that the mere existence of a social practice justifies it and makes it right, and does so while still acknowledging the importance of social practice and shared understandings in determining what ethics and the law require. Appealing to social practices and norms in determining what is right doesn't imply a "democratic relativism" that defines right as whatever a majority vote dictates; not just because majority votes may diverge from what social practice dictates; but also because one can acknowledge that practices are involved in the application of principles without holding that whatever our practice is, by definition, is right.

Scanlon's position is that even where an action we regard as a wrong explicitly violates a practice, to explain why it is wrong we need a mediating moral principle. He then implies that we can rely exclusively on mediating moral principles without making reference to practice in determining what ethics requires. It is this further implication that I want to challenge by emphasizing the role social practice plays both in developing and applying moral principles.

CONCLUSION: PRACTICES AND THE OBLIGATION TO KEEP PROMISES

MacCormick, Bentham, Hare, and Scanlon all seem right to insist that moral questions be decided by critical thinking, rather than by deferring to the authority of custom or practice. But the relation between practices and principles is complex. We may know how to formulate the moral principles that explain the wrong of promise-breaking because of the existence of a social practice of promising. To engage in a practice is to act with a point that others can understand. We can reflect on what the point of the practice is, or whether we should even have the practice. And if we are unclear what the practice requires in a hard case, we might want to appeal to an articulated version of its point, expressed as a principle, for many of our practices lack fixed rules to cover all cases. But the principles to which we appeal either in criticizing a practice or acting within it when the rules of the practice are indeterminate needn't be seen as independent of the existence of social practice. While agreeing with the position that determinations of right and wrong should be based on critical thinking and rational principles rather than on blind deference to the authority of custom, tradition, and practice, I have taken issue with the claim that critical thinking takes place in a vacuum, as if customs, traditions, and practices were of no account. Locke, MacCormick, and Scanlon all maintain that practices are not necessary for an obligation. MacCormick and Scanlon argue that the obligation to keep promises is an instance of a more general class of wrongs that does not depend on social practice. They start with intuitions (which they have in part because they are familiar with the practice of promising and other of our practices), develop a principle to account for their intuitions, and then claim that practices can be disregarded. They imagine an obligation could arise between two people without any knowledge of their political or cultural identity. While praising their search for principles to help us when we are unclear what our practice requires, or to justify our practice when we are in doubt about a particular obligation, I am critical of the general position they take of discarding practice in deciding what's right. Sometimes it is important to be sensitive to culturally variant practices.

We have covered lots of ground in this chapter, and considered many ways in which practices and shared understandings may be involved in principled moral reflection. In this concluding section, I want to identify from our earlier discussion five distinct ways practices can come into play.

The strongest role we have seen some theorists give to social practices is what we might call a constitutive role: practices define our obligations. Rawls takes this position (in "Two Concepts of Rules"), as do Searle, Pitkin, and others. One reason this position has not persuaded philosophers such as Scanlon is that it is hard to see how the fact that a practice requires us to keep promises provides a moral reason for doing so. Rawls compares the obligation to keep promises to a baseball player's obligation to adhere to the rules of baseball:

> In a game of baseball if a batter were to ask "Can I have four strikes?" it would be assumed that he was asking what the rule was; and if, when told what the rule was, he were to say that he meant that on this occasion he thought it would be best on the whole for him to have four strikes rather than three, this would be most kindly taken as a joke. One might contend that baseball would be a better game if four strikes were allowed instead of three; but one cannot picture the rules as guides to what is best on the whole in particular cases.[142]

Rawls's point is that just as the baseball player, once "inside" the game, is bound by its rules and not free to ask whether it would be best on the whole to diverge from what the game requires, so too the promisor, "inside" the practice of promising, is bound by its rules and not free to ask whether it would be best on the whole not to keep the promise. But promising is not like baseball; even if it were, Rawls shows only that the baseball player (and promisor) has an institutional

---

[142] Rawls, "Two Concepts of Rules," 90.

obligation to adhere to the rules, and institutional obligations in themselves have no moral force.

There *is* an important truth in what Rawls says: that social practices exist sometimes means they must be taken into account even if on reflection we think they aren't justified and that we'd be better off without them, because practices set up expectations on which people rely. They do this most notably by imposing sanctions and rewards; the sanctions associated with breaking promises, for example, must be taken into account by an act-utilitarian in deciding whether to keep a particular promise. Sometimes it is inappropriate to criticize the rules of a practice, as in the middle of a baseball game or when a judge is charged with following the legislator's sentencing guidelines. Some practices define roles, and while in one of these roles it may be inappropriate to subject the practice to critical scrutiny.

The weakest role practices have in moral deliberation are as a means to invoke principles. Invoking a social practice is one way to satisfy the conditions stipulated in an obligation principle. Scanlon acknowledges that practices and conventions can play this role. He notes, for example, that promising is a conventional way of satisfying principle F: uttering "'I promise' creates the conditions of mutual knowledge required "with great economy."[143] But in Scanlon's view, that there are conventions for satisfying the conditions of principle F does not show that principle F is not a natural principle, so long as without these conventions, for example, in a state of nature, the conditions could be satisfied in a way that gives rise to a moral obligation. Scanlon insists that principle F can be satisfied in ways other than "by making a promise."[144] In other words, the social practice is not a necessary condition for an obligation.

There are, however, other ways in which we appeal to social practices in applying a principle. Sometimes only by invoking, or choosing not to invoke, the practice of promising can we distinguish cases in which reliance is induced, but where no moral obligation arises because reliance is not reasonable, from those in which a moral obligation does arise. We saw that MacCormick's principle R could not always determine whether B's reliance on A's doing x is reasonable without appealing to practice. Scanlon, however, claims that principle F states the conditions under which B has a *right* to rely on A's doing x.[145] In Scanlon's view, no appeal to social practice is needed to decide if reliance is reasonable. Fulfilling the conditions of principle F *establishes* that reliance is reasonable. But just as not all cases in which MacCormick's principle R are satisfied generate moral obligations, so too are there cases in which principle F is satisfied but no moral obligation arises, precisely because conventional methods of promising were not invoked. We need the practice to delimit the scope of obligations. Consider the case discussed earlier in which reliance is induced but no obligation arises—the example of "low-price Lou." All six conditions of principle F seem to

---

[143] Scanlon, "Promises and Practices," 214; cf. 211.
[144] Ibid., p. 210.
[145] Ibid.

be satisfied. Lou intends to lead his customers to expect he will charge the lowest prices, he knows they want this assurance, and he takes measures to provide this assurance by setting the lowest prices and occasionally reminding his customers that he has the lowest prices. Lou intends for the customers to know he is trying to win their business. All of principle F's knowledge conditions seem to be met. Yet there is no obligation for Lou to lower prices below those of a newly opened store or to tell his customers that lower prices can now be found there. There would be a moral obligation had he promised or guaranteed the lowest prices, and he has a moral obligation not to lie if asked by customers whether his prices still are the lowest. That he *could* have promised but didn't is crucial in accounting for the lack of a moral obligation in this case. The example shows that whether a principle leads to a judgment in a particular case in a society depends on that society's norms and practices. Principle F does have an "exception" clause: no obligation arises if there is "special justification." But if social practice determined what counts as a "special justification," and if this clause played a role in lots of cases, then what is left of Scanlon's claim that the principle does not refer to social practice? Practices, then, sometimes are needed to interpret whether a principle applies in a particular case. They are a standard for determining whether it is reasonable to apply the principle in a particular case, or whether there are any special justifications for not applying the principle in a particular case.[146]

There is still another role for social practices: practices and shared understandings are a source of our intuitions about whether obligations exist in particular cases, intuitions which may be the basis for selecting our moral principles. At one point Scanlon comes close to acknowledging this role of convention. He says we would agree to principle F because we value assurance; in this respect, he notes, there is a conventional "element" in promises.[147] Scanlon does not fully acknowledge this final role of social practice, but only "comes close." His position is that if a people value assurance, they have reason to live by a moral principle promoting assurance and ought to conform with that principle *even if it is not generally adhered to or recognized by them.* Scanlon does not explain how we could value x without generally adhering to or recognizing a principle promoting x; nor does he explain the argument he apparently holds that if we value x, we ought gener-

---

[146] There are at least two other ways in which social practice bears on the application of principle F. First, for conditions 2 and 4 of principle F to be met, A must know something about B, and B must know something about A; but if they come from very different places with very different practices, it is unlikely these knowledge conditions could be met. A similar point was made earlier regarding MacCormick's principle of reliance. Second, principle F requires that A *voluntarily* creates an expectation in B. As I shall discuss in chapter four, what counts as "voluntary" will sometimes depend on practices and norms.

[147] Scanlon, "Practices and Promises," 222. J. L. Austin makes a related point: "The social habits of the society may considerably affect the question of which performative verbs are evolved and which . . . are not." For example, our society seems to approve of censuring and reprimanding, and so we have the performative "I reprimand you," "I censure you"; but on the other hand, since apparently we don't approve of insulting, we have not evolved a simple formula 'I insult you'" (*Philosophical Papers* [Oxford: Oxford University Press, 1961], 232.

ally to adhere to or recognize a principle promoting x. This needs explanation and defense because it seems reasonable for a society to think certain promises—deathbed promises, or at least John's deathbed promise in our earlier example—needn't be kept, even though the society values assurance. There are of course relativist implications once we acknowledge this role for social practices. Recall the possibility in Scanlon's example that the strange man is well aware that I made the equivalent of a lying promise, but rather than judge me as having wronged him, he praises my cleverness. Can we say that he is mistaken in his judgment? Or rather, would he be mistaken only for us, given our ways?

Gilbert Harman argues that when we say that A ought not to have done something we are making an "inner judgment": we are saying that A's action was inconsistent with motivational attitudes—goals, desires, and intentions—that A shares with us. If we do not share A's motivational attitudes then we cannot properly make this inner judgment. If A acts in a way that is consistent with her motivational attitudes but inconsistent with ours, we cannot say she ought not to have acted in that way, for this would be improperly to make an inner judgment; we *can* say that what A did ought not to have happened, that her action was consistent with her motivational attitudes but that she ought not to have those attitudes—here we invoke what Harman calls the "normative" sense of *ought*.[148] Harman argues that we can properly say "Hitler ought not to have killed the Jews" if we mean that what Hitler did ought not to have happened, that it was a bad thing that Hitler had the moral considerations that led him to do what he did. In saying this we are invoking the normative sense of *ought;* but, Harman continues, we cannot properly say "It was wrong for Hitler to kill the Jews." We cannot say to someone who does not give any weight to our moral considerations that he "ought not" to do x. All we can do is call him a criminal. To say "he ought not to do" x (which we cannot say) is different than to say "it ought not to be the case that he has his moral considerations" (which we *can* say). To invoke the moral as opposed to the normative *ought* is to make an inner judgment, and we can properly make inner judgments only if certain conditions hold. In an inner judgment, some speaker S says that an actor A ought to do some action D. S assumes there are motivational attitudes shared between S and A.[149] If the action D we are talking about is my walking away with my spear without attempting to return the boomerang in Scanlon's example, then for S to say that I ought not to do D, S has to share my motivational attitudes, and those motivational attitudes have to lead to the conclusion S makes. The relativistic claim Harman defends—that we cannot properly use the moral *ought* to make inner judgments of actions of those who do not share our motivational attitudes—is, as Harman says, "a soberly logical thesis about logical form."[150]

---

[148] Gilbert Harman, "Moral Relativism Defended," *Philosophical Review* 84 (1975): 3–22. Harman distinguishes four senses of *ought*, of which I refer to two: what he calls the moral sense, that concerns inner judgments, and the normative sense, that concerns a judgment about whether it is a good thing that someone has the moral considerations that they have.

[149] Ibid., 5–6, 8–9.

[150] Harman, "Moral Relativism Defended," 4.

If we accept Harman's thesis, then it is possible for someone, S, to say that I ought not to have done D because that violates some moral principle, only if both myself and S accept and agree to live by that principle. Otherwise S cannot properly say I ought not to have done what I did, though he could make the normative judgment that I ought not to exclude the relevant moral principle from my motivational attitudes. It is unclear how one would justify that normative judgment. Scanlon's account is contractualist: we would agree to certain moral principles, and our obligation to adhere to them derives from hypothetical, not actual, agreement.[151] We would agree to these principles not because we already actually do, the argument goes, but because it is reasonable to and because these principles accord with our intuition. It seems to me plausible to suppose that this intuition derives from what we are accustomed to, to the reactions we see, to legal decisions; and that it is reasonable to agree to the principle because assurance is a value both required by and requisite for many of our practices. While at a high level of abstraction a principle may be universally regarded as reasonable, when applied in a particular situation, what society regards as reasonable may depend on that society's practices, assuming the society is even in agreement as to what is reasonable.

In Scanlon's example it may seem that what is reasonable would be so for any rational human being, regardless of their particular cultural background. A society that made no moral distinction between keeping and not keeping one's word would not be a very attractive one. There are good reasons for us to respect the principle of fidelity. But societies not radically different from ours, such as eighteenth century England, perhaps would not have adhered wholeheartedly to this principle.[152] In chapter five we shall turn to a set of ethical and legal issues concerning privacy for which there is considerable disagreement about what is reasonable among members of different societies and even among members within the same society. One point of resisting Scanlon's and MacCormick's move, following the development of principles, of disregarding social practice is to help us better confront such situations. Even if the possibility of different societies that don't value assurance may have little weight for us in thinking about promising, sensitivity to cultural variations in expectations and judgments of reasonability is important as we confront many other ethical and legal issues, and may be important in determining how to apply a principle that promotes the value of assurance in a particular case.

[151] Scanlon, "Promises and Practices," 220. In this respect the argument parallels Harman's. Harman argues that moral obligations arise from an agreement in intentions, but Harman seems to mean an actual agreement.

[152] See Atiyah, *Promises, Morals, and Law,* 64–65, discussed earlier.

Contracts

Problems in Contract Law

In chapter three we considered why promises give rise to moral obligations. In this chapter we consider which promises should be enforced by courts—we turn to the law of contract. One reason for doing so is to extend the discussion of promises in chapter three. There I showed how social practice plays an important role in our having a moral obligation to keep promises. Our concern was primarily with the abstract question of whether the wrong of breaking a promise is a natural wrong. In this chapter we consider promising from a more practical perspective: Which promises give rise to obligations? Under what circumstances is a promisor not obligated to keep a promise? Another reason for turning to contract law is to extend the argument about the role social practices and principles play to a case of legal (as distinct from moral) judging.

I shall consider only a few of the many issues arising in contract law in the United States. My concern is less with the blackletter law, which practicing attorneys must know, more with how we determine what the law *should* require of promisors. In approaching contract law, we need to go beyond the discussion of moral obligations. Even if we knew with certainty which promises give rise to moral obligations, that would not tell us which promises the state should enforce. When a promise is broken, the sanction might be "moral indignation, riposte in kind, withering contempt, public condemnation, sending to Coventry, withdrawal of friendship."[1] Failure to fulfill a promise giving rise to a clear obligation reflects on one's character.[2] Breaking a contract *might* similarly reflect on one's character or evoke moral condemnation since contracts *can* give rise to moral obligations. But not everyone agrees they must. Many contracts involve commercial transactions, and sometimes for economic reasons it is in one's interest to breach a contract and pay damages rather than to fulfill the contract.[3] Some argue that doing so does not mean one is untrustworthy or bad.[4] Not all legal obligations are moral obligations. So too, not all promises that *do* give rise to moral

---

[1] Colin McGinn, *Moral Literacy or How to Do the Right Thing* (Indianapolis: Hackett, 1992), 88: discussing the enforcement of morality in general.

[2] Richard Brandt, "The Concepts of Obligation and Duty," *Mind* 73 (1964): 381.

[3] Depending on the nature of the contract, the breaching party might be required either to perform what the contract required (specific performance), or to compensate the other party. Compensation might be for losses suffered by the breach (reliance damages) or for the benefit the other party would have received had the contract been fulfilled (expectations damages).

[4] See Eugene F. Mooney, "Old Kontract Principles and Karl's New Kode: An Essay on the Jurisprudence of our New Commercial Law," *Villanova Law Review* 11 (1966): 213–58.

obligations should be enforceable by a court. Not all immoral acts are illegal. Even someone holding passionately to the conviction that it is immoral to eat red meat might agree that it is no business of the state to punish people who do so.

How are we to determine which promises should be legally enforced? One way would be to look at existing contract law, to see which promises *are* legally enforced. This would be similar to the move made by those philosophers we considered in chapter three for whom the obligation to keep a promise is an institutional obligation, an obligation that arises only by invoking an institution or practice. In their view, to answer the question of whether one is bound to keep a promise, we turn to the rules of the moral practice of promising. One problem with this approach is that it is sometimes unclear where to turn to find the rules of moral practices or an authoritative arbiter when there are disputes about what the practice requires. This is less a problem with contract law, which does have knowable, detailed rules and arbiters with recognized authority. But there is another problem with deciding what ethics and the law should require by simply consulting the dictates of existing practice. That I violate the rule of a practice does not mean I have acted badly unless we have a moral reason for adhering to the rule. This was the objection of moral philosophers who claim that the wrong of breaking a promise is an instance of a more general wrong that is explained by appealing not to the fact that a practice-rule was violated but to some moral principle, such as a principle of reliance or fidelity or the principle of utility. The case for deferring to existing contract law to decide which promises should be legally enforced is similarly weak. That a judge one day decides to enforce a man's promise to marry a woman doesn't mean that is what the law should be. Moreover, in contract law authoritative sources for what the law is disagree: some judges, for example, do enforce promises to marry, others do not.[5]

No theorist of contract law suggests that in deciding which promises the state should enforce we should simply defer to whatever the law of contract happens to be. Most of the legal theorists we shall consider turn to some reason or principle to determine this, just as many of the moral philosophers discussed in chapter three, in determining what morality requires of promisors, did not simply defer to the practice of promising, but invoked some principle. Just as in chapter three I argued that we need to refer to moral principles, but that the application of these principles is constrained by social practices and customs, in this chapter I shall argue that in determining what the law should require of promisors we should want to use sound principles that may be critical of existing law, *but our use of such principles is constrained by social practices and customs.*

---

[5] Breach-of-promise-to-marry actions succeeded in *Wildley v. Springs*, 840 F Supp 1259 (1994); *Langley v. Schumacker*, 46 Cal 2d 601, 297 P 2d 977 (1956); *Piccininni v. Hajus*, 429 A 2d 886 (1980); *Bryan v. Lincoln*, 285 SE 2d 152 (1981); *In re Marriage of Buckley*, 133 Cal App 3d 927 (1982). Many states have enacted legislation prohibiting such actions. A recent case in which the action failed is *Askew v. Askew*, Cal App LEXIS 225 (1994). See also *Bradley v. Somers*, 322 SE 2d 665 (1984). For discussion of breach-of-promise-to-marry actions, see Lauren Kim, "Reexamining Judicial Interpretation of Heartbalm Statutes and Actions" (undergraduate honors thesis, Stanford University Department of Political Science, May 1995).

In considering the problem of which promises the state should legally enforce, let us begin with the following examples:

1. *Mills v. Wyman:* Mills gave shelter and comfort to Levy Wyman until Levy died. After hearing of this, Levy's father, induced by a transient feeling of gratitude, promised in writing to pay Mills for the expenses he incurred but later decides not to pay.[6]

2. *McDevitt v. Stokes:* Stokes, a horse breeder who stood to gain over $25,000 if a certain horse won a race, promised McDevitt, the jockey of that horse, $1,000 for winning the race. The jockey was already legally bound to try and win the race by virtue of an employment contract with the horse's owner. McDevitt wins the race, but Stokes refuses to pay the $1,000.[7]

3. *Balfour v. Balfour:* Mr. Balfour verbally promises his wife that he will give her 30 pounds a month while they are apart, he in India, she at home receiving medical care.[8]

4. *Garcia v. von Micsky:* Garcia, not wanting to become pregnant ever again, received a tubal ligation from Dr. von Micsky. Prior to the operation she signed an agreement acknowledging the possibility that she may not be completely or permanently sterile after the operation. Five months after the operation, von Micsky allegedly said to Garcia "that she had nothing to worry about, that it was impossible for her, you know, to have any more children and to try to relax and to take it easy." Garcia became pregnant shortly after.[9]

5. *Stephen K. v. Roni L.:* Roni L. had promised Stephen K. that she was taking birth control pills. He relied on this promise in having sexual intercourse with her. The promise turned out to be false, and Roni L. gave birth to Stephen K.'s child.[10]

In each of these cases, with the possible exception of *Garcia,* a promise was made.[11] In each case the promisor or promisor's administrator failed to carry through on the promise. While some and perhaps all of these promises gave rise to moral obligations, none were legally enforced.

Consider now five other promises:

6. *Webb v. McGowin:* Webb risked his life to prevent a seventy-five-pound block from falling on his boss McGowin, and was badly crippled for life as a result. Almost a month later, McGowin verbally promised to maintain Webb for the rest of Webb's life at $15 every two weeks. McGowin died and his administrators ceased payments.[12]

7. *Ricketts v. Scothorn:* Ricketts promised his granddaughter Scothorn $2,000

[6] 3 Pick. 207 (Supr Jud Ct of Mass, 1825).

[7] 192 SW 681 (1917).

[8] 2 KB 571 (1919).

[9] 602 F 2d 51 (1979), at 52.

[10] 164 Cal Rptr 618 (1980).

[11] Arguably there was no promise in *Garcia.* As the dissenting judge acknowledged, there was no manifest intention to act or refrain from acting. But Dr. von Micsky did provide assurance "of a condition or fact upon which the doctor could fully have expected his Patient to act."

[12] 27 Ala App 821, 168 So 196 (1936).

with the hope that this would encourage her to quit her job. The promise was not conditioned on her actually quitting. She quit in reliance on the promise. Ricketts died and his administrators refused to fulfill the promise.[13]

8. *Feinberg v. Pfeiffer Company*: The president of Pfeiffer, in recognition of long and faithful service, promised Feinberg $200 per month for life upon retirement, adding that she was welcome to continue working as long as she would like. Feinberg continued to work for about a year and a half and then retired. Some payments were made, but after the president died and a new accounting firm questioned the payments, they ceased.[14]

9. *Marvin v. Marvin*: Lee Marvin makes an oral promise with his nonmarital partner Michelle Marvin to share equally all property accumulated while they lived together, in return for Michelle's services "as a companion, homemaker, housekeeper and cook." When they decide to split up, Lee Marvin denies having any obligation.[15]

10. *Sullivan v. O'Connor*: Sullivan, a professional entertainer, sought plastic surgery on her nose from Dr. O'Connor. The doctor had promised to improve her appearance. In fact he made her nose worse, and she sues for damages upon a broken promise.[16]

In each of these cases a promise was made, some and perhaps all of which gave rise to a moral obligation, and the promise was broken, either by the promisor, or if he died, by his administrator. But unlike the first five promises, the latter five promises all *were* legally enforced by the courts.

It may be that we can distinguish the first five promises from the latter five and explain why only the latter should give rise to legal obligations. Or it may be that it is inconsistent for the law to enforce McGowin's promise but not Wyman's, Ricketts' promise but not Balfour's, Dr. O'Connor's promise but not Dr. von Micsky's, or Lee Marvin's promise but not Roni L.'s, and that some of the decisions are simply bad decisions. In either case we need some basis for deciding which promises are contracts giving rise to legal obligations.

One reason some promises are not legally enforced is that they are regarded as private matters with which it is inappropriate for the state, through the courts, to get involved. In *Stephen K. v. Roni L.* (example 5), the California Court of Appeals refused to enforce Roni L.'s promise when Stephen K. filed suit for wrongful birth. The court held that "as a matter of public policy the practice of birth control, if any, engaged in by two partners in a consensual sexual relationship is best left to the individuals involved, free from any governmental interference."[17]

There are other reasons commonly given by judges and legal commentators for

[13] 57 Neb 51, 77 NW 365 (1898).

[14] 322 SW 2d 163 (1959).

[15] 557 P 2d 106 (1976).

[16] 296 NE 2d 183 (1973).

[17] 164 Cal Rptr at 621. See also Hugh Collins, Review of Atiyah's *Promises, Morals, and Law*, in *Modern Law Review* 45 (March 1982): 230: law courts consider, besides the morality of a promisor's behavior, whether "there is a reason for the state to interfere." Collins argues that courts don't enforce unilateral gratuitous promises, not because they think one ought not to keep these promises, but because "it is no business of the state to force people to."

why not all promises should be legally enforced. In a contract the parties express an intention to be legally bound; many promisors express no such intention; the argument is that courts should enforce only those promises in which the promisor intended, as part of the promise, for the promisee to be able to seek a legal remedy for breach.[18]

Another reason courts don't enforce all promises is that some promises are made casually, without precision, and with no paper trail, so that it would be virtually impossible for a judge to decide what the promise actually was, assuming it even existed at all. This is one reason many judges only enforce promises that conform with legal rules, although which rules they must comply with is a matter of dispute. Most contracts constitute a bargained exchange and courts have held that they must comply with common law or statutory rules that there be a proper offer, acceptance, and consideration. Consideration refers to a mutuality of obligation. According to the requirement that there be consideration, a promise is legally enforceable only if it is bargained for, that is, only if the promisor gets something in return for the promise. *Mills v. Wyman* (example 1) is a classic example of a promise not enforced for lack of consideration. The court held that "if there was nothing paid or promised for it, the law, perhaps wisely, leaves the execution of it to the conscience of him who makes it."[19] (It was crucial that Mills incurred the expenses *prior to* the making of the promise, and not in reliance on it.) Another formal rule is that most contracts must be written.[20] Promises not complying with these rules may not be regarded as contracts, and may give rise to no legal obligation, although, as I have indicated, the importance of certain requirements are disputed; for example, consideration is not always necessary for a promise to be legally enforced.[21]

Courts, however, do enforce some promises that are not, strictly speaking, contracts. According to the doctrine of promissory estoppel, promises that do not conform with the formal requirements of contracts but that reasonably induce detrimental reliance, may be legally enforced.[22] In *Ricketts v. Scothorn* (example 7)

---

[18] Randy E. Barnett, "A Consent Theory of Contract," *Columbia Law Review* 86 (1986): 304–5.

[19] 3 Pick 207.

[20] Which contracts must be written is established by the statute of frauds, which has its roots in the English statute of 1677. For discussion see, for example, E. Allan Farnsworth, *Contracts*, 2d ed. (Boston: Little, Brown, 1990), chap. 6.

[21] In *Webb v. McGowin* (ex. 6), the judge found consideration in the promise: "Where the promisee cares for, improves, and preserves the property of the promisor, though done without his request, it is sufficient consideration for the promisor's subsequent agreement to pay for the service, because of the material benefits received"(168 So at 197). But consideration was found only by stretching that concept beyond recognition. The point of the doctrine of consideration is to enforce only bargained-for promises. A promise made subsequent to the benefit received by the promisee could not have been bargained for. This case illustrates Andrew Kull's point that judges often extend the concept of consideration as a pretext for enforcing unrelied-on gratuitous promises. See Andrew Kull, "Reconsidering Gratuitous Promises," *Journal of Legal Studies* 21 (January 1992): 40–44.

[22] *Restatement (Second) of Contracts*, sec. 90 (1): "A promise which the promisor should reasonably expect to induce action or forbearance on the part of the promisee or a third person and which does induce such action or forbearance is binding if injustice can be avoided only by enforcement of the promise."

there was no consideration for Ricketts' promise to his granddaughter, since he didn't make the promise conditional on his granddaughter actually quitting. The granddaughter did quit, though, in reliance on the promise, and the court enforced the promise using the remedy of promissory estoppel. The court declared that "it would be grossly inequitable" not to enforce the promise even though it was not bargained for.[23]

In determining which promises should be regarded as contracts giving rise to legal obligations, it is not enough to turn to existing law, for it is conflicting; what the law is depends on which decisions we read or how we interpret the decisions.[24] One judge may enforce only promises with adequate consideration, while another will enforce a wholly gratuitous promise. One judge may say she enforces a promise because she finds consideration in it, while another judge will enforce the same promise, having found that it lacked consideration, but not thinking consideration is a requirement for a legal obligation to keep a promise. *Should only bargained-for promises give rise to legal obligations? Should all promises promisees rely on to their detriment be legally enforced?*

There is another sort of issue arising in contract law that we shall consider as well, regarding which existing law is also unsettled. The issue concerns not whether it is the proper role of the state to bring to bear the sanction of law on those who break promises giving rise to moral obligations but whether promises the state would otherwise enforce should not be enforced on moral grounds, either because they were made under duress or for other reasons are unconscionable, or because they were not made in good faith. Bargained-for promises are a form of advantage-taking and we need to decide which forms of advantage-taking are legitimate and which are not.[25] Some promises are extracted from the promisor by taking advantage of one's mental incapacity, or through deception, threat, economic coercion, or failure to disclose information.[26] We might think such promises give rise to no obligation, either moral or legal.

Moral philosophers are divided about whether there is a moral obligation to fulfill coerced promises.[27] I take the most reasonable position to be that whether

---

[23] 77 NW 365, at 367.

[24] Case law has been characterized as "schizophrenic" by Jay Feinman, "Critical Approaches to Contract Law," 30 *UCLA Law Review* (1983): 830, 833; cf. pp. 834, 839, 847, 849, 853, 856; cf. Grant Gilmore, *The Death of Contract* (Columbus: Ohio State University Press, 1974), 59–60. P. S. Atiyah writes that "there is no hope of reducing the whole body of contract, or even its main outlines, to a single principle." P. S. Atiyah, Review of Charles Fried, *Contract as Promise*, 95 *Harvard Law Review* 509 (1981): 528.

[25] Cf. Anthony Kronman, "Contract Law and Distributive Justice," *Yale Law Journal* 89 (1980): 480.

[26] Ibid., 478–79.

[27] See the discussion of Hobbes's account in Carole Pateman, *The Problem of Political Obligation* (Berkeley: University of California Press, 1985), 44, 52, 53, and the discussion of David Hume's and Adam Smith's accounts in R. S. Downie, "Three Accounts of Promising," *Philosophical Quarterly* 35, no. 140 (July 1985): 261–62. Hugo Grotius concedes that "there is great diversity of opinion" on this topic, in *The Rights of War and Peace*, trans. A. C. Campbell (Washington, D.C.: M. Walter Dunne, 1901), chap. 11, sec. 7, p. 137. Henry Sidgwick, in *The Methods of Ethics*, 7th ed. (Indianapolis: Hackett, 1981), says the question of whether coerced promises bind is uncertain: in some cases they

the promisor has this obligation depends on the extent of coercion used to extract the promise. Many promises are made under some pressure. But there is a difference between being pressured by obligations of friendship or reciprocity to promise to take a friend to the airport, being pressured by a desire to complete a coin collection into promising to pay an exorbitant price for a particular coin, being pressured by economic necessity to promise to do work at a wage lower than the going market rate, and being pressured by fear of death into promising to pay a ransom. We need to determine when the pressure used in extracting a promise is legitimate and when it is unduly coercive. Consider the following promises or agreements:

11. *Alaska Packers' Association v. Domenico:* Sailors had a contract with Alaska Packers' Association, some to work for $50 plus 2 cents per fish caught for the season, others to work for $60 plus 2 cents per fish. While in Alaska, they stopped work and demanded payment of $100 instead of the $50 or $60 originally agreed to. Since replacements were unavailable, the company promised to pay the $100, although the company superintendent noted that he lacked authority to make the promise.[28]

12. *Henningsen v. Bloomfield Motors, Inc.:* Mr. Henningsen purchased a new car from Bloomfield Motors, having signed a contract with a clause in small font and technical language, reading, "it is expressly agreed that there are no warranties, express or implied," except that the "manufacturer . . . warrants each new motor vehicle . . . to be free from defects in material or workmanship" for ninety days, and that this warrant is "limited to making good at its factory any part" determined by the manufacturer (Chrysler) to be defective if shipped to them. Shortly after purchase Mrs. Henningsen was injured in an auto accident that appeared to be caused by a faulty steering wheel mechanism, and the Henningsens sued for damages caused from negligence, apparently in breach of their agreement to the limited warranty excluding such claims.[29]

13. *O'Callaghan v. Waller and Beckwith Realty Company:* O'Callaghan signed an exculpatory clause in her lease with her landlord that released the landlord and his agents from any liability for personal injuries to O'Callaghan caused by any act or neglect of the landlord or his agents. After this, O'Callaghan injured herself in a fall while crossing the paved courtyard of her apartment building and sued for injuries caused by defective pavement.[30]

14. *Schwartzreich v. Bauman-Basch, Inc.:* Schwartzreich had a contract to work for Bauman-Basch for $90 a week. Before beginning his tenure, Schwartzreich got a better offer from another firm, and through an agreement the details of which

---

don't bind the promisor, but other cases are less clearcut. He notes that in contract law some coerced promises are enforced, but he adds, "Still, this does not settle the moral question" (306).

[28] 117 F 99 (1902). Cf. *Post v. Jones*, 60 US 150 at 159–160 (1856): the master of a sinking ship agrees to sell cargo at auction to two nearby ships; the court voided the agreement as it wasn't genuine but coerced, and as such was an "unreasonable bargain."

[29] 32 NJ 358; 161 A 2d 69 (1960).

[30] 15 Ill 2d 436; 155 NE 2d 545 (1959).

are disputed, Bauman-Basch, which claimed it would not be able to get a comparable replacement, promised to pay him $100 a week.[31]

In each of these four cases, a promise was made but the promisor claims to be under no obligation because the promise was extracted under duress. The contracts Henningsen and O'Callaghan signed were form contracts the clauses of which are not negotiable: if one wants a car or an apartment, one has no choice but to agree to the terms of the contract—thus the argument that the promises were made under duress. In *Alaska Packers Association* and *Henningsen,* the promises were not enforced, but in *O'Callaghan* and *Schwartzreich* they were. It may be that we can distinguish the former promises from the latter and explain why only the latter should be enforced. Or it may be that it is inconsistent for the law to enforce O'Callaghan's and Bauman-Bausch's promises but not the sailors' or Henningsen's and that some of these decisions are simply bad decisions. In either case we need some basis for deciding *which promises were made under such duress as to make their enforcement unconscionable.*[32]

Some promises are made because the promisor has mistaken beliefs and what looks to be a good bargain turns out to be improvident.[33] Sometimes the promisor has mistaken information through the promisee's deception or failure to disclose accurate information, and we might think such promises should not be enforced. Consider the following two examples:

15. *Swinton v. Whitinsville Savings Bank:* Swinton purchased a house from the defendant, who knew the house was infested with termites and who concealed this fact from Swinton. Swinton discovered the termites nearly two years later and sued for damages.[34]

16. *Obde v. Schlemeyer:* Obde purchased a house from the Schlemeyers, who

---

[31] 131 NE 887 (1921). Cf. *Watkins and Son, Inc. v. Carrig,* 21 A 2d 591 (1941): Watkins and Son agreed to excavate a cellar for Carrig for a stated price. Solid rock was encountered, and Carrig orally promised to pay a new price that was about nine times greater than the price stipulated by the written contract. The new oral promise was enforced by the court.

[32] Sometimes the court will infer coercion if an agreement is grossly inequitable; see *Jones v. Star Credit Corp.,* 298 NYS 2d 264 (1969). There, Jones agreed to purchase a freezer unit with retail value of about $300 under credit terms such that the purchase price totaled $1,234.80. The court refused to enforce the agreement: "The value disparity itself leads inevitably to the felt conclusion that knowing advantage was taken of the plaintiffs" (at 267). The Court refers to a "gross inequality of bargaining power" in this case, as well as in a similar and well-known case, *Williams v. Walker-Thomas Furniture Co.,* 350 F 2d 445 (1965).

[33] In addition to the cases discussed below, see *Wood v. Boynton,* 25 NW 42 (1885): Wood agrees to sell a stone for $1 to Boynton. It turns out that what both Wood and Boynton thought was a valueless but curious stone was an uncut diamond worth between $700 and $1,000. Wood sues to get her stone back, but the agreement was enforced. In *Beachcomber Coins, Inc. v. Boskett,* 166 NJ Super 442; 400 A. 2d 78 (1979), a retail coin dealer agrees to purchase a dime from Boskett for $500, which Boskett had acquired earlier for $450. Both parties are "certain" the coin was Denver-minted, but in fact it was counterfeited, and when the dealer finds out he seeks to rescind the sale and succeeds. Both these cases involve sales and not promises, although they are usually treated as "contracts" cases.

[34] 42 NE 2d 808 (1942).

knew there may be a termite problem and failed to disclose this fact. Upon discovery of termites, Obde sued for damages.[35]

In each of these cases a promise was extracted that most likely would not have been had the promisee disclosed crucial information. *When does a promisee's failure to disclose information invalidate the promise?* Again a line must be drawn between legitimate and illegitimate forms of advantage-taking, a line courts have drawn differently. Swinton lost, Obde won. Assuming the facts of these cases are not essentially distinguishable, how do we decide which decision expresses what the law should be?

PRINCIPLES

In chapter three we saw that some philosophers determine what morality requires of promisors by turning to the practice of promising. Rawls, Searle, and Pitkin all seem to imply that a promisor reflecting on whether he or she must keep a promise need only turn for an answer to the rule of the practice that promises must be kept. Most of us would agree that not *all* promises must be kept, though. As Rawls acknowledges, when the consequences of keeping a promise are extremely severe, it need not be kept; and promises extracted under gunpoint or under false pretenses do not obviously give rise to a moral obligation. But if we want to know precisely what exceptions to the rule that promises must be kept the practice allows, it isn't clear where we turn. Atiyah suggests we turn to the law of contract. But apart from the fact that the law does not necessarily articulate the demands of morality, we have seen that the law of contract is divided about what is required of promisors. We need, then, to turn to standards beyond what the law simply is.

In determining what the law requires of promisors, legal theorists have developed various principles. It is natural to want to know not simply what the law is but what it should be, especially when courts have issued conflicting decisions, and this has motivated theorists to find principles that could prescribe correct or optimal resolutions to contractual disputes. In some cases these principles offer conflicting prescriptions. In chapter three we saw that there were different principles to explain the wrong of promise-breaking. Just as my purpose there was not to show that one of the principles was right and the others wrong but that all of these principles were constrained by social practice, so too the purpose of this chapter is not to argue that one principle of contract law is superior to the others, but to show how application of any of these principles is constrained by social practice. This chapter is another case study intended to show both the necessity

---

[35] 56 Wash 2d 449; 353 P 2d 672 (1960). Cf. *Weintraub v. Krobatsch*, 317 A 2d 68 (1974): seller failed to disclose that house purchased was infested with roaches. Cf. *Holcomb v. Zinke*, 365 NW 2d 507 (1985): seller of home fails to disclose problems with the sewer system and appliances. Cf. *Simmons v. Evans*, 206 SW 2d 295 (1947): seller of home fails to reveal to buyer that the local water company supplies water only during the daytime. In each of these cases, the court held the seller liable for mere nondisclosure.

for rational principles in determining what ethics and the law require, and the limitation of abstract principles; it emphasizes how the theorist—in this case the legal theorist—in stepping back from in order to criticize conventions and norms, cannot entirely abstract from them.

As a way of introducing some of the leading principles of contract law that might be used to resolve the problems laid out in section one, consider one final example:

17. *Britton v. Turner*: Britton signs a contract to work for Turner for one year in return for $120. He quits without reason after nine months and demands payment for his nine months of work. Turner refuses to pay Britton anything, since the contract to which he agreed stipulates that payment is for a year's work. Britton sues.[36]

Should Britton recover anything for the time he worked?

The Will Theory

In one view—a particular interpretation of what is called the "will theory"— Britton should not recover. Turner's obligation, in this view, is limited to the promissory obligation expressed in the signed contract, and as its terms were not met, Turner has no obligation to pay. On the will theory, a contract is an expression of a will to be bound to an agreement or promise.[37] Turner promised to pay Britton only for a full year's work; if in the contract he promised nothing but that, then he has no contractual obligation to pay Britton for anything short of a year's work.

We shall see that on other theories Britton should recover, at least so long as the benefit Turner received from the nine months' work outweighed any harm Britton's early departure caused Turner to suffer in reliance upon Britton's promise to work a full year. The court that decided this case held, in favor of Britton, that if "a party actually receives labor, or materials, and thereby derives a benefit and advantage . . . the law thereupon raises a promise to pay to the extent of the reasonable worth of such excess."[38] The law, the court said, creates an implicit promise, and a legal obligation, based on "the general understanding of the community" that receipt of benefits in such cases demands compensation even though this obligation was not agreed to by the parties of the contract. This reasoning seems to fly in the face of a will theory grounding contractual obligations in promises explicitly made by the parties.[39]

[36] 6 NH 481 (1834).

[37] Cf. Grotius, *De Jure Belli ac Pacis*, bk 2, chap. 11: contractual obligations arise from an agreement which is itself binding by "a rule of natural law that promises and agreements are binding obligations"; cited in P. S. Atiyah, *Promises, Morals, and Law* (Oxford: Oxford University Press), 10.

[38] 6 NH 481, at 492. In fact Turner was able to find a replacement for Britton, so there was no significant detrimental reliance in this case.

[39] 6 NH at 493. This decision can be seen as an example of a trend that Grant Gilmore labeled the "death of contracts," by which he means the fall of the will theory and the rise of nonpromissory bases

The will theory of Anglo-American contract law came to dominance in the nineteenth century, as evidenced by William Story's declaration that "every contract is founded upon the mutual agreement of the parties."[40] Morton Horwitz argues that the will theory developed with the rise of widespread markets in government securities and commodities around 1815.[41] Prior to this the law reflected a "medieval tradition of substantive justice." Goods or services had an "objective value," as determined by the "community's sense of fairness" and reflected in customary prices. "The prices of most goods and services were conceived of as settled." But with the rise of markets, value came to be seen as subjective, something determined by the convergence of wills. On the new theory, obligations arose from agreements, not from standards of justice external to the wills of the parties. Even freely entered contracts that appear unjust to an onlooker are binding, on this view, for, as Horwitz notes, "where things have no 'intrinsic value,' there can be no substantive measure of exploitation."[42]

The will theory was not then, nor is it now, entirely subjectivist. Few if any versions hold that obligations are created by purely internal acts of will. "An external manifestation of the intentions [of the parties] is always needed," so that an obligation based on a convergence of wills could not be avoided by some secret reservation by one of the speakers.[43] In *Lucy v. Zehmer*, Lucy sought to enforce a written contract for the sale of Zehmer's farm. Zehmer claimed he signed the note in jest, while drunk, although there was evidence that he was not that drunk. The court enforced the contract: "We must look to the outward expression of a person as manifesting his intention rather than to his secret and unexpressed intention." "The law imputes to a person an intention corresponding to the reasonable meaning of his words and acts."[44]

An "objective will theory" appeals not to intentions, but to what was said. It appeals to a bargain reflecting convergent wills of the contracting parties, but to the bargain objectively understood. Objectively to understand a bargain may require not just going beyond intentions to words, but even looking "beyond the

---

of obligation. In *Death of Contracts*, Gilmore argues that "with the growth of the ideas of quasi-contract and unjust enrichment [principles of restitution that support Britton's claim against Turner], classical consideration theory was breached on the benefit side. With the growth of the promissory estoppel idea, it was breached on the detriment side"(87–88). But, as we shall see below, the decision in *Britton* can be reconciled with some interpretations of the will theory.

[40] William Story, *Treatise on the Law of Contracts* (1844), cited in Morton Horwitz, *The Transformation of American Law, 1780–1860* (Cambridge: Harvard University Press, 1977): 185.

[41] P. S. Atiyah traces the will theory further back, at least to the writings of the "natural lawyers" of the sixteenth and seventeenth centuries, including Grotius and Pufendorf, who held a bare promise morally binding on its face. See Atiyah, *Promises, Morals, and Law*, 10.

[42] Horwitz, *Transformation of American Law*, 160–61, 166–73.

[43] Atiyah, *Promises, Morals, and Law*, 15; cf. Gilmore, *Death of Contract*, 42–43.

[44] 196 Va 493; 84 SE 2d 516 (1954). See also Learned Hand's decision in *Eustis Mining Co. v. Beer, Sondheimer and Co.*, 239 F 976 (SD NY 1917): "It makes not the least difference whether a promisor actually intends that meaning which the law will impose upon his words. The whole House of Bishops might satisfy us that he had intended something else, and it would make not a particle of difference in his obligation. That obligation the law attaches to his act of using certain words, provided, of course, the actor be under no disability."

words and acts which constitute the transaction to the nature of the relationship between the parties and the circumstances surrounding their actions."[45] In *Garcia v. von Micsky* (example 4), the court held that when Dr. von Micsky told Garcia she would not get pregnant following her tubal ligation, he was not making an enforceable promise, but merely offering "therapeutic reassurance": "To hold as appellants urge in this case would be to elevate the deceased doctor's therapeutic reassurance of his patient to the status of a guaranty, made without contract or compensation and at the risk of absolute liability. This does not make good sense, either medically or legally."[46] Farber and Matheson note that the court, in reaching this conclusion, appealed to a common understanding that physicians do not give warranties.[47] The will theory explains the absence of an obligation because Dr. von Micsky's words, the argument is, could not reasonably be taken as a promise or as the undertaking of an obligation. Farber and Matheson imply that it is unreasonable simply given this common understanding. Absent evidence that the doctor intended to undertake a legal obligation with his words, then we use the common understanding to infer the doctor's intentions.[48] In other words, even if we choose to adopt the will theory as our basis for a principle with which we could decide which promises legally to enforce, in applying the principle that courts shall enforce voluntarily undertaken obligations, we would have to appeal to the customs and practice from which we derive our common understandings of precisely what was voluntarily undertaken by the promisor.[49] There are at least two ways, then, in which the principle that contract disputes should be resolved by enforcing the wills of the parties involved is practice-dependent: first, the very adoption of the will theory captures intuitions that arguably arise only among a people sharing a certain understanding of value associated with the rise of markets; second, application of the principle may require that we appeal to an objectively reasonable definition of what the parties agreed to, and this is done by appealing to common understandings.

The decision of the *Garcia* court does not simply defer to common understandings, but implies that there are good reasons, apart from the fact that a common understanding exists, to construe the doctor's words not as a guarantee or en-

---

[45] Daniel A. Farber and John Matheson, "Beyond Promissory Estoppel: Contract Law and the 'Invisible Handshake,'" 52 *University of Chicago Law Review* (1985): 915 n. 45.

[46] 602 F 2d 51, 53.

[47] Farber and Matheson, "Beyond Promissory Estoppel," 915–16.

[48] The doctor had died before the case went to court, so there was no way of knowing what his actual intentions were.

[49] Sometimes the reasonable meaning of one's words will be ambiguous, and in such cases the objective will theory will be indeterminate. Thus *In re Soper's Estate* (*Cochran v. Whitby*), 196 Minn 60; 264 NW 427 (1935): Soper is married to two women. He commits suicide, and his insurance policy is to be paid to "the wife." See also *Raffles v. Wichelhaus*, 2 H and C 906; 159 Eng Rep 375 (1864): A contract was made to purchase cotton from the ship "Peerless" from Bombay; the defendant meant the Peerless sailing in October, the plaintiff, the Peerless sailing in December; the court held there was no contract. See also *Williams v. Curtin*, 807 F 2d 1046 (1986): a contract is made concerning "slaw cabbage": in Georgia that means large cabbage; in the interstate cole slaw trade it means all cabbage suitable for making cole slaw; the court used interstate trade usage.

forceable promise but merely as therapy; the court says taking the doctor's therapeutic reassurance as an enforceable guaranty would "not make good sense, either medically or legally."[50] To say that application of a will theory is constrained by social practice is not to say that the resulting judgment is ungrounded. There should be good reasons for the customs and practices that are the basis for the understandings it is reasonable to impute to a person's words or actions. Perhaps we think that patients should realize that if doctors made guarantees they would be subject to damaging lawsuits that would destroy the patient-doctor relationship. But once a common understanding is established and accepted, it shapes expectations upon which people reasonably rely, and it is simply the common understanding of the doctor's words, not the justification for society imputing that understanding to those words, that we defer to in deciding whether it was reasonable for the patient to construe the words as a promise. The patient should have just known that no one would take the doctor's words as a guarantee, because doctors just don't make guarantees.[51] Even if a common understanding existed for which there was no particularly good reason, the fact that it is the prevailing understanding members of the society have may make it reasonable *at that time.*

In another case, a landlord and lessee agreed to a written lease that allowed extension upon written notice. The landlord had apparently twice extended the lease upon oral notice. The landlord died and the trustee terminated the lease for lack of a written extension. The court held that an implied promise existed allowing oral notice.[52] Even if there were no good reasons for the landlord to have extended the lease without written notice, the fact that he did meant an expectation was created in the tenant, and it was reasonable for the tenant to have assumed there was an agreement that the lease could be extended orally. Both this case and *Garcia* are consistent with an objective will theory that finds obligations only in bargained-for promises but which appeals to common understandings or practice to determine whether there was a promise, and if there was a promise, what it meant.

That background understandings can impart to words a meaning beyond what the speaker may have intended accounts for how a will theory could support the court's decision in *Britton v. Turner* (example 17). The decision to force Turner to pay Britton for what work he did perform appears contrary to the will theory precisely because in refusing to pay Turner is not breaking his promise, or showing himself to be untrustworthy. The court "raised" a promise, and in doing so we

[50] 602 F 2d 53.

[51] If the doctor did say "I guarantee there is no chance of your getting pregnant" and said this with the intention of encouraging Garcia to have the operation, I think we should say that this *was* a promise and that the doctor is culpable for lying (since he should know what he says isn't true). But there is no evidence the doctor said this; moreover, Garcia should have known pregnancy was still a possibility after the surgery, as she signed a written authorization for the proposed surgery that stated "it is possible that I may not be completely or permanently sterile after the operation" (602 F 2d at 52).

[52] *Wachovia Bank and Trust Co., N.A., v. Rubish,* 293 SE 2d 749 (1982); discussed in Farber and Matheson, "Beyond Promissory Estoppel," 917.

might think it really based Turner's obligation to compensate Britton for the work done not on promissory but on restitution grounds. Restitution is a legal response to unjust enrichment: if you receive benefits from me even though you never promised to pay me for them, a court may, under certain conditions, make you compensate me to avoid your unjust enrichment. But it is possible to reconcile the decision with the will theory by saying the reasonable meaning of Turner's promise to pay is that while Britton was expected to work one year, he would still be paid in proportion to the work he actually performed. Only had Turner explicitly said he would not pay Britton even a penny for anything short of a year's work should Britton recover nothing, according to this interpretation of the objective will theory.

The objective will theory makes reference to social norms and understandings in deciding how bargains should be understood.[53] But it still derives contractual obligations from the consent of the parties. It might seem incoherent to turn to social norms or objective understandings while claiming to derive obligations from individual wills. P. S. Atiyah suggests the objective will theory is a paradox: "The theory that promises arise from acts of the will is based on the idea that a person is bound to do something because he has willed that obligation upon himself by an internal mental act, an act of will. It is not easy to marry this idea with a further need for communication."[54] But a contract reflects a *common* will. An agreement must be expressed through formal gestures or signs, by a specific declaration in language.[55] The declaration must be understood by both parties if a common will is to be formed.[56] In cases where one of the parties was misunderstood due to reasonable ambiguity in his words, we should say no common will was formed. But sometimes it is unreasonable to disavow an intention having uttered certain words. Expressing a declaration creates an obligation to be bound to the reasonable meaning of one's offer, if it is accepted.

The objective will theory provides a principle to determine which contracts should be legally enforced—agreements embodying a mutual will should be enforced in a way that complies with the parties' wills objectively understood. Use of the principle signals a rationalist approach to contract law that does not blindly defer to whatever existing contract law is to decide cases; rather, appeal is made to a principle, a principle immanent in the law but which can be used to criticize particular opinions. We might ask *why* courts should adhere to the will theory and enforce the wills of the parties. Charles Fried, a leading advocate of the theory, provides an answer in his book *Contract as Promise*. Fried seeks an ac-

[53] Fried, *Contract as Promise*, 86: an agreement is interpreted "against the background of normal practices and understandings." Pufendorf also introduces the idea of social norms into his will theory; for discussion, see Cheryl Welch and Murray Milgate, "Implicit Contracts: Social Norms as Rational Choice" (paper presented at the 1993 Western Political Science Association Meeting, Pasadena, California, March 1993).

[54] Atiyah, *Promises, Morals, and Law*, 20. See also Barnett, "A Consent Theory of Contract," 272–73.

[55] This is a point made by Hegel; see his *Philosophy of Right*, ed. Allen Wood (Cambridge: University of Cambridge Press, 1991), par. 78.

[56] Cf. Ibid., par. 79 Remark.

count of the principles immanent in contract law so he can use these principles to determine how particular cases should be decided so as to comply with the purpose of contract law. For Fried, that purpose is to promote the values underlying the moral practice of promising.[57] In turning to Fried's account, I shall emphasize how, just as objective will theorists in applying their theory need to appeal to conventional understandings to determine if an agreement exists and what it is, so too Fried in applying his "promise principle" must appeal to conventions and shared understandings that are external to the promise principle.

Fried sees the wrong of breaching a contract as the wrong of breaking one's promise, which, on Fried's Kantian account of promising, is the wrong of failing to respect individual autonomy and of violating trust.[58] Fried isn't a consistent Kantian, though. He draws on Kant's account of autonomy, and at times expresses a Kantian anti-empiricism that rejects appeals to "what is done." Fried echoes Kant in writing that "the validity of a moral, like that of a mathematical truth, does not depend on fashion or favor."[59] But unlike Kant, Fried acknowledges the important role the existence of a convention of promising plays—his reliance on Kant, then, is selective. Unlike Kant's account of promising, or for that matter the accounts of Scanlon or MacCormick discussed in chapter three, in Fried's account the existence of a practice of promising is important in explaining the wrong of promise-breaking; but what makes it wrong to break a promise, in Fried's view, is not that in doing so one violates a practice-rule; it is, rather, that in doing so one abuses a shared institution intended to invoke bonds of trust and thereby uses another person.[60] Not to hold a person to his promise not only victimizes or uses the promisee, but fails to "take [the promisor himself] seriously as a person."[61] As I argued in chapter 2, when discussing Kant's theory of promising, some appeal to social practice or shared understandings is presupposed in holding that breaking a promise to someone counts as using him and is therefore morally wrong. As we shall see, Fried ends up appealing to conventions and norms also in determining whether the breaking of a particular promise is not only a moral but a legal wrong.

We can see the critical force, as well as the limitations, of the promise principle

[57] Fried gives one of the most extensive defenses of the promise principle, but there are others as well. See Friedrich Kessler's discussion in Kessler, Gilmore, and Kronman, *Contracts,* 3d ed. (1986), defending contractual obligations on the ground of individual autonomy, excerpted in Peter Linzer, ed. *A Contracts Anthology* (Cincinnati: Anderson, 1989), 4–12. See also the comments of Williston in the "Debate on Sec. 88 (later Sec. 90) of the Restatement of Contracts," *American Law Institute Proceedings* 4 (1926): appendix, 85–114, in Linzer, *Contracts Anthology,* 222–32.

[58] Fried, *Contract as Promise,* 16: "The obligation to keep a promise is grounded not in arguments of utility but in respect for individual autonomy and in trust." Cf. 57. Fried refers to this as a "Kantian principle of trust and respect" (17).

[59] Ibid., 2.

[60] Ibid. Cf. Fried, Review of Atiyah's *Rise and Fall of Freedom of Contract, Harvard Law Review* 93 (1980): 1863: "Promis[ing] is a social convention that will commit when invoked"; and 1864: "Reasonable reliance presupposes obligation, which can be supplied by the invocation of the convention of promising." Fried does not take up explicitly whether a promissory obligation could arise absent a social practice.

[61] Ibid., 21.

by considering how it would resolve the issues discussed in the previous section. The first issue concerned which promises should be legally enforced. Should the state enforce promises lacking consideration? Are there any promises that it is no business of the state to enforce?

Fried defends state enforcement of gratuitous or gift-promises even if they are economically "sterile."[62] So long as there was an intention to create a legal relation, and the promise was made freely, fairly, rationally, and deliberately, Fried argues it should be enforced by courts.[63] What does this imply for the promises made in examples 1 through 10? There is little reason to think any of these promises were coerced, and so according to the principle they should be enforced insofar as they manifested an intention to be legally bound. Dr. von Micsky probably did not intend to undertake a legal obligation, and the reasonable meaning of his words do not imply that in offering assurance he was providing a legally enforceable guarantee. Several of the other promises in these examples involved relatives, and when one makes a promise to a relative one might not intend for the promise to be enforceable by a court. Fried suggests as much when he notes that there are a class of promises, which he calls "social promises," that typically lack the requisite intention to be legally bound that the promise principle requires for state enforcement. An example of such a promise would be a promise to take a friend out to a movie; it is generally recognized that breaking such dates is not a cause for legal action. A harder case is a promise to marry—some breach-of-promise-to-marry actions have succeeded.[64] Fried argues that whether enforcing social promises does violence to the intention of the parties is a "task for interpretation."[65]

The promise principle, then, leaves to interpretation the task of resolving whether the promises made between relatives or those involved in intimate relations (examples 3, 5, 7, 9) should be enforced, or rather, regarded as social promises lacking the necessary intention to be legally bound. It also leaves to interpretation the alleged promises in examples 4 and 10 between doctor and patient—these promises should be enforced only if according to societal norms the statements made by the doctors in those cases would reasonably be understood to express an intention to be legally bound.

Fried's promise principle needs to make reference to social practices and shared understandings if it is to distinguish from all the promises giving rise to moral obligations, the breaking of which fails to respect the dignity and autonomy of the promisee and violates trust, those promises which give rise to legal obligations. As with objective will theories in general, the promise principle

---

[62] Ibid., 36–37. Cf. 29, 35, 38, 228 on the doctrine of consideration. Fried bases his conclusion on both utilitarian and Kantian grounds. He says that allowing people to promise a gift and secure an expectation promotes utility (37); but adds in a footnote that there is a moral obligation to keep such promises, as well (37 note).

[63] On the requirement that there be an intention to create a legal relation, see Fried, *Contract as Promise,* 38 and n.

[64] See note 5, above.

[65] *Contract as Promise,* 38 n.

requires criteria for determining whether there was the necessary intention to undertake a legal obligation, and societal understandings and norms are one important source for determining this.[66]

Fried uses his promise principle also to address the issue of which bargained-for promises should not be enforced because they involve illegitimate advantage-taking. Fried argues that the value of autonomy requires limits on the enforcement even of unambiguous contracts. Certain conditions must obtain if a contract is to be an expression of the wills of autonomous individuals and therefore worthy of state enforcement. If a contract is to respect the autonomy of the individual parties, it must be entered into freely and fairly, rationally and deliberately.[67] When I am coerced or deceived into agreeing to do something, holding me to my promise does not respect my autonomy. It is sometimes argued that according to the will theory, contract law should be governed by a caveat emptor rule of enforcing whatever the parties objectively agree to, and that the state should not question the propriety or fairness of agreements. This is what Grant Gilmore, one of the theory's leading critics, suggests in saying that in the will theory's view, "no man is his brother's keeper; the race is to the swift; let the devil take the hindmost."[68] But according to Fried's promise principle, we hold people to their promises as a way of respecting their freedom and rationality.[69] Holding

---

[66] There is a deep problem with the principle: Fried does not really explain why the state should use any of its scarce resources to impose on promisors a legal obligation; the principle does not explain why we need the added and expensive mechanism of state enforcement to transform moral into legal obligations. At least one commentator has suggested that a promise principle implies that *no* promises should be legally enforced, because "personal autonomy is limited, not promoted, by enforcing contracts. Every act of enforcement restricts the freedom of the party who disavows the earlier agreement" (Jay Feinman, "Critical Approaches to Contract Law," *UCLA Law Review* 30 [1983]: 841). Other commentators disagree, arguing that the state has a legitimate role in promoting the plans individuals are left free to make with each other and that a respect for individual autonomy implies the state should enforce at least some promises. See Andrew Kull, "Reconsidering Gratuitous Promises," *Journal of Legal Studies* 21 (January 1992): 61; and Melvin Eisenberg, "The Principles of Consideration," *Cornell Law Review* 67 (1982): 640, on how legal enforcement of promises facilitates reliance on promises.

There are reasons not to supplement moral and social sanctions with legal sanctions. For one, it is expensive to bring cases through the court system. In addition, bringing a case to court usually requires a public airing of the dispute, and there may be occasions where an agreement was made in private that one or both parties would not want to be made public. If casual remarks or agreements between those involved in intimate relationships could be construed as legally enforceable, this could stifle such remarks, upset those relationships (see Craswell and Schwartz, *Foundations of Contract Law,* 244). Fried's promise principle seems unable to justify the use of the legal sanction without appealing to standards external to the promise principle, be they considerations of economic efficiency, privacy, or social custom. This is to say not that the promise principle is useless in contract law, only that it needs to be supplemented.

[67] Fried, *Contract as Promise,* 38, and chaps. 6–7.

[68] Gilmore, *Death of Contract,* 95.

[69] Fried, *Contract as Promise,* 57; cf. 20: "Respect for others as free and rational requires taking seriously their capacity to determine their own values." The requirement of voluntariness appears in Scanlon's promissory principle, discussed in chapter 3. Principle F requires that the promisor "voluntarily and intentionally" creates expectations in the promisee. See p. 93, n. 146. The ensuing discussion of how what counts as "voluntary" depends on practices and norms suggests another way application of Scanlon's principle of fidelity requires appeal to social practice.

someone to a promise they were unduly coerced into making does not respect their freedom and therefore is *ruled out* by the principle.

But how do we distinguish when the pressure used in extracting a promise is legitimate, from when it is unduly coercive? Were the promises extracted from Henningsen (example 12), O'Callaghan (example 13), or the agents of Alaska Packers Association (example 11) or Bauman-Basch, Inc. (example 14) the result of such coercion that enforcement of these promises would fail to respect the promisor's freedom? To determine this Fried invokes the criterion that "a proposal is not coercive if it offers what the proponent has a right to offer or not as he chooses. It is coercive if it proposes a wrong to the object of the proposal."[70] I needn't be held to my promise to give an armed robber my money when that promise was extracted by threat, since the proposal inducing the promise ("your money or your life") proposes a wrong to me. But if someone who offers me the right to use a path on his land extracts a promise of money from me, I can be held to it since as the landowner he has a right to make this offer and proposes no wrong to me in doing so.[71] The issue, for Fried, turns on what rights people have. But *that* is decided independent of the promise principle. As Fried acknowledges, what rights we have is largely a matter of convention.[72]

In both *Alaska Packers' Association* (example 11) and *Schwartzreich* (example 14), a party already under a contractual obligation made a proposal that conflicted with its obligation. In each case the proposal might be construed as a threat to breach the existing obligation, a proposal the promisor would have no right to make, in which case Fried's promise principle would dictate that the new promise should not be enforced. But if the proposal was construed, not as a wrongful threat but as an invitation for a voluntary, mutual waiver of the original bargain, then the resulting new promise should be enforced. Fried does not discuss *Alaska Packers' Association* but there is some indication he would see the proposal made by the sailors in that case as a wrongful threat.[73] However he implies that the promise extracted from Bauman-Basch to pay Schwartzreich more than was already agreed to (example 14) was not unduly coercive and should be enforced.[74]

The court in *Alaska Packers' Association* characterizes the action by the sailors as a wrong, while the court in *Schwartzreich* maintains that no undue coercion was involved in encouraging the waiver of the prior contract.[75] But *why* should we regard the sailors' action as wrongfully coercive while viewing Schwartzreich's action as legitimate advantage-taking? Why should we think Schwartzreich has the right to threaten to rescind as a means to gain a release from his prior obliga-

[70] Fried, *Contract as Promise,* 97; cf. 98–99.

[71] Ibid., 95–96, 98.

[72] Ibid., 97; cf. 98–99; and 100: "Rules of property are very largely conventional."

[73] Fried discusses a case similar in some ways to *Alaska Packers Association—Post v. Jones—* arguing that the court properly refused to enforce the contract (see ibid., 109–111).

[74] Ibid., 35 and n. 26

[75] In *Alaska Packers Association,* the court held that to enforce the new contract "would be to offer a premium upon bad faith, and invite men to violate their most sacred contracts *that they may profit by their own wrong*" (117 F 99, 103; emphasis added).

tion, while the sailors have no such right? In both cases an employee under contractual obligation threatens to cease working or to work elsewhere; and in both cases the employer had little option but to accede to the threat.[76]

Some standard external to the promise principle must be at work to distinguish these judgments, although Fried does not make explicit what this standard might be.[77] In his discussion of Henningsen (example 12) and cases similar to O'Callaghan (example 13), he does make explicit his use of an external standard to justify enforcing the latter contract but not the former.[78] While acknowledging that there is a difference in bargaining position between the parties in both cases, he suggests it would be unfair to relieve O'Callaghan of his obligation to adhere to his promise, because this would force particular persons (landlords) to bear the burden of remedying unfair background conditions, and this should be society's burden instead.[79] But he would relieve Henningsen of his obligation because the other party of the contract is a monopoly or cartel, and to enforce bargains reached only because of the unequal bargaining power of a monopoly would be to promote economic inefficiencies associated with monopolies or cartels.[80] Fried is forced in applying his Kantian promise principle to appeal to some criterion external to the principle to explain why Chrysler's extraction of Henningsen's promise is illegitimate advantage-taking while Waller and Beckwith Realty Company's extraction of O'Callaghan's promise is not. Here he appeals, not to convention, but to another principle.

Fried resorts to sources external to the promise principle also in considering the requirement to bargain in good faith by disclosing information. Fried compares Obde v. Schlemeyer (example 16) with a hypothetical example in which an oil company, conducting an expensive geological survey, identifies a site with oil potential. It buys the land without revealing the information it acquired from its

[76] In Schwartzreich the employer claimed that he would not be able to get another comparable designer to replace Schwartzreich (231 NY 196, 199).

[77] According to one standard, we decide when compulsion becomes duress by looking to "the quantitative reasonableness of the terms"—divergence from market rates suggests duress. See Robert Hale, "Bargaining, Duress, and Economic Liberty," Columbia Law Review 43 (1943): 603, in Contracts Anthology, ed. Linzer, 348–49. Hale concedes, however, that there may be duress even when an agreement is at normal market rates.

[78] On Henningsen see Ibid., 107. Fried does not discuss exculpatory clauses such as that found in O'Callaghan, but he does discuss hard bargains with private individuals who are not cartels; see 103–4 and 106.

[79] Ibid., 106: "it is unfair (and in the end counterproductive) to force particular persons, who are making their private arrangements against the background of conditions they did not create, to bear the burden of remedying these conditions."

[80] Ibid., 107: "By refusing to enforce the no-warranty clause, we force automobile manufacturers to give up their monopoly profits to consumers, and the result will be greater economic efficiency." Other legal theorists reject the view that when a party to a contract has monopoly power the contract was necessarily the result of coercion. See Alan Schwartz, "A Reexamination of Nonsubstantive Unconscionability," Virginia Law Review 63 (1977): 1053; and Duncan Kennedy, "Distributive and Paternalist Motives in Contract and Tort Law, with Special Reference to Compulsory Terms and Unequal Bargaining Power," Maryland Law Review 41 (1982): 563—relevant passages from each article are excerpted in Foundations of Contract Law, ed. Craswell and Schwartz, 306–7, 310.

survey and pays the going price for farm land. The company acted through a broker so as not to reveal its identity. Is the seller bound to the terms of the agreement, despite his ignorance of the information the buyer had acquired?

Courts generally would enforce the latter contract but not the contract in *Obde v. Schlemeyer,* in both cases favoring the buyer.[81] We might expect the advocate of the will theory to enforce both contracts, on the grounds that individuals should be held responsible for their decisions. But will theorists reach for ways to void unjust contracts. Grotius argues that "natural justice" requires equality of terms and that "a seller is bound to discover to a purchaser any defects which are known to him . . . a rule not only established by civil laws, but strictly conformable to natural justice."[82] Grotius specifically criticizes fraudulent concealment, as when a seller conceals that his house is infected with the plague; however Grotius adds that to sell corn at a high price without revealing knowledge that ships laden with grain will soon arrive is *not* fraudulent concealment. He is not clear about the basis for this distinction, saying only: "That only is a fraudulent concealment which immediately affects the nature of the contract."[83]

Fried appeals not to natural or civil law but to the liberal value of autonomy to support a good-faith requirement.[84] But when he tries to give an account of when there is lack of good faith, he must appeal to convention: "Where the better informed party cannot compensate for the other's defects without depriving himself of an advantage *on which he is conventionally entitled to count,* his failure to disclose will not cause the equities to tilt against him."[85] Although he appeals to economic efficiency in explaining why the contract in *Henningsen* is not enforced, Fried refuses to appeal to efficiency to distinguish *Obde* from the oil company example. He notes that the principle of economic efficiency yields the right results, but he says it does so for the wrong reason: "The oil company wins not because we want to encourage future investments but because it would be unfair to defeat its past reasonable expectations."[86] These expectations are reasonable not because

[81] Craswell and Schwartz, *Foundations of Contract Law,* 78–82, and 148 n. 17, citing a Canadian case, *Leitch Gold Mines, Ltd. v. Texas Gulf Sulphur,* 1 Ont. Rep. 469, 492–3 (1969), and *Laidlaw v. Organ,* 2 Wheat. (4 US) 178 (1817) as analogous to the oil company hypothetical. Kronman ("Contract Law and Distributive Justice," 428 n. 28), notes that "in many jurisdictions, a seller is now required by law to disclose the presence of termites in a dwelling, despite the buyer's failure to make inquiries." In this case the obligation is statutory, not contractual.

[82] Hugo Grotius, *The Rights of War and Peace,* trans. A. C. Campbell (Washington, D.C.: M. Walter Dunne, 1901), 147 (chap. 12, secs. 8, 9, 10–11).

[83] Ibid., 148 (chap. 12, sec. 9).

[84] Fried, *Contract as Promise,* 77: a requirement of honesty ensures that one does not use another as a means. Cf. 78–79: to enforce promises made in bad faith would be to "invoke *against* the victim the very morality of respect and trust that the liar betrayed."

[85] Ibid., 83, my emphasis. Cf. *Restatement of Contracts,* 2d ed. (St. Paul: American Law Institute, 1981), on the need to turn to social conventions in determining what good faith in performance requires: "[Good faith performance] excludes a variety of types of conduct characterized as involving 'bad faith' because they violate community standards of decency, fairness or reasonableness." Sec. 205, comment a.

[86] Fried, *Contract as Promise,* 83. Fried is responding to Anthony Kronman's efficiency argument; see Kronman, "Contract Law and Distributive Justice."

respecting them is efficient, but simply because they are recognized and relied upon. "The recourse to prior conventions permits individuals to plan, to consider and pursue their own ends. And once they have made and embarked on plans against this background it would be unjust to change the rules in midcourse by requiring unexpected disclosures and sharing just in case the plans succeed."[87] The fact that a prevailing understanding exists, even if there is no particularly good reason for it, makes it reasonable at the time it is relied upon. We should want to change that understanding if it is irrational, but prevailing understandings are the measure of reasonableness at the time agreements are made.

Fried, committed to rational, principled criticism of contract law, develops a principle to resolve contract disputes, but to apply it he has to appeal elsewhere, either to other principles, or to conventions and shared understandings that themselves are not subject to immediate critical scrutiny. Fried does this even though at times he emphasizes the Kantian roots of his project, as when he writes that determining what's right is not a matter of "fashion or favor." The point I have emphasized is the same point discussed in chapter two about Kant and in chapter three about MacCormick, Bentham, and Scanlon: while following their call for principled criticism, I have objected to the tendency, less marked in and at times explicitly disavowed by Fried, and most prevalent in MacCormick and Scanlon, to be overly detached from social practices, to the point even of seemingly denying *any* role to practice and shared understandings in ethical and legal deliberation.

Fried, we've seen, *does* appeal to conventions as well as other principles in interpreting the promise principle. His entire project, of finding a principle immanent in contract law that best explains and fulfills its purpose, reflects how for Fried theory is not distinct from but tries to account for practice. I shall say more in the final section about why an account such as Fried's, tied as it is to an understanding of the purpose of contract law and its connection to the practice of promising, is preferable to an account that makes no reference to the point of contracts or the practice of promising. At that time we will have had an opportunity to consider such an account.

Fried has been *criticized* for his reliance on conventions by other theorists who do not think he takes his commitment to rational principles far enough, who fault him for failing to abstract himself enough from existing norms and conventions. Richard Craswell argues that Fried's promise principle is indeterminate. Pointing to how Fried is forced to appeal to standards external to the promise principle to resolve specific contract issues, Craswell writes: "Fried relies on people's existing expectations; sometimes he uses economic arguments; sometimes he rests on principles of "fault" or "altruism"; and sometimes, as in the case of expectation damages, he advances no justification at all. Such a scattershot approach to the selection of default rules does little to advance our understanding of contract law."[88] While I shall not here defend Fried's interpretation of the will theory as a

[87] Fried, *Contract as Promise*, 84.

[88] Richard Craswell, "Contract Law, Default Rules, and the Philosophy of Promising," *Michigan Law Review* 88 (1989): 523.

better account than other theories of contractual obligation, Craswell's judgment seems unduly harsh. Fried's acknowledgment of the role social practice and convention play in a theory of contract law is one of the strengths of his theory, though at times he seems to deny their role, as when he speaks of the validity of a moral truth not depending on "fashion or favor." Where Craswell points to this aspect of Fried's account as one of its weaknesses, I see it as a necessary feature of principled accounts of ethical and legal judging, especially when principles are applied to resolve issues in which people's expectations are involved.

The Reliance Principle

Fried acknowledges other bases for liability besides the promise principle. "There is nothing at all in my conception of contract as promise that precludes persons who behave badly and cause unnecessary harm from being forced to make fair compensation. Promissory obligation is not the only basis for liability."[89] Because Fried insists that the basis of contractual obligation is promise, yet also acknowledges other sources of liability, he has been charged with being inconsistent or incoherent. P. S. Atiyah, for example, notes that Fried favors the decision in *Hoffman v. Red Owl Stores*,[90] in which Red Owl Stores was found liable for inducing detrimental reliance in Hoffman by getting him to believe they would offer him a franchise, even though they made no formal promise. Atiyah claims there is a discrepancy between this position and Fried's promise principle, which should hold that one is not generally justified "in relying on anything short of a promise."[91] Fried responds by saying that *Hoffman* illustrates how a reliance principle "need not compete with the promise principle, but may comfortably supplement it."[92] A principle of restitution might provide a basis of relief for Britton, for example (example 17); for Fried this would be a noncontractual basis of relief.[93] A tort principle could provide relief where someone relies to their detriment on something short of a promise.[94] In the latter case what Fried sees as a noncontractual source of obligation to supplement the promise principle, others see as the central basis of contractual obligation.

In chapter three we saw that MacCormick and Scanlon explain the wrong of promise-breaking by appealing not to the fact that a social practice of promising was violated, but to the fact that in promising one creates expectations or provides assurances upon which others may rely to their detriment. The wrong of breaking a promise is the wrong of disappointing such expectations. Insofar as it is possible to create these expectations without actually promising, a moral obligation could arise absent a promise. In their view a promise is not a necessary

---

[89] Fried, *Contract as Promise*, 24.

[90] 133 NW 2d 267 (1965).

[91] Atiyah, Review of Fried's *Contract as Promise*, *Harvard Law Review* 95 (1981): 521.

[92] Fried, review of Atiyah's *Rise and Fall of Freedom of Contract*, *Harvard Law Review* 93 (1980): 1867.

[93] Fried discusses *Britton v. Turner* in *Contract as Promise*, 27, noting that the promise principle and restitution principle "appear to point in opposite directions in this situation," then hinting that these principles can "work together," without saying exactly how he would have decided this case.

[94] Fried, *Contract as Promise*, 69–71.

condition for a moral obligation nor is it a sufficient condition; a promise that did not provide assurance (Scanlon) or have the potential of inducing detrimental reliance (MacCormick) might not be wrong to break.

Some legal theorists, most notably P. S. Atiyah, have taken a similar position with respect to contracts. In Atiyah's view, a promise is neither a necessary nor sufficient condition for the existence of an obligation. Legal obligations will be imposed when one knowingly induces detrimental reliance in another, whether this was done by promising or in some other way.

Atiyah, like Fried, claims to be giving an account of existing contract law.[95] His purpose, like Fried's, is to develop a principle that explains existing law and which could at the same time serve as a guiding tool in resolving hard cases or cases about which the law is unclear. His account of contract law differs significantly from Fried's. But like Fried's promise principle, and to an even greater extent and with more explicit acknowledgement on Atiyah's part, Atiyah's principle—a reliance principle—relies for its interpretation on social practices and shared understandings. Atiyah does not defer to whatever a judge happens to declare the law to be, but in stepping back from the law in order to theorize he does not step back too far. Some will say he doesn't step back far enough.

Atiyah, looking at existing contract law, finds it significant that "some promises are read in by the law which are not explicitly stated."[96] The law of sale, for example, treats the seller as "impliedly" promising to supply goods of merchant-

---

[95] Atiyah also claims to give an account of morality, of the obligation to keep promises. He argues that promise-keeping lacks the sanctity many moral philosophers think it has—"The breach of a promise which has not been paid for or relied upon is a relatively venial wrong" (Atiyah, *Promises, Morals, and Law*, 142)—and supports this position by turning to the law of contract (27–28; 65–67). Atiyah has been sharply criticized for inferring insights into the moral philosophy of promising by looking at the law courts. Hugh Collins, in his review of Atiyah in *Modern Law Review*, writes that "the courts are not tribunals of morality but agencies of the state, and they behave accordingly." William Howarth makes a similar criticism: "One wonders whether the philosophical difficulties raised by promising are properly thought of as problems for empirical or rational enquiry. If the latter is actually the case, as I suspect it is, it is not very helpful for Atiyah to 'enlighten' philosophers by presenting them with a host of examples from the law of contract that purport to show that their paradigm of a promise is the wrong one. The supposition that the behavior of the courts in deciding contract cases should be the central concern of moral philosophers trying to elucidate the rational character of promises seems a dubious one." See his review of Atiyah in *Cambrian Law Review* 13 (1982): 77–80. See also *Michigan Law Review* 81 (March 1983): 899–903; and Raz, "Promises in Morality and Law," 919–20: "It is normally thought that morality is the arbiter of law, that the law can be justified only if it conforms to morality. Atiyah's comments . . . suggest that he wishes to reverse their roles and to make law the arbiter of morality."

Atiyah's position is particularly precarious in that not only does he use contract law as a standard of judgment, but he also criticizes that law. For example, he criticizes the law insofar as it enforces mutual-executory contracts (which involve promises without reliance or benefit): "We are prone to think of mutual executory promises as having a more binding character than is in truth warranted by the reasons" (212; cf. 195). Raz wonders how Atiyah can appeal to the law and common practice, yet go on to criticize the law and practice by saying such promises should not be morally binding (924). But see Mark Tunick, *Punishment: Theory and Practice* (Berkeley, University of California Press, 1992), 12–13, for a discussion of how one can appeal to principles immanent in a practice to criticize features of that practice.

[96] Atiyah, *Promises, Morals, and Law*, 151.

able quality. The resulting obligations do not arise from the intent of the promisor and may arise, rather, from a "sense of justice arising from social policy."[97] Not only are some promises read into the law, "some promises which are explicitly stated are struck out by the law as void."[98] As an example, Atiyah points to an English case, *Lazenby Garages v. Wright*.[99] Wright promised to sell his used car to a car dealer. The car dealer, acting in reliance, sold the car to a third party for the price he agreed to pay Wright. Wright breaches. Since the car dealer suffered no loss, the court awarded no damages. While the court did not deny the binding force of the promise, by refusing to award any damages it in effect gave the promise no legal backing. On a reliance theory, an enforceable obligation arises only where there is detrimental reliance on the promise.[100]

Fried sees promises as the source of contractual obligations: the reason it is wrong to breach a contract is that in doing so one fails to fulfill a promissory obligation and violates trust. Atiyah rejects this account of contracts. For Atiyah, promises are not the source of contractual obligations, but are admissions of *preexisting* obligations:

> The promise is evidence, is an admission, of the existence of some other obligation already owed by the promisor. By making an explicit promise, the promisor concedes or admits the existence and extent of the pre-existing obligation. Indeed, I shall argue that this is in truth the paradigm of an explicit promise.[101]

Atiyah writes that a purchaser's obligation to pay "surely derives from his purchase of the goods, rather than from his promise; . . . the implication of a promise to pay the price may be the result, rather than the cause of holding the transaction to be a purchase."[102] Preexisting obligations might arise from the receipt of benefits—this would be the basis of recovery for Britton—or from someone hav-

---

[97] Ibid., 148. Others argue that the law imposes (or should impose) an obligation when a certain point has been reached in negotiations to go forward and make a contract, an obligation arising prior to any meeting of wills. See Charles Knapp, "Enforcing the Contract to Bargain," *New York University Law Review* 44 (1969): 673, in *Contracts Anthology*, ed. Linzer, 188–92; and E. Allan Farnsworth, "Precontractual Liability and Preliminary Agreements: Fair Dealing and Failed Negotiations," *Columbia Law Review*, 87 (1987): 217–94.

[98] Atiyah, *Promises, Morals, and Law*, 151. Cf. Ian Macneil, "The Many Futures of Contract," *Southern California Law Review* 47 (1974).

[99] 1 WLR 459 (1976).

[100] Atiyah, *Promises, Morals, and Law*, 6. In *Lazenby* the court does not decide the contract at issue is void, but, still, it refuses to give force to the contract by rewarding expectation damages or requiring specific performance. Atiyah's point seems to be not merely that no damages are to be awarded for breaches of unrelied upon promises, but that there is no legal obligation to keep such promises.

[101] Ibid., 184.

[102] Ibid., 143–44. But see p. 202: "No final answer can be given to the question, Is the promise itself the source of the obligation?" Commentators of Atiyah's work have noted that this last passage, and the section in which it is included, in which Atiyah seems to take back in some measure his earlier and vehement rejection of the promise principle, is obscure. See Hugh Collins, Review of Atiyah, *Promises, Morals, and Law, Modern Law Review* 45 (March 1982): 228–29; and Joseph Raz, "Promises in Morality and Law" (review of Atiyah, *Promises, Morals, and Law*), *Harvard Law Review* 95 (1982): 927 n. 19.

ing caused detrimental reliance. In the former case obligation is based on the principle of unjust enrichment; in the latter case, on promissory estoppel.

What is the source of these preexisting obligations? Atiyah, suspicious of rationalist approaches that rely on abstract principles and pure reflection rather than on "positive social morality," says they arise from a social judgment:

> The social group today is still willing to delegate considerable autonomy to its members; and it does this largely by enabling them to admit . . . that circumstances exist in which the group recognizes the existence of obligations. But the modern social group has much more difficulty in recognizing the right of individuals to create obligations in circumstances where the group itself does not recognize the existence of obligations.[103]

"It is the social group which makes the decisions and creates the obligations or entitlements."[104]

Precisely what Atiyah means by this isn't always clear. At times he implies that the social group refers to decision makers, who may decide the scope of our obligations by conducting a balancing of interests. He writes that "the source of promissory liability" lies in what augments utility.[105] However Atiyah does not consistently take a utilitarian position. Shortly after suggesting we do a "balancing exercise" to decide when consents are revocable, he suggests we decide the issue by appealing to the "social group": "whether a consent is or is not expressed in a form which amounts to a promise, its revocability is a matter to be settled by external factors: a decision by the social group (or the judges appointed by the group) is necessary before one can say whether the consent is irrevocable."[106] At times he appeals to a "positive social morality." In saying that the source of preexisting obligations is determined by the social group, and in referring to this source as a positive social morality, he seems to mean that the content of these obligations are relative to social practice, conventions and norms. Atiyah is critical of those, like John Searle, who derive obligations from the rules of discrete practices—for, he notes, we need reasons for thinking we should be bound to such rules. But while he doesn't think a discrete practice of promising is necessary to create a promissory obligation, he does think that certain values or understandings must be presupposed. We presuppose, for one, the very idea of obligation, which "in modern times," he says, "is the social and legal morality of a group of persons."[107] The content of obligations also reflects a judgment that is relative to particular societies and their practices. If practices change, so too, on this view, will our obligations. Atiyah notes that presently negligence is required for liability, and if a company is not negligent, we will not imply a promise or warrant

---

[103] Atiyah, *Promises, Morals, and Law*, 194. For Atiyah's criticism of rationalist approaches that use internal reflection and reason rather than appealing to "positive social morality," see ibid., 25–28, 169.

[104] Ibid., 130–31.

[105] Ibid., 131. Cf. 181–82 ("balancing exercise"); and 145–46: the purpose of promises is to further one's interests, and this provides their justification.

[106] Ibid., 183.

[107] Ibid., 111–13, 121; cf. 68–69, 179–29, 135, 192.

on its good. But if the law changes to strict liability, we will say a manufacturer *does* impliedly promise her goods are safe, and eventually, that she intends to, and "people may come to feel that the obligation arises from the implied promise or warranty." "The justification for the obligation arising from express and implied promises is the same; but that justification is in both cases derived from an amalgam of ideas of fairness and policy created by the social group."[108]

Like MacCormick and Scanlon, Atiyah sees the obligation to keep promises as deriving from another obligation. Atiyah, like MacCormick, emphasizes in particular the obligation not to induce detrimental reliance. But unlike MacCormick, Atiyah is convinced that the extent of this obligation—the situations in which the obligation arises—has to do with societal norms not universally valid moral principles.

The rationalist will wonder why Atiyah thinks we should defer to the ideas of the social group, unless of course they are themselves justified by rational principles. Apart from a few references to utility and a balancing of interests, Atiyah implies that these underlying values are not up for grabs, or at the very least, change slowly. As was the case with Fried's promise principle, Atiyah's principle of reliance and the idea of preexisting obligations to which it appeals make reference to shared understandings of when reliance is reasonable, or what one's obligations are. I have suggested that while it is possible for a theorist to subject these understandings to principled scrutiny, until that occurs and understandings are transformed, existing understandings provide the standard of reasonableness upon which people form their plans. Principled scrutiny of these understandings may *not* be appropriate at the point where we are resolving a particular ethical or legal issue. This is especially applicable to promises and contracts, the primary purpose of which is to let people have firm expectations about the actions of others so that they can proceed with their own plans without being frustrated.

Atiyah's reliance principle offers some guidance when we turn to the specific cases discussed in the previous section. As we shall see, it sometimes reaches conclusions in conflict with Fried's promise principle, and in those cases we would need some basis for choosing between those principles. Again my purpose here is not to decide whether Fried's or Atiyah's account is superior but to show that, as with Fried's principle, in some cases how we apply Atiyah's reliance principle depends on social norms and conventions, or other standards external to the principle, as Atiyah himself often recognizes.

Consider the problem of which promises the state should enforce. Atiyah's reliance principle dictates that we not enforce the promises in *Mills* (example 1) and *Webb* (example 6), as they were not relied upon. There might be a basis for siding with Webb, on Atiyah's theory, if the "social group" recognized a beneficiary's obligation to reward a Good Samaritan; but while Webb's society recognized an obligation of gratitude, that obligation did not entail providing monetary rewards. The reliance principle probably would dictate that we not enforce the promise in *McDevitt* (example 2), since even though the jockey might have relied

---

[108] Ibid., 174–75, 176.

on the promise by riding with increased diligence, there was no detriment in this reliance since he was under a prior obligation to ride as hard as he could. The other case in which there was no reliance, *Balfour* (example 3), is more difficult. While Atiyah's reliance principle may seem to dictate that the husband's gratuitous promise to his wife to pay her a monthly sum of money should not be enforced, it might be argued that, at least at the time the promise was made, there was an obligation of the husband to support his wife, and his promise might be regarded as evidence of this preexisting obligation. If this were the case— whether it is is a question of what Atiyah calls "positive social morality"—then on the reliance principle we should enforce the promise.

In each of the six other cases, there was detrimental reliance on a promise or statement. Yet it isn't clear Atiyah would insist all of these promises should be enforced by courts. If according to "the social group" it is unreasonable to rely on a girlfriend's promise that she is taking contraception (example 5), a doctor's therapeutic reassurance (example 4), or a relative's or employer's promise (examples 7, 8), then Atiyah might say even these relied upon promises should not be enforced. Whether reliance is reasonable in these cases will depend on shared understandings and norms.[109]

Atiyah says little about whether coerced promises, or promises extracted through failure to disclose information, constitute illegitimate forms of advantage-taking and therefore ought not to be legally enforced. In the case where an original agreement was modified after one party in effect threatened a unilateral breach to obtain more favorable terms (examples 11, 14), the reliance theory would enforce the original agreement if it induced detrimental reliance. For example, if Alaska Packers Association lost the opportunity to hire other workers at $50 in reliance upon the agreement by the original sailors to work at this rate, then the sailors should be held to their original agreement. In the case of promises extracted by those with greater bargaining power (examples 12, 13), it might be said that the powerful party is not really relying on the promise and so there would be no reason to enforce the terms of the contract. But this might be unconvincing. Landlords, for example, probably do rely on the signing of exculpatory clauses: given a choice between renting to those who do and those who don't accept the terms of such clauses, they would choose to rent to those who do, and so the tenant's agreement means something to the landlord, who relies on the tenant's promise by foregoing other opportunities. The reliance principle still could justify nonenforcement of exculpatory clauses, however, if we could say that the landlord's reliance was not reasonable, which we might do by appealing to a source external to the reliance principle itself.

Relational Theory

We have seen that proponents of an objective will theory appeal to social norms to determine the meaning of a promise. Fried, in his version of a will theory, must

---

[109] Other principles, such as a principle of utility, might help tell us whether these promises should be enforced. As we saw in chapter three and shall see in the discussion of economic efficiency later in this chapter, convincing application of these principles also is constrained by practice.

appeal to conventions in applying the promise principle. Atiyah, rejecting the will theory, applies a principle of reliance, but also appeals to social norms to determine whether reliance is reasonable, or whether there are other preexisting obligations for which promises serve as evidence and which are the basis of contractual obligations. There is another sort of theory that also turns to norms and customs not just to find the meaning of a promise, but to determine whether it is of the sort that creates an obligation, or to find nonpromissory sources of contractual obligations. Proponents of this approach note, as does Atiyah, that obligations arise not just from consent, but from context: "Rights and duties come into existence in ways other than conscious assent to terms at the moment a contract is formed."[110]

Atiyah, contrary to liberal will theorists, bases contractual obligations on social norms, or judgments of what he elusively refers to as the "social group." These other theorists, also rejecting the will theory, appeal to social practice as a basis of obligation but refer more specifically to the economic relationships of the parties concerned as the source of norms from which contractual obligations arise, giving what is called a "relational theory"[111] of contract.[112]

Most relational theorists acknowledge their debt to Stuart Macaulay, who argues that "contract planning and contract law, at best, stand at the margin of important long-term business relations." Surveying businessmen and lawyers, Macaulay found they rely not on express agreements but on customs arising from their economic relations.[113] Perhaps the leading advocate of the relational approach presently is Ian Macneil. He suggests that contractual obligations arise from the fact of ongoing economic relations. Macneil rejects the will theory of contracts. He asks rhetorically:

Is the world of contract a world of discrete transactions . . . or is it a world of *relation*, an ongoing dynamic state, no segment of which . . . can sensibly be viewed independently from other segments? Is it a world entirely of segmental personal engagements, or is it one tending to engage many aspects of the total personal beings of the participants?[114]

In Macneil's view, promises are made within a relational structure that itself creates expectations, so that promises don't even need to be said: "The dependence, the motivations, and inevitably the obligations, arising from such relations may

[110] Peter Linzer, "Uncontracts: Contexts, Contorts and the Relational Approach," *Annual Survey of American Law*, 1988, vol. 1; cited in Linzer, *Contracts Anthology*, 82.

[111] While I place the relational theory in the section entitled "Principles," as we shall see, the theory doesn't emphasize application of principles, focusing more on practices and customs of ongoing relationships.

[112] *Relational contract* is a term used to refer to most agency relationships (franchises, joint ventures) or long-term contractual involvements. Sometimes the term is given a more specific construction; see Charles J. Goetz and Robert E. Scott, "Principles of Relational Contracts," *Virginia Law Review* 67 (1981): 1089.

[113] See Stuart Macaulay, "Non-Contractual Relations in Business: A Preliminary Study," *American Sociology Review* 28 (1963): 55, reprinted in Linzer, *Contracts Anthology*, 18–21; cf. Stuart Macaulay, "An Empirical View of Contract," *Wisconsin Law Review* (1985): 465.

[114] Ian Macneil, "The Many Futures of Contract," *Southern California Law Review* 47(1974): 694.

affect future exchange just as rigorously as any promise."[115] Macneil adds, "Contracts have never approximated the pure independent promise that transactions would suggest," and specifically criticizes modern advocates of a promise principle, including Fried and Kronman, who he says are held "hostage to promise."[116]

Macneil does not *deny* that promises create obligations. But he believes that at least sometimes the prima facie obligation they create is outweighed by other considerations arising from our being situated in relations, and these considerations are essential features of contractual obligations.[117] As an example, Macneil considers a service station operator who

> is far more concerned about his perhaps vague future economic relations with his supplier or its distributor than he is with the fact that the last delivery of motor oil was short several cases of a popular weight. Based on that concern he is likely to make tradeoffs about the shortage which he most certainly would not have made had he bought the motor oil in a transactional and non-relational market.[118]

In Macneil's view, obligations and their specific content largely arise from "customs, general principles or internalizations all arising from relation."[119] He speaks of contracts occurring in a "social matrix," which has its own "ancient evolutionary origins." Macneil argues that "ignoring the always present role of the social matrix in contract is akin to ignoring the role of DNA in the interaction of parts of a living body."[120] "Customary practice" and "myriads of accompaniments" constantly "shadow" promise. "Even promises made on the commodity exchange—the purest of transactions—are made against a backdrop of regulations, customs and ongoing relations among brokers, the commodity exchange, and usually customers."[121]

The relational theory, like Atiyah's reliance theory and Fried's promise prin-

---

[115] Ibid., 719.

[116] Ibid., 734; and Ian Macneil, "Relational Contract: What We Do and Do Not Know," *Wisconsin Law Review* (1985): 520–21.

[117] At one point Macneil writes, "the social obligation may very well be as non-legal and diffuse as simple internalizations by the parties of 'ought'" or may be "derived from social sources external to the transaction itself"(Ibid., 785). Macneil here refers to nonlegal social obligations, which might be understood to be distinct from contractual obligations. But the thrust of Macneil's work, as I understand it, is rather to suggest these social obligations are contractual obligations, that is, are to be taken into account by a judge deciding who wins in a dispute. Macneil, after all, speaks of the world of relation as the world of contract (694). By saying they are "non-legal," Macneil, I think, means that they do not derive from a discrete transaction or convergence of wills.

[118] Macneil, "Many Futures of Contract," 733.

[119] Ibid., 740 (quote taken from Macneil's chart).

[120] Ibid., 710. Cf. pp. 785, 791 n. 280 on the "social matrix."

[121] Ibid., 731–32. Cf. 715: "Command, status, social role, kinship, bureaucratic patterns, religious obligation, habit and other internalizations all may and do achieve [projections of exchange into the future]"; 717: "Economic exchange can be projected into the future without present specificity" of the degree associated with the will theory; and 783: in pure transactions, "the exclusive source of the content of obligation undertaken is to be found in genuinely expressed, communicated and exchanged promises of the parties. Such a transaction is, in a sense, unknown in the real world, since *some* of the content is the bindingness of the obligation, and *some* of the bindingness always comes from external sources residing in the social structure in which the transaction occurs."

ciple, appeals to existing conventions and understandings to determine whether an obligation arises. For relational theorists, to know what the law requires of parties to a contract we turn not to the will theory, a reliance principle, a promise principle, or any other principle; rather, we consult the custom and practice of those engaged in the transaction—we consult commercial practice. Precisely because they do not rely on principles to guide judges in resolving particular disputes, it is hard to see how the relational theorists provide any guidance when there are disputes, like some of those in the numbered examples we considered in the previous section, where the parties either are not involved in an on-going relation, or, where they are, they are in a relation where the dispute at issue arises so rarely that customs or norms associated with the relation provide no guidance.

Atiyah's and Fried's approaches differ strikingly from that of the relational theorists precisely because their approaches are principled. But all three approaches are similar in making reference to social practice, customs, and shared understandings. Turning to these three approaches lets us see the different degrees a theory can rely on social practice. Relational theorists rely on practice at a fundamental, constitutive level. Just as for Rawls the fact that we are involved in a practice means we have certain obligations, for the relational theorist the fact that parties in an ongoing relation share certain norms of interaction creates an obligation to abide by those norms. Practice enters more indirectly in the theories of Atiyah and Fried. In their views, obligations arise when the conditions of a principle are satisfied, but we need to appeal to practice to decide whether these conditions are satisfied. For Fried we need to appeal to practice to decide whether a promise was entered into freely and fairly, with an intention to undertake a legal obligation. For Atiyah we turn to social norms to decide whether reliance is reasonable, or whether a preexisting obligation exists of which the promise in question is an admission.

Relational theories seem less attractive precisely because they defer, seemingly with blind eyes, to existing practice and offer little hint that there are principles we could use to determine whether it is reasonable to adhere to practice. Atiyah and Fried both offer principles that themselves point to reasons to support a legal system based on these principles; Fried, for example, argues that we resolve contract disputes by invoking the promise principle, and that this is justified because by doing so we promote important liberal values.

While offering principled criticism, Atiyah and Fried do rely on practices and shared understandings in applying their principles and, like relational theorists, generally leave unanswered the question why we should accept them. Surely we can ask, for example, whether reliance on a doctor's therapeutic reassurance *should* be regarded by society as reasonable. But I have argued that the fact that expectations exist upon which people do rely and make plans is itself a good reason for taking these expectations into account and giving them their due, even if upon reflection we think that we'd be better off with a different practice in which these expectations would not arise. This is not to say that we should never reflect on our practices and try to make them better.

Economic Efficiency

Some advocates of the final approach we shall consider claim to offer a principle that not only can determine which promises should be legally enforced, but that subjects to critical scrutiny the shared understandings and norms to which other theories implicitly or explicitly appeal. On this approach, we decide whether the state should enforce particular promises by regarding this as an economic problem to be resolved using the tools of economics. In this view cases should be decided by appealing not to values such as individual liberty or autonomy, or to existing social understandings, but to a principle of economic efficiency—in a contract dispute the victor and remedy should be chosen on the basis of what most promotes social wealth or utility, or a just distribution of resources, or some other criterion of efficiency.[122] If courts never enforced promises, we should expect reliance upon promises to decrease. This would reduce detrimental reliance, thereby augmenting social utility; but it would also reduce beneficial reliance, thereby diminishing social utility. In deciding what level of promise-enforcement courts should adopt, efficiency theorists examine these costs and benefits, seeking an optimal balance. Goetz and Scott, for example, develop a formula that balances detrimental and beneficial reliance, and takes into consideration as well the administrative and error costs of calculating detrimental and beneficial reliance.[123] Legal enforcement of promises reassures the promisee, who can decrease his "social protection costs" with the knowledge that promises will be enforced. In other words, if a contractor knows that she will be awarded damages if you fail to deliver the supplies she needs to build a house, the contractor needn't take out as much insurance to protect her from being sued for not building the house on time. With legal enforcement not only is the promisee provided added assurance, but the promisor is as well, and this may mean an increase in the utility of the promisor (what economists call interdependent utility).[124] Some promises bind not only the promisor but the promisor's administrators; with legal enforcement I can be sure that my promise of support to my children will be assured even after I die, and knowing this brings me utility. However, there are costs to legal enforcement: if all promises were strictly enforced, then "a promisee might be tempted to extend his reliance beyond any objectively reasonable point"; the flip side of this risk is that legal sanctions may

---

[122] See Richard Posner, "Gratuitous Promises in Economics and Law," *Journal of Legal Studies* 6 (1977): 411–26; Posner, *Economic Analysis of Law,* 4th ed. (Boston: Little, Brown, 1992), chap. 4; Charles Goetz and Robert Scott, "Enforcing Promises: An Examination of the Basis of Contract," *Yale Law Journal* 89 (1980): 1261; Melvin Eisenberg, "The Bargain Principle and Its Limits," *Harvard Law Review* 95 (1982): 741. For the just distribution argument, see Anthony Kronman, "Contract Law and Distributive Justice," *Yale Law Journal* 89 (1980): 472. Economic theories of law do not precisely correspond with utilitarian theories because there is a difference between the economic concept of value and the moral concept of utility. See Tunick, *Punishment,* 79, n. 48.

[123] Goetz and Scott, "Enforcing Promises," 1270–71, 1290. Their model aims to specify the "socially optimal" level of promising.

[124] Ibid., 1278. The point about interdependent utility is taken from Posner, discussed below.

encourage the promisor to make "qualitative precautionary adjustments," that is, to establish conditions on the promise to avoid regret costs, thereby diminishing beneficial reliance.[125] Moreover, there are significant administrative costs whenever courts get involved with private dealings. Richard Posner, a leading efficiency theorist, writes, "The design of optimal rules of substantive law must always take into account the costs of enforcement. Promises should not be enforced where the enforcement cost—to the extent not borne by the promisor—exceeds the gain from enforcement."[126] Whether the social cost of enforcing a promise exceeds the benefits to social wealth may depend on the size of the transaction and length of period of transfer—the case for enforcement is stronger the larger the size.[127] Posner notes that for social promises such as "I promise to take you to dinner," the size of the transaction is small, the legal costs and risk of error in enforcing the promise great, so we don't enforce such promises.[128] Charitable pledges, on the other hand, are typically enforced, and should be, because their size often is large and the donor desires to spread out payments; the ability to do so increases his utility, placing more weight on the social benefits side of the balance.[129]

The economics approach is at odds with Fried's promise principle, for according to the efficiency argument the fact that a promise was freely and deliberately made in itself does not dictate that it should be enforced by the state.[130] On the economics approach, promises are treated as commercial transactions, and promisors as economic actors who consider the costs and benefits of fulfilling their promises.[131] Fried would find this to be an inappropriate assumption to make inasmuch as when one promises that means that one is not supposed to make the sort of calculation of costs and benefits in deciding whether to keep one's word—after all, one *promised*. But on the economics approach, the only reason *legally* to enforce promises is that doing so leads to an efficient outcome—just as the only good reason to keep a promise is to promote social utility on some of the versions of utilitarianism we considered in chapter three. We can see this from Posner's discussion of why a false promise should be actionable. Posner has us consider a case where A offers a box of candy to B and assures B it is candy so that B relies and does not check to make sure, but really the box contains cat food. He argues

---

[125] Ibid., 1280–81. Cf. Craswell and Schwartz, *Foundations of Contract Law*, 244: legal enforcement of casual remarks could "significantly increase the costs of communicating by requiring that even the most innoccuous [sic] remarks . . . be accompanied by a disclaimer clearly disavowing any intent to make a binding promise."

[126] Richard Posner, "Gratuitous Promises in Economics and Law," *Journal of Legal Studies* 6 (1977): 414.

[127] Ibid., 415.

[128] Ibid., 417.

[129] Ibid., 420.

[130] Fried argues that efficiency theories sacrifice the will principle and individual autonomy for the sake of wealth maximization (*Contract as Promise*, 5, 9). However, above we saw that at times Fried himself appeals to an efficiency argument, as in his discussion of *Henningsen*.

[131] For example, Goetz and Scott build their model on the assumption that "each promise carries both potential benefits and harms that must be balanced" ("Enforcing Promises," 1287).

that if the false promise is not actionable B and those similarly situated will have to incur inspection costs, and that is wasteful.[132] The idea that it would be morally wrong to make a false promise has no place in the analysis.

The efficiency theory also differs from those approaches that defer to conventions or shared ethical norms.[133] Whether a particular form of advantage-taking should be allowed is decided not by whether it happens to be allowed by convention but on the basis of whether it works to the long-run benefit of social welfare, or, for those theorists concerned with a just distribution of wealth, to the long-run benefit of those disadvantaged by the form of advantage-taking.[134]

What does the efficiency theory tell us about our ten examples concerning whether only bargained-for promises, or promises upon which the promisee detrimentally relied, give rise to legal obligations? It may tell us different things. An offshoot of utilitarian theory, efficiency theory is subject to the same ambiguity that in chapter three we found in utilitarianism: in considering the effect of legal enforcement of a particular promise should we consider the consequences of enforcing only that particular promise (an approach an act utilitarian would take), or the consequences of enforcing a *rule* that would cover that particular promise (the approach Rawls takes)?[135] Posner at one point suggests that we enforce a rule that we abide by parties' intentions, presumably even if in a particular case doing so is not efficient:

> If the law is to take its cues from economics, should efficiency or intentions govern? Oddly, the latter. The people who make a transaction—thus putting their money where their mouths are—ordinarily are more trustworthy judges of their self-interest than a judge (or jury).[136]

While he allows for exceptions to this rule of abiding by the wills of the parties, for example cases of mistake or incapacity, his conclusion is surprisingly close to Fried's, that promises, even economically sterile gratuitous promises, should be enforced. Posner thus supports the enforcement of McGowin's promise to Webb (example 6). "Making B's [McGowin's] promise binding will convey useful information to A [Webb]—that he can really count on this money for the rest of his life. This information makes the gift more valuable to A, and therefore to B as well, for he must derive satisfaction from A's satisfaction or he would not make the gift." Unlike Fried, then, for Posner the reason we enforce gratuitous promises, when we do, is that doing so augments utility. Enforcement would promote beneficial reliance that increases the utility not only of the promisee but of the promisor, who may derive utility from helping out the promisee.[137]

[132] Posner, *Economic Analysis of Law*, 112.

[133] Goetz and Scott say their economic welfare model rejects appeals to such practice-standards, which, they add, are not helpful in "explaining the observable limits that the law sets on enforcing the sanctity of promises" ("Enforcing Promises," 1264 n. 15).

[134] See Kronman, "Contract Law and Distributive Justice," 486, 474–75.

[135] See the discussion of rule utilitarianism in chapter three.

[136] Posner, *Economic Analysis of Law*, 93.

[137] Ibid., 96. This points to another ambiguity in utilitarian theories: do we approve of actions

Beyond the ambiguity in economics approaches of whether to consider the consequences of enforcing a rule of respecting parties' intentions, or the consequences of each case at hand, efficiency theory leaves ambiguous how to weigh beneficial reliance against the costs of enforcement. The efficiency principle may point in different directions when applied to our ten examples. In the case of "social" or "family" promises (examples 3, 5, 7, 9, and possibly 1), Posner finds an economic reason for (a rule of) nonenforcement—to spare courts the cost.[138] But on an efficiency theory it isn't clear why the utility these promises provide is any less worth the cost of enforcing than McGowin's promise. There *are* reasons for drawing a distinction between promises between friends and family, and promises between those involved solely in a business relationship, but it isn't clear efficiency theory provides the most persuasive reason.

The parallels between efficiency theory and utilitarian moral theory suggest a further ambiguity in the former theory. In chapter three we saw a fundamental ambiguity in Bentham's utilitarianism: To know how to apply the principle of utility we need to know whether to regard preferences, "pangs of guilt," and societal responses of praise and blame as simply given, to be uncritically entered into the utility function, or, rather, as themselves to be justified or criticized by the principle of utility.[139] Must the utilitarian presume social practices engendering such preferences, pangs of guilt, or societal responses, or is her task, rather, to decide what social practices should be without presuming any? This ambiguity arises in contract law: Efficiency theorists have us consider in deciding whether to enforce a promise factors such as beneficial and detrimental reliance, and the interdependent utility of the promisor; this raises the question of whether we are to take as given whatever results from the promisor's utility function, and to enter into our calculation of costs and benefits the consequences of whatever a promisee does in reliance, no matter how unreasonable. Posner at one point suggests that we don't just take a promisee's reliance as a fact, the consequence of which we are to weigh; but that we ask whether this reliance is reasonable; he says reliance must not be "precipitate" or "imprudent"—but he doesn't say how we decide whether it is.[140] The discussion of Atiyah's reliance principle suggests that deciding this would involve appeals to norms and shared understandings.

Advocates of the economics approach use their theory not only to identify the proper scope of judicial involvement in the enforcement of private agreements but also to determine how to police bargains; efficiency theory is used to identify which promises should not be enforced because they are extracted with undue coercion; and to determine when failure to disclose information is bargaining in bad faith and justifies nonenforcement of any resulting contract.

In deciding whether a promise is extracted with undue coercion, an economics approach might consider whether allowing coercive measures would shift re-

according to the tendency they *appear* to have to augment utility, or to the tendency they in fact have? Here Posner implies that we appeal to the relevant party's subjective assessment.

[138] Ibid., 97.

[139] See chapter three, "The Principle of Utility and Social Practice: I."

[140] Ibid., 95.

sources to nonproductive uses. Kronman, for example, rules out the use of threats of physical harm as a means of advantage-taking by noting that allowing such threats "would give people an incentive to shift scarce resources . . . to nonproductive [uses] (the development of more powerful weapons and better bullet proof vests) that improve no one's position but merely maintain the status quo."[141] None of the four examples we considered that raise the issue of duress involve threats of physical harm. A further argument has been used to defend nonenforcement of promises extracted under threats of *nonphysical* setbacks, for example, the promise in *Alaska Packers' Association* (example 11): by holding to the original agreement and not enforcing the forced modification, the court "assures prospective contract parties that signing a contract is not stepping into a trap, and by thus encouraging people to make contracts promotes the efficient allocation of resources."[142] On this reasoning the modification in *Schwartzreich* (example 14) should not be enforced. However if by not enforcing the modified contract Schwartzreich, in being bound to the original contract, would receive less than what the market is willing to pay him, nonenforcement of the modification arguably results in an inefficient allocation of resources—one criterion of efficiency requires that commodities be allocated so that they are possessed by those who most highly value them. In the context of discussing bargains in which a promisor is manipulated through his incapacity into making a promise, Melvin Eisenberg notes that "the promisee . . . has engaged in activity that the economic system has no reason to encourage. . . . In [such] cases . . . the promisee may very well move the commodity, at least temporarily, away from the knowledgeable consumer who would value it most highly, and thereby frustrate the market mechanism."[143] In *Schwartzreich*, however, a commodity (labor) would be moved away from a consumer who would most value it if the new promise were not enforced. There are reasons to prevent modifications by insisting on legal enforcement of the original contract. We should want to prevent prospective contract parties from stepping into a "trap." But until the economist can explain why such traps are necessarily inefficient, it seems more plausible to rely on moral notions of autonomy and trust to explain why.

Efficiency theorists resist appealing to such moral notions. Sometimes their desire to avoid moral notions and to explain everything with the tools of economics leads to distinctly odd and unconvincing accounts. Consider Posner's efficiency argument for nonenforcement of coerced promises. Posner gives the

---

[141] Kronman, "Contract Law and Distributive Justice," 490. Recall that Kronman adopts an economic approach that is concerned with distributive justice. He would use the principle that "a particular form of advantage taking should be allowed if it works to the longrun benefit of those disadvantaged by it, but not otherwise" (486). His singling out of physically threatening forms of coercion, however, seems motivated by commitment to some other moral principle than a principle of distributive justice.

[142] *Selmer Co. v. Blakeslee-Midwest Co.*, 704 F 2d 924 (7th cir, 1983), referring to *Alaska Packers' Association*. Cf. Posner, *Economic Analysis of Law*, 98: "This is the correct economic result, as once it is well known that such modifications are unenforceable workers in the position of the seamen in the *Domenico* case will know it will do them no good to take advantage of their employers' vulnerability."

[143] Eisenberg, "Bargain Principle and Its Limits," 765–66.

paradigmatic case of coercion: A extracts a promise from B by pointing a gun to B's head. He argues that we don't enforce this promise but *not* because "B was not acting of his own free will. On the contrary, he was no doubt extremely eager to accept A's offer. The reason is that the enforcement of such offers would lower the net social product, by channeling resources into the making of threats and into efforts to protect against them."[144] The conclusion is right but not the explanation. B was eager to accept, but he should not have had to choose. A's pointing a gun to B's head wronged B, and the nature of that wrong seems to me not best explained by appealing to the costs prospective B's have to incur to prevent being thrust in B's position.

An efficiency theory has been used also to determine when failure to disclose information invalidates a promise. Where the undisclosed information arises from expertise that is expensive to acquire, the theory holds that courts should not require disclosure. Kronman claims that the law tends to recognize a property right in information obtained by deliberate search, and doing so enhances "efficiency in resource allocation."[145] A party with geological information can buy land cheap if not obligated to disclose the value he knows the land to have on the basis of his information. A duty of full disclosure would discourage investments yielding such information and this may lead to an increase in the price of oil, thereby making sellers of land worse off in the long run.[146]

Posner takes a similar position: "The question of liability for nondisclosure should turn on which of the parties to the transaction, seller or consumer, can produce, convey, or obtain the pertinent information at lower cost."[147] He justifies the decision in *Obde* (example 16) by arguing that "in general, if not in every particular case, the owner will have access at lower cost than the buyer to information about the characteristics of his property and can therefore avoid mistakes about these characteristics more cheaply than prospective buyers can. This is why the seller of a house is liable to the buyer for latent . . . defects."[148] If there were no legal remedies against misrepresentations or failures to disclose, unnecessary expenditures would be made by buyers for self-protective measures.[149] Posner uses the same principle of efficiency to explain why disclosure would not be required for hard-to-get information: "If we do not allow people to profit from information by keeping it to themselves, they will have less or no incentive to obtain it in the first place, and society will be the loser."[150]

---

[144] Posner, *Economic Analysis of Law*, 113.

[145] Anthony Kronman, "Mistake, Disclosure, Information, and the Law of Contracts," *Journal of Legal Studies* 7 (1978): 1–34.

[146] Kronman, "Contract Law and Distributive Justice," 489. Kronman adds that "adopting a rule [allowing deliberate, fraudulent misinformation, on the other hand] would give everyone an incentive to invest in the detection of fraudulent representations" and this would be "nonproductive" (490).

[147] Posner, *Economic Analysis of Law*, 111.

[148] Ibid., 102.

[149] Ibid., 110.

[150] Ibid., 109. The quote appears in the context of discussing *Laidlaw v. Organ*, 15 US (2 Wheat) 178 (1817), where a merchant got a windfall from selling tobacco due to his knowledge of the signing of the Treaty of Ghent prior to the making of the contract.

The above examples reveal again that determining what solutions efficiency requires will be a difficult and controversial task. In particular, it may be difficult to "draw a workable line between information that alters the use of resources in a socially valuable way and information whose only effect is to redistribute existing gains."[151] It is possible that rigorous pursuit of an efficiency theory, one that resolves the dispute between act and rule-utilitarianism, which provides a basis for determining when reliance is reasonable and which convincingly weighs beneficial reliance against costs of enforcement, would provide unambiguous solutions to many contract disputes. The principle of promoting social wealth is a powerful tool. In discussing Fried's promise principle, we saw that in many cases it was indeterminate, and an efficiency principle could be helpful in filling it out, or in filling the gaps of Atiyah's reliance principle, or relational theories.

Some efficiency theorists, though, believe that their approach is the only suitable one for deciding which promises should be enforced. In addressing the issue of whether we should legally enforce promises made under duress, the authors of one article maintain that we get nowhere appealing to philosophical accounts of coercion, and state their intention "to escape the sterility of metaphysical concepts, such as the 'overborne will'" and instead "proceed to develop an economic framework."[152] In the next section, I shall raise the issue of whether, insofar as the efficiency argument ignores the "philosophical" element—ignores the values of autonomy and freedom central to the practice of promising, or the obligation not to induce detrimental reliance and thereby cause harm, or preexisting obligations that arise from conventions and practices from which expectations arise—it fails to give an adequate account of why promises should or shouldn't be enforced. The efficiency argument is an important tool. However, its account of contract law becomes unconvincing when it becomes a totalizing theory that sees the only purpose of contract law as promoting social wealth. It falls short by ignoring the purposes in contract law of enforcing promises that give rise to moral obligations and of thereby promoting the value of individual autonomy and enforcing preexisting obligations. But even if the goal of some efficiency theorists of achieving a purely economic account that freely ignores moral concepts was worthy, it isn't clear it could be met. Moral judgments that themselves are not deducible from a principle of economic efficiency may secretly enter into the economic analysis. Consider Posner's economic rationale for the *Alaska Packers' Association* decision. He argues that by not enforcing the extracted modification, seamen will "know it will do them no good to take advantage of their employers' vulnerability."[153] However Posner argues that the Henningsens were not similarly vulnerable when they signed their contract to purchase an automobile. The shipping company had the choice of paying more money or returning without fish; the Henningsen's had a choice of agreeing to waive liability

[151] Craswell and Schwartz, *Foundations of Contract Law,* 172.

[152] Varouj A. Aivazian, Michael Trebilcock, and Michael Penny, "The Law of Contract Modification: The Uncertain Quest for a Bench Mark of Enforceability," *Osgoode Hall Law Journal* 22 (1984): 173, reprinted in *Foundations of Contract Law,* ed. Carswell and Schwartz, 212.

[153] Posner, *Economic Analysis of the Law,* p. 98.

claims or not buy a new car. Posner, I believe, cannot explain why bargaining with the employers in this instance is taking advantage of someone who is vulnerable, but why Chrysler was not taking advantage of a vulnerable Mr. and Mrs. Henningsen, without appealing to some moral norm itself unexplained by efficiency theory.[154]

PRACTICES AND PRINCIPLES IN CONTRACT LAW

Contract law differs from the practice of promising because it involves legal enforcement, hence it brings into play institutional considerations absent when we think about where our moral obligation lies. Yet contract law has a point apart from the augmentation of social wealth, and its point is connected with the practice of promising. Economic efficiency is an important standard for deciding which promises should be legally enforced and what remedy for breach is appropriate. It provides a reason that we lack when we merely defer to conventions and norms. It can fill in the gaps left by other principles that theorists find in the law of contract, such as the promise principle or the principle of reliance. But if efficiency theory becomes totalized and abstracted from the practice, it leads to odd explanations, such as Posner's efficiency argument for nonenforcement of coerced promises.

The moral idea that one ought to keep one's promise may be the historical basis for the legal institution of contracts. The law of contract did not simply emerge by design in accordance with economic theories; rather, it evolved from earlier practices and custom. Anglo-American contract law, for example, has its roots partly in the canon law of the medieval English Church and the *fidei laesio*.[155] Still, contract law's genealogy needn't dictate blind deference to custom. Judges and lawmakers should appeal to principles in deciding how contract law should continue to evolve or, when the law is ambiguous, how it should be interpreted in a particular case. In doing so there is an important role for the principle of economic efficiency. The fact that the moral ideal that one ought to keep one's promises is expressed in institutions means that institutional considerations, including considerations of economic efficiency, are not inappropriate to take into account, at least in deciding the issue of which promises should be enforced by courts.[156] However, there is a

---

[154] Ibid., 115: Posner argues that the Henningsens still had "a real choice," even if it were the case that the product they were buying was monopolized. See also his discussion of *Williams v. Walker-Thomas*: "The case is totally unlike 'Your money or your life.' . . . hard-up consumers may benefit both ex ante and ex post from 'harsh' terms when the alternative would be to pay higher prices"(116). His placing of scare quotes around "harsh" is telling; he seems to deny that there are standards for determining fair terms apart from what's agreed to in this case, but not in *Alaska Packers' Association*.

[155] R. H. Helmholz, "Assumpsit and Fidei Laesio," *Law Quarterly Review* 91 (July 1975): 406–32.

[156] This is not to say that we need agree with the specific conclusions of a particular economic theory. Andrew Kull, for example, disputes some of the assumptions made by Posner and Goetz and Scott regarding how non-bargained for promises are more likely to have greater administrative and error costs, in his "Reconsidering Gratuitous Promises," *Journal of Legal Studies* 21 (January 1992): 39–65.

danger in totalizing that principle, in divorcing it from the practice of promising and the moral point of that practice.

Just as Scanlon and MacCormick develop principles to determine when moral obligations arise by trying to capture intuitions that they have in part because they share the practice of promising, so too advocates of all three principles articulate the principle they find immanent in contract law, and this is one way in which the bearer of principles makes reference to practice. We've seen that Fried and Atiyah attempt to provide an account of the principle immanent in contract law, and some efficiency theorists say they explain existing law as well.[157] Rather than starting from nowhere, building up a system of laws from scratch according to abstract principles, they interpret existing law, developing a theory of the purpose of that law. For Fried it is to promote individual autonomy; for Atiyah, to enforce preexisting obligations, including the obligation not to cause harm by inducing detrimental reliance in someone and then letting them down. For efficiency theorists, it is to increase social wealth. The theorists disagree about what the essential purpose of contract law is, but their accounts are derived from their understanding of the law and of the practice of promising.

One problem efficiency theorists sometimes run into is that they mistake an institutional consequence for the central purpose of contract law. They rightly observe that developing a system of law to enforce private agreements requires us to take into account economic concerns, but they take these economic concerns as the essential purpose of contract law. Craswell doesn't think judges or legal theorists dealing with contractual disputes need to spend much time if any with the question of why promises are binding or with the underlying values that may explain why promises are binding.[158] While he may be right that these underlying values won't help us choose between expectation or reliance damages as a remedy in a particular dispute, I think he is wrong to suggest that an account such as Fried's, which focuses precisely on these underlying values, "does little to advance our understanding of contract law."[159] Whether or not we enforce Wyman's, Stokes', Balfour's, von Micsky's, Roni L's, McGowin's, Ricketts', Pfeiffer's, Marvin's, or O'Connor's promises is not decided simply by doing an economic calculation. It makes a difference to us whether there was detrimental reliance on the promise (although it may be difficult to determine whether reliance was reasonable or not); it makes a difference whether an explicit promise was made; it makes a difference whether there was an intention to undertake a *legal* obligation, or whether the promise was a "private" promise. Whether we hold to a reliance principle or to a promise principle will shape our thinking about whether these promises should be legally enforced. Economic considerations enter as well. Not only do we want to avoid using up scarce resources on trials involving trivial

---

[157] Goetz and Scott, for example, say they "explain" the "patterns of promissory liability observed in actual practice" ("Enforcing Promises," 1264–65). Both Kronman and Posner also claim to "explain" features of the law with economic principles: see Kronman, "Contract Law and Distributive Justice," 496; and Posner, *Economic Analysis of Law,* 416 n. 11.

[158] Craswell, "Contract Law, Default Rules, and the Philosophy of Promising," 528.

[159] Ibid., 523.

amounts of money, but we may want to use economic principles to establish rules of when reliance is reasonable in certain cases. But economic calculations alone aren't enough to determine whether the expectations generated by promises are reasonable.

Not only are the principles of contract law we've looked at constrained by practice inasmuch as they attempt to interpret existing law—the principles are chosen to account for our practice; but also, application of the principles hinges on what settled expectations and notions of reasonableness are. Economic efficiency may tell us it is rational to have certain expectations, but that doesn't mean the expectation will be there. That certain expectations exist—even if they exist for no good reason, purely as an arbitrary convention, or perhaps for a reason that once was a good reason but is one no longer—means people may rely on these expectations, and doing so would be reasonable. Consider a problem arising under the rubric of "quasi-contracts": A, a painter, is supposed to paint B's house but paints C's house by mistake. A has conferred a benefit on C, but there was no agreement between A and C. Does C have an obligation to compensate A? The answer is, in most circumstances, no, and the will theory gives us a persuasive explanation of why—C never promised A compensation, and so no obligation arises. But in salvage law, if A and C are at sea, and A rescues or in certain other ways benefits C, then the courts require C to grant some restitution to A even though C never promised to compensate A. Why the divergence of common and salvage law? John Wade argues that "no adequate explanation has been given . . . other than the historical development [of the law]. . . . The practical explanation of the difference between the common law and the maritime law may be that they are two different systems of law, with entirely different backgrounds." There is no reason to distinguish land from marine cases, he suggests; "The only real difference is that custom has now developed so that the salvor at sea always expects compensation and there is no presumption of gratuity."[160]

It may be irrational to draw this difference. But the fact that certain expectations do exist is crucial in judging particular actions that were undertaken on the basis of these expectations. Of course the law can be used to change expectations, and lawmakers may want to use efficiency principles to make new laws that eventually instill in us new expectations (although we should not assume that economic efficiency is the only principle that ought to guide lawmakers—there are important reasons to draw a line between private (social, family, date) promises and commercial promises, for example, a line that efficiency theory does not readily explain). But given that contract law is tied to the practice of promising and guided by that practice's point—the fact that we dispute what the primary point is doesn't mean there is no point or that the point can be ignored—then the values served by that practice, be they individual autonomy, or the value of being able to rely on the words of others—are relevant for resolving some contractual disputes. Determining whether these values have been flouted sometimes re-

---

[160] John A. Wade, "Restitution for Benefits Conferred without Request," *Vanderbilt Law Review* 19 (1966), 1183–1214, reprinted in *Contracts Anthology*, ed. Linzer, 219–20.

quires us to refer to customs and conventions. Consider the doctrine of unconscionability, where agreements are not enforced if their terms are unconscionable. In trying to explain why charging much higher prices than the norm is unconscionable in law, Melvin Eisenberg appeals to the principle of fairness; but in explaining why it is unfair to charge a higher price, he is forced to appeal to a modern convention: "Today . . . haggling is the exception, not the rule."[161] In other words, for societies where haggling is the norm, it is not unconscionable to get more for your goods—it means you are practicing well; but where haggling is not the practice, and there is no expectation that prices are negotiable, paying more is regarded as unfair. What counts as fair, then, ultimately depends on what practices we share.

Both practice and principles play a crucial role in an adequate account of contract law. Throughout this chapter I have pointed to various ways in which appeal to social practices, customs, and shared understandings enter into judgments about which promises the state should enforce. In chapter six we shall consider some of the implications of the fact that culturally variant practices play an essential role in the formation of ethical and legal judgments. There is also an important implication for contract law in particular. Accepting that there is an essential conventional element to contractual obligations, then whether a promise should be legally enforced or, absent an explicit promise, a legal obligation implied will sometimes depend on the cultural background of the parties involved. For example, a judge may need to take into account cultural differences to decide whether a party to a contract could reasonably be expected to have shared the understanding of the agreement, or to have undertaken a legal obligation, or whether a person's reliance was reasonable.

I have also emphasized the role of principles in contract law. My target was both unprincipled deference to custom and convention, and rationalist appeal to principle that ignores the importance of practice. My purpose was *not* the ambitious one of developing an approach we are all supposed to agree resolves contract disputes. It was to show how some of the important principles that have been developed are constrained by social practices and conventions.

By showing the ways in which social practice is involved in principled approaches to contract law, and how sometimes uncritical deference to social practice is appropriate and justified, this chapter has sought to further the important aims of this book: to show precisely how social practices and principles interact when we make ethical and legal judgments, and to challenge the problematic and perhaps unattainable rationalist ideal that seeks to apply critical thinking to everything on the mistaken premise that everything is always up for grabs.

161 Eisenberg, "Bargain Principle and Its Limits," 780.

CHAPTER FIVE

Privacy

SOCIAL PRACTICES play a number of roles in ethical and legal judging. At an abstract level, they are the basis of intuitions on which we may rely in developing and justifying principles—this was a central point of chapter three. We've seen also that moral principles may make reference, implicitly or explicitly, to the idea of reasonableness, as with a principle of detrimental reliance,[1] and that social practices provide the basis of expectations on which people rely and that bear on what is objectively reasonable. This was also one of the points of chapter three, and which in chapter four was explored in greater detail in the context of legal as opposed to moral judgment. Social practice also provides standards for interpreting moral principles in other ways. A moral principle may declare that it is wrong to harm others, but we need to know what counts as harm, and social practices help determine this. Practice also plays an important role in shaping the preferences that are inputted into utilitarian calculations.

Now we turn to a final case study that lets us further explore the role of social practices and their interaction with principles, this time with regard to an important issue in U.S. constitutional law: determining whether an expectation of privacy is reasonable. This case is especially appropriate because it lets us see more clearly how practice works to shape expectations by showing how family structure, architecture, technology, as well as ideology influence expectations of privacy. Privacy is well-suited as a topic for us also because in one way it provides a contrast with the discussion of promises. In chapter three I had argued that the principle of fidelity underlying promissory obligations is one most societies share; but with privacy, there are significant variations among and within societies regarding what is reasonable.

THE PROBLEM

Mr. Katz entered a phone booth in Los Angeles in order to transmit wagering information to Miami and Boston. He was unaware that FBI agents were listening in on his conversations with an electronic listening and recording device.

The Laguna Beach Police Department, in response to information suggesting that Mr. Greenwood traffics in narcotics, asked Greenwood's neighborhood trash collector to pick up the plastic garbage bags at Greenwood's curb and turn them

---

[1] One version of this principle holds that when I knowingly or intentionally induce you to rely on my doing x, you'd suffer by my not doing x, and you do so rely, and this reliance is reasonable, then it is wrong for me not to do x. In chapter three, I argued that MacCormick's version of this reliance principle, to be persuasive, must include the requirement that reliance is reasonable.

over without mixing their contents with other garbage. The police searched Greenwood's garbage, finding evidence of narcotics use.

Mr. Riley lives in a mobile home on five acres of rural property, surrounded by wire fence and DO NOT ENTER signs. Police, responding to an anonymous tip that Riley was growing marijuana, piloted a helicopter four hundred feet above a greenhouse on Riley's property and observed marijuana by looking through an exposed area of the greenhouse roof.

Officer Char of the Hawaii police department, having received a tip from an anonymous informant that marijuana was being grown in Penny-Feeney's home, flew over the home in a helicopter and pointed a forward looking infrared (FLIR) device to detect heat ventilation from the home's garage. The device indicated an unusual amount of heat generating from the garage, suggesting that high-wattage light bulbs used to grow marijuana were operating inside.

Police in Connecticut, searching for a murder suspect who was said to be living in an area underneath a bridge abutment, went to the area and, finding a make-shift home, proceeded to search the contents of a duffel bag and cardboard box there.

In each of these cases law-enforcement agents conducted warrantless searches in an effort to uncover criminal activity. In each case, the suspect under surveillance claimed he had a reasonable expectation of privacy that the law-enforcement agents violated.[2] Was it reasonable of the police to conduct these warrantless searches for the purpose of uncovering possible crime? How are we to weigh the competing interests we have in privacy on the one hand, and publicity, exposure, and law enforcement on the other?

These are questions not just of ethics but of law. The Fourth Amendment to the U.S. Constitution holds, "The right of the people to be secure in their persons, houses, papers, and effects, against unreasonable searches and seizures, shall not be violated, and no Warrants shall issue, but upon probable cause."[3] The Supreme Court has interpreted the amendment to hold that the government may conduct searches without a warrant so long as the searches pass a two-pronged test. The first part of the test holds that if the person affected by a search had no expectation of privacy in the object of or information revealed by the search, then the search is reasonable. For example, if a police officer enters a public restroom and observes a person using an illicit drug by a sink, this would not be regarded

---

[2] See *Katz v. U.S.*, 389 US 347 (1967); *California v. Greenwood*, 486 US 35 (1988); *Florida v. Riley*, 488 US 445 (1989); *U.S. v. Penny-Feeney*, 773 F Supp 220 (1991) and 984 F 2d 1053 (1993); and *State v. Mooney*, 588 A 2d 145 (1991).

[3] In this chapter I focus on the Fourth Amendment's protection of privacy. But privacy is not the only value it protects. See Anthony Amsterdam, "Perspectives on the Fourth Amendment," *Minnesota Law Review* 58 (1974): 358; and Scott Sundby, "Everyman's Fourth Amendment: Privacy or Mutual Trust between Government and Citizen," *Columbia Law Review* 94 (October 1994): 1755–58. Justice Stewart, in his opinion in *Katz*, notes that the Fourth Amendment protects more than just privacy—it protects against activity that might not violate privacy, such as unwarranted public arrests (389 US at 350–51, n. 4). But while privacy is not the only value protected by the Fourth Amendment, it certainly is a core value that the Court sees as central to the amendment.

as an unreasonable search.[4] The drug user probably had no expectation that he would not be observed. But even if he did have a subjective expectation of privacy that the officer frustrated, the search is still permissible if it passes the second prong of the Court's test: a search is reasonable even if it frustrates a subjective expectation of privacy if that expectation of privacy is not one society recognizes as objectively reasonable.[5] If the drug user claimed that he did expect that no one would observe him, a judge would respond that he was in a public place in plain view and *should* have known others might see him—his subjective expectation of privacy was objectively unreasonable.

In deciding which warrantless searches government may undertake, courts ultimately must decide what expectations of privacy it is reasonable to have. In thinking about this problem, we are drawn to the issues we have been considering in the previous chapters. In deciding what expectations of privacy it is reasonable to have, do we simply defer to existing social practices and customs by asking what expectations of privacy our society does in fact respect? Or are there principles that can tell us what expectations of privacy we ought to respect regardless of what our practices happen to be, principles we could use to criticize existing practice? I shall argue that whether an expectation of privacy is reasonable depends on our social practices and norms. For example, in our society one knocks at the front door and waits to be let in to a neighbor's home, and this practice is associated with an expectation of privacy we have in our homes. But in some societies it is common simply to enter a neighbor's home without advanced warning. For example, Native Americans had to be taught the unfamiliar practice of knocking at the door first and asking leave to enter before coming in;[6] and in the Soviet Union, as a rule it was unnecessary to knock in order to enter the room of a neighboring family.[7] Whether a police officer's warrantless search of a home violates expectations of privacy society recognizes as reasonable will depend on, among other things, whether in that society people are expected to knock first before entering. As Justice Harlan wrote, "Our expectations, and the risks we

---

[4] Some legal scholars would insist that in this case there isn't even a "search," and so the Fourth Amendment proscription against *unreasonable* searches isn't even implicated. See, for example, Christopher Slobogin and Joseph Schumacher, "Reasonable Expectations of Privacy and Autonomy in Fourth Amendment Cases: An Empirical Look at 'Understandings Recognized and Permitted by Society,'" *Duke Law Journal* 42 (1993): 728–29. Whether it is a search would depend on the officer's intent: did he enter the restroom to look for crime? Courts are divided about the general question of whether the purpose of an officer's action bears on the reasonableness of the expectation of privacy the action frustrates, but this needn't concern us here. It makes little difference whether we say the officer did not search, or the officer conducted a reasonable search; in either case his action is permissible under the Fourth Amendment.

[5] The two-pronged test was first articulated by Justice Harlan in his concurring opinion in *Katz v. U.S.* (389 US 347 at 361). Harlan establishes a rule that he understands to have emerged from prior decisions: "First that a person have exhibited an actual (subjective) expectation of privacy and, second, that the expectation be one that society is prepared to recognize as 'reasonable.'"

[6] See David Flaherty, *Privacy in Colonial New England* (Charlottesville: University Press of Virginia, 1967), 88–89.

[7] Vladimir Shlapentokh, *Public and Private Life of the Soviet People* (New York: Oxford University Press, 1989), 181.

assume, are in large part reflections of laws that translate into rules the customs and values of the past and present."[8]

But, my argument continues, it is ethically problematic to accept all social practices of discovery as legitimate simply because they exist as social practices. Existing practices may be unacceptable. Eavesdropping was so prevalent in Nazi Germany and the Soviet Union that few in these societies could expect privacy in their homes. But this empirical fact does not itself justify the level of exposure to which people in these societies were subjected. That few German or Soviet citizens could expect privacy in their homes does not mean that Soviet or German citizens should not have been able to expect privacy. We might want to say that the surveillance practices that shaped expectations in these societies violated moral principles by which a free society must live.

Another reason we cannot simply defer to existing practices shaping expectations of privacy is that with the rise of new technologies of surveillance there is no obvious practice to turn to in deciding whether novel surveillance techniques violate reasonable expectations of privacy. Does Penny-Feeney have a reasonable expectation of privacy in his heat waste? Because heat detection devices are so new, most of us do not know that our heat waste can be revealed. While our ignorance may mean we lack a subjective expectation of privacy in our heat waste, this does not mean we have no privacy interest against this sort of surveillance. Use of the device might be compared to the use of other devices, and the practice of using these other devices may help us think about expectations of privacy regarding heat detection. But heat detection may be so distinct from familiar sorts of surveillance that there are no established practices to guide us, so that we have to turn to principles in thinking about its appropriateness or constitutionality.

Even if a practice is established, why should we defer to it? Suppose a drug dealer makes a transaction on a cordless phone and the police listen in with inexpensive equipment available at a local electronics store. In determining whether the police violated a reasonable expectation of privacy, someone appealing solely to social practice would want to know how prevalent interception of cordless phone calls is, and if it were the case that people commonly did overhear these calls, might conclude that there is no reasonable expectation of privacy in conversations on these phones. But even if it were common for people to listen in on cordless phone conversations, we might want to say that doing so is nevertheless wrong. We might appeal to moral principles to criticize prevailing surveillance practices.[9] In the dissenting opinion quoted above, Justice Harlan, having noted that our expectations of privacy largely reflect customs and values of the past and present, adds a crucial caveat to this view: "Since it is the task of the law to form and project, as well as mirror and reflect, we should not, as judges, merely recite the expectations and risks without examining the desirability of

---

[8] *U.S. v. White,* 401 US 745, 786 (1971), dissenting opinion.

[9] We also might try to consult surveillance practice regarding similar technologies. We don't allow tapping of conventional phones. But we allow people to listen in on radio transmissions. So do we compare cordless phones to conventional phones or to radio transmitters? Simple deference to practice can't answer this question.

saddling them upon society."[10] Law, notes Harlan, does not merely reflect—it also projects. A judge needn't be bound by a prevailing practice of cordless phone interception, even if it is so prevalent that people do not expect their conversations to be private. If, upon reflection and consideration of relevant principles and values, a judge thinks interception of these conversations is wrong, the judge can declare them to be wrong; the practice of interception would become less prevalent, and expectations of privacy in cordless phone conversations might come to be regarded by society as reasonable.

In this book I argue that in deciding what ethics and the law require, it is essential for us to turn both to existing norms and practices and to principles that might be critical of existing practice. The topic of privacy is especially propitious to consider because it forces us to think about issues with tremendous present and future implications for which there are no settled norms or practices. John Gilliam writes:

> By all accounts, we are at the beginning of a wave of technical advances in the means of surveillance. DNA testing, hair follicle and saliva testing, AIDS testing, computer matching, and other techniques all promise to increase the depth, breadth, and density of the state's ability to survey and control. At the same time, we face an apparent rise in the need to control. . . . those of us who don't smoke, don't use drugs, don't drive drunk, don't have AIDS or tuberculosis, don't exceed the speed limit, or don't have genetic illnesses that overload insurance programs, face an increasing motivation and ability to discover and control those who do and thereby threaten us.[11]

Technology now exists for computers to read an electronic tag mounted inside a car's windshield and automatically deduct tolls from a preestablished account. One privacy advocate has noted how this "offers unprecedented opportunities to monitor the movements of drivers. It would create a bank of personal information that the Government and private industry might have difficulty resisting." Information could be obtained through this technology about a person's movements that "might be a key fact in forcing an out-of-court settlement in a divorce or worker's compensation case."[12] Technological advances have also produced a millimeter-wave camera that can detect concealed weapons at up to twelve feet and may lead to a sensor that by detecting gravity fluctuations may reveal contraband in closed containers.[13] With the increasing use of voice mail, courts will be asked to decide whether employers violate employees' privacy by listening in on voice mail for "quality assurance."[14] In the previous chapters of this book, I have emphasized the importance social practice and norms play in determining what is right. In this chapter we shall see how courts are asked to determine what

[10] U.S. v. White, 401 US 745 at 786 (1971).

[11] John Gilliam, *Surveillance, Privacy, and the Law: Employee Drug Testing and the Politics of Social Control* (Ann Arbor: University of Michigan Press, 1994), 132.

[12] Simson Garfinkel, "Op-ed," *New York Times*, May 3, 1995.

[13] On the gun detector, see *New York Times*, Mar. 10, 1995, A11; on the latter device, see *Aviation Week and Space Technology*, Sept. 16, 1991, 66; cited in Lisa J. Steele, "Waste Heat and Garbage: The Legalization of Warrantless Infrared Searches," *Criminal Law Bulletin* 19 (1993): 39, n. 94.

[14] See *San Francisco Chronicle*, Jan. 23, 1995, A6, concerning a federal lawsuit involving a boss at McDonald's listening in on voicemail to check on business-related conversations.

social practice will be when there is no past practice as a guide. My argument is that principles can be decisive; but, as I have argued in the previous chapters, our application of principles is constrained by social practice. I shall defend a certain principle to resolve privacy ethics issues, while arguing at the same time that this principle yields judgments of reasonableness that are not universal or culturally invariant. Judgments of reasonableness, while principled, are shaped by practices and norms that are not universally shared.

Answering the question of whether an expectation of privacy is reasonable requires us not merely to consult expectations people do have but to reflect on the value of privacy. We need to ask what would be lost if courts allowed the police to search a homeless person's duffel bag, or Greenwood's garbage (and not just Greenwood's but yours or mine).

In considering the value of privacy, we should be clear about what privacy means. By an interest in privacy we might mean an interest in solitude or physical isolation.[15] But that is not the only sense of privacy, for one can utterly lack physical isolation yet still lead a private life. When Ernst van den Haag writes that "privacy actually cannot be preserved in urban life" because "the urban resident must join streams of traffic as soon as he leaves his residence," he assumes that privacy means nothing but isolation, so that only if one is physically alone does one have privacy.[16] But private lives can be lived in densely populated areas. Granville Hicks once noted how living in a rural town, he had physical privacy but was gossiped about and scrutinized by others, and he contrasted this with someone living in New York City, lacking physical privacy but leading a private life of another sort—a life of anonymity.[17] Of course even the most public of figures can lead a sort of private life. Citizen Kane was recognized by everyone, but the hopes and dreams closest to his heart remained a mystery to all but himself. Welles shows the emptiness and alienation resulting from this privacy, but there is also great value in retaining an inner sanctum shielded from exposure.

An interest in privacy might refer to an interest in not being subject to intrusions by others so that one can retain cherished solitude; or in not having others find out information about you or having that information publicized, so that one can retain cherished anonymity. Only by protecting our private aspirations and secrets from indiscriminate exposure can we choose to whom we reveal ourselves. Without this protection we would be less able to form intimate relations with friends and loved ones, so that our interest in privacy can be seen as an interest in preserving these relationships.[18] Schoeman captures these senses of

[15] Flaherty, *Privacy in Colonial New England*, 1; citing Alan F. Westin, *Privacy and Freedom* (New York, 1967).

[16] Ernest van den Haag, "On Privacy," in *Privacy*, ed. J. Roland Pennock and John W. Chapman (NOMOS XIII) (New York: Atherton Press, 1971), 162.

[17] Granville Hicks, "The Invasion of Privacy (3): The Limits of Privacy," *American Scholar* 28, no. 2 (spring 1959): 185–93. Cf. Flaherty, Privacy in Colonial New England, 2, citing Westin, on privacy as anonymity.

[18] See Charles Fried, "Privacy," *Yale Law Journal* 77 (1968): reprinted in *Philosophical Dimensions of*

privacy at stake when government officials conduct surveillance to protect society against criminals when he defines privacy as "a state of limited access to a person."[19]

The senses of privacy so far discussed are sometimes referred to under the rubric "the right to be let alone," a phrase made famous by Justice Brandeis.[20] This very broad depiction of the interest in privacy also characterizes the distinct value of "autonomy," which is often associated with privacy.[21] Privacy as autonomy refers to the interest in making one's own choices without interference by others. But as Hyman Gross notes, privacy and autonomy should be distinguished: "While an offense to privacy is an offense to autonomy, not every curtailment of autonomy is a compromise of privacy." Gross notes that an attempt by government to regulate personal affairs implicates autonomy but not necessarily privacy.[22] In this chapter we shall be concerned with the interest in not having government find out information about our lives and not with the interest in not having government dictate how we conduct our personal affairs.

Not everyone cherishes privacy understood as a state of limited access to a person.[23] Some Americans are exhibitionists, willing to reveal their darkest secrets to a viewing public of millions when egged on by Oprah or Geraldo. Some see the concern with privacy as a symptom of an overly individualist society, or as a product of capitalism.[24] Privacy has been criticized as perpetuating shame and inhibitions.[25] Films such as *Sorry, Wrong Number* and *Rear Window* convey the message that while eavesdropping can get you into trouble, it may save someone's life. Enforcement of norms and laws requires that concealed activities be exposed.

But even Puritan society, which generated norms that viewed a demand for privacy as a subversive shield from wrongdoing, recognized *some* value in privacy.[26] While not everyone wants a lot of privacy, and too much privacy may prevent us from obtaining other goods, some level of privacy seems essential. Clearly some balance needs to be reached between privacy and exposure. We need to weigh the interest most of us have in privacy against "the claim of fair and effective law enforcement," as well as that of "the citizenry to be fully informed about what is going on about them."[27]

Privacy: An Anthology, ed. Ferdinand Schoeman (New York: Cambridge University Press, 1984); James Rachels, "Why Privacy Is Important" ; and Robert Murphy, "Social Distance and the Veil," both also in Schoeman.

[19] Ferdinand Schoeman, "Privacy: Philosophical Dimensions of the Literature," in his *Philosophical Dimensions of Privacy*, 3.

[20] *Olmstead v. U.S.*, 277 U.S. 438 at 478 (1928), dissenting opinion.

[21] See Jed Rubenfeld, "The Right to Privacy," *Harvard Law Review* 104 (February 1989): 4.

[22] Hyman Gross, "Privacy and Autonomy," in *Privacy*, ed. Pennock and Chapman, 180–81.

[23] Flaherty notes that "a few may consider personal privacy of no importance whatsoever" (*Privacy in Colonial New England*, 20).

[24] H. W. Arndt, "The Cult of Privacy," *Australian Quarterly* 21, no. 3 (September 1949): 68–71.

[25] Bruno Bettelheim, "The Right of Privacy Is a Myth," *Saturday Evening Post*, July 27, 1968.

[26] Flaherty, *Privacy in Colonial New England*, 14–15.

[27] William H. Rehnquist, "Is an Expanded Right to Privacy Consistent with Fair and Effective Law Enforcement?" *Kansas Law Review* 23 (1974): 12.

The Court, in applying the Fourth Amendment, seeks this balance in part by drawing on the idea of reasonableness. Privacy is respected by prohibiting government searches that violate reasonable expectations of privacy; but the government may, in its need to expose, uncover information that people should not reasonably expect to remain shielded. Information about ourselves is revealed to others all the time. We don't expect when we walk down the street talking to a friend that others avert their eyes or cover their ears. If we want privacy in the fact that we are with someone, or in our conversation, we must take measures to protect this information from the sorts of exposure society accepts as legitimate. But we shouldn't have to hide in a dark basement and talk in whispers to protect this information. Society has norms of permissible (noninvasive) and impermissible (invasive) methods of gathering information about others, and we should have to protect what we don't want exposed only against permissible methods of exposure.[28] But what some people regard as unduly invasive others may see as proper. Many judges have held that there is nothing wrong in searching through another person's garbage; but other judges have declared that such snooping is reprehensible and that "a free and civilized society should comport itself with more decency."[29]

When is it reasonable to expect privacy? Katz may have a legitimate claim against the FBI agents who used technologically sophisticated equipment to overhear his phone conversation, but would he have a similar claim had the agents simply listened hard from the next table in a restaurant? Some of us might think Riley has a legitimate claim against the officers who flew over his property in a helicopter, but would his charge that his privacy has been invaded be persuasive if his marijuana crop had been seen through an uncurtained window by a passerby on a sidewalk? Was it reasonable of Greenwood to expect that the contents of his garbage would not be divulged to snoops? How do we decide what expectations of privacy it is reasonable to have? The point of this chapter is to explore what role principles and practices play in deciding this.

DETERMINING THE REASONABLENESS OF EXPECTATIONS OF PRIVACY: PRACTICE OR PRINCIPLES?

Imagine you are exploring an isolated area of a large park in the city and, in a corner almost completely hidden from view of the pathway that you had left in

---

[28] Judith Jarvis Thomson, in considering the argument that right-bearers shouldn't have to take precautions to protect their rights, gives the example that I have a right that a pornographic picture I keep locked in my wall safe not be torn or looked at and I needn't put it in platinum to shield it from a long-distance picture-tearer. But she also notes that *some* protective measures must be taken to claim the right; for example, you can't leave the picture in a "place such that another person would have to go to some trouble if he is to avoid tearing it," in "The Right to Privacy," *Philosophy and Public Affairs* 4, no. 4 (Summer 1975): 295–314; reprinted in *Philosophical Dimensions of Privacy*, ed. Schoeman, 275–77. We still need to make a judgment about what trouble it is reasonable for a person to have to go to to protect a right.

[29] *State v. Hempele*, 576 A 2d 793 at 815 (NJ, 1990).

your wandering, you notice a shopping cart with some personal items inside and a cardboard sign lying atop that says PROPERTY OF HENRY. Next to the cart there is a closed cardboard box, also marked PROPERTY OF HENRY, and a duffel bag. No one is in sight. Would it be proper to look inside the box or duffel bag? Would it be proper if you were a police officer and suspected Henry of committing a crime? The latter question, if asked in court upon a constitutional challenge by Henry, would depend on whether the court believes Henry has a reasonable expectation of privacy in his box and duffel bag.

I believe you have no business rummaging through the box or bag and that if you were a police officer you should examine their contents only with a warrant. But others will say there is no reason for anyone not to examine the box or bag, for they are unguarded, in plain view, easily accessible to animals or children or any passerby; had Henry wanted to secure privacy in his belongings, he shouldn't have left them in a public park. Does my reluctance to search a box left in a park reflect an unreasonable concern for privacy? Would Henry be justified in expressing outrage were he to spot someone going through his belongings? How do we decide what is reasonable?

The idea of reasonableness is elusive. Judges would disagree about whether Henry's expectation of privacy is reasonable.[30] They disagree not only about whether homeless people reasonably can have expectations of privacy in shopping carts, cardboard boxes, or duffel bags in which they keep their belongings, but about whether it is reasonable to have an expectation of privacy in our garbage, in public restrooms, in open fields beyond the curtilage of our homes, or in the contents of our urine.[31] Some judges, for example, find government-mandated urine tests to detect drug use "offensive to personal dignity"[32] and a "quite substantial intrusion."[33] Justice Scalia has referred to employment drug testing as "particularly destructive of privacy and offensive to personal dignity."[34] Yet others have "wonder[ed] a little bit about this supersensitivity about . . . urine

---

[30] Compare *State v. Mooney*, 588 A 2d 145 (1991), *Committee for Creative Nonviolence v. Unknown Agents*, 797 F Supp 7 (1992), and *State v. Dias*, 62 P 2d 637 (1980) with *Commonwealth v. Cameron*, 561 A 2d 783, *U.S. v. Ruckman*, 806 F 2d 1471 (1986), and *Amezquita v Hernandez-Colon*, 518 F 2d 8 (1975).

[31] On expectations of privacy in our garbage, compare *California v. Greenwood*, 486 US 35 (1988), *State v. De Fusco*, 606 A 2d 1 (1992), and *State v. Schultz*, 388 So 2d 1326 (1980) with *State v. Tanaka*, 701 P 2d 1974 (1985), *State v. Hempele*, 576 A 2d 793 (1990), *State v. Boland*, 800 P 2d 1112 (1990), and *People v. Hillman*, 821 P 2d 884 (1991). On expectations of privacy in the toilet stalls of public restrooms, compare *Smayda v. U.S.*, 352 F 2d 251 (1965) with, for example, *Bielicki v. Superior Court of L.A. County*, 371 P 2d 288 (1962). On open field doctrine, compare the majority and dissenting opinions in *U.S. v. Dunn*, 480 US 294 (1987) and *Oliver v. U.S.*, 466 US 170 (1984). On urinalysis drug testing, compare *Acton v. Vernonia School District 47J*, 23 F 3d 1514 (1994) with *Schaill v. Tippecanoe County School Corp.*, 864 F 2d 1309 (1988); and compare the majority and dissenting opinions in *Vernonia School District v. Acton*, 518 US , 115 S Ct 2386, 132 L Ed 564 (1995).

[32] Judge Wachtler, in *Patchogue-Medford Congress of Teachers v. Board of Education*, 517 NY S 2d 456, 461 (1987).

[33] *AFGE v. Weinberger*, 651 F Supp 726, 734 (1986).

[34] *National Treasury Employees Union et al. v. Von Raab*, 489 US 656, 680 (1989)(dissent).

collection,"[35] and in another case involving testing of student athletes, the same Justice Scalia who finds the monitoring of urine offensive to personal dignity dismisses the concerns of those challenging the tests, saying that "school sports are not for the bashful." He adds that the privacy interests compromised here are "negligible."[36] Justice O'Connor disagrees, arguing that monitoring of student athletes' excretory functions is intrusive and more severe than other searches the Court has struck down.[37] Another striking example of disagreement is *Hudson v. Palmer,* in which the Court, in a 5–4 decision, held that prisoners have no expectation of privacy against searches of their prison cells.[38] Chief Justice Burger, writing for the majority, declared that "society is not prepared to recognize as legitimate any subjective expectation of privacy that a prisoner might have in his prison cell" and added that "we are satisfied that society would insist" on this, and that "we believe that it is accepted by society."[39] But four dissenters, led by Justice Stevens, disagreed with the majority's "perception of what society is prepared to recognize as reasonable." Stevens notes that the majority's assessment isn't "based on any empirical data" and merely reflects their perception. Stevens adds that "most inmates have family or friends who retain an interest in their well being" and so "one must acknowledge that millions of citizens may well believe that prisoners should retain some residuum of privacy and possessory rights."[40] Justice Stevens, unwilling to rely solely on his assessment of what society believes to be reasonable, appeals also to an argument that respecting prisoners' privacy, in respecting their dignity, would promote reform; Stevens says this is a point recognized by "sociologists."[41]

Still another notable instance in which justices simply disagree about what society recognizes as reasonable is *Oliver v. U.S.*[42] In that case, Kentucky police, acting on a lead, drove past Oliver's house to a locked gate with a NO TRESPASSING sign, walked around the gate, passed a barn and camper, and traversed a secluded field, bounded by woods, fences and NO TRESPASSING signs posted at regular intervals, eventually finding a marijuana grow over a mile from Oliver's house. The search was conducted without a warrant. A 6–3 majority held that the search was not unreasonable. Justice Powell, for the majority, argued that no reasonable expectation of privacy was violated: "By their very character as open and unoccupied, [open fields] are unlikely to provide the setting for activities whose privacy is sought to be protected by the Fourth Amendment."[43] But Justice

---

[35] Oral Arguments, *National Treasury Employees Union v. von Raab,* in *Landmark Briefs and Arguments of the Supreme Court of the United States,* ed. Philip B. Kurland and Gerhard Casper (Washington, D.C.: University Publications of America, 1990), 813.

[36] *Vernonia School District v. Acton,* 63 LW 4653, at 4656.

[37] Ibid., at 4660.

[38] 468 US 517 (1984).

[39] 468 US at 526, 528.

[40] 468 US at 553, n. 28.

[41] 468 US at 552.

[42] 466 US 170 (1984).

[43] 466 US at 179.

Marshall, in dissent, appealed to custom and practice to reach the opposite conclusion. He noted:

> Many landowners like to take solitary walks on their property, confident that they will not be confronted in their rambles by strangers or policemen. Others conduct agricultural businesses on their property. Some landowners use their secluded spaces to meet lovers, others to gather together with fellow worshippers, still others to engage in sustained creative endeavor.[44]

Justice Marshall also gave a consequentialist argument to support his position that the government trespass was unreasonable: allowing police to trespass might lead to land owners using self-help to expel them, raising a risk that police officers will get into violent confrontations with landowners, "with potentially tragic results."[45] How do we decide whether an intrusion is or isn't an affront to personal dignity or whether an expectation of privacy is or isn't reasonable when thoughtful and intelligent people within the same society disagree? In a case involving a school official's search of a student's purse, Justice White ruled that school officials could search students without probable cause and according to a standard of reasonableness because it would be too difficult to instruct the officials in "the niceties of probable cause" and is easier simply to "permit them to regulate their conduct according to the dictates of reason and common sense." But it isn't so obvious what "reason and common sense" dictate. What for Justice White was a reasonable search, for the New Jersey Superior Court was unreasonable. To Justice White, New Jersey's highest court used "a somewhat crabbed notion of reasonableness."[46] How do we arrive at an uncrabbed notion of reasonableness?

One answer is that there is, objectively, no such thing, and that whether an expectation of privacy is reasonable depends finally on the subjective predilections of judges, a position suggested by Chief Justice Rehnquist when he writes:

> Because we are dealing with questions of political and philosophical accommodation of values, the point of intersection of the curves [between government and private interests] will, in the last analysis, remain a matter of individual judgment.[47]

This position, besides being of limited use in reflecting upon these questions, isn't entirely convincing, because we *can* speak of resolutions that are arbitrary, and those that are supported by reasons; and of judgments that are more persuasive than others. Rather than fall back on the position that whether it is reasonable to rummage through Henry's belongings is simply a matter of personal taste, we shall explore different theoretical approaches to determining whether an expectation of privacy is reasonable, as Chief Justice Rehnquist himself does when deciding cases for the Court.

Does the Constitution itself provide any guidance? Not very much. The Fourth

---

[44] 466 US at 192.
[45] 466 US at 194 n. 19.
[46] *New Jersey v. TLO,* 469 US 325 at 343 (1985).
[47] Rehnquist, "Expanded Right to Privacy," 14.

Amendment, while proscribing unreasonable warrantless searches, does not say what counts. In often cited dicta, the Court acknowledged this, declaring: "Legitimation of expectations of privacy by law must have a source outside of the Fourth Amendment, either by reference to concepts of real or personal property law or to understandings that are recognized and permitted by society."[48] The reference to "real or personal property law" refers to the view that a privacy interest is coextensive with a property interest, and that an invasion of privacy is akin to a trespass. In this view, a reasonable expectation of privacy was violated if a property right was violated, and we determine this by appealing to property law. Ever since *Katz v. U.S.*, however, the Court no longer sees the violation of property rights as a necessary condition for declaring a privacy interest to be violated.[49] In *Katz*, the Court held that electronic eavesdropping of Katz's conversation in a phone booth violated his Fourth Amendment privacy interests even though there was no physical trespass onto Katz's property.[50] Prior to *Katz*, a physical penetration such as a physical trespass or seizure of a material object was required to implicate Fourth Amendment privacy interests.[51] While the violation of property rights is no longer required to implicate the Fourth Amendment, such a violation by government does in some cases suggest that the government's search may be unreasonable. If the police failed to respect Henry's property rights in our example above, this would be an important reason for thinking Henry's expectation of privacy has been wrongly violated. But one can have a privacy interest without ownership, as did Katz in the phone booth, as do guests in motels or at a friend's home,[52] and as does a person using a toilet stall in a public restroom.[53] To deny Henry a privacy interest in a public park because he doesn't own the land would be wrongly to reduce privacy interests to property interests.[54] Since *Katz*, courts, in deciding whether an expectation of privacy is rea-

---

[48] *Rakas v. Illinois,* 439 US 128, 143 (1978). Original-intent theorists might argue that the society whose understandings we refer to should be that of the Framers. In this chapter I do not engage with the further complexity of how our theory of constitutional interpretation shapes our understanding of the Fourth Amendment. That is a separate issue distinct from the concerns of this book.

[49] However, some recent cases have returned to the idea in *Olmstead v. U.S.* (277 US 438, 1928) that privacy is not invaded unless there is an invasion of property interests. For example, in *U.S. v. Ruckman,* 806 F 2d 1471 (1986), the court held that Ruckman had no reasonable expectation of privacy in the cave he inhabited because the cave was on government land. See "Comment: Privacy and the Growing Plight of the Homeless: Reconsidering the Values Underlying the Fourth Amendment," *Ohio State Law Journal* 53 (Summer 1992): 880, 887–88.

[50] 389 US 347 (1967).

[51] See *Olmstead v. U.S.,* 277 US 438 (1928).

[52] *Jones v. U.S.,* 362 US 257 (1960)—houseguest with key may challenge search; *Minnesota v. Olson,* 495 U.S. 91 (1990)—guest has privacy interest.

[53] *Ward v. State,* 636 So 2d 68 (1994)—peeking through a closed stall door violates privacy; see also *Bielicki v. Superior Court of L.A. County,* 371 P 2d 288 (1962); *Brown v. State,* 238 A 2d 147 (1968); *State v. Bryant,* 177 NW 2d 800 (1970); *Britt v. Superior Court of Santa Clara County,* 374 P 2d 817 (1962).

[54] In *U.S. v. Ruckman,* 806 F 2d 1471 (1986) the Court held that Ruckman had no privacy interest in his habitat and personal items as he was trespassing on government-owned land (at 1473–74). The decision, while still the law, has been properly criticized as reducing privacy interests to property

sonable, turn primarily to "understandings that are recognized and permitted by society" as well as to a balancing test that weighs other values besides privacy in determining how much leeway to allow law enforcement.

As the Constitution itself does not tell us whether an expectation of privacy is reasonable, we need to turn elsewhere, and one place we might turn is to societal understandings of reasonableness. One way we might determine what these are would be to ask people what they regard as reasonable and tally up the results. On the view of one pair of commentators, Slobogin and Schumacher, "if most people felt that, say, police confrontation of a bus passenger was a significant restraint on freedom, the Court would be torturing the concept of reasonableness to hold that such a perception was 'unreasonable.'"[55] In their view, it is "better to assess [community] values by asking representative members of the community about them than by relying on what nine members of a rather isolated Court might conjecture."[56] The pair proceeded to survey 217 individuals—undergraduates and law students as well as twenty-five citizens of a college town—and on this basis concluded that "some of the Court's decisions regarding the threshold of the Fourth Amendment and the warrant and probable cause requirements do not reflect societal understandings."[57]

Surveys certainly help discern what society *regards* as reasonable. Of course we should be careful about how the survey is conducted. Polling primarily college students or relying on a brief, one-sentence description of a scenario to stimulate a judgment among participants, as do Slobogin and Schumacher in their survey, may be insufficient for assessing societal standards of reasonableness. But even representative and thorough surveys do not necessarily tell us what is reasonable. If the great majority of respondents say that they find a warrantless search of garbage left out at a curb reasonable, this does not make the search reasonable. Nor does it even necessarily mean society recognizes the search as reasonable.

Well-done surveys might be useful indicators of what is reasonable, but they cannot be decisive because the respondents of a survey may be wrong. Polling people about what they regard as the cause of crime won't tell us what the cause of crime is; it only tells us what people believe. When we are concerned not with

---

interests: "An individual does not desire privacy in a living area merely because he owns it"— "Comment: Privacy and the Growing Plight of the Homeless," 887. In *Pottinger v. City of Miami,* 810 F Supp 1551 (1992), a federal district court held that homeless persons do have a privacy interest in their personal possessions, even if they are situated in a public park. The *Pottinger* court does not divorce privacy interests from property interests but allows that one can retain a property interest in items that are left in a public park so long as these items are "reasonably distinguishable from truly abandoned property" (1559; cf. 1571).

[55] Slobogin and Schumacher, "Reasonable Expectations," 746.

[56] Ibid. Their survey is an important and valuable effort to fill a gap in privacy research.

[57] Ibid., 732. For other surveys regarding expectations of privacy, see Dorothy K. Kagehiro, "Psychological Research on the Fourth Amendment," *Psychological Science* 1, no. 3 (May 1990): 187–93, surveying college students about the reasonability of third-party consent searches; John Gilliam, *Surveillance, Privacy, and the Law,* surveying employee attitudes about drug testing; Alan Westin, *Privacy and Freedom,* 207, citing media studies of privacy; and Louis Harris and Associates, Inc. and Alan Westin, *The Dimensions of Privacy: A National Opinion Research Survey of Attitudes Toward Privacy* (New York: Garland, 1981).

objective causes but judgments of reasonability, then respondents' judgments are more directly indicative of what we seek to know. But even a majority of respondents can be mistaken in their judgment. Slobogin and Schumacher appeal to a principle of reasonability at least twice to challenge the responses of what they call "errant participants." One of the subjects ranked a body cavity search as less intrusive than a roadblock, and the authors take this to be a flawed response. Another subject ranked all the scenarios as not intrusive at all, and yet another, as maximally intrusive, and again the authors criticize these rankings as errant.[58] In rejecting these responses, the authors assume some criteria of intrusiveness against which to measure the responses. If there are such criteria, why bother taking a poll? The point is not just that there may be a few aberrant respondents who diverge so significantly from the normal response that we want to classify them as errant; but that the responses of the participants taken as a whole can be challenged. For example, Slobogin and Schumacher's respondents as a whole viewed the intrusiveness of a search as a function of the purpose of the search; but the authors criticize this view by invoking a principle that the purpose of a search should be irrelevant to its intrusiveness.[59] Again we must ask, if the authors know this principle to be valid, why do they bother taking a poll?

While surveys are not the most reliable method of determining what is reasonable, they would appear to be ideally suited for determining at least what society *regards* as reasonable. Some caution should be taken even here. Most surveys are unlikely to convey the complexities of the fact situations typically involved in the cases about which courts have to make judgments or to provide participants with adequate time to consider all of these complexities. As we shall see in the final section, a judgment about reasonability can involve the weighing of numerous factors. Well-done surveys can be extremely helpful in determining what society regards as reasonable. But we needn't turn just to what people say. We can turn as well to what people do. We can turn to social practice. Or we can turn to principles. Each may shape the intuitions motivating a survey respondent's answers. Of course in a survey we can ask for a judgment about a particular situation. (Is it reasonable to search Woodgreen's garbage given he is suspected of being a terrorist who plans to explode a bomb in downtown Miami next week?) Whereas in consulting practice we can uncover only general expectations of privacy. (Do people generally expect that what they throw away will remain private?) Judgments of particular situations may weigh various factors; but there is no reason to think that the most suitable weighing of factors will be discerned by a poll. In the following sections we shall consider how each bear on a judgment of whether an expectation of privacy is reasonable.

A Practice Approach

The determination of what is reasonable necessarily requires consulting cultural norms. This is not to say that cultural standards of reasonableness cannot be

---

[58] Slobogin and Schumacher, "Reasonable Expectations," 745.
[59] Ibid., 771.

criticized by appeal to principles. But it is to say that the expectations of privacy a person reasonably has are a function of aspects of her society such as its architecture, family and work structure, and shared understandings and practices. These expectations will be different for people of different societies and of different historical periods. They will also be different for different individuals within the same society where that society has conflicting or unsettled practices or has no shared understandings regarding whether an expectation of privacy in a particular situation is reasonable. Expectations may differ even depending on whether or not an individual shared a bedroom with siblings while growing up, or ever lived in a dormitory or living group with others. In this section we shall see some ways in which our culture shapes our expectations of privacy and consider why we might regard these existing expectations as reasonable. But that culture shapes expectations doesn't mean it uniquely determines them. Another important qualification must be added. We shall address the question of reasonable expectations of privacy generally, without focusing on particular fact situations. But what is reasonable in one situation may be unreasonable in another: for example, it may generally be unreasonable to require persons to urinate in a bottle to see whether they use alcohol; but if lots of commercial jets have crashed because of inebriated pilots, it could be reasonable to give pilots urine tests before flights. The intrusiveness of a search is an important factor in determining its reasonableness, but other factors also play a role, such as the purpose and importance of the search. In a later section we shall consider how a judgment of reasonableness often entails a balancing of privacy interests against other important interests.

A favorite example for those who emphasize the cultural relativity of expectations of privacy is the alleged difference between Americans and Britons. Americans are said to care less about privacy with respect to fellow citizens but care more about privacy against government intrusions than their British counterparts.[60] Americans are also said to close their doors and prefer to be left alone in their rooms, whereas Britons are said generally to lack the luxury of having a room to themselves, and instead "internalize a set of barriers" and adopt mannerisms such as speaking more softly and directing their voice carefully as a way of preserving privacy within a shared space.[61] American attitudes toward privacy have been contrasted with German attitudes as well: "An American does not feel that a person walking close to a group or a home has 'intruded' on privacy; Germans will feel this a trespass."[62]

It is tempting to dismiss such generalizations as impressionistic stereotypes. But a convincing case can be made establishing cultural and historical variations in expectations of privacy when these expectations are linked to concrete differences in social structure, practices, and architecture. A few studies effectively expose these links.

One striking example of cultural variation in attitudes about privacy and how

[60] Herbert J. Spiro, "Privacy in Comparative Perspective," in *Privacy*, ed. Pennock and Chapman, 132–33.

[61] Edward Hall, *The Hidden Dimensions* (Garden City, N.Y.: Anchor, 1969), 131–35; cited in Flaherty, *Privacy in Colonial New England*, 8, and in Westin, *Privacy and Freedom*, 29–30.

[62] Hall; cited in Westin, *Privacy and Freedom*, 29.

it can be derived from concrete differences in the way a people live their lives is provided by Thomas Gregor's study of the Mehinaku Indians of Brazil. The physical layout of this small tropical-forest tribe's village leaves few private areas—"it is nearly impossible to walk across the central plaza without being seen. . . . Someone is almost always sitting in the front door of one of the houses or staring outside just to see what is going on."[63] Doors are left open all day; residents enter without announcement or restriction.[64] The bathing area is another very public region, allowing for direct observation of what in most other societies remains private.[65] Exposure comes not only from direct but from indirect observation. Gregor notes how everyone's footprint is known to all. "The print of heels or buttocks on the ground may be enough to show that a couple stopped and had sexual relations alongside the path."[66] It is difficult for the Mehinaku to remain anonymous; it is also difficult for them to live in physical solitude, given Mehinaku living arrangements. Hammocks are tied just a few feet apart from each other, and people are awoken routinely, as when food is being passed around. The only way a Mehinaku can completely evade unwanted social engagement is to leave the village, and trips are common. In addition, customs have developed to satisfy the need for seclusion such as the use of partitions behind which one is required to stay at certain points in one's life, such as after the death of a spouse, or when there is a birth.[67]

A. R. Holmberg has also linked expectations of privacy to domestic architecture in his study of the Siriono Indians of eastern Bolivia. For the Siriono "privacy is almost impossible to obtain" because young children sleep with their parents, the mother-in-law's hammock is hung not three feet away, and up to fifty hammocks occupy the hut. Consequently, "much more intercourse takes place in the bush than in the house."[68]

Vladimir Shlapentokh argues that living arrangements in the Soviet Union played a critical role in diminishing Soviet expectations of privacy. One reason for the "lack of a clear concept of privacy in the Soviet mentality of the past," he writes, is that most city residents lived in communal apartments, where several families shared a kitchen, bathroom, and phone.

> A single family occupied one room for itself (rarely two rooms) and quite often several generations . . . shared this one-room apartment. In such a case there was absolutely no isolation for an individual. People could not even have sexual relations there without

---

[63] Thomas Gregor, "Exposure and Seclusion: A Study of Institutionalized Isolation among the Mehinaku Indians of Brazil," in *Secrecy: A Cross-Cultural Perspective*, ed. Stanton K. Tefft (New York: Human Sciences Press, 1980), 82–83.

[64] Ibid., 83. But see 86: there is a code of etiquette that "prevents a Mehinaku from casually entering any dwelling but his own." Gregor does not explain this apparent discrepancy.

[65] Ibid.

[66] Ibid.

[67] Ibid., 88–94.

[68] Cited in Carl D. Schneider, *Shame, Exposure and Privacy* (Boston: Beacon Press, 1977), 58; also cited in Westin, *Privacy and Freedom*, 15.

other members of their family present, who pretended to sleep while sexual intercourse was going on.[69]

As individual apartments became more prevalent, Shlapentokh argues, so too did the "emergence and spread of the concept of privacy in Soviet life."[70]

One of the most comprehensive treatments of the effects of architecture and social structure on privacy expectations is David Flaherty's book on privacy in colonial New England. Flaherty notes how colonial homes were often places of business or used to house lodgers, thereby compromising privacy.[71] In the winters there was even less chance of privacy as it was too cold to be outdoors and one had to share the room with a fireplace. More than one-third of the families in Massachusetts in 1764 lived with another (though often related) family.[72] Not just homes were crowded, or bedrooms, but even beds. Flaherty tells us that "few recognized any invasion of their personal privacy in [the] custom of sharing beds." Strangers happening upon the same public inn might find themselves strange bedfellows, in part from lack of beds, in part from the expense of heating and lighting.[73]

Colonists also had reduced expectations of privacy in their letters, at least in the seventeenth century prior to the enactment of legislation providing for greater security in the mails. Letters would be delivered by friends or, if by post, sometimes they would be left in the open for anyone to read, perhaps on a table in a pub. Flaherty notes that "because receipt of a letter was still something of a rarity, letters were objects of intense curiosity. An isolated population constantly sought news from abroad or even the nearest colony."[74] People would sometimes use codes if they wanted the contents of their letters to remain private.[75] They would resort to this precisely because they did not expect privacy in their letters. Flaherty's point is not that there was no desire for privacy in colonial New England. Rather, he argues that the colonists *did* want privacy, but the privacy they could expect was constrained.[76]

It seems likely that there is a universal desire for privacy in some form, but

---

[69] Shlapentokh, *Public and Private Life of the Soviet People,* 181.

[70] Ibid., 181–82.

[71] Flaherty, *Privacy in Colonial New England,* p. 71. Cf. Ariès and Duby, *History of Private Life,* 5:13: "Where work was done at home, the worker's home was to some degree inevitably open to strangers." "In one sense the person who worked at home ceased to have a home."

[72] Ibid., 66–74, 51.

[73] Ibid., 76–78.

[74] Ibid., 117.

[75] Ibid., 118–19.

[76] Flaherty writes, "A New England resident believed he had a right to privacy from the outside world within his home and the privilege of repelling anyone who challenged that right," yet he also notes that "doors were often left unlocked, and visitors sometimes entered homes without knocking"(*Privacy in Colonial New England,* 88, 91). Flaherty is not careful in his account to distinguish wanting privacy, having an expectation of privacy, and believing one has a right to privacy. He fails to explain how he can say the colonists believed they had a right to privacy yet also say that they couldn't expect privacy. This has created some confusion among Flaherty's readers. For example, Ferdinand Schoeman reads Flaherty to say that what we consider a right to personal privacy was "not operative in colonial times"(Schoeman, *Privacy and Social Freedom,* 125–26). Flaherty, however, repeatedly emphasizes the ways in which people desired and demanded privacy.

factors such as domestic architecture shape the sort of privacy that will be available and therefore the privacy expectations people will have.[77] The Roman household was densely occupied, and slaves often slept at the door to the master's bedchamber. The omnipresence of slaves, notes one commentator, was akin to "constant surveillance."[78] The layout of apartments in nineteenth century France, to give another example, affected the expectations of privacy among its inhabitants:

> Walls were thin (and squeaking beds told what was going on on the other side), windows left open on summer evenings turned courtyards into resonance chambers that magnified marital quarrels and disputes between neighbors. . . . A key figure in every apartment house was the concierge, who was almost invariably a woman. . . . She was feared because of her intermediate position, straddling public and private, between tenants and landlords and at times in cahoots with the police . . . who sought to recruit her as a spy. . . . No visitor or street singer could enter the courtyard without her permission. Those who lived in buildings with direct access to the street had greater control over their privacy.[79]

As the last sentence of this passage suggests, even within a society expectations of privacy will vary. Sometimes they will vary along class lines. For the bourgeoisie of the Belle Epoque, there were public rooms for displaying what was presentable and other rooms to hold what needed to be shielded from "indiscreet eyes." But "living conditions of peasants, workers, and the urban poor did not permit concealing from strangers a part of life that became, by virtue of its very concealment, 'private.'"[80] Sartre describes a scene in a poor section of Naples where tiny rooms "open directly onto the street"—"people are drawn into the street," which "is an extension of their living quarters, they fill it with their private smells and objects." Tables and chairs are dragged outside. "If a woman falls ill and stays in bed all day, it's open knowledge and everyone can look in on her."[81] The poor, then, may have reduced expectations of privacy in their homes; or as options for privacy dwindle, places that wealthier people regard as public may come to be "private" places.[82]

---

[77] Westin argues this in *Privacy and Freedom* (cited in *Philosophical Dimensions of Privacy*, ed. Schoeman, 60); Westin cites an unpublished paper by Clifford Geertz in which Geertz notes that in Java, the lack of physical barriers in the household leads to psychological barriers in the form of etiquette and emotional restraint: "It is not . . . that the Javanese do not wish or value privacy"; rather, domestic architecture doesn't allow it, so other barriers are set up (64–5).

[78] Ariès and Duby, *History of Private Life*, 1:73.

[79] Ibid., 4:229–30.

[80] Ibid., 5:4.

[81] Ibid., 5:4–5; quoting Sartre, in *Lettres au Castor et a quelques autres* (Paris: Gallimard, 1983), J, 79. On the role of architecture and family life in shaping private life, see also Philippe Ariès, *Centuries of Childhood: A Social History of Family Life*, trans. Robert Baldick (New York: Random House, 1962), 391–99.

[82] See Gary B. Melton, "Minors and Privacy: Are Legal and Psychological Concepts Compatible?" *Nebraska Law Review* 62 (1983): 455–94. Discussing privacy of children, Melton writes that "as options for privacy decrease, spaces which suburban, middle class people may regard as public may take on meaning as 'private' places for inner-city, lower-class children" (491).

Architecture is not the only basis for variation in expectations of privacy. Attitudes toward the body, for example, will affect expectations of privacy. Norbert Elias notes a trend of "modernity" of keeping private acts that once were public, such as wiping one's nose, defecation, and lovemaking, and argues that this privatization of bodily functions reflects a change in individuals' attitudes toward the body.[83]

Political ideology also will affect expectations of privacy. In Nazi Germany people spoke in whispers and with the gramophone playing. They kept the windows closed and the drapes drawn. One woman "took to popping a thick tea cozy over the telephone" when anything sensitive was discussed. Passwords would be used. People at the next table in a restaurant might crane their necks to hear a conversation. One billboard read, "'Be on your guard in conversations! The enemy is listening!' The picture showed soldiers and civilians at a tavern table, and behind them the looming black outline of an eavesdropper."[84] During the French Revolution, notes Lynn Hunt, private life endured "the most systematic assault ever seen in Western History." "Privacy was equated with the secrecy that facilitated plotting."[85] In the Soviet Union, communal apartments contributed to the feeling that "life without privacy was normal" but so did the "collectivist ideology."[86] Arguably domestic architecture only facilitated invasions of privacy that were motivated either by ideology or self-interest. Shlapentokh writes:

> The lack of privacy in communal apartments, in particular the necessity to use the same telephone in the lobby, was a situation actively exploited by the political police, who demanded neighbors spy on each other and report any suspicious event that happened in the apartment. Informers pressed into service were joined by millions of voluntary ones who often settled personal scores with neighbors. Motives for informing might be envy, sadism, the hope of taking over an additional room (in case the individual would be jailed), and so on.[87]

While the account above is admittedly cursory, providing only snippets of anecdotal evidence, it is my hope that it effectively illustrates how expectations of privacy vary in history and among cultures or subcultures.

Why Defer to Practice?

Architecture, technology, the level of trust within a society, the amount of political freedom accorded its citizens, work habits, attitudes toward sexuality and the body—all manifested in social practices—shape expectations of privacy. Where we share rooms with others, walls are thin, doors are open, or we are told the enemy may be listening, we will expect to have to take measures to keep informa-

---

[83] Norbert Elias, *Civilizing Process* (1939), cited in Ariès and Duby, *History of Private Life*, 4:2.

[84] Bernt Engelmann, *In Hitler's Germany* (New York: Schocken Books, 1986), 57, 59, 100, 157, 165.

[85] Ariès and Duby, *History of Private Life*, 4:13–14, 17–18.

[86] Shlapentokh, *Public and Private Life of the Soviet People*, 181.

[87] Ibid.

tion about us unexposed—we might need to talk in whispers or in code or to find a more secure place for our private activities. But does the fact that social practices shape expectations of privacy mean that those expectations are reasonable? Is it reasonable for someone to *have* to talk in whispers or seek refuge in a secluded bush just because this is what everyone else does when they want privacy?[88]

In our society when one enters a toilet stall in a public restroom, closes the door behind and latches it, one expects that he has privacy and will not be observed. This expectation is associated not only with the idea that in our society evacuation is regarded as a private function,[89] but with the meaning that a closed door has. If someone were to stare fixedly through the space under the stall door, or peek through a hole in the partition or ceiling, then outrage would be appropriate. The expectation of privacy we have is regarded by our society as reasonable.[90] It is reasonable not because it accords with universally shared principles but because the expectation is widespread in our society and accords with ideas widely shared in this society regarding evacuation and the meaning of a closed door. We might imagine other societies with different attitudes about evacuation, in which an expectation of privacy would not be prevalent or regarded as reasonable.[91] If we were brought up with different practices, we would have different expectations of privacy, a point brilliantly illustrated in a striking scene from Luis Buñuel's film *Phantom of Liberty*. In the scene, guests arrive at a professor's home and are brought into another room, where they are seated around a table, not in chairs but on toilets. They all pull down their clothes as one does before sitting on a toilet, and then begin conversing naturally. A little girl at the table mentions that she has to eat and is scolded for talking so obscenely at the table. Meanwhile the discussion at the table has turned to the problem of how the world is to

[88] Cf. *Lorenzano v. Superior Court*, 9 Cal 3d 626, 636 (1973): "There is no requirement that a person 'enclose himself in a light-tight, air proof box'"; cf. Robert Power, "Technology and the Fourth Amendment: A Proposed Formulation for Visual Searches," *Journal of Criminal Law* 80 (spring 1989), n. 105: "There are limitations in the precautions that must be taken to preserve" privacy.

[89] See Schneider, *Shame, Exposure and Privacy*, 72: "If one wants to find assured privacy in our culture, one flees to the bathroom. . . . [I]t symbolizes utmost privacy. Intrusion into the bathroom symbolizes violation of the private sphere of the person." See also Power, "Technology and the Fourth Amendment," 89: "Our society demands privacy for evacuation and nudity."

[90] Courts have repeatedly declared it impermissible for officers to peer into a closed stall in a public restroom: *Ward v. State*, 646 So 2d 68 (1994); *Britt v. Superior Court of Santa Clara County*, 374 P 2d 817 (1962); *Bielicki v. Superior Court of L.A. County*, 371 P 2d 288 (1962); *Brown v. State*, 238 A 2d 147 (1968); *State v. Bryant*, 177 NW 2d 800 (1970). In *Ward v. State*, for example, the court held: "Objectively, society must grant Ward and all others so situated, the expectation of privacy under these circumstances if it is to exist *anywhere* in a public place. If not, then society must be willing to accept the prospect of being observed by hidden cameras, 2- way mirrors, or clandestine peeking while engaged in one's natural functions in a closed toilet stall in any public building. We doubt society is prepared or willing to accept that prospect" (at 72). But see *Smayda v. U.S.*, 352 F 2d 251 (1965) for a contrary view, upholding a park worker's looking through a ceiling hole into a public restroom stall; and *U.S. v. Billings*, 858 F 2d 617 (1988), upholding an officer's looking through the gap between the floor and bottom of the stall door.

[91] Alan Westin writes that evacuation is more open in nonliterate societies, in *Philosophical Dimensions of Privacy*, ed. Schoeman, 14.

dispose of human waste given the rapid rise of the global population. One guest then excuses himself, asking where he may take in some food. The host points the way and the guest gets up and walks to a room at the end of the hall, enters, locks the door behind him, sits, and serves himself food and drink from a cabinet next to his seat. Shortly after, another guest, also feeling hungry, leaves the table, walks to the "dining room," and knocks on the door. The man inside responds that the room is occupied and the woman, embarrassed at having disturbed someone during so private and shameful an act, returns to the table and takes her seat at her toilet, to resume the public conversation. Things are topsy-turvy in the world Buñuel depicts; what for us is a public act, in that world is private, and what for us is a deeply private function—a topic not suitable for dinner conversation—in that world brings no shame. Who is to say which world is right about what should be public and private?

What we can say is that given our practices, which may lack any justification apart from their being accepted, we have certain expectations of privacy. These expectations are reasonable in part because the practices giving rise to them are socially accepted. In some cases people rely upon or order their lives on the basis of these expectations. To frustrate the expectations would, in some cases, be unfair, and this also explains why frustrating an expectation is unreasonable: not because doing so is intrinsically wrong, but simply because there was this expectation.[92]

Expectations of privacy arising from the existence of practices lacking any justification apart from their being accepted may be reasonable just because the practices are accepted. Or practices may be reasonable because they are an accepted accommodation to externally imposed constraints. Such practices, of course, may not be the only or even the best possibility. In our society we expect that sexual intercourse remain private, unseen by others, and this is in accordance with fundamental attitudes about what is public and private, and our practices reflect these attitudes, which we have been taught. But perhaps we needn't have these attitudes and practices and would be better off with others. Richard Wasserstrom suggests just that:

> We are embarrassed if others watch us having sexual intercourse—just as we are embarrassed if others see us unclothed. But that is because the culture has taught us to have these attitudes and not because they are intrinsically fitting. Indeed our culture would be healthier and happier if we diminished substantially the kinds of actions that we now feel comfortable doing only in private. . . . Sexual intercourse could be just as

---

[92] See the discussion in chapter four on reliance upon expectations in contract law. It is helpful here also to consider the idea prevalent in property takings cases of investor-backed expectations. If a state has historically allowed unregulated development in a particular region, investors will have the expectation that they can develop there without fears of costly regulation, and will make their economic decisions accordingly. If suddenly the state implements regulations limiting development, investor-backed expectations may be frustrated. Not only will this discourage economically worthwhile investments in the future, but it is unfair, and this is one reason courts have regarded such regulations as a taking of property requiring just compensation.

pleasurable in public (if we grew up unashamed) as is eating a good dinner in a good restaurant. Sexual intercourse is better in private only because society has told us so.[93]

But that our practices could be different, even better, does not mean they are unreasonable. We are used to them, and rely upon them. They instill in us and reflect fundamental attitudes that are expressed in other of our practices and institutions, so that to change the one practice would require changing many others.

But not all practices widely accepted are *acceptable,* and we still may want to say expectations of privacy arising from unacceptable but prevailing practices are *not* reasonable. On the Shetland Islands, it is common practice for people to observe their neighbors with pocket telescopes. Erving Goffman traces this practice to the Islands' "strong maritime tradition"—one would "check constantly what phase of the annual cycle of work one's neighbors were engaged in"; but this provided the opportunity also to check on "who was visiting whom."[94] The maritime tradition might explain how this practice of surveillance arose, but does it mean the practice and the expectations of privacy that result are *reasonable?* If in a society people regularly use telescopes to peer through neighbors' windows, and this is accepted and does not lead to reactions of outrage or civil suits, then members of this society will expect that they may be observed if they are visible through an uncurtained window. They will order their lives on the basis of this expectation. They may avoid doing activities they don't want others to know about from positions in their home that are within the line of sight of someone outside looking in. But should we say that it is *unreasonable* for people in this society to expect privacy in activities they conduct within their homes? Perhaps not, for there are other standards of what a society should recognize as reasonable expectations of privacy apart from the expectations people in that society in fact have. As Scanlon argued with respect to promises, we may think there is a principle that declares such exposure to be wrong even if the principle is not recognized or generally adhered to.

There are some cases about which we should say that despite prevailing practices of surveillance that frustrate expectations of privacy, it is reasonable for people still to expect privacy. An expectation of privacy can be objectively reasonable even if there is no subjective expectation of privacy. In an often quoted passage, Anthony Amsterdam argues:

An actual, subjective expectation of privacy obviously has no place . . . in a theory of what the Fourth Amendment protects. It can neither add to, nor can its absence detract from, an individual's claim to Fourth Amendment protection. If it could, the government could diminish each person's subjective expectation of privacy merely by an-

[93] Richard Wasserstrom, "Privacy: Some Arguments and Assumptions," in *Philosophical Dimensions of Privacy,* ed. Schoeman, 330–31.

[94] Erving Goffman, *Behavior in Public Places* (New York: Free Press, 1963), 15, n. 3.

nouncing half-hourly on television that 1984 was being advanced by a decade and that we were all forthwith being placed under comprehensive electronic surveillance.[95]

Amsterdam's argument doesn't quite work: a government announcement that we should no longer expect privacy in our home would violate an already existing subjective expectation of privacy, an expectation that is objectively reasonable, and therefore the new surveillance would be unreasonable. The misleading example, though, should not obscure the underlying point that someone might not exhibit or hold an expectation of privacy yet still it would be reasonable to have one.[96] This underlying point has received some judicial recognition. For example, the Supreme Court of Washington has argued that the protection of privacy afforded by the Washington Constitution is "not confined to the subjective privacy expectations of modern citizens who, due to well publicized advances in surveillance technologies, are learning to expect diminished privacy in many aspects of their lives."[97]

A state might implement surveillance practices that take hold so effectively that people no longer expect privacy where once they had it, but this does not mean it would be unreasonable still to have an expectation of privacy against that surveillance. This is what I think needs to be said about privacy in the home in Nazi Germany and the Soviet Union: despite a prevailing practice of exposure and lack of a subjective expectation of privacy, at least some of the invasions of privacy there were unreasonable. They may have been reasonable in the sense that they conformed with widespread practice and norms, and may even have been recognized as valid; but *that* standard of reasonableness isn't always adequate, for in some cases existing practices and norms, even if accepted, are unacceptable. However, there are other cases where prevailing practices negate expectations of privacy, yet we should say that the want of an expectation of privacy is not unreasonable—I take this to be what we should say generally about the lack of privacy in the home in certain periods of colonial New England or among the

[95] Amsterdam, "Perspectives on the Fourth Amendment," 384. Cited in, for example, Richard Wilkins, "Defining the 'Reasonable Expectation of Privacy': An Emerging Tripartite Analysis," *Vanderbilt Law Review* 40 (1987): 1115; and in *U.S. v. Scott*, 975 F 2d 927, 930 (1992).

[96] Cf. Edward Bloustein, "Privacy as an Aspect of Human Dignity," in *Philosophical Dimensions of Privacy*, ed. Schoeman: our dignity can be affronted even absent a "subjective sense of being wronged. . . . the wrong involved is the objective diminution of personal freedom" (178).

[97] *State v. Young*, 123 Wash 2d 173; 867 P 2d 592 (1994): striking down a police search of a home using a forward-looking infrared device, under both state and federal constitutions. Cf. Justice Stewart, in *Coolidge v. New Hampshire*, 403 US 443 (1971), at 455: "If times have changed, reducing everyman's scope to do as he pleases in an urban and industrial world, the changes have made the values served by the Fourth Amendment more, not less, important." Cf. Samuel Warren and Louis Brandeis, "The Right to Privacy," *Harvard Law Review* 4 (1890), reprinted in *Philosophical Dimensions of Privacy*, ed. Schoeman, who argue that the fact of advances in photography that allow surreptitious pictures to be taken suggests a greater need to protect privacy (85). Cf. *U.S. v. Kim*, 415 F Supp 1252 (1976), which rejects the argument that increased use of telescopes by private citizens means government can use high-powered telescopes without a warrant: "the fact that Peeping Toms abound does not license the government to follow suit" (1256). But see *Commonwealth of Pennsylvania v. Hernley*, 263 A 2d 904 (1970), in which a search was upheld because defendant didn't curtain his windows, thus showing "little regard for his privacy" (at 907).

Mehinaku or Siriono. Other cases, including perhaps the practice in the Shetland Islands of spying with pocket telescopes, are less clear cut.

Why in some cases should we accept as unreasonable expectations of privacy where certain social practices frustrate those expectations, but in other cases say that expectations that are frustrated are nevertheless reasonable, and should not be frustrated despite the fact that they are? How can we distinguish the practices in colonial New England, or among the Mehinaku and Siriono, from those in Nazi Germany, the Soviet Union, or Orwell's 1984? Are there principles by which we can judge any practice or expectation of privacy arising from it, as reasonable or unreasonable? If so, do these principles provide us with a universal standard of privacy ethics so that we can say what is reasonable is culturally invariant or not relative to social practice? Are some invasions of privacy natural wrongs?

Applying Principles

We might think the difference between the practices in colonial New England or among the Mehinaku and Siriono, on the one hand, and those in Nazi Germany or the Soviet Union, on the other, is that the diminished expectations of privacy in the former societies seem to be primarily the consequence of architecture, village layout, or other structural features, rather than of politics or ideology. These practices—sharing beds or bedrooms with strangers or relatives, bathing in public—were less a product of choice than of necessity. The fact that heating was scarce in colonial New England required sharing confined spaces with others. While the necessity of our having certain expectations of privacy arising from features such as architecture or social structure may not be the necessity one means in saying a physical law is necessary, we might speak of these expectations as resulting from practical necessity, and this may make them reasonable: we have them as a result of a reasonable accommodation to a situation not readily subject to change. Given the constraints imposed by physical or practical need, activities that people might wish to be private are exposed without much effort. On this view, the diminished expectations of privacy in colonial New England or among the Mehinaku and Siriono are reasonable according to a principle that one cannot reasonably expect privacy where the expectation is readily frustrated by virtue of physical or social structure or by practices that are physically or practically a necessary accommodation to circumstances. According to this principle, where, for example, architecture requires we share a room with others so that there is no visual or auditory barrier between us and them, we cannot reasonably expect privacy in that room. An expectation of privacy is unreasonable because exposure is physically or practically unavoidable. According to this principle—let's call it the "unavoidability principle"—a demand for privacy that can't be met is an unreasonable demand; and an expectation of privacy where privacy can't be had is an unreasonable expectation.

The unavoidability principle has some force. Consider the following example. A couple is staying in the motel room next to yours. They are talking at a normal conversational level, but you can hear every word because the walls are so thin. Should you listen in on their exchange, or, rather, take active measures not to hear, such as focusing your attention elsewhere, covering your ears, or putting on the television? Listening in may seem wrong, especially if it is apparent that the conversation is on an intimate subject. Straining to hear seems very wrong. But that the couple can be heard without effort and perhaps even unavoidably strongly suggests that they do not have a reasonable expectation of privacy in their conversation.

We might think the unavoidability principle is one we could apply universally to determine reasonable expectations of privacy, without having to make reference to social practices. But it is not, for three reasons. Most obviously, the results the principle dictates will be a function of culturally variant features such as architecture or social structure: certain societies leave more unavoidably exposed than others. There is, in other words, what Bentham calls a "geographical" basis for variation in reasonable expectations of privacy.[98] Second, it's not just that whether an activity is subject to unavoidable exposure varies with architecture and other cultural variables, but that *what counts* as unavoidable varies according to a society's norms. There is what Bentham refers to as a moral basis for variation in reasonable expectations of privacy. Finally, while the principle tells us when an expectation of privacy is unreasonable due to exposure being unavoidable, it cannot tell us which expectations of privacy are unreasonable when exposure *is* avoidable. These last two points require elaboration.

The principle says unavoidable exposure isn't protected. But it does not say what is unavoidable. We might think that whether exposure is or isn't avoidable is just a matter of physics. A thick wall makes it impossible for a person on the other side to see me or hear my voice, and so I have a reasonable expectation of privacy; but were there no wall, I could be seen or heard, therefore I would have no reasonable expectation of privacy. So say the laws of physics. But things are not so simple. First, walls create physical barriers to be sure, but communication is almost always still possible. Holes can be drilled in walls to see, a glass or stethoscope can be put to walls to hear (though, of course, we can avoid taking such measures). Social norms as well as physics are responsible for the barrier to social interaction a wall presents, as Erving Goffman points out:

> The work walls do, they do in part because they are honored or socially recognized as communication barriers, giving rise . . . to the possibility of "conventional situational closure" in the absence of actual physical closure.[99]

The unavoidability principle tells us that where exposure is unavoidable, there can be no reasonable expectation of privacy. But there is almost no such thing as physically unavoidable exposure. It is nearly always possible to take measures to avoid seeing or hearing what is possible to see or hear, unless one is kept in place, eyes forced open. The principle of unavoidability doesn't tell us what measures it is reasonable to have to take; but social norms do require us occasionally to look

---

[98] However, to say architecture is a geographical variable implies it is only a function of geography (climate, terrain). While geography does shape architecture, so too does a people's aesthetic sense. Architecture may be a sociological or cultural basis for variation as well. The reference to Bentham is to his "On the Influence of Time and Place in Matters of Legislation," discussed in chapter three.

[99] Goffman, *Behavior in Public Places*, 151–52.

the other way to avoid uncovering what is physically exposed but regarded as private. Stanley Benn notes that some acts—sexual, excretory—are private not only in the sense that one is entitled to immunity from observation, but also in that "some care ought to be taken that they are not generally observed."[100] The unavoidability principle requires us to appeal to social norms to decide what counts as "avoidable" and "unavoidable."

That a principle makes reference or appeals to social practice is no reason to reject it. The argument of this book is that principles, generally, must do this, if not explicitly then implicitly. We need to go beyond the unavoidability principle not because it relies on social practice, but because it offers so little critical guidance. The unavoidability principle cannot by itself tell us against which among all avoidable exposures it is reasonable to have an expectation of privacy. If we took the unavoidability principle to proscribe any observation we could avoid making, it would rule out observations all of us would agree are reasonable, including observations made in plain view. Interpreted in this light the principle must be rejected. Often it is unreasonable to expect privacy in an activity the exposure of which by others is avoidable: I leave clues to a crime on a sheet of paper I clumsily left on a park bench; I discuss with a friend a murder I am plotting while sitting in a restaurant with patrons nearby; I harbor an illegal alien in my car as I cross the border; I conceal a weapon as I board an airplane. It is of course possible in all these cases for private citizens, police, immigration and airport security officers not to observe or listen to me, but this does not mean I have a reasonable expectation of privacy in my activities. The fact that in each of these examples exposure would reveal a crime isn't what makes the expectation of privacy unreasonable. It would be unreasonable if the sheet of paper contained a love poem, the restaurant conversation was about football, my car's passenger was a dog, or all I was carrying on me as I boarded the plane was my ticket.

The unavoidability principle can be salvaged only if interpreted to hold that if exposure is avoidable an expectation of privacy *might* be reasonable. But this interpretation, while necessary if the principle is to be valid, leaves it virtually useless as a guide. Where rooms may be crowded, walls thin, doors open, windows uncurtained, it is possible for us to look the other way, just as it is possible where exposure is difficult to use our ingenuity to pierce veils; whether the latter is permissible or the former is expected is not adequately explained by appealing to the unavoidability principle.

Recall the example of the motel with thin walls. While the unavoidability principle seems persuasively to explain why there is no reasonable expectation of privacy if the couple's conversation could not but be heard next door, it cannot tell us whether it would be wrong to put a stethoscope or a glass or even an ear to the wall to hear the conversation. We might think use of a stethoscope or glass is wrong because we are using a sense-enhancing device, and argue for a *sense-enhancement principle* that proscribes observations using devices enhancing our

---

[100] "Privacy, Freedom and Respect for Persons," in *Philosophical Dimensions of Privacy*, ed. Schoeman, 224.

natural senses. This principle is inadequate because it leads to too many false positives and false negatives. I have no reasonable expectation of privacy in an activity I do in plain view whether it is observed by someone across the street or by someone much further away using binoculars. The sense-enhancement principle leads to false positives in wrongly proscribing searches that do not violate reasonable expectations of privacy. In singling out the wrong criterion for an unreasonable search, the sense-enhancement principle also leads to false negatives. It seems just as wrong to put an ear to a wall to listen to a conversation as it does to use a glass or stethoscope, but the sense-enhancement principle would rule out only the latter two searches.

Where a conversation can remain private but can also easily be heard either accidentally or by a resourceful snoop, we need some other principle to tell us whether an expectation of privacy is reasonable in that conversation. It seems to make a big difference whether the conversation was overheard accidentally or by a resourceful snoop. We should seek a principle that captures this difference. One such principle holds that an expectation of privacy in a place or activity is unreasonable, not if exposure is unavoidable practically or physically but when exposure can occur by mischance. The unavoidability principle holds that where exposure is avoidable, there *may* be a reasonable expectation of privacy, but the principle cannot tell us whether there is. On the revised principle—I call it the *mischance principle*—where an effort to discover an activity or uncover information reveals what could not be accidentally observed by a nonsnoop (someone not intending to uncover information in which someone has a privacy interest) using legitimate means of observation or inquiry, there *is* a reasonable expectation of privacy against such exposure. But if information about us *could* be discovered by a nonsnoop engaged in legitimate or normal means of observation or inquiry, we have *no* reasonable expectation of privacy in that information. The mischance principle does not protect us against all possible exposures. It leaves us exposed to accidental observations but protects us against snoops. I believe that is all the protection it is reasonable to have.

Some courts interpreting the Fourth Amendment, without explicitly acknowledging the fact, have used the principle that where an activity would not likely be discovered by mischance, an expectation of privacy in that activity is reasonable.[101] Thus there is a "plain view" exception to the warrant requirement: where an activity is seen in plain view by an officer, courts don't consider this a violation of a reasonable expectation of privacy.[102] Justice Powell, in *Robbins v. California*,

---

[101] See *Ward v. State*, 636 So 2d 68, 71 (1994) and cases cited below.

[102] See *Ponce v. Craven*, 409 F 2d 621, 625 (1969); *U.S. v. Minton*, 488 F 2d 37 (1973); *State v. Dawson*, 675 SW 2d 127 (1984); *U.S. v. Billings*, 858 F 2d 617 (1988); *State v. Daniel*, 319 So. 2d 582 (1975). Cf. Justice Stevens' dissent in *Robbins v. California*, 453 US 420 (1981), at n. 5: "It would seem rather clear to me that a brick of marijuana wrapped in green plastic would fall in the nonprivate category. I doubt if many dealers in this substance would be very comfortable carrying around such packages in plain view." See also *Smayda v. U.S.*, 352 F 2d 251, 256 (1965): defendant chose "to commit crimes where they may be seen" and therefore takes the risk of exposure. *Smayda* is an odd and thoroughly unconvincing application of the "plain view" exception to the warrant requirement,

writes that the reasonability of an expectation of privacy in the contents of a container depends on "whether the possessor had taken some significant precaution, such as locking, securely sealing or binding the container, *that indicates a desire to prevent the contents from being displayed upon simple mischance*."[103] In *Commonwealth v. Lemanski,* a search of a home and greenhouse off of a dead-end dirt road in a rural area, where the officer parted brush and shrubbery and used a binocular and zoom lens, was not allowed: "The setting does not invite casual intrusion; the location of the home and the greenhouse is a clear indication to us of appellant's expectation of privacy."[104] In *State v. Kaaheena,* the court found unreasonable a search where an officer used a crate to peer through a gap in blinds at a height of six feet; the gap was high enough to make observation unlikely ("no one could look in unassisted").[105] The idea that searches are unreasonable if affirmative measures beyond "normal inquiry or observation" are taken in their pursuit appears in tort cases as well. In *Nader v. GMC,* the court held: "Privacy is invaded only if the information sought is of a confidential nature and the defendant's conduct was unreasonably intrusive. . . . the plaintiff must show that the appellant's conduct was truly 'intrusive' and that it *was designed to elicit information which would not be available through normal inquiry or observation*."[106] As we shall see, there are several cases in which courts have reached conclusions the opposite of what the mischance principle requires. In pointing to cases in which courts do apply something like the mischance principle, I am not invoking a legal descriptive standard; that is, I am not arguing that the fact that some courts have adopted something close to the mischance principle justifies the principle. It does show, however, that some of the cases point to what I regard as a better resolution of the issue than the cases discussed below in which the mischance principle is rejected or misapplied.

Where the unavoidability principle merely leaves open the possibility that avoidable searches violate reasonable expectations of privacy, the mischance principle draws a sharper line between those avoidable searches that are and are not reasonable. Consider the case *U.S. v. Mankani.* A DEA agent checked into a hotel room adjacent to a suspect, moved a piece of furniture, knelt down to a hole that fortuitously was in the wall separating the two rooms, and which had been obstructed by the furniture, and put his ear to the hole. Without taking these measures the agent could not have heard the conversation next door. His hearing the conversation was not, and could not have been, the result of mischance. According to the mischance principle, the agent's action violates a reasonable

---

though, because the defendant, who was in a public toilet stall with the door closed, was observed by an officer looking through a hole he had arranged to have cut in the ceiling—hardly in plain view. In *Bielicki v. Superior Court of L.A. County,* 371 P 2d 288 (1962), the court found a search unreasonable where an officer peered into a toilet stall by looking through a ceiling pipe from the roof; the court noted that what was seen was *not* "in plain sight" (at 291).

[103] 453 US 420, 434 (1981), my emphasis.

[104] 529 A 2d 1085 (1987).

[105] 575 P 2d 462 (1978), discussed in Power, "Technology and the Fourth Amendment," 30.

[106] 255 NE 2d 765, 769 (1970), my emphasis.

expectation of privacy.[107] This seems to me to be the correct result. The federal court of appeals held otherwise, upholding the warrantless search. Judge Cardamone wrote that "the Fourth Amendment protects conversations that cannot be heard except by means of artificial enhancement."[108] I believe Judge Cardamone's opinion is in error, and that the mischance principle explains why.

The principle also appears to distinguish exposure among New England colonists and the Mehinaku on the one hand, and in the Soviet Union and Nazi Germany on the other. In the former societies, architecture or social structure imposed constraints on privacy by facilitating unintentional exposure—what is viewed is viewed not surreptitiously but casually. The colonial or Mehinaku busybody takes no measures that rise above normal inquiry or observation, and what they discover could have been exposed by chance. But the snoops in Nazi Germany or the Soviet Union acted in secret, and uncovered what would not be exposed by chance by nonsnoops using normal inquiry or observation. Though eavesdropping there was *prevalent,* it can be distinguished from *normal* means of observation that aren't intended to but which might accidentally expose what one wants to keep private.[109]

The mischance principle does not proscribe all intentional discovery by snoops. Such searches are allowed if what they uncover could have been uncovered unintentionally by legitimate means. Sometimes what snoops find out could be discovered by accident, without an intention to snoop. The opening of letters was common practice in colonial New England among people who didn't expect or intend to find out any particular information or incriminating evidence. Flaherty, we saw, notes that letters were rare and would be read just because people were starved for public news from abroad. He also speculates that many letters would be read by others because the addressee may have been illiterate.[110] A colonist couldn't reasonably expect privacy in his letters, even against snoops, given social practice there. Similarly, if I use an FM radio or bearcat scanner to listen in on your cordless phone conversation, I have not violated a reasonable expectation of privacy just because I intended to uncover information, so long as your cordless phone conversation could have been accidentally exposed by anyone with an FM radio or bearcat scanner who was randomly turning the dial to pick up whatever might be out there.[111] The user of a cordless phone can't reasonably expect privacy in her conversation if her phone shares frequencies with FM radios or scanners given how in our society such devices are legitimately used for nonintrusive purposes. Conversely, if I *do* have a reasonable expectation

---

[107] The mischance principle would also seem to declare it wrong simply to put one's ear to a wall to hear so long as it is not normal for people to put their ears to walls. This conclusion might not accord with some people's intuitions. For them, the example shows a fault with the principle in its presently stated form.

[108] 738 F 2d 538, 543 (1984); he added that the outcome might have been different had the agent created the hole or enlarged it (544).

[109] There is a further reason to distinguish these cases, which I discuss below.

[110] Flaherty, *Privacy in Colonial New England,* 117.

[111] See *U.S. v. Smith,* 978 F 2d 171 (1992).

of privacy against invasion by snoops or spies, the expectation of privacy doesn't become unreasonable simply because the exposer didn't intend to uncover private information about me. When you go through my diary, you violate my privacy just as much when your purpose is to expose intimate details of my life as when it is to look for a lost ticket stub or find out the date of a concert.

But why should we regard reading mail or imprints in the sand or listening in on cordless phone conversations through FM radios or bearcat scanners as acceptable "normal inquiry" or discovery by mischance against which an expectation of privacy would be unreasonable, but not the surreptitious surveillance in Nazi Germany or the Soviet Union? It won't do simply to say that in the former cases observation was likely and therefore does not violate reasonable expectations of privacy.[112] If in a society lots of people use telescopes to peep into neighbors' windows, then observation is likely, yet we still might want to say that a reasonable expectation of privacy has been violated. Suppose in a society a norm is established that one carries binoculars wherever one goes and uses them regularly to read street signs or the numbers on buildings. This practice creates the possibility for accidental exposure of what takes place in one's home. It is easy to imagine a binocular moving, by mischance, from the number on a home to its window. Is an expectation of privacy against such observation unreasonable simply because of this society's norm regarding binocular use? And in any case, why not say that the prevalence of eavesdropping in the Soviet Union or Nazi Germany makes it part of normal inquiry and therefore acceptable in the same way that in colonial New England the fact that it was common practice to read other people's letters meant there was no reasonable expectation of privacy in one's letters?

The mischance principle provides a potentially powerful tool for distinguishing reasonable and unreasonable expectations of privacy. When we want privacy, it is reasonable for us to expect to have to take measures to protect ourselves only from permissible methods of exposure. If we adopt the mischance principle, this means we need only protect ourselves from normal or legitimate inquiries or from what could be revealed by mischance by nonsnoops. Application of the principle requires us to refer to social practice. Where doors can be entered without knocking, to secure privacy one must be discreet even in one's home or else risk exposure by mischance. Where windows must be left open due to summer heat, criminal plottings must be made in whispers lest revealed by mischance. In a society where evacuation and nudity are shameful and deeply private, we should expect that when we enter a restroom or dressing room we will not be watched or accidentally discovered—one knocks first before attempting to enter. The mischance principle, then, confronts the same constraint as did the

---

[112] Where observation is likely, an expectation of privacy is weak. However, an observation may be unlikely but still unprotected by the Fourth Amendment. A drug deal may take place in a remote part of Central Park late at night, where observation is unlikely; but if a police officer by chance happens to be passing by and sees it, he has not violated a reasonable expectation of privacy. The example is taken from "Private Places," 983, and is discussed in Robert Power, "Technology and the Fourth Amendment," n. 101.

unavoidability principle: its application requires appeal to sources external to the principle. As with the unavoidability principle, the mischance principle draws on norms and practices that vary among cultures. The point is not just that results from applying the mischance principle will vary depending on culturally variant features such as architecture that help determine what can be uncovered by mischance; but that what *counts* as normal or legitimate inquiry or discovery by mischance itself is a judgment that will vary among societies depending on their customs and practices, architecture, and other culturally variant factors. But we are then led to ask whether this means that in using the principle we are stuck deferring to social practices that establish what counts as normal or legitimate inquiry, so that we have no way of criticizing surveillance practices in Nazi Germany or the Soviet Union or Orwell's 1984, or, for that matter, exposure practices in colonial New England or among the Mehinaku. If a society practices aerial surveillance, or accepts rifling through garbage, or the use of heat detection devices or bearcat scanners as part of "normal or legitimate inquiry," thereby expanding the scope of what is observable by mischance, must we accept as reasonable the diminished expectations of privacy that result?

The mischance principle protects us only against exposure that could not occur accidentally by a nonsnoop. A cordless phone conversation is not protected if the conversation could be detected by an FM radio or bearcat scanner, since these devices can be legitimately used in nonintrusive ways that accidentally expose the conversation. Similarly, the mischance principle offers no protection from people climbing up a tree to get a better view, since tree-climbing is a legitimate practice that might accidentally expose what we'd like to be private. The mischance principle may protect us against an officer climbing a ladder or using binoculars to look into a second-story apartment, if the inside of that apartment would not otherwise be observable by a nonsnoop engaged in legitimate or normal means of observation. Of course in our society people do legitimately climb ladders or use binoculars in nonintrusive ways, but when practiced in the accepted ways, these activities would not accidentally expose what goes on inside one's home. But suppose a society comes to adopt a practice of binocular viewing of homes or ladder-climbing near apartment dwellings? While the mischance principle does rely for its application on existing norms and practices, this does not prevent us from criticizing as unacceptably intrusive certain sorts of inquiries or means of exposure or practices that provide opportunities for accidental but intrusive exposure, even if they are prevalent.

The mischance principle is constrained by prevailing norms of acceptable inquiry. But what we *allow* to count as normal inquiry or exposure by mischance is not *just* a function of social practice. Certain forms of inquiry, though prevalent, may be incompatible with principles that we cherish. The fact that practices of exposure have been established that make it necessary to go to great lengths to secure privacy does not mean we are stuck with these practices. We might appeal to principles or values to criticize these practices and argue that even where there is no expectation of privacy there ought to be one. The court in *State v. Young,* recognizing that "as technology races ahead with ever increasing speed, our subjective expectations of privacy may be unconsciously altered," insists that "our legal rights to privacy should reflect thoughtful and purposeful choices rather than simply mirror the current state of the commercial technology industry."[113] Justice Warren, dissenting in *Breithaupt v. Abram,* notes that in *Rochin v. California* the Court held that forced stomach pumping violates due process and our sense of justice, even though stomach pumping is "common and accepted."[114] He implies that a practice's acceptance doesn't make it acceptable. Justice Douglas, also dissenting, invokes libertarian principles and a conception of human dignity to criticize the forced extraction.[115] For Douglas, even if this form of seizure were common practice, that would not justify it. Other judges and commentators have appealed to what is consistent with a free and civilized society to criticize prevalent practices of discovery. Justice Brennan, dissenting in *New Jersey v. TLO,* writes, "Considerations of the deepest significance for the freedom of our citizens counsel strict adherence" to the warrant and probable cause requirement.[116] Justice Douglas, dissenting in *U.S. v. White,* criticizes the Court for allowing the use of a wire on an invited guest to record and transmit a conversation directly to government agents, appealing to the value of freedom and an open society: We "must be free to pour out [our] woes or inspirations or dreams to others"; Douglas complains of the "chilling effect" of living in fear that our every word may be transmitted or recorded.[117]

We might think we shouldn't have to burn our papers before tossing them in the trash, curtain our tenth-floor windows to prevent an observer with binoculars from looking in from a hill a quarter mile away, speak in code in restaurants even when we are speaking at a level that could not normally be overheard, or worry either that our friends are spies and that what we reveal to them will be made known to the police, or that what we do in our backyards will be seen by government agents flying in helicopters overhead. Even in societies practicing garbage sifting, binocular observing, eavesdropping, spying, or low-flying observations, in which such exposure might occur accidentally in the process of a legitimate endeavor, we could still criticize these examples of "normal inquiry" by appealing to a conception of liberty or autonomy. To apply the mischance principle convincingly, we will need not merely a descriptive account of normal modes of inquiry but also something like a liberty-limiting principle that one invokes in arguing that what some may regard as legitimate inquiry really isn't legitimate.[118]

---

[113] 123 Wash 2d 173, 184 (1994).

[114] 352 US 432, 442; see *Rochin v. California,* 342 US 165 (1952).

[115] 352 US at 442–43.

[116] 469 US 325, 361 (1985).

[117] 401 US 745, 763, 765 (1971). Justice Marshall, dissenting in *Oliver v. U.S.,* writes that "if the police are permitted routinely to engage in such behavior, it will gradually become less offensive to us all" and this is a "serious danger" (466 U.S. 170, 196 n. 21 [1984]). Cf. Justice Brennan's dissent in *California v. Greenwood,* 486 U.S. 35 (1988). See also Amsterdam, "Perspectives on the Fourth Amendment": we should consider the capacity of the intrusion "to choke off free human discourse that is the hallmark of an open society" (388). Amsterdam concedes, though, that this isn't an administrable rule (416).

[118] In this chapter I am unable to say much about how such a principle might work with the mischance principle beyond the brief discussion in the application sections below.

Sometimes practice is unacceptable and needs to be criticized. If we lived in Orwell's 1984, I think we should do all we could to change the practices that frustrate expectations of privacy we ought to enjoy. They don't accord with the values of a free society. Living in colonial New England, though, we might think it reasonable to reconcile ourselves with many of the practices there and accept the expectations of privacy that result as reasonable, even if the practices could be better. There are cases where we will disagree about whether reconciliation or principled criticism is required.

But—and this is a crucial point—that we appeal to principles, such as a liberty-limiting principle, sometimes to criticize practices, does not mean we can use such principles—what in earlier chapters I called abstract principles—to decide all reasonable expectation of privacy issues. Existing practices provide a starting point, or ground, for determining reasonability. That we can criticize these practices if need be doesn't mean we don't need the starting point. Many of our judgments of reasonability are not subject to principled criticism "all the way down." For example, in our society it is reasonable to expect that when you enter a public restroom stall you will have privacy. If a critic asks why, we can respond that in our society evacuation is regarded as private. But if the adamant rationalist continues to ask why that should be and demands justification of the practice of evacuation in public restrooms (perhaps he finds it an unnecessary waste of re-sources to build stall doors, or destructive of communal spirit, so that he thinks it *is* in need of justification), it seems enough to say simply that this is the way it is and that given our practices, the expectation of privacy is reasonable.

In determining whether an expectation of privacy is reasonable, I have argued, we can appeal to the mischance principle, which itself appeals to practices of normal inquiry that shape what is subject to chance observation. We ask, first, whether what is exposed by an intentional search could have been accidentally discovered by a nonsnoop engaged in legitimate or normal means of observation or inquiry. If the answer is yes, before we can conclude that no reasonable expec-tation of privacy was violated we need to ask the further question whether society should require that we take measures to avoid the possibility of accidental expo-sure, that is, whether the means of exposure *should* be regarded as acceptable normal inquiry.

In this section I have argued for one particular principle of privacy ethics, a principle that no doubt needs further development for it persuasively to resolve the variety of issues brought before the courts in Fourth Amendment chal-lenges.[119] I have argued that application of this principle is constrained by social practices and norms. Other commentators have suggested still other principles determining whether an expectation of privacy is reasonable, and it is worthwhile

[119] The mischance principle invokes a conception of "legitimate means" of discovery; and reason-able people may well disagree about whether a means of discovery is legitimate. In deciding this we might use a descriptive standard, such as social practice; or intuitions; or we might use normative standards: I mention a conception of liberty or autonomy as an example, but say very little here about that conception or how it could be used. Precisely what practices of discovery a conception of liberty or autonomy would permit as legitimate, and what reasons would support restriction of liberty is a complex question requiring further work.

briefly addressing them, if only to show that these other principles, too, are also constrained by social practices.

Edward Bloustein appeals to a principle of "inviolate personality" in explaining why privacy should be protected and determining when it is unreasonably invaded. Those searches that are "an affront to personal dignity" are considered unreasonable.[120] But deciding what counts requires appeal to social practice. Bloustein gives an example of a tort case where the defendant was an unwanted spectator to the plaintiff's giving birth, and suggests this was an affront to the plaintiff's "individuality and human dignity."[121] But if childbirth is so shameful that observance affronts the mother's dignity, this is true only of certain cultures. Such shame is not universally experienced, and I am aware of no valid principles that would imply that it ought (or ought not) to be experienced. Similarly, when Bloustein writes that "a man whose home may be entered at the will of another, whose conversation may be overheard at the will of another . . . is less of a man, has *less human dignity* on that account," he implies what is simply not true for certain societies.[122] Colonial New Englanders, Javanese, or people living in the poorer sections of Naples are surely not "less human" because they happen not to have the practice of knocking on doors before entering. The principle may be true that exposure that affronts human dignity is unreasonable, and this principle helps explain why we should generally regard certain particularly invasive searches as unreasonable; for example, forced surgical extraction of a bullet for evidence or body-cavity searches.[123] But what counts as affronting human dignity depends on social practices.

Seeing the need for guidance in determining what is reasonable, some commentators have attempted to provide it by articulating still other principles. Noting how whether we have a reasonable expectation of privacy seems to depend on where we are located, one commentator has suggested that the reasonability of an expectation depends on the "degree to which society honors the intimacy or privacy of the activity normally carried on in [the place in question]."[124] Richard Wilkins, formulating a similar principle, sees it as one of three principles of reasonability: places bound with "intimate activity" and "privacies of life" get more protection; a search is unreasonable if "a given form of surveillance impermissibly intrudes upon the person"; and the reasonability of a search depends on the object of the search: interpersonal conversations are specially protected, for example, but fingerprints and handwriting is not.[125] All of these principles are

---

[120] Edward Bloustein, "Privacy as an Aspect of Human Dignity," in *Philosophical Dimensions of Privacy*, ed. Schoeman, 163. Bloustein is primarily concerned with cases of appropriation or publicity, where a man is made "part of commerce against his will," which he regards as degrading (176).

[121] Ibid., 164.

[122] Bloustein, "Privacy as an Aspect of Human Dignity," 165.

[123] The Court invalidated the use of surgery to retrieve a bullet in *Winston v. Lee*, 470 US 753 (1985); but it upheld body cavity searches of pretrial detainees in *Bell v. Wolfish*, 441 US 520 (1979) over Justice Marshall's vigorous dissent, in which he characterizes such searches as "one of the most grievous offenses against personal dignity and common decency" (at 576–77).

[124] Note, "Private Places," 983–84.

[125] Richard Wilkins, "Defining the 'Reasonable Expectation of Privacy': An Emerging Tripartite Analysis," *Vanderbilt Law Review* 40 (1987): 1103, 1112, 1116, 1121–22.

also constrained by social practice, in the sense both that they merely characterize social norms (or Supreme Court decisions); and that to know how to apply them we need to appeal to social practice. For example, to know what counts as "intimate activity," or as "impermissibly intrusive," or to know which objects of a search are specially protected, we need to go beyond these principles.[126] This is the case, too, with two other principles judges have used. In *State v. Schultz,* which concerned whether a search of garbage violated a reasonable expectation of privacy, Judge Anstead, dissenting from the majority's opinion upholding the search, decides the issue by invoking what might be called a principle of empathy. He has us imagine a man leaving his trash out on collection day only to have his neighbor rifle through it. The reaction to be expected is that "he would be absolutely incensed," and "the principle, of course, applies equally to the police."[127] The sort of reflection this principle requires us to undertake is one of appealing to intuitions that have their source and are reflected in social practice. I would be incensed if my neighbor looked through my garbage but only because this sort of thing is not done in my society and I don't expect it to be done.[128] Relying on this norm, I might not think much about discarding papers I don't want others to read, or think that I had better shred or burn them first. But suppose our practice was different. Suppose concern with the environment increased dramatically and recycling took on extreme urgency; severe moral condemnation comes to be expressed at those who throw away what can be recycled. Or imagine a society that deals with the needs of the poor by encouraging food scavenging, and the more well-to-do purposely discard excess food in their trash bins as a way of redistributing wealth. Members of these societies may well shred documents they don't want exposed, precisely because they cannot expect privacy in their garbage.[129] Whether incense is an appropriate response to a neighbor's rifling through one's garbage, then, depends on social practice.

In *Soli v. Superior Court of Mendocino County,* the court determines whether an expectation of privacy is reasonable by appealing to a principle of personal security: we apply not "differing constitutional standards to various locales," but rather

---

[126] "Private Places," 983–84.

[127] 388 So 2d 1326, 1331 (1980).

[128] In some municipalities it is against the law to seize garbage once it is put by the curbside for pickup. See *State v. Boland,* 800 P 2d 1112 (Washington 1990), at 1114. Some of these ordinances are motivated by health rather than privacy concerns (see 800 P 2d at 1120, dissent).

[129] Justice White, in *California v. Greenwood,* 486 US 35 (1988), argues that there is no reasonable expectation of privacy in one's garbage in our society in part because he believes garbage is frequently rummaged through by scavengers. He cites a nationally syndicated consumer columnist who "has suggested that apartment dwellers obtain cents-off coupons by 'mak[ing] friends with the fellow who handles the trash' in their buildings, and has recounted the tale of 'the "Rich lady" from Westmont who once a week puts on rubber gloves and hip boots and wades into the town garbage dump looking for labels and other proofs of purchase' needed to obtain manufacturers' refunds" (40, note 3). Justice White fails to distinguish these instances where garbage of many people intermingled together is gone through, from the facts in *California v. Greenwood,* where Greenwood's trash was purposely not mixed with trash from his neighbors so that the police could find out something about Greenwood. The case is discussed further below.

a single standard of reasonableness to all places in accordance with a fundamental understanding that a particular intrusion into one domain of human existence seriously threatens personal security, while the same intrusion into another domain does not.[130]

Again, what counts as seriously threatening personal security will depend on social practice. Entering a home without knocking may be threatening in our society but is not threatening in others.

Incorporating Practice and Principle in Fourth Amendment Reasonable-Expectation-of-Privacy Analysis: The Mischance Principle Applied

Courts sometimes decide whether an expectation of privacy is reasonable or unreasonable simply by deferring to current practices of protection and exposure. In *Minnesota v. Olson,* the Court confirms that guests in homes have a legitimate privacy expectation, noting: "To hold that an overnight guest has a legitimate expectation of privacy in his host's home merely recognizes the everyday expectation of privacy that we all share. Staying overnight in another's home is a long-standing social custom that serves functions recognized as valuable by society."[131] Sometimes courts may appeal to a practice of regulation the prevalence of which is said to undermine any claim to a reasonable expectation of privacy. In *Schoemaker v. Handel,* for example, the court, in holding that drug testing of jockeys doesn't violate reasonable expectations of privacy, appeals to a history of regulation in the industry that makes any expectation of privacy there unreasonable: "The Commission historically has exercised its rulemaking authority in ways that have reduced the justifiable privacy expectations of persons engaged in the horse-racing industry."[132]

Practice shapes judgments of when expectations of privacy are reasonable. But the existence of practices of surveillance doesn't necessarily justify them.[133] The lack of privacy among the colonists, Mehinaku and Siriono was in many cases a reasonable response to constraints; the lack of privacy in the Soviet Union or Nazi

---

[130] 103 Cal App 3d 72, 162 Cal. Rptr. 840 (1980); citing *People v. Dumas,* 9 Cal 3d 871, 881–3.

[131] 495 US 91, 98 (1990).

[132] 795 F 2d at 1142. See also *Camara v. Municipal Court of the City and County of San Francisco,* 387 US 523, 548–50, 554 (1967), Justice Clark dissenting, on how a common practice of administrative searches means they are reasonable; *Schaill v. Tippecanoe County School Corp.,* 864 F 2d 1309, 1319 (1988): the "pervasiveness of drug testing in professional and collegiate athletics in this country and in the Olympic games" implies a reduced expectation of privacy on the part of high-school athletes against random urine drug testing.

[133] Cf. *Entick v. Carrington,* (K.B. 1765) 19 Howell's St. Tr. 1029, 95 Eng Rep 807, in which Lord Camden ruled that the British government's use of general warrants are invalid. They were defended as consistent with custom, and Lord Camden replies that the existence of a practice of issuing warrants is no defense of them (at 1067–68).

Germany was often not. We get nowhere in explaining why if we simply defer to prevailing practices. I have argued for a principle of privacy ethics—the mischance principle—that can help us distinguish permissible and impermissible forms of exposure. In considering a form of exposure we ask, first, whether it reveals what could not be accidentally discovered by a nonsnoop using legitimate or normal means of observation or inquiry. Asking this question requires making reference to social practices and norms of acceptable inquiry or observation. But this does not end the inquiry, for even if we regard an activity as subject to accidental exposure through normal or legitimate inquiry or mischance, we can ask the further question whether it *ought* to be so regarded. In answering that question, we might find that while society might not regard as reasonable an expectation of privacy against a form of exposure, it ought to, perhaps because in analogous situations expectations of privacy are respected, perhaps because not regarding such an expectation of privacy as reasonable would be incompatible with the values of an open and free society. In this section we turn to specific applications of the mischance principle to show both how the principle can be used as a critical tool in adjudicating Fourth Amendment cases, and how application of the mischance principle requires appeal to and is shaped by social practices and norms.

Garbage

In *California v. Greenwood,* police officers asked the trash collector in respondent Greenwood's neighborhood to pick up the plastic garbage bags that Greenwood left on the curb in front of his house, and turn them over before their contents were mixed with garbage from other houses. Searching through the rubbish, the officers found items indicating narcotics use and used this evidence to secure a warrant to search Greenwood's home, where they discovered cocaine and hashish. Greenwood was convicted of felony narcotics charges and challenged the conviction by arguing it relied on evidence obtained in violation of his Fourth Amendment rights. Justice White, writing for a majority of six Justices, argued that while Greenwood may have had a subjective expectation of privacy in the contents of his garbage, society is not prepared to accept that expectation as objectively reasonable.[134]

Justice White bases this conclusion primarily on what looks like an application of the mischance principle. He argues:

> It is common knowledge that plastic garbage bags left on or at the side of a public street are readily accessible to animals, children, scavengers, snoops, and other members of the public. [M]oreover, respondents placed their refuse at the curb for the express purpose of conveying it to a third party, the trash collector, who might himself have sorted through respondents' trash or permitted others, such as the police, to do so . . .

[134] 486 US at 37–38 (1988). The decision was 6–2. Justice Kennedy took no part in the case.

[T]he police cannot reasonably be expected to avert their eyes from evidence of criminal activity that could have been observed by any member of the public.[135]

For the majority, the possibility of accidental exposure of Greenwood's trash and therefore of the evidence of narcotics use reasonably negates any expectation of privacy Greenwood might have in his garbage.

We have seen that the mischance principle does not hold simply that if exposure is physically possible there is no reasonable expectation that whatever can be exposed remain private. We should have to protect ourselves only from exposure that can reasonably happen by accident, and this requires an idea of what sorts of normal inquiries or unintentional exposures our society should tolerate. Social norms require us sometimes to look the other way to avoid uncovering what is physically exposed or to prevent taking affirmative measures even if exposure could occur by accident.

Justice White suggests several different ways garbage might be exposed, without critically examining whether the possibility of exposure in each instance is of a sort against which it is reasonable to expect us to have to take measures to protect our privacy. His first suggestion that "snoops" might rifle through our garbage can easily be dismissed. That objectionable behavior occurs doesn't mean we should tolerate it. Snoops do frustrate our expectations of privacy. Given the threat of snoops, some of us take protective measures, such as ripping up or burning important papers. Before discarding expired plastic credit cards, one might cut them into many pieces so they don't come into the wrong hands.[136] But that I take this precaution does not mean I have no reasonable expectation of privacy in my garbage, just as the fact that most of us put locks on our doors does not mean we shouldn't or don't expect privacy in our homes.[137] Most of us look down on snoops.[138] Justice White, perplexingly, uses the snoop as a standard of

---

[135] 486 US at 40–41.

[136] See *New York Times*, Oct. 13, 1995, A7, on a sophisticated fraud ring that stole more than $10 million partly by recovering discarded checks, deposit slips, and credit card receipts from dumpsters and trash cans.

[137] See the dissent in *California v. Greenwood*: the possibility of burglary doesn't negate an expectation of privacy in one's home (486 US at 54). Cf. the dissent in *State v. Schultz*, 388 So 2d 1326: that scavengers and snoops rummage through garbage doesn't make it right for the police to do so: "two wrongs do not make a right" (1331).

[138] See *State v. Hempele*, 576 A 2d 793 (1990), "most people seem to. . ." (803); "A free and civilized society should comport itself with more decency" (815); also, the *Greenwood* Court and other courts that deny there is a reasonable expectation of privacy in one's garbage "are flatly and simply wrong as the matter [sic] the way people think about garbage" (814–15); *State v. Boland*, 800 P 2d 1112 (1990): "Average persons would find it reasonable to believe the garbage they place in their trash cans will be protected from warrantless governmental intrusion" (1116); *State v. Tanaka*, 701 P 2d 1974 (1985): "People reasonably believe that police will not indiscriminately rummage through their trash bags to discover their personal effects" (1276); *State v. Schultz*, 388 So 2d 1326 (1980), dissent: "I think the average person does, in fact, have an expectation of privacy in this situation, and the pervasiveness of that expectation demonstrates its reasonableness" (1331); Justice Brennan, dissenting in *Greenwood*: "The American society with which I am familiar 'chooses to dwell in reasonable security and freedom from surveillance,' . . . and is more dedicated to individual liberty and more sensitive to intrusions on the sanctity of the home than the Court is willing to acknowledge"; and

acceptable conduct. The mischance principle is designed to prevent using the snoop's behavior as a standard for reasonableness, by declaring that we forfeit a reasonable expectation of privacy in an activity only if our activity can be observed by a *nonsnoop* using legitimate or normal means of observation or inquiry. The mischance principle assumes that the prevalence of snooping, or the prevalence of technologies of surveillance intended to uncover information in which someone has a privacy interest, cannot serve as a bootstrap for defining legitimate means of observation or inquiry.

Justice White's other examples, unlike that of the deviant snoop, or the equally deviant curious and enterprising trash collector, involve instances of accidental exposure of garbage. He notes that garbage is often rummaged through by scavengers. Scavengers, unlike snoops who intend to expose private facts, usually are just looking for something to eat. Justice White's argument seems to be that our society condones scavenging—and given this accepted practice, we can't expect that what we put in our trash will remain private.[139] This argument, too, needs critical scrutiny. If most scavenging occurs at dumpsters, than its prevalence says nothing about the reasonability of expectations of privacy in *nonintermingled* trash. The trash in the opaque containers left out for pickup is not subject to accidental exposure by scavengers going through public garbage cans or dumpsters. But even if the scavenger does practice in single-home neighborhoods, what he practices is unlikely to expose the intimate details of our lives that we want to keep private, unless the scavenger becomes a snoop. When he does, then the same arguments advanced for why the prevalence of snoops does not mean we forfeit reasonable expectations of privacy in our garbage can be applied to the scavenger.

The scavenger can also expose what we want to keep private in the same way animals and children might when they rifle through one's nonintermingled garbage. While few scavengers and children and no animal would read the scribble on our discarded papers, all may undermine the integrity of garbage containers, leaving its contents exposed to the wind. The dissent in *Greenwood* notes: "Had Greenwood flaunted his intimate activity by strewing his trash all over the curb for all to see, or had some nongovernmental intruder invaded his privacy and done the same, I could accept the Court's conclusion that an expectation of privacy would have been unreasonable."[140] Had "'animals, children, scavengers, snoops, [or] other members of the public' . . . *actually* rummage[d] through a bag of trash and expose[d] its contents to plain view," police may have been justified in searching for we then could not expect them to avert their eyes.[141]

Washington Post, editorial, July 10, 1975, criticizing National Enquirer reporter Jay Gourley's searching of Henry Kissinger's trash: "It is a question first of all of the way decent people behave in relation to each other, a question of how we permit one another to live."

[139] See 486 US at 40, n. 3, where Justice White notes an example of rummaging through a dumpster. See also *State v. Schultz*, 388 So 2d 1326 (1980), where the Court, in declaring an expectation of privacy in one's garbage unreasonable, argues that the "social practice of rummaging through garbage made the expectation of privacy unreasonable"(1029).

[140] 486 US at 53.

[141] Ibid.

The dissent seems right that it matters that this is not how the police in this case came to observe the contents of Greenwood's garbage. Consider the following, more restrictive version of the mischance principle: unless an act of exposure is of a sort of activity that society regards as legitimate but which could be employed by a nonsnoop in a way that accidentally exposes information, there is a reasonable expectation of privacy against this exposure. We might call this the *search-relative mischance principle* because it focuses on the means of intrusion, rather than the object being exposed. On this principle the search in *Greenwood* would clearly be invalid absent a warrant. The police in *Greenwood* did *not* simply view papers scattered in the wind; the activity they undertook, rather, was the securing of nonintermingled trash, and that is not an act of a sort that could be employed by a nonsnoop in a way that accidentally exposes information.

There are reasons to prefer the search-relative mischance principle to the formulation of the mischance principle we so far have used, which we might call the *object-relative mischance principle*. Suppose I bury something in my backyard. A dog might dig it up, but does this fact warrant police officers without a warrant, or snoops, from doing the same? On the object-relative mischance principle it may, and that seems wrong. That it seems wrong intuitively is supported by considering that it would be normal and reasonable to express outrage at someone digging up what I've buried in my backyard, an outrage beyond that which we would express merely because someone has trespassed. The example shows the force of the more restrictive search-relative mischance principle. According to the principle, it is unacceptable for police to use extremely invasive techniques of surveillance without a warrant on the grounds that what they uncover *could* have been discovered in legitimate ways. This is particularly so if the legitimate means of exposure is unreliable or uncertain, as in the case of a dog by chance digging up evidence in someone's backyard and carrying it to the street or sidewalk, or of children happening to knock over a garbage can and the wind blowing evidence onto the street. In such instances the use of more invasive techniques reveals what in all likelihood would not have been uncovered. Of course more invasive techniques of surveillance often will reveal information that could not possibly be exposed by normal or legitimate means of observation or inquiry, and this is why they will generally be ruled out by the less restrictive "object-relative" mischance principle.

Because it is more restrictive, not all of us will want to adhere to the search-relative mischance principle. In defending the mischance principle by appealing to intuitions or to societal norms regarding what methods of discovery are appropriate, our results will be convincing only where we share the same intuitions or where society is in agreement about norms of appropriate discovery, and this may not always be the case. When employing the less restrictive object-relative mischance principle, warrantless police searches of garbage may seem valid on the grounds that what the police discovered might have been discovered by a nonsnoop using otherwise legitimate or normal means of observation or inquiry. But this conclusion is reached too quickly. It assumes, first, that the contents of one's garbage could have been accidentally discovered in legitimate ways. It may be reasonable to expect people who want the contents of their garbage to remain private to take measures to prevent animals or children from exposing nonintermingled trash if it is likely or even merely possible that this will occur. But if I live in an adults-only complex where animals and children aren't allowed, it would be unreasonable to expect this. On the logic of the mischance principle, a version of which he himself implicitly invokes, Justice White should allow that there *can* be a reasonable expectation of privacy in garbage that is reasonably secured against accidental exposures. Leaving aside snoops, he should allow that if I place my trash in an opaque bag securely tied, and place the bag in a metal garbage can with a lid, and secure the lid with a heavy piece of wood, then I have a reasonable expectation of privacy in my trash.[142]

Justice White's conclusion that Greenwood lacks a reasonable expectation of privacy also assumes that our society regards it as legitimate and nonintrusive to look upon open trash—Justice White's conclusion assumes the possibility of such "normal inquiry" exposing Greenwood's use of narcotics. In other words, from the fact that animals and children occasionally undermine the integrity of garbage bags, Justice White leaps to the conclusion that rummaging through exposed nonintermingled trash in pursuit of private information is normal inquiry or legitimate. Even if he were right about the likelihood of exposure of the contents of the bags to the wind, and of a nonsnoop legitimately scrutinizing exposed trash, we could still argue that our society *should* not accept nonpurposive rummaging through nonintermingled, exposed trash as "normal inquiry." One could argue persuasively that our society ought to have a norm requiring people to avoid carefully scrutinizing exposed nonintermingled trash, if indeed such a norm does not already exist.

If the mischance principle's application to *Greenwood* is at least complicated by the fact that garbage cans can be knocked over and plastic bags ripped by animals, leaving private papers exposed to the wind and available to the curious eye, its application to a more recent garbage case is clearcut and provides what I take to be a compelling criticism of the law as it now stands. In *U.S. v. Scott,* the IRS suspected respondent Scott of filing false income tax returns. They seized his garbage without warrant and combed through it. The contents included papers that Scott had shredded. The agents patiently pieced together 5/32-inch shredded strips, and used the resulting evidence to request various search warrants that let them secure additional evidence to indict Scott. The Court of Appeals for the first circuit, reversing the district court, allowed the seizure.[143] On *any* plausible interpretation of the mischance principle, this is a bad decision because what was exposed could not have been discovered by accident. Scott's expectation of pri-

---

[142] These were the facts in *State v. Boland,* 800 P 2d 1112 (1990), which found a search of garbage to violate the Washington state constitution. Cf. Bush and Bly, "Expectations of Privacy Analysis and Warrantless Trash Reconnaissance after Katz," *Arizona Law Review* 23 (1981), 314–16: reasonability of expectations of privacy in garbage depends on factors such as where the garbage is placed and whether it is in a covered metal can.

[143] *U.S. v. Scott,* 975 F 2d 927 (1992).

vacy was reasonable, and if agents must have the evidence to convict Scott, they should get a warrant.[144]

Aerial Surveillance

One of the examples introducing this chapter concerned a police search of a greenhouse behind the respondent Riley's mobile home from a helicopter flying four hundred feet overhead. The Court upheld that warrantless search, citing as precedent a case decided three years previously.[145] In that case, *California v. Ciraolo,* police had received an anonymous telephone tip that marijuana was growing in the respondent's backyard. Unable to observe the yard from ground level due to a six-foot outer and a ten-foot inner fence, officers trained in marijuana identification secured a private plane and flew over the house at 1,000 feet, observing a marijuana grow and photographing it with a 35mm camera. With this evidence they secured a warrant of the home and seized evidence used to convict the respondent. The respondent sought to suppress the evidence as the fruit of an unconstitutional search.[146]

A 5–4 majority upheld the warrantless search in *Ciraolo,* implicitly invoking the mischance principle. Chief Justice Burger argued that the marijuana was seen "in plain view." While the respondent may have had a subjective expectation of privacy in his backyard, especially as he enclosed it with fences, this expectation is unreasonable because, despite the fences, the contents of the yard still could be observed accidentally through normal inquiry: "[A] 10-foot fence might not shield these plants from the eyes of a citizen or a policeman perched on the top of a truck or a two-level bus."[147] Exposure, Burger suggests, could reasonably be the result "of a casual, accidental observation."[148] Of course, unless the plants were fairly tall and there was a line of sight from the street to the yard, they couldn't possibly be seen even by someone on the top deck of a two-level bus. Even if there *were* any double-decker buses in California, or people were to perch themselves on top of trucks, and assuming Riley's backyard was not obstructed from the view of someone on the street, it is still unclear that the marijuana plants could be observed. The closer I stand to a wall, the less visible I become to someone on the other side. The further away the person on the other side stands from the wall the higher the vantage point they would need. If a fence is f feet tall and of negligible width, and marijuana within the fence border is positioned d feet from the fence, and if h is the height one must be at to see the very top of the marijuana when positioned outside the fence, x is the distance one stands outside the fence, and a is the height of the marijuana, then $h = [f(x + d) - ax]/d$. So if the

---

[144] The question is not just what tax evaders must do, but what you and I must do as well. In *U.S. v. Scott,* the court based its decision primarily on the dubious notion that criminals don't have Fourth Amendment rights.

[145] *Florida v. Riley,* 488 US 445 (1989).

[146] 476 US 207 (1986).

[147] 476 US at 211.

[148] 476 US at 212.

marijuana plants are 6 feet high, 10 feet on the inside of a 10 foot fence, and a double-decker bus is driving along a road at a distance of 30 feet from the fence, someone on the bus would have to be at a height of 22 feet to see the very top of the marijuana and at 40 feet to see the full plant. If the same marijuana were placed 2 feet inside the fence, the observer would have to be at a height of 70 feet to see the very top, and at 160 feet to see the entire plant. Perhaps realizing this, Chief Justice Burger does not rely solely on this example of casual accidental observation and adds that the respondent's marijuana plants could have been accidentally observed also by "any member of the public flying in this airspace who glanced down."[149] To support this claim Burger notes that "private and commercial flight in the public airways is routine."[150]

The same argument was invoked in *Florida v. Riley*. Justice White, writing for a plurality of four Justices, noted that helicopters flying at four hundred feet are not "sufficiently rare in this country to lend substance to respondent's claim that he reasonably anticipated that his greenhouse would not be subject to observation from that altitude."[151] "Any member of the public could legally have been flying over Riley's property in a helicopter at the altitude of 400 feet and could have observed Riley's greenhouse."[152] Justice White implies that such observation should not be unexpected given that more than ten thousand helicopters are registered in the United States.[153] Justice O'Connor, concurring, and Justice Blackmun, in dissent, agreed that whether Riley's expectation of privacy is reasonable hinges on "the frequency of nonpolice helicopter flights at an altitude of 400 feet."[154] Justice Blackmun, however, would put the burden of proof on the prosecution to establish this frequency, and remand the case.

The decisions in both *Riley* and *Ciraolo* defend aerial surveillance on the ground that it is so prevalent that people should not reasonably expect that activities that can possibly be seen from the skies remain private. Presumably this means that nude sunbathers should not reasonably expect to remain unobserved. Justice White, at the very end of his decision in *Florida v. Riley*, casually suggests that it made a difference that "no intimate details connected with the use of the home or curtilage were observed" but does not otherwise distinguish acceptably and unacceptably intrusive aerial observation, apart from adding that aerial sur-

---

[149] 476 US at 213.

[150] 476 US at 215.

[151] 488 US 445, 451 (1989).

[152] 488 US at 451. In both *Riley* and *Ciraolo*, it was relevant that the officers were complying with FAA safety regulations so that they were where they had a right to be. See *California v. Ciraolo*, 476 US at 213 ("from a public vantage point where he has a right to be"); and *Florida v. Riley*, 488 US at 451. O'Connor, in her concurrence to *Riley*, argues that the majority makes too much of the helicopter's compliance with FAA safety regulations: "the relevant inquiry after *Ciraolo* is not whether the helicopter was where it had a right to be under FAA regulations. Rather, consistent with *Katz*, we must ask whether the helicopter was in the public airways at an altitude at which members of the public travel with sufficient regularity that Riley's expectation of privacy from aerial observation was not 'one that society is prepared to recognize as "reasonable" '"(454).

[153] 488 US at 450, note 2.

[154] 488 US at 455 (O'Connor); 488 US at 467 (Blackmun).

veillance may be unduly intrusive if it creates undue noise, wind, dust, or threat of injury.[155]

There are two ways to criticize the decisions in *Riley* and *Ciraolo*. One way is to object to their acceptance of aerial surveillance as "normal inquiry" by arguing that despite the possibly widespread use of new technologies of exposure, we should not condone their use in undermining society's interest in privacy. In other words, we can appeal to the value of privacy and related values of liberty and autonomy to criticize the spread of technology, to take a stand against the spread of new practices of exposure. In doing so we would be promoting a norm that requires us to avoid uncovering what is physically exposed when in a plane or helicopter. The version of the mischance principle I have sketched, while appealing to descriptive norms of inquiry, also leaves room for criticizing even a prevalent practice as illegitimate.

The dissenters in both *Riley* and *Ciraolo* at times take this approach. Justice Brennan, dissenting in *Florida v. Riley*, appeals to principles to criticize the practice of aerial surveillance. For Brennan the issue is not the prevalence of this practice of surveillance but rather

> whether, if the particular form of surveillance practiced by the police is permitted to go unregulated by constitutional restraints, the amount of privacy and freedom remaining to citizens would be diminished to a compass inconsistent with the aims of a free and open society.[156]

Merely because technology is available doesn't mean we should legitimate its use. The fact that it comes to be used, and even that it frustrates expectations of privacy, does not mean an expectation of privacy against the exposure the technology facilitates is unreasonable. Justice Brennan writes that "the extent of police surveillance traffic cannot serve as a bootstrap to demonstrate public use of the airspace."[157] But neither can it serve as a bootstrap to demonstrate the reasonability of this practice of surveillance.

Justice Powell also appeals to the value of privacy and related values to criticize the trend of aerial surveillance. Dissenting in *California v. Ciraolo*, he writes that

---

[155] 488 US at 452. A distinction between acceptably and unacceptably intrusive observations is at work in *U.S. v. Cuevas-Sanchez*, 821 F 2d 248 (1987). Here the court refused to extend *Ciraolo* to video surveillance of defendant's backyard from a power pole bordering his property, because government surveillance was not a minimal intrusion but allowed a continuous record of all activity in defendant's backyard. See John Wesley Hall, *Search and Seizure*, 2d ed. (New York: Clark Boardman Callaghan, 1991), 1:541. See also *Commonwealth v. Oglialoro*, 579 A 2d 1288 (1990): police hovered over a barn at fifty feet for fifteen seconds and made three or more passes lasting five minutes or so; the defendant's wife testified that she experienced loud noise, and vibration of the house and windows. The court held that this search endangered people or property on the ground and thus was unreasonable. See also *U.S. v. Saltzman*, 992 F 2d 1219 (1993). But see *Moss v. State*, 878 SW 2d 632 (1994): an aerial search was upheld despite the fact that the helicopter used created a great disturbance, damaged tomato and other plants, and frightened children. The court noted that flights were common and this particular flight complied with FAA regulations.

[156] 488 US at 456.

[157] 488 US at 465.

"it is not easy to believe that our society is prepared to force individuals to bear the risk of this type of warrantless police intrusion into their residential areas."[158] In developing this point, Powell observes that "few build roofs over their backyards";[159] while he notes this in order to respond to the Court's suggestion that people "knowingly expose their residential yards to the public," the observation helps advance this first criticism: people should not *have* to build roofs over their backyards just because a new method of surveillance has become available.

To criticize the outcomes in *Riley* and *Ciraolo,* though, it is unnecessary to reach the question of whether aerial surveillance ought to be accepted as normal inquiry. For the police searches at issue in these cases fail the first step of the mischance principle test. The Court is simply wrong in holding that the searches revealed what could be accidentally exposed by nonsnoops through normal inquiry.

Exposure from the observations of plane passengers or pilots is not the sort of contingency we typically take into account or should have to take into account in ordering our lives (for example, in deciding whether in our backyard we should sunbathe nude, dance around when in a giddy mood, practice martial arts, or even grow marijuana).[160] Such exposure might happen, just as snoops might rummage through our garbage or burglars might wrongfully enter our home. But if it happens, it's not the result of mischance. Identifying marijuana or any activity in a backyard while flying overhead at one thousand or even four hundred feet (let alone above ten thousand feet, where most commercial passengers fly) requires a concentrated effort, not a mere glance. To identify an activity as well as the particular location where it occurs would require seeking out details of the house that could allow its address to be discerned. In other words, any aerial surveillance that could invade privacy necessarily requires affirmative measures and can't be done accidentally by a nonsnoop. Such exposure from the skies, while perhaps possible (at least from four hundred feet), is not prevalent or "commonplace."[161] While exposure would have to be intentional to uncover what Riley and Ciraolo concealed, the point is not that it is never permissible to be a snoop—that position was rejected earlier. The point, rather, is that no legitimate form of observation or inquiry by a nonsnoop could accidentally reveal what Riley and Ciraolo concealed, and so their expectations of privacy were reasonable. To see what they concealed, one did not merely have to fly a plane within legal airspace (which is legitimate), but fly slowly, hover, identify a place, squint. The license to fly is not normally the license to conduct surveillance.

---

[158] 476 US at 225.

[159] 476 US at 224.

[160] There are other reasons for not growing marijuana in our backyard. There is the moral reason that doing so is against the law. And there are prudential reasons: police may conduct aerial searches with a warrant; the marijuana may be discovered by a neighbor (and evidence from private searches may be the basis for probable cause to obtain a warrant).

[161] 488 US at 460: "the question before us must be . . . whether public observation of Riley's curtilage was so commonplace that Riley's expectation of privacy in his backyard could not be considered reasonable."

In *California v. Ciraolo,* Justice Powell, in dissent, argues that "members of the public use the airspace for travel, business, or pleasure, not for the purpose of observing activities taking place within residential yards."[162] "The actual risk to privacy from commercial or pleasure aircraft is virtually nonexistent."[163] In our society there is no general norm of observation from airplanes or helicopters that would support the claim that observation of private activities from the skies can occur by accident. What we regard as exposed to "plain view" depends on what we regard as "plain" ways of viewing. Viewing from a plane is not plain viewing. Justices Powell and Brennan both adhere to the mischance principle, as do the majorities in *Riley* and *Ciraolo,* but provide a more convincing account of the prevalence of the practice of aerial surveillance—as distinguished from aerial *travel.* That aerial surveillance is not generally part of normal inquiry in our society, I think, convincingly shows the error of *Riley* and *Ciraolo* and makes it unnecessary to appeal to the second-prong of the mischance principle test.

However, relying on the first prong of the test, we leave open the possibility that some aerial surveillance may be constitutional. *People v. Mayoff* concerned a search conducted by aerial surveillance in Humboldt County, California. Agent Brown flew at an altitude of one thousand to fifteen hundred feet to identify areas where marijuana was being cultivated. He conducted a general exploratory search that happened to uncover a marijuana grow on the defendant's property. The court upheld the warrantless search by invoking the mischance principle. The court noted that

> Defendant's land is in a rugged, mountainous, wooded area that is sparsely populated. . . .[164]
>
> The record indicates that commercial carriers, private planes, Forest Service planes, and livestock investigators have been seen flying over Humboldt County. The Humboldt tax assessor flew over the entire county. Humboldt County admittedly has a paucity of good roads in its remote, wooded rural areas. However, these areas are also subject to forest fires. . . . The only practical method of law enforcement and assistance is through the use of aircraft patrol.[165]

Given local conditions, and "the other private and official flights passing over the land," the defendant should have expected such surveillance.

According to the mischance principle, we should have to protect ourselves only from exposure that can happen by accident (without an intention to uncover information in which someone has a privacy interest) through otherwise normal or legitimate means of observation or inquiry. In Humboldt County aerial surveillance is an accepted and *justified* practice, and as a result expectations of privacy against exposure that can result from aerial surveillance are unreasonable. The exposure in this case falls within a sort of activity society regards as legitimate and which could be employed by nonsnoops in a way that accidentally exposes infor-

---

[162] 476 US at 224.

[163] 476 US at 223.

[164] 197 Cal Rptr 450, 452 (1983).

[165] 197 Cal Rptr 450, 453. Cf. Note, "What Is a Reasonable Expectation of Privacy?" *Washington State University Law Review* 12 (1985): 854.

mation. But in most other places in the country, aerial surveillance, as opposed to aerial travel, is not commonplace, nor acceptable normal inquiry; and the mischance principle, which requires that we take into account both the role of technology as well as its accepted normal use as manifested in social practice, does not dictate that we generally forfeit reasonable expectations of privacy in the face of this means of exposure.

Heat Detection (FLIR Devices)

A third example of police searches without warrant that raises Fourth Amendment concerns involves a forward-looking infrared (FLIR) device, which highlights manmade heat sources. The device can detect a human form through an open window when the person is pressing against a curtain or leaning against a relatively thin barrier such as a plywood door.[166] The device also can disclose which rooms a homeowner is heating, perhaps his "financial inability to heat the entire home," and possibly the number of people in the home.[167]

The FLIR device has been characterized as "a passive, non-intrusive instrument. . . . It does not send any beams or rays into the area on which it is fixed or in any way penetrate structures within that area."[168] Normal uses include locating missing persons in a forest, identifying inefficient building insulation, and detection of forest fire lines through smoke.[169] The device is increasingly used by law enforcement agents to detect marijuana growing labs. One National Guard captain testified that an infrared tracking device was used to view structures more than fifty times to apply for twelve warrants and uncovered ten marijuana grows.[170] A DEA agent testified to having used the device at least forty-two times.[171]

In *U.S. v. Penny-Feeney*, the federal district court for the district of Hawaii upheld the use of an FLIR device from a helicopter flying three hundred to six hundred feet above the petitioner's residence. The device revealed that a significant amount of heat was being released from the garage, leading the officer conducting the warrantless search to conclude that the structure was being used "for the purpose of cultivating marijuana under artificial lighting."[172] In rejecting the defendant's motion to suppress evidence obtained in a search pursuant to a warrant issued in part on the basis of the results of the FLIR search, the court declared that there is no legitimate expectation of privacy in "heat waste." There is no subjective expectation of privacy "since [petitioners] voluntarily vented [the heat waste] outside the garage where it could be exposed to the public and in no way attempted to impede its escape or exercise dominion over it." Even if there were a subjective expectation

[166] *State v. Young*, 123 Wash 2d 173, 177 (1994).
[167] 123 Wash 2d at 183.
[168] *U.S. v. Penny-Feeney*, 773 F Supp 220, 223 (1991).
[169] 773 F Supp 220, 223 n. 4.
[170] *U.S. v. Casanova*, 835 F Supp 702, 704 n. 2 (1993).
[171] *U.S. v. Porco*, 842 F Supp 1393 (1994).
[172] 773 F Supp at 224.

of privacy, the court held, *Greenwood* implies that it is not one "that society would be willing to accept as objectively reasonable."[173] Another consideration for the court was that use of the FLIR device is not very intrusive: "Use of the FLIR . . . entailed no embarrassment to or search of the person."[174] Several courts have followed *Penny-Feeney* in upholding FLIR searches. In *U.S. v. Porco,* the federal district court of Wyoming found the FLIR device "non-intrusive" and declared that the defendant had no subjective expectation of privacy in his heat waste, having done nothing to prevent heat from escaping apart from covering his windows; and that even if he did, *Greenwood* dictates that such an expectation would be unreasonable.[175] In another case, *U.S. v. Kyllo,* which also allowed a warrantless FLIR search, the government defended its use of the device by arguing it does not "reveal intimate details as to the inside of the home," adding that "intimacy," "personal autonomy," and "privacy" are not threatened. The government also compared discovery of heat waste to discovery of smoke from a chimney.[176] At least two courts have struck down FLIR searches.[177]

We might think the issue of whether FLIR searches are permissible is easily decided by application of the mischance principle. As one of the two courts disallowing both aerial and ground FLIR searches observed, "the thermal images recorded by this technology were not in plain view from the aircraft or the ground."[178] The court suggested that had the law enforcement agent simply "felt" excessive heat being released from the building no reasonable expectation of privacy would be violated, but the use of a "high tech sensory device" makes the invasion of privacy unreasonable.[179] The other court finding a warrantless FLIR search unconstitutional similarly noted that the device enables police to see more than the respondent left exposed.[180] Both courts implicitly invoke a mischance principle. If heat waste were discoverable simply by walking along a sidewalk and feeling the emission, then we could not reasonably expect to keep private the amount of heat we release. But to discover the amount of heat used in a marijuana grow laboratory a sophisticated device not in common use is required. Use of the

---

[173] 773 F Supp at 226.

[174] 773 F Supp at 227. The Ninth Circuit Court of Appeals affirmed the district court decision denying suppression of the evidence obtained from warrants eventually issued, but on the ground that there was probable cause for the warrants independent of the FLIR search; the constitutionality of FLIR searches was not considered by the appellate court. See *U.S. v. Feeney,* 984 F 2d 1053 (1993).

[175] 842 F Supp 1393 (1994), at 1398, 1397.

[176] *U.S. v. Kyllo,* 809 F Supp 787, 792 (1993). See also *U.S. v. Domitrovich,* 852 F Supp 1460 (1994), finding unreasonable an expectation of privacy in heat waste and arguing that use of the FLIR device is not unduly invasive (at 1474); *State v. De Fusco,* 606 A 2d 1 (1992); *U.S. v. Pinson,* 24 F 3d 1056 (1994); *U.S. v. Robertson,* 39 F 3d 891 (1994); and *Boren v. State,* 1991 WL 268467.

[177] See *State v. Young,* 123 Wash 2d 173 (Supreme Court of Washington, 1994), striking down an FLIR search of a home under both Washington state and federal constitutions; and *U.S. v. Ishmael,* 843 F Supp 205 (U.S. District Court for the Eastern District of Texas, 1994), rejecting *Penny-Feeney* in striking down an FLIR search of "business curtilage."

[178] *U.S. v. Ishmael,* 843 F Supp 205, at 212.

[179] See *U.S. v. Ishmael,* 843 F Supp at 213.

[180] *State v. Young,* 123 Wash 2d 173, 183.

device is not part of normal inquiry, and what the device exposes is not otherwise exposed by accident or mischance. The mischance principle, it would seem, leads to the conclusion that there is a reasonable expectation of privacy against FLIR searches. Suppose a society chronically suffered from drastic energy shortages. Use of FLIR devices by ordinary citizens might become prevalent and justified, and in this society the practice of heat detection may indeed diminish expectations of privacy in heat waste and make such an expectation unreasonable. But, the argument would go, in our society there is no such practice and so exposure by mischance is not a contingency against which we do, or should have to, take measures to protect privacy.

There is something troubling about this conclusion. Precisely what privacy interest does one defend in arguing that we should not have to take measures to guard against exposure from heat detection devices? The reason the decision in *Penny-Feeney* and the several cases following it seem correct is that it is hard to see how privacy is at stake when heat detection devices are used. The heat-detection cases lead us to a point we have put off discussing so far: Fourth Amendment adjudication requires some balancing of interests, where we weigh the benefits to society of allowing searches that can detect crime against the intrusiveness of these searches. Looking down from the sky can stifle intimate activities even if people don't know who exactly you are. Fortunately aerial peeping toms are not prevalent, but if they were, we might say that their activities are unacceptable to a free society that values privacy. But FLIR searches might be justified on the grounds that they do not expose intimate details but only criminal activities and that really privacy is not at stake.

The court in *State v. Young* believes otherwise. It notes that "the device discloses information about activities occurring within the confines of the home, and which a person is entitled to keep from disclosure absent a warrant."[181] "One could not stand near an open window or any part of the home constructed of material such as plywood" without being revealed.[182] If the FLIR device was indeed capable of exposing intimate details that people (not just criminals, of course, but law-abiding citizens as well) have an interest in shielding, then the mischance principle could explain why warrantless searches using the device would be unacceptable. But in light of the testimony concerning the capabilities of this technology presently, it seems more convincing to conclude that privacy is not really at stake.

The Need to Balance Interests

The discussion of the heat-detection case reminds us that privacy is a value to be weighed. Protecting privacy has its costs, and sometimes those costs are great. If the privacy interest itself is minimal or the benefit of the search is great, we might want to conclude that a search frustrating the privacy interest is justified on

181 123 Wash 2d at 184.

182 123 Wash 2d at 193. Cf. Steele, "Waste Heat and Garbage," 34: "[The FLIR device] is capable of discerning what lays behind the solid walls of a dwelling."

balance and consequently reasonable. In concluding this chapter it is appropriate to point to some of the other factors entering into a judgment of reasonableness apart from whether society regards the expectation of privacy frustrated by a search as generally reasonable.

The discussion in the early parts of this chapter referred to expectations of privacy we have against invasions, not just by government but by anyone. We might think a society accords to individuals different expectations of privacy against government as opposed to private intrusions. We may think we have more protection against government, perhaps because we expect government to follow rules of civility and to express trust in its citizens.[183] Or we might think we have less of an expectation of privacy against government as opposed to private surveillance, perhaps because citizens should expect to give up some privacy to government as part of their obligation as citizens to promote an ordered society.[184] Or we may think there is no fundamental difference between government and private invasions of privacy.[185] The question of whether an expectation of privacy is reasonable as it arises in U.S. constitutional law concerns expectations of privacy against government invasions since the Fourth Amendment proscription against unreasonable searches is a proscription only against state action and not against private citizens.[186] In considering the reasonability of government invasions of privacy it is essential to consider the purpose usually motivating such invasions—the control of crime.

I have argued that in resolving the issue of whether a warrantless police search violates reasonable expectations of privacy we cannot rely on universal principles of privacy in a way that ignores social norms and practices. There is a role for principles, but our use of them is constrained by cultural norms and practices, some of which may be justified simply because they have generated expectations upon which people rely.[187] Up to now we have considered how to determine

---

[183] Cf. *U.S. v. Kim*, 415 F Supp 1252 (1976): "The fact that Peeping Toms abound does not license the government to follow suit" (1256).

[184] See Note, "Private Places," 979.

[185] See Edward Bloustein, "Privacy as an Aspect of Human Dignity," in *Philosophical Dimensions of Privacy*, ed. Schoeman, 166, 181.

[186] For example, the Fourth Amendment does not constrain private security guards—see *State v. Hutson*, 649 SW 2d 6 (1982); *U.S. v. Francoeur*, 547 F 2d 891 (1977); and *U.S. v. Lima*, 424 A 2d 113 (1980). However, principles concerning expectations of privacy against private intrusions may be relevant: we may want to use tort law (statutory or common law), used to constrain nongovernment invasions of privacy, as a source in determining what society recognizes as a reasonable expectation of privacy for the purposes of determining constraints on government—see Note, "Private Places," 979.

[187] The position here is generally but not wholly sympathetic with that taken by Ferdinand Schoeman in *Privacy and Social Freedom* (Cambridge: Cambridge University Press, 1992). Schoeman rejects the view of morality as "a type of rationality" that "can be explicated without reference to a particular culture" (4). Rather, he argues, moral philosophy must aim "at understanding our social character" (5). We need to appreciate our "cultural embeddedness" without "ritually and unreflectively mimicking whatever others do" (5). There is an irrationalist streak in some of what Schoeman says; for example, he writes that "it is good that we accept much that we cannot defend, if challenged" (7). At times he seems to deny the possibility of judging practices at all, even though he rejects "unreflective mimicking": "No one occupies the Olympian perspective from which her own culture can be evalu-

generally whether an expectation of privacy is reasonable. But what is reasonable in one situation may be unreasonable in another. Courts deciding the issue are always faced with a particular fact situation. Their judgment of reasonability will hinge not just on whether people generally have an expectation of privacy against a certain sort of intrusion; it may depend not only on the intrusiveness of the search but also on the likelihood of the search revealing crime, the seriousness of the crime, and the societal interest in addressing the problem of crime.

Practice helps shape expectations of privacy; but to decide whether those expectations are reasonable in a particular situation, we may need to consider factors specific to the situation. The point here is two-fold. First, a search of a particular sort of place may be intrusive in one situation, nonintrusive in another. In *U.S. v. Dunn,* the Court had to decide whether the defendant had a reasonable expectation of privacy in his barn. Normally a barn might be considered within the curtilage of a home and therefore normally there may be a reasonable expectation of privacy against searches of barns. But the majority held that in this case, given the nondomestic, commercial use of this particular barn, it should not be considered part of the curtilage, and the Court upheld the warrantless search.[188]

We may need to turn to the particular fact situation to determine not only the extent to which privacy is implicated, but also whether a frustration of an expectation of privacy is justified by the promotion of other values that outweigh the diminution in privacy. Whether a search is intrusive is not decisive for determining whether it is reasonable. Involuntarily extracting blood without a warrant is very intrusive, but it is more reasonable in some circumstances than in others. Doing this immediately after an automobile accident to determine a driver's blood-alcohol level is more reasonable than doing it to a suspected rapist to check if his blood type matches the blood found at the scene of a rape. In the former case, if police wait for a warrant to be issued, alcohol could dissipate and crucial information would be lost; there is no similar reason not to secure a warrant to extract blood from a rape suspect. Whether or not we think involuntary blood tests are ever reasonable, clearly the *level* of reasonability is a function of more than its intrusiveness.

---

ated objectively" (93). At times, however, he appeals to the value of "human freedom" in defending privacy against "overreaching social pressures" (97, 106; cf 94, 113). I have tried to go beyond merely recognizing the need to be attentive to both practice and principle by specifying concretely how practices and principles interact in privacy ethics and by developing a more precisely formulated principle.

[188] 480 US 294 (1987). See also Justice Powell's concurrence in *Robbins v. California,* 453 US 420 (1981): that a container can possibly or conceivably be used for personal effects does not mean that it is "inevitably" associated with an expectation of privacy (at 434). Cf. *People v. Ingle,* 53 Cal 2d 407, 412 (1960): "There is no exact formula for the determination of reasonableness. Each case must be decided on its own facts and circumstances . . . and on the total atmosphere of the case." Some Justices oppose a case-by-case approach. The dissent in *Dunn* argued that the Court "should refuse to do a case-by-case analysis of the expectation of privacy in any particular barn and follow the general rule that a barn is in domestic use. What should be relevant . . . is the typical use of an area or structure." See also the majority opinion in an earlier open-fields case, *Oliver v. U.S.,* 466 US 170, 181 (1984).

An intrusive search may be reasonable upon considering the purpose of the search. Courts, adhering to this principle, have adopted a balancing test in establishing the reasonableness of searches.[189] Not all Justices approve of the indiscriminate use of a balancing test. Justice Blackmun insists that the Court may subject Fourth Amendment privacy interests to a balancing test only in cases of "special needs":

> Only in those exceptional circumstances in which special needs, beyond the normal need for law enforcement, make the warrant and probable cause requirement impracticable, is a court entitled to substitute its balancing of interests for that of the Framers.[190]

Justice Brennan, one of the most outspoken opponents of balancing tests, says that "all of these 'balancing tests' amount to brief nods by the Court in the direction of a neutral utilitarian calculus while the Court in fact engages in an unanalyzed exercise of judicial will."[191]

Justice Brennan's criticism is perhaps best seen as a criticism of certain applications of a balancing test. There are examples where the balancing of interests the Court undertakes is less than convincing. Justice Kennedy upholds drug tests of certain customs workers using a balancing test. He cites as a compelling government interest that outweighs any privacy interest the claim that custom officers have been stabbed, and that nine have died, without linking these consequences to drug use or showing that drug testing would address the government interest in the health and safety of its workers.[192] Another example of an utterly unconvincing application of a balancing test is *Bell v. Wolfish.* Justice Rehnquist upheld body cavity searches of pretrial detainees based on a "balancing of the need for the particular search against the invasion of personal rights that the search entails."[193] The argument is that body cavity searches are needed following contact visits to ensure that visitors don't slip weapons to inmates which they might

---

[189] See *U.S. v. Brignoni-Ponce,* 422 US 873, 878 (1975): the constitutionality of a particular search depends on a "balance between the public interest and the individual's right to personal security free from arbitrary interference by law officers." See also, for example, *Acton v. Vernonia School District,* 23 F 3d 1514 (1994); *In re Tyrell J.,* 876 P 2d 519 (1994); *AFGE v. Roberts,* 9 F 3d 1464 (1993); *Piroglu v. Coleman,* 25 F 3d 1098 (1994); *State v. Young,* 867 P 2d 593 (1994); Rehnquist's dissent in *Michigan v. Clifford,* 464 US 287 (1984); *Bell v. Wolfish,* 441 US 520 (1979); *Hudson v. Palmer,* 468 US 517 (1984); *New Jersey v. TLO,* 469 US 325 (1985); *Winston v. Lee,* 470 US 753 (1985); *Skinner v. Railway Labor Exec. Assn,* 489 US 602 (1989); *U.S. v. Place,* 462 US 696 (1983); *Commonwealth v. Hernley,* 263 A 2d 904 (1970); *Breithaupt v. Abram,* 352 US 432 (1957); *Camara v. Municipal Court,* 387 US 523 (1967).

[190] *New Jersey v. TLO,* 469 US 325 (1985), at 321 (concurrence).

[191] *New Jersey v. TLO,* 469 US 325, 369. Cf. Brennan's concurrence in *U.S. v. Place,* 462 US 696, 718 (1983): "The protections intended by the Framers could all too easily disappear in the consideration and balancing of the multifarious circumstances presented by different cases, especially when that balancing may be done in the first instance by police officers engaged in the 'often competetive enterprise of ferreting out crime'" (Citing *Dunaway v. NY,* 442 US 200, 213 [1979] which in turn quotes *Johnson v. U.S.,* 333 US 10, 14 [1948]).

[192] In *National Treasury Employees Union v. Von Raab,* 489 US 656 (1989), at 670. Justice Scalia gives a compelling criticism of Kennedy's weighing of interests at 682–83.

[193] 441 US 520 (1979), at 559.

insert into the vaginal or anal cavity. But Justice Marshall, in dissent, notes that the searches, which are *very* invasive, have little benefit: "inmates are required to wear one-piece jumpsuits with zippers in the front. To insert an object into the vaginal or anal cavity, an inmate would have to remove the jumpsuit, at least from the upper torso."[194] Also, "contact visits occur in a glass-enclosed room" that is monitored continuously, so concealing a weapon in a body cavity would be "extraordinarily difficult"; "before entering the visiting room, visitors and their packages are searched thoroughly by a metal detector, fluoroscope, and by hand." Moreover, "visual inspection would probably not detect an object once inserted."[195]

While the Court's scale is sometimes skewed, some balancing of interests is necessary to arrive at a judgment of reasonableness.[196] For example, use of a magnetometer to detect weapons in federal buildings or airports would be ruled out by the mischance principle but is reasonable in light of the compelling state interest in preventing terrorist acts and is therefore justified on a balancing test.[197] This shows how intrusiveness on its own is an insufficient determinant of reasonable expectations of privacy.

Many considerations may enter into a balancing test. Primarily the intrusiveness of the search must be weighed against the public interest in crime control. A minor intrusion, such as a brief stop at an automobile checkpoint, may be reasonable if it would effectively promote drug interdiction or prevent illegal immigration or drunk driving.[198] On the other hand, there are limits to what government may do to address crime:

> We do not permit a search of every house on a block merely because there is reason to believe that *one* contains evidence of criminal activity. . . . Nor can the success of massive testing justify its use. We would not condone the beatings of suspects and the admissibility of their confessions merely because a larger number of convictions resulted.[199]

---

[194] 441 US at 577.

[195] 441 US at 578.

[196] One factor skewing the scale may be a hindsight bias. Slobogin and Schumacher (1993) argue that there is a hindsight bias because judges typically know that defendants are guilty and this leads them to "underestimate the privacy and autonomy interests infringed on by police actions" (732; cf. 761, 735, 760). Justice Stevens suggests evidence of a hindsight bias in noting that since 1982 "the Court has heard arguments in 30 Fourth Amendment cases involving narcotics. . . . All save two involved a search or seizure without a warrant or with a defective warrant. And, in all except three, the Court upheld the constitutionality of the search or seizure"(*California v. Acevedo*, 500 US 565, 600 [1991], dissent, citations omitted).

[197] One might argue that these searches are reasonable because we consent to them, but many of us have little choice in boarding airplanes, so the consent isn't genuine.

[198] See *U.S. v. Martinez-Fuerte*, 428 US 543 (1976), upholding checkpoint border searches; and *Michigan Dept. of State Police v. Sitz*, 496 US 444 (1990), upholding sobriety checkpoints.

[199] *Capua v. City of Plainfield*, 643 F Supp 1507, 1511 (1986). Cf. Justice O'Connor's dissent in *Vernonia School District v. Acton*, 94–590, 63 LW 4653 (1995): suspicionless drug testing may be more effective, but "Fourth Amendment protections come with a price" (4663).

Other factors may enter into a judgment of reasonableness. Some commentators, for example, argue that the reasonableness of a search depends on the likelihood of innocence of the searchee.[200]

We cannot consider here all the complexities involved in a balancing test, nor all of the criticisms that might be made of courts' applications. The point relevant for us is that practice and principle both come into play in an evaluation of the privacy interest to be weighed on the balance. For example, in *Acton v. Vernonia School District* the court balances the privacy interest in one's urine against the government interest in discouraging drug use.[201] In figuring the privacy interest, the court appeals to tradition, social custom, and law and finds a significant interest in privacy when passing urine. These traditions and customs are not themselves subject to critical evaluation. They are foundational, although they are not universal—no doubt the feelings were different in Rome when public latrines were used.

[200] See Arnold Loewy, "The Fourth Amendment as a Device for Protecting the Innocent," *Michigan Law Review* 81 (1983): 1229–72. Loewy argues that there is no Fourth Amendment right to be secure from the government's finding evidence of a crime: "If a device could be invented that accurately detected weapons and did not disrupt the normal movement of people, there could be no Fourth Amendment objection to its use" (1246; cf. 1229, 1247). Cf. *Michigan Dept. of State Police v. Sitz*, 496 US 444, 452, 465 (1990). Drawing on *People v. Evans*, a 1977 case which gives an example of a device developed that could only detect cocaine (an example strikingly similar to Loewy's in his later article), Justice Brennan disagrees that there would be no Fourth Amendment bar to pointing it at anyone or in any building (*U.S. v. Jacobson*, 466 US 209 [1984]).

[201] 23 F 3d 1514 (9th Cir., 1994); reversed in *Vernonia School District v. Acton*, 63 LW 4653 (1995).

CHAPTER SIX

Practices, Principles, and Contemporary Political Theory

EDMUND BURKE, the great theorist of conservatism, defends tradition and opposes abrupt change and untested reforms. "Rage and phrenzy will pull down more in half an hour, than prudence, deliberation, and foresight can build up in an hundred years."[1] Burke's deference to long-standing practices and custom has been seen by some as irrational and subservient. Why do something just because it has been done for time immemorial? The antitraditionalist argument is perhaps most forcefully expressed by Jeremy Bentham. For Bentham, by deferring to tradition the conservative virtually acknowledges himself

> not to possess any powers of reasoning which he himself can venture to think it safe to trust to: incapable of forming for himself any judgment by which he looks upon it as safe to be determined, he betakes himself for safety to some other man, or set of men, of whom he knows little or nothing, except that they lived so many years ago; that the period of their existence was by so much anterior to his own time—by so much anterior, and consequently possessing for its guidance so much the less experience.[2]

Bentham, thoroughly disgusted with blind deference to the past, implies that the uncritical conservative "should be considered as a person labouring under a general and incurable imbecility."[3] In this book I have supported the idea, to which Bentham so enthusiastically adheres, that in thinking about what ethics and the law require of us, we sometimes need to engage in principled criticism and not rest content adhering to the requirements of our existing practices and law, even if they are deeply rooted in our past.

But siding with Bentham does not mean denying any role to social practices in ethical and legal judging. One can both acknowledge the importance of principled criticism and appreciate the importance of tradition and long-standing social practices. Burke himself, while at times suggesting that we should unthinkingly accept the pleasing illusions of the past, at other times advocates reforms and principled criticism of corrupt practice when they are necessary and prudent.[4]

---

[1] Edmund Burke, *Reflections on the Revolution in France* (Garden City, N.Y.: Doubleday, 1973), 183.

[2] Jeremy Bentham, *The Book of Fallacies,* in *Works,* ed. John Bowring (Edinburgh: William Tait, 1838), 392.

[3] Ibid.

[4] In his speech on the impeachment of Hastings, Burke says: "Will your Lordships submit to hear the corrupt practices of mankind made the principles of government? No! It will be your pride and glory to teach men intrusted with power, that, in their use of it, they are to conform to principles, and not to draw their principles from the corrupt practice of any man whatever" (Edmund Burke, *Selected Writings and Speeches,* ed. Peter J. Stanlis [Gloucester, Mass.: Peter Smith, 1968], 396). Burke advocates prudent reform, and even revolution when necessary, in *Reflections,* 42, 184, 265–66. Yet else-

Burke does not oppose *all* social criticism; he opposes a certain sort of criticism that assumes that *everything* is subject to principled scrutiny, that all is up for grabs, that we could build an ideal society from scratch in accordance with abstract principles, oblivious to the fact that people plan their lives on the basis of expectations that arise from existing practices and customs: "I cannot stand forward, and give praise or blame to any thing which relates to human actions, and human concerns, [a]s it stands stripped of every relation, in all the nakedness and solitude of metaphysical abstraction."[5] For Burke it is arrogant and presumptuous for a theorist or politician to consider his country "as nothing but carte blanche upon which he may scribble whatever he pleases." A good politician, rather, "always considers how he shall make the most of the existing materials of his country."[6]

In chapter two we saw that Hegel, like Burke, also is critical of utopian theorists who, in thinking of the practices a society ought to have, believe they can disregard how members of that society have already been shaped by a system of practices and laws. Burke does sometimes give the impression that we should accept these deeply ingrained practices uncritically; he surely does not *emphasize* the need for social criticism or the role principles can play in such criticism.[7] Hegel, unlike Burke, makes the idea of principled criticism central to his political philosophy. Hegel emphasizes that practices, no matter how long-standing, must be justified—they must be rational—if we are to be free under them. One point of turning to Hegel was to see that one can engage in principled criticism of social practices without denying their importance.

We have explored a debate between those who hold that there are principles of rational conduct, principles that do not depend on the existence of or make reference to social practices, and which we can and should use to guide our conduct, or to establish, reform, criticize, or explain the features of practices; and, on the other hand, those who hold that to answer the question of where our duty or obligation lies, or what action is morally proper, we must turn not to abstract principles but to our existing practices and shared understandings, and that if any principles guide us they are principles already implicit or immanent in these practices. I have argued that we need to recognize the importance of both principles and practice—there is truth in what both Bentham *and* Burke say. I have done this by showing how development and application of principles in particular cases of ethical and legal judging are constrained by social practice. The point is not simply that to be a good moral or legal theorist one needs to be attentive to practice. By examining some of the complicated ways in which practices and

---

where in *Reflections* he recommends that we avoid thinking too much and just accept our practices and prejudices: see, for example, 100: "You see, Sir, that in this enlightened age I am bold enough to confess, that we are generally men of untaught feelings; that instead of casting away all our old prejudices, we cherish them to a very considerable degree"; and pp. 90–91, 104, 174.

[5] Burke, *Reflections*, 19.

[6] Ibid., 172.

[7] Indeed, in the passage cited from the Hastings speech (footnote 4 above), Burke's criticism of practice might be construed as criticism of an individual's singular practice not of a social practice.

principles interact, we see that sometimes uncritical deference to practice is appropriate and justified, that everything is not always up for grabs. In this concluding chapter, after reviewing some of the ways social practice comes into play in principled criticism, I shall consider some of the implications of the argument for contemporary debates in political theory between liberals and communitarians, and between cultural relativists and universalists.

The Role of Social Practice in Ethical and Legal Judging

I have argued throughout the book that social practice plays an important role in ethical and legal judging. I have argued against the Kantian position that we should not consult social practice to determine what morality requires by pointing to examples of how a determination of right is contingent on social practice. I have argued *not* that something is right because it is recognized as right in practice (although sometimes the fact that a norm exists itself establishes a good reason for adhering to it or makes adhering to it reasonable); but that there are ways in which social practice—both discrete, rule-governed practice and practice more broadly understood, bears on or constrains principled determinations of what is right.

One reason we are unlikely ever to realize the Kantian ideal, the ideal that in deciding what morality requires we make no reference to social practice and rely solely on valid moral principles, is that moral principles often refer, implicitly if not explicitly, to conditions or standards the interpretation of which requires appeal to social practice. In chapter two we turned to Kant's categorical imperative, which declares an action to be wrong if it would not be possible for everyone universally to consent to a maxim of willing that action. The categorical imperative requires that the action in question not undercut the agency of anyone else so that it remains possible for everyone to consent to the maxim. Kant claims that the categorical imperative rules out false promising; but being the victim of a false promise doesn't make me incapable of consenting or withholding my consent to a maxim that false promises be allowed. Making a false promise does victimize the promisee, but a more persuasive explanation than Kant gives for why it does so is that it frustrates expectations arising from a social practice.

In chapter three we considered a variety of moral principles, each of which made reference to social practice. MacCormick's principle of reliance held that when I knowingly or intentionally induce you to rely on my doing x, you'd suffer by my not doing x, and you do so rely, then it is wrong for me not to do x. But there are cases where these conditions are met yet no wrong is committed. MacCormick's reliance principle, to be convincing, must implicitly include the requirement that your reliance on my doing x is reasonable, and whether reliance is reasonable depends in part on social practice. Application of Bentham's principle of utility also varies depending on what social practices one is brought up with: what leads to happiness in one place may not lead to happiness in another, and what is regarded as yielding happiness in one place may not be so regarded in another, sometimes simply because people socialized by different practices come to have different preferences. Scanlon's principle of fidelity has at least two provisions, one being a requirement that A voluntarily leads B to have a certain expectation, the other a "special justification" clause, the interpretation of which may depend on social practice. Whether any of these principles leads to a judgment in a particular case in a society depends on that society's norms and practices.

In chapter four, on contracts, we considered principles similar to the principles used by moral philosophers to explain the wrong of promise-breaking—Fried's Kantian "promise" principle, which sees the wrong of breaking a promise as the wrong of failing to respect individual autonomy and violating trust; Atiyah's principle of detrimental reliance; and a variation of a principle of utility that resolves contractual disputes by invoking a principle of economic efficiency. Application of these principles makes implicit or explicit reference to social practice. For example, only promises made with an intention to be legally bound give rise to a legal obligation, and Fried's promise principle needs to make reference to social practices and shared understandings to distinguish from all the promises giving rise to moral obligations, the breaking of which fails to respect the dignity and autonomy of the promisee, those promises undertaken with the requisite intent. In addition, the promise principle dictates an obligation only when a promise was not extracted through coercion or bad faith, but to decide what counts as undue coercion or as lacking good faith, we may need to appeal to convention. Atiyah explicitly recognizes that his principle of detrimental reliance relies on judgments of a "social group. In a technologically advanced society, it makes sense for the state to step in and protect consumers lacking the requisite technical expertise to judge with competence the fairness of their bargains, whereas in a less-advanced society a principle of caveat emptor may be practiced; whether reliance on a promise is reasonable in a particular case may depend on whether we live in one or the other society. Social norms bear on judgments of whether particular promises should be enforced in other ways as well. In a society where haggling is common practice, it may not be unconscionable for a merchant to get $250 from a customer for an item that could have been bought for half the price at the store next door; but where other norms for price-setting are established, this may be regarded as unreasonable.[8]

In chapter five I pointed to a principle we might use to determine whether an expectation of privacy is reasonable—the mischance principle. At the same time,

---

[8] Custom and shared understandings are important in interpreting principles in the law of torts as well. For example, matters made public in an offensive way so as to invade privacy must be offensive to a "reasonable man of ordinary sensibilities," and in interpreting this "reasonable man" standard, one of the leading theorists of torts argues that we appeal to "customs and ordinary views of the community" (William Prosser, "Privacy: A Legal Analysis," *California Law Review* 48 (1960): 338–423, reprinted in *Philosophical Dimensions of Privacy: An Anthology*, ed. Ferdinand Schoeman [New York: Cambridge University Press, 1984], 111–12). In deciding whether an actor was negligent, we consider whether he used "reasonable care," and, argues Prosser, custom "bears upon what others will expect the actor to do, and what, therefore, reasonable care may require the actor to do"(*Prosser and Keeton on the Law of Torts*, 5th ed., 193; cited in Ferdinand Schoeman, *Privacy and Social Freedom* [Cambridge: Cambridge University Press, 1992]).

I noted several ways in which application of this principle makes reference to social practices. Architecture, technology, work habits, attitudes toward sexuality and the body, political ideology, all shape expectations of privacy, and determine whether an activity is subject to discovery by mischance. If we were brought up with different practices, we would have different expectations of privacy. Living in the world Buñuel depicts in *Phantom of Liberty*, a police officer's search of a toilet stall might not be regarded as unreasonable.[9] The point is not just that manners vary among cultures, that in some places it is impolite to enter a room without knocking while in other places it is acceptable; these differences have important moral and legal implications. When they are taken into account when we apply the mischance principle, they will determine whether a search is or isn't reasonable and perhaps whether someone ends up in prison.

It is possible to ask whether we should live in the world Buñuel depicts or our own world, to ask which world is better. We can ask whether it is better to live in a society that practices haggling or one that prohibits it. We can ask whether it is best to have a practice of promising. But if we do live with the practices of Buñuel's world, or in a society with haggling or promising, then, unless these practices are insufferable, it is reasonable to respect the expectations arising from our having these practices. We may want or even need to ask whether these practices are justified; but there are appropriate and inappropriate times for doing so. A lawyer in a courtroom arguing about the reasonability of a police officer's warrantless search of a motel room or of a dressing room in a retail store, will consider whether this search violated expectations of privacy that society recognizes as reasonable; to answer this question we would appeal to practices in that society such as that one knocks on doors before entering a person's residence, or that when one comes upon a stranger getting dressed one averts one's eyes. Arguing the particular legal issue of the reasonableness of the officer's search is not the appropriate context for considering whether these deeply entrenched practices are desirable. In that context it is unreasonable to expect principled criticism "all the way down." Rather, it is appropriate to defer to expectations created by existing practices, even if they may not be the only, or even the best possibility.

There are levels of justification. In the context of deciding whether to sentence a convicted criminal with five, ten, or twenty years in prison, a judge or jury will appeal to prevailing standards of our criminal justice system. Some people don't think we should *even have* the practice of punishment and might argue that any level of incarceration is unjustified because punishment is barbaric and indefensible. But this criticism, this demand for justification, is misplaced in the context of deciding on a particular sentence. When we are justifying the practice of punishment, we are at a different level of justification than when we are justifying a particular sentence, and the sorts of arguments appropriate at the former level of

---

[9] In the scene from *Phantom of Liberty* to which I refer, Buñuel depicts a world in which eating is regarded as a deeply private function done in isolation behind locked doors, while evacuation is regarded as a public act, done together at a table over conversation: see chapter five.

justification may be inappropriate when we are at the latter level. Once we are within the practice it is reasonable to appeal to its standards. If we don't think we should have this practice at all, we certainly can present our reasons in an appropriate forum, but the forum of deciding on the convicted criminal's sentence is not the appropriate one.[10] It is unreasonable to think that in justifying a particular action we must subject to critical scrutiny all of the assumptions and claims underlying our judgment.

The mere fact that a social practice exists may lead people to form expectations upon which they rely, and once these expectations are established and relied upon, there is a moral reason not to frustrate them, even if on reflection the social practice is not as defensible as an alternative. The moral reason has to do with fairness. This is one of the points underlying Burke's conservatism. Burke criticized the French Revolution in part because it undermined established property rights, thereby frustrating expectations. Burke writes:

> When men are encouraged to go into a certain mode of life by the existing laws, and protected in that mode as in a lawful occupation—when they have accommodated all their ideas, and all their habits to it—when the law had long made their adherence to its rules a ground of reputation, and their departure from them a ground of disgrace and even of penalty—I am sure it is unjust in legislature, by an arbitrary act, to offer a sudden violence to their minds and their feelings; forcibly to degrade them from their state and condition, and to stigmatize with shame and infamy that character and those customs which before had been made the measure of their happiness and honour.[11]

It is unfair to frustrate expectations upon which people reasonably rely, even if we can imagine a different world with different practices in which these expectations would be unwarranted.[12]

Even if fairness is not at stake, there are occasions where we can still say that an action complying with custom or long-standing practice may be reasonable simply in virtue of the fact that it conforms with custom. If according to common law and settled police practice, it is permissible for an officer to detain suspicious persons for the purpose of demanding that they give an account of themselves, then it is difficult to see how we could say an officer following this practice acts unreasonably; in this case it is not that it would be unfair not to allow the officer to do what the common law allows but that adherence to customary practice is inherently reasonable. There may be good reasons to change this practice, but until new norms are implemented, the officer is not acting in bad faith or unrea-

---

[10] This idea of levels of justification, and of the distinction between justifying a practice and justifying an action falling within a practice, was first developed in detail by John Rawls in "Two Concepts of Rules," *Philosophical Review* 64 (1955), which is discussed in chapter three; see also Mark Tunick, *Punishment: Theory and Practice* (Berkeley: University of California Press, 1992), chap. 1.

[11] Burke, *Reflections,* 171.

[12] For treatments of the idea of fairness and how it generates obligations, see George Klosko, "Presumptive Benefit, Fairness, and Political Obligation," *Philosophy and Public Affairs* 16, no. 3 (Summer 1987): 241–59; George Klosko, *The Principle of Fairness and Political Obligation* (Lanham, Md.: Rowman and Littlefield, 1992); and John Rawls, "Legal Obligation and the Duty of Fair Play," in *Law and Philosophy,* ed. Sidney Hook (New York: NYU Press, 1964), 3–18.

sonably in adhering to existing practice. Similarly, if a common understanding exists that the therapeutic reassurance a doctor provides to her patient is not a legally enforceable guarantee, then even if there is no particularly good reason for not holding doctors legally accountable for statements made to their patients upon which patients might rely to their detriment, the fact that this is the common understanding at the time the doctor speaks to her patient would make it unreasonable to interpret what she says as a legally binding promise.[13]

Other theorists considering the role of social practice in ethical and legal judging have suggested general reasons why we should draw upon already existing shared understandings. One is that in doing this the theorist is more likely to be persuasive. Another is that some existing understandings are so entrenched that to implement radically different practices would require massive coercion.[14] Another still is that culture has authority in part by its being the solution to coordination problems: it "has authority because it indicates which method of coordination is the adopted one."[15] These general arguments may provide convincing reasons on some occasions; whether an argument for deference is persuasive will likely depend on the particular situation. For this reason I have confined my claim that it is reasonable to respect expectations arising from existing social practices to specific examples, without asserting a rigid, general rule. Turning to the case studies of chapters three through five, I have argued that sometimes it is reasonable to defer to existing practices and norms, for reasons having to do with fairness and the inherent reasonableness of acting in accordance with certain long-settled norms. I have not meant to imply that all our traditions are worth our respect, or that all aspects of culture have, or should have, authority, or that it would never be worth the turmoil of massive coercion to alter some entrenched practices that are oppressive and insufferable.

Another way social practice enters into principled accounts of moral and legal judging is as a source of intuitions upon which a theorist may rely to formulate and ground principles. One of the dominant approaches in contemporary political philosophy is to formulate principles that account for our intuitive convictions. For example, in thinking about whether a warrantless search violates a reasonable expectation of privacy, we might list instances of clearly wrongful searches and of clearly reasonable searches, then identify features common to the former instances that are absent in the latter and incorporate these features into a principle that would define when a reasonable expectation of privacy has been violated. That principle could then guide us when thinking about examples about

---

[13] See the discussion of *Garcia v. Von Micsky* in chapter four. Ronald Dworkin offers an example that makes a similar point: "The fact that a practice of removing hats in church exists justifies asserting a normative rule to that effect . . . because the practice creates ways of giving offense and gives rise to expectations of the sort that are good grounds for asserting a duty to take off one's hat in church or for asserting a normative rule that one must" (*Taking Rights Seriously* [Cambridge: Harvard University Press, 1977], 57).

[14] Michael Walzer, *Spheres of Justice* (New York: Basic Books, 1983), xiv, 44.

[15] Ferdinand D. Schoeman, *Privacy and Social Freedom* (Cambridge: Cambridge University Press, 1992), 77.

which we have no clear intuitions. The principle we arrive at in this manner is justified because it coheres with our intuitive sense of what is reasonable.[16] In chapter three we saw that Scanlon takes something like this approach when trying to explain the wrong of breaking promises. The moral principles developed using this approach are concerned with social practice in that they are immanent in our practices: the principles are chosen because they best accord with the intuitions we have as a result of sharing certain practices and norms.[17]

Some philosophers might object to this approach to justification, equating it with "intuitionism," which they regard as ultimately subjective. R. M. Hare, for example, writes, "the appeal to moral intuitions will never do as a basis for a moral system." For Hare, intuitions offer "no ground or argument"; that a theorist bases a claim that something is right on the claim's cohering with intuition makes that claim contingent on the theorist just happening to have certain intuitions.[18] It would be a mistake to equate the sort of appeal to intuitions made by contemporary philosophers such as Scanlon with a thoroughly subjective intuitionism that appeals simply to what the theorist "feels" to be right. Some intuitions are more grounded than others. Some intuitionists phrase their appeals to intuitions in a way that makes them seem ungrounded and subjective. Sir David Ross, for example, in defending his belief that promises give rise to moral obligations, writes, "To me it seems as self-evident as anything could be, that to make a promise, for instance, is to create a moral claim on us in someone else. Many readers will perhaps say that they *do not* know this to be true. If so, I certainly cannot prove it to them; I can only ask them to reflect again, in the hope that they will ultimately agree that they also know it to be true."[19] Other appeals to intuition, however, are of a more objective character. For example, I might claim that a police officer's warrantless search of nonintermingled garbage in a residential neighborhood seems "intuitively wrong" and use this intuition to help formulate and justify a principle of reasonable and unreasonable searches. But this claim is not entirely subjective, because it can be supported by pointing to social practice: while there are snoops, many of us look down on them, and this social fact, that snooping through garbage warrants some form of condemnation, provides some objective, if contested, support for the intuition.

[16] See, for example, Will Kymlicka, *Contemporary Political Philosophy: An Introduction* (Oxford: Oxford University Press, 1990), 7: Kymlicka implies that ultimately the test for a theory of justice is that it coheres with our "intuitive sense of right and wrong." George Klosko also appeals to a coherence theory of justification that "justifies moral convictions according to the degree of their coherence with our overall moral views." This method ultimately "relies on the presumed integrity of our moral and political intuitions and principles" (*Principle of Fairness and Political Obligation*, 20–21, 25).

[17] Cf. J. L. Mackie, *Ethics: Inventing Right and Wrong* (London: Penguin, 1977), 36: moral disagreement reflects "people's adherence to and participation in different ways of life." For example, "People approve of monogamy because they participate in a monogamous way of life"; it's not that "they participate in a monogamous way of life because they approve of monogamy."

[18] R. M. Hare, *Moral Thinking: Its Levels, Method and Point* (Oxford: Oxford University Press, 1981), 12, 151.

[19] Sir David Ross, *The Right and the Good* (Oxford, 1930), 21, n. 1; cited in P. S. Atiyah, *Promises, Morals, and Law* (Oxford: Oxford University Press, 1981), 88.

Still another way the existence of social practices needs to be taken into account, at least on utilitarian theories, is as a source of rewards and sanctions. For example, an act-utilitarian deciding whether to keep a particular promise will need to take into account the loss of reputation he would suffer in breaking the promise, a sanction he would suffer simply because the practice exists.

CONTEMPORARY POLITICAL THEORISTS ON THE ROLE OF SOCIAL PRACTICE

While defending principled deliberation in ethics and the law, I have argued that in important instances of ethical and legal deliberation, we cannot rely solely on principles to the exclusion of social practice. I have argued against a tradition of political philosophy, most prominently represented by Kant, which, convinced that moral reflection involves not an inquiry into what accepted practice is but rigorous application of moral principles, proceeds to deny any role in moral reflection to social practice. On this view there are natural principles, which do not refer to the existence of social practices, and these principles point to natural wrongs. In this section I shall turn to contemporary theorists who object, implicitly or explicitly, to the view that there are natural principles and natural wrongs, and who emphasize the conventional nature of morality. The argument I have presented in this book is one by example, showing concretely the role social practice plays in actual instances of moral or legal judging. It complements the more abstract and general arguments for the importance of social practice offered by these theorists. However, my argument is to be distinguished from the arguments of some of these theorists who, in insisting that morality is purely conventional, adhere to the antithesis of a principle conception; I have argued that we need, rather, a synthesis: practices *and* principles.

One of the leading theorists to recognize the importance of social practice and shared understandings in deciding what justice requires is Michael Walzer. Although he does not oppose the application of general principles in resolving issues such as how we should justly distribute goods, Walzer argues that when we apply these principles we must make reference to shared understandings, the sorts of understandings that arise from our sharing in social practices. Walzer's main thesis in his book *Spheres of Justice* is that "no social good x should be distributed to men and women who possess some other good y merely because they possess y and without regard to the meaning of x."[20] While this is a general principle which can be used to criticize existing social practices, its application requires us to refer to the "meaning of [social good] x." "Social goods have social meanings, and we find our way to distributive justice through an interpretation of those meanings."[21] The general principle will dictate that certain exchanges should be blocked, to prevent those with more wealth (good y) from having undue access to good x just because they possess y. But in deciding which ex-

---

[20] Walzer, *Spheres of Justice*, 20.
[21] Ibid., 9, 19.

changes *should* be blocked, Walzer argues, we must turn to those that *are* blocked or conventionally deplored, or to other evidence of the social meaning of good x.[22] For example, the general principle might dictate that one's access to cultural events such as drama should not depend on one's personal wealth, but it might not; whether it does depends on "what the drama means in this or that culture." Similarly, "we don't know whether the sale of guns should be a blocked exchange, until we know how guns are used on particular streets."[23] Certain wants or needs may be regarded as so important that everyone within the community is regarded as having a right to satisfy them regardless of their status; but *which* wants or needs are so regarded must be defined by a particular community's "culture, its character, its common understandings."[24]

In Walzer's view social practices don't merely fill in the gaps left by general principles or provide the information we need to apply principles; they also are the *source* of principles. Walzer sees the principle-wielding social critic not as standing outside the city, looking on from a distance, judging it with principles uncorrupted by the practices of the city, but, rather, as standing "in the cave, in the city, on the ground." We find justice not by looking outward for external principles; a just society is "already here," "hidden, as it were, in our concepts and categories."[25] When engaged in criticism, Walzer appeals to principles that are "internal":

> Social critics commonly don't, and certainly needn't, invent the principles they apply; they don't have to step outside the world they ordinarily inhabit. They appeal to internal principles, already known, comprehensible to, somehow remembered by, the people they hope to convince.[26]

In answering the question "How ought we to x?" Walzer looks to how we do x, finding implicit principles that make sense of the practice of x'ing.[27] These prin-

---

[22] Ibid., 97. In saying we must turn to convention, Walzer does not think we turn only to existing laws. If we are considering whether the wealthy should have been able to buy exemptions from conscription in the 1860s, it won't suffice simply to point to the Enrollment and Conscription Act of 1863, which permitted the purchase of exemptions for $300. This existing law has no normative force, for Walzer: it was never reenacted, and it violated "a deep sense of what it meant to be a citizen of the state—or better, of this state, the United States in 1863" (99). In other words, social understandings are just as important a source for determining what is "conventionally deplored." A law might not adequately reflect social understandings, just as Supreme Court decisions, which have the force of law, do not always reflect social understandings (see chapter five).

[23] Ibid., 231.

[24] Ibid., 76. Cf. p. xv: what rights we have follows "from shared conceptions of social goods; they are local and particular in character."

[25] Ibid., xiv.

[26] Michael Walzer, rejoinder to Dworkin, *New York Review of Books,* 21 July 1983, 65–68.

[27] Ronald Dworkin challenges Walzer's appeal to social conventions, arguing instead for the need to turn to reflection and general principles, on the grounds that "we cannot leave justice to convention and anecdote." Walzer responds by suggesting that appeal to social practice and convention is unavoidable. He argues that even Dworkin's model judge Hercules "is not privy to some universal theory of justice" and appeals, rather, to his own tradition, teasing out the deepest understanding of the existing legal community (ibid.). Richard Rorty has also objected to Dworkin's argument: "Intra-

ciples, which are part of the "logic" of institutions, can be used to criticize existing practice, because sometimes the community lacks the readiness "to live up to the logic of its own institutions." For example, our legal system makes a public commitment to equal resources for rich and poor, but this ideal, immanent in the system, is not lived up to in practice.[28] Principles immanent in practices can be used to criticize practice.[29]

Walzer conveys the idea that principles derive from or presuppose practices and shared understandings again in his more recent book *Thick and Thin*. There he notes that there are moral principles that seem to hold universally and which constitute what he calls a "minimalist" morality that perhaps all societies share.[30] But this moral minimum "is not a free-standing morality. It simply designates some reiterated features of particular thick or maximal moralities."[31] The moral principles that are universally shared are "thin" principles that are derivative of particularistic and parochial thick moralities. "Morality is thick from the beginning, culturally integrated, fully resonant, and it reveals itself thinly only on special occasions." In Walzer's view we start thick. "Maximalism in fact precedes minimalism."[32] Thin principles may be universally shared, but they are not natural principles; they derive from social practices, minimal features of which may be common to the practices of virtually all human societies.

This argument for the priority of practice over principles has implications similar to those of an argument other theorists make for the priority of particular judgments over general rules. Martha Nussbaum and Amartya Sen argue that "universal rules and other ethical generalizations have worth only insofar as they correctly summarize particulars; they are rules of thumb and cannot, in general, take precedence over concrete perceptions."[33] Nussbaum has recently developed a theory of judgment that, while not rejecting, points to the limits of rule-governed moral reasoning and application of universal principles, instead emphasizing how "storytelling and literary imagining . . . can provide essential ingredients in a rational argument."[34] Rather than relying solely on "abstract general principles" in

societal tensions . . . are rarely resolved by appeals to general principles of the sort Dworkin thinks necessary. More frequently they are resolved by appeals to what he calls 'convention or anecdote' " (Richard Rorty, *Objectivity, Relativism, and Truth: Philosophical Papers* [Cambridge: Cambridge University Press, 1991], 1:201).

[28] Walzer, *Spheres of Justice*, 85.

[29] See Tunick, *Punishment: Theory and Practice:* "Immanent criticism is possible because it is possible for us to have ideals that in principle guide us, but for us occasionally (or even often) to act against those ideals. Actuality, or a practice as it is actually carried out, can diverge from the practice as it would be if it were consistently carried out according to its ideals" (12–13; cf. 17–18, 65–66, 110, 115–16).

[30] Michael Walzer, *Thick and Thin* (Notre Dame, Ind.: University of Notre Dame Press, 1994), xi, 1–2, 6.

[31] Ibid., 10.

[32] Ibid., 4, 13.

[33] Martha Nussbaum and Amartya Sen, "Internal Criticism and Indian Rationalist Traditions," in *Relativism: Interpretation and Confrontation*, ed. Michael Krausz (Notre Dame, Ind.: University of Notre Dame Press, 1989), 315.

[34] Martha Nussbaum, *Poetic Justice* (Boston: Beacon Press, 1995), xiii.

ethical and legal judging, Nussbaum wants us to bring "our evolving sense of principle and tradition to bear on a concrete context." We use "historically grounded and yet principled reasons."[35] Nussbaum draws on Aristotle, who held that principles are correct "only insofar as they do not err with regard to the particulars."[36] Nussbaum emphasizes the importance of being contextual, concrete, of putting ourselves in a particular situation, with all its complexity, and of using our emotions, empathy, and imagination in judging. She does not frame her argument as calling for an appeal to conventions and social practices, but insofar as these influence our responses to particular situations, then her argument, intended in part as a criticism of a purely Kantian, universalist principle conception of judgment, might be seen as among other things a call to recognize the importance of social practice.[37]

Nussbaum insists that there still is a role in judging for principles, even universal principles.[38] We've seen that Walzer agrees. Peter Steinberger is another theorist who suggests the priority of practice to principle yet who doesn't reject rational application of principles. In Steinberger's view, "Judgment in politics presupposes membership in a political community." "To judge in politics," writes Steinberger, "is thus to participate in a community and to help that community recall exactly which claims it regards as valid and sensible."[39] Judgments, in his view, arise from insight, operating "in light of the often implicit conceptual and theoretical materials that compose the intellectual foundations of a culture," though, he adds, they must be "reconstructed rationally."[40]

But some theorists who emphasize the importance of social practice in moral judgment seem to imply that we have no standards for judgment other than what our practices dictate, or that even if there are standards we should not employ them. Michael Oakeshott seems to devalue the role of principled criticism. In his view,

> moral ideals are not, in the first place, the products of reflective thought, the verbal expressions of unrealized ideas, which are then translated (with varying degrees of accuracy) into human behavior; they are the products of human behavior, of human practical activity, to which reflective thought gives subsequent, partial and abstract expression in words.[41]

[35] Ibid., 80, 84, 85.

[36] Martha Nussbaum, Love's Knowledge: Essays in Philosophy and Literature (New York: Oxford University Press, 1990), 69.

[37] It isn't clear, however, that Nussbaum would reject the idea that there are natural wrongs, or natural principles. In Poetic Justice she notes that it is possible to recognize human needs "that transcend boundaries of time, place, class, religion, and ethnicity" (45). She sometimes suggests that certain emotional responses are natural, as in writing "we will naturally be most concerned with the lot of those whose position is worst" (91).

[38] See, for example, Nussbaum, Love's Knowledge, 27.

[39] Peter Steinberger, The Concept of Political Judgment (Chicago: University of Chicago Press, 1993), 286.

[40] Ibid., 247–48.

[41] Michael Oakeshott, Rationalism in Politics and Other Essays (Indianapolis: Liberty Press, 1991); reprinted in Daly, ed., Communitarianism, 250.

For Oakeshott, a moral life is rooted in "habit of affection and behavior" rather than in reflective thought.

> We acquire habits of conduct, not by constructing a way of living upon rules or precepts learned by heart and subsequently practised, but by living with people who habitually behave in a certain manner: we acquire habits of conduct in the same way as we acquire our native language.[42]

What we learn can be formulated in rules and precepts, but we do not learn by learning rules and precepts; we learn by "imitation." This sort of moral education "does not give the ability to explain our actions in abstract terms, or defend them as emanations of moral principles." But it is more secure. "It is not subject to the kind of collapse which springs from the detection of some flaw or incoherence in a system of moral ideals. Intellectual error with regard to moral ideas or opinions does not compromise a moral life which is firmly based upon a habit of conduct."[43] Oakeshott does see some role for principled reflection; but reflection, if dominant, can lead to "sudden and ignominious collapse." "The constant analysis of behavior tends to undermine, not only prejudice in moral habit, but moral habit itself, and moral reflection may come to inhibit moral sensibility."[44]

Similar skepticism, not merely of the desirability of but of the very possibility of principled criticism, is expressed by Mounce and Phillips, in their book *Moral Practices*. They note an objection to the position that the rules of social practices, and not abstract principles, dictate what is right: surely we can ask whether we *should* have the moral rules that we do have, and in deciding whether we should, surely we need to appeal to abstract principles. Their response to this objection is that it is misleading "to regard our moral practices as something we justify by appeal to wider considerations."[45] They do not deny "that our reasons for acting in a certain way can be given in terms of moral considerations or moral principles" but say that it is mistaken to push moral inquiry to a further level that demands justifying why we have the moral rules we do. In their view, certain things just can't be questioned: "In order for a man to hold a moral position at all, there must be certain things it does not make sense for him to question. In our society, for example, it does not make sense to ask whether honesty is in general good, or murder bad, or generosity admirable."[46] Morality, in their view, is grounded in our forms of life, which are not themselves up for grabs or subject to justification.[47]

This takes deference to social practice too far. *Of course* we can intelligibly ask

---

[42] Oakeshott, *Rationalism*, 244–45. Of course some linguists, most notably Noam Chomsky, would reject Oakeshott's account of how we acquire language.

[43] Ibid.

[44] Ibid., 251, 248. Oakeshott gives the historical example of Christianity: "The urge to speculate, to abstract and to define, which overtook Christianity as a religion, infected also Christianity as a way of moral life" (253).

[45] D. Z. Phillips and H. O. Mounce, *Moral Practices* (New York: Shocken Books, 1970), 19–20.

[46] Ibid., 17.

[47] Ibid., 70; cf. 73–74.

whether we should have our practices.[48] The view I have taken, while sympathetic to Mounce and Phillips' position, does not fully embrace it. Sometimes the mere existence of a social practice is reason enough to conform to its demands; but other times it is not. There are contexts in which it is appropriate, even necessary, to consider the justification of our practices, and to do this we need to appeal to some standard(s).

PRACTICES AND PRINCIPLES

One point I have emphasized is that appreciation of the importance of social practice does not entail an irrational conservatism. I have argued for the importance of principled criticism and rejected the argument that we should adhere to tradition for the sake of tradition. I have also argued that at times it is appropriate to defer to expectations created by existing practices, even if these practices may not be the only or the best possibility. Practices and traditions can create expectations upon which it is reasonable to rely, and if people do so rely, it may be unfair suddenly to frustrate these expectations; or it may be unreasonable to admonish someone who acts in good faith in accordance with norms that are recognized as valid. This does not mean we should not, at an appropriate time, suggest reforms or even radical change in practices that would eventually lead to new expectations. With respect to some practices, *any* time would be appropriate to suggest reform or radical change.

Sometimes there are good reasons to defer to long-standing practice and traditions, other times there are not. We should defer only when it is reasonable or there are good reasons to do so. Because this is an important point, I want to develop it further. Recently the U.S. House of Representatives debated the "Defense of Marriage Act." Proposed in response to a state court's decision to require that gays and lesbians be allowed to have a marriage recorded as a state decree, the act would prevent any state from having to recognize any law passed by any other state respecting a relationship between persons of the same sex that is treated as a marriage; and it would define marriage for the purpose of interpreting federal law as a "legal union between one man and one woman as husband and

---

[48] Cf. Richard Flathman's criticism of Hanna Pitkin's "semantic rule approach" in his *Political Obligation* (New York: Atheneum Press, 1972). Pitkin argues it is a sign of "philosophical disorder" to seek reasons for precepts or general rules, such as that one must obey law or keep promises. In Pitkin's view, it simply is a conceptual truth, part of the meaning of promising, that one must keep promises; to ask whether we ought to keep a promise signals that one doesn't understand the concept of promising. Flathman responds that while it is important to understand concepts, we still can ask, meaningfully, why obey law, or why keep promises. Pitkin, he says, implies we can't ask for reasons for the general rule (that promises must be kept, that law must be obeyed) because this "implies a degree of freedom of choice on our parts which we do not in fact have." Pitkin never denies that it is possible to ask why we have our practices: "We can, under certain circumstances, competently and meaningfully question what is conventionally taken to be obligatory" (*Wittgenstein and Justice* [Berkeley: University of California Press, 1972], 227; cf. p. 201). This apparent discrepancy in Pitkin's account may disappear once we see there are different levels of justification (see discussion above).

wife."[49] One effect of the law would be to prevent legal recognition of homosexual marriage. The act raises many difficult issues: whether Congress has authority under the Constitution to allow states not to recognize laws enacted by other states; whether the federal budget can bear the burden legal recognition of homosexual marriage would impose; whether refusal to provide benefits to homosexual couples denies them equal protection of the law; whether it is proper to force those who oppose homosexuality to have their tax dollars be used to provide the benefits to which homosexual couples would be entitled if their marriages received legal recognition. But I shall leave aside these issues in order to address an issue raised by the Defense of Marriage Act that is central to the argument of this book: When we are deciding whether to radically change the institution of marriage so that it includes homosexual marriages, what force does the fact that the institution of marriage traditionally has been exclusively heterosexual "for time immemorial" have?[50]

My argument has been that we should not defer to a tradition simply because it is tradition; rather, we should have good reasons for adhering to it. I also argued that in some contexts it is reasonable to respect expectations upon which people rely even if they arose from a practice that we would choose not to have given the opportunity; even, perhaps, if there are no particularly good reasons for the practice. Suppose A hires B to be the head of a local Boy Scout troop on the assumption that B leads a stable, normal married life. A will not hire any single man because the fact that a man is single, in A's mind, means he is probably homosexual, and it is unacceptable in A's mind to have a homosexual as head of a Boy Scout troop. A assumes B is married to a woman because he asked B if he is single, and B answered no. It turns out B is married, but to another man. Had A known this he would not have hired B. We may challenge the reasonableness of A's beliefs about the suitability of homosexual men to lead Boy Scout troops or about the likelihood that being single implies one is homosexual, but nevertheless we might say that it would be reasonable for A to think he has no obligation to keep his promise to hire B once he finds out B is homosexual, because in making the promise he relied on an understanding of what it is to be married, an understanding that is reasonable given the fact that marriage traditionally has been exclusively between man and woman. In this context, deference to a tradition of exclusively heterosexual marriage may be reasonable even if we don't approve of this tradition.[51] But when Congress debated the Defense of Marriage Act, it was not concerned with such unlikely situations in which individuals rely on expectations arising from the tradition that marriage is uniquely between man

[49] H. R. 3396, section 2 and section 3; cited in *Congressional Record*, July 12, 1996 (House), H7480 (hereafter *CR*).

[50] Representative Canady of Florida used the phrase "time-immemorial": "Should the law elevate homosexual unions to the same status as the heterosexual relationships on which the traditional family is based, a status which has been reserved from time immemorial for the union between a man and a woman?" (*CR*, H7491)—his answer was of course no.

[51] Of course B might challenge A's decision not to keep his promise on constitutional grounds or on the basis that A's assumptions are flawed.

and woman. Many people would be surprised or even shocked to come across a homosexual married couple, but this does not necessarily mean they ever *rely* on an expectation that marriage is heterosexual. Needless to say, none of the representatives defending the act on the floor of the House argued that we need to respect expectations arising from a tradition upon which people reasonably rely. When Congress debated the act, it was concerned with what public policy should be, and in this context it is appropriate to subject the tradition, no matter how entrenched, to critical scrutiny. When doing *that,* it won't do simply to defend traditional ways because they are traditional.

Many of the act's defenders argued that the institution of marriage between man and woman is a bedrock of our society and that homosexual marriage would uproot our ethical foundations. They offered essentially a Burkean argument that what is old is good because it is old. Representative Bryant opposed legal recognition of homosexual marriage because "it would be against the traditional marriage of husband and wife."[52] William J. Bennett, in an editorial included in the *Congressional Record*, argues that "to insist that we maintain this traditional understanding of marriage is not an attempt to put others down. It is simply an acknowledgment and celebration of our most precious and important social act. Nor is this view arbitrary or idiosyncratic. It mirrors the accumulated wisdom of millennia and the teaching of every major religion."[53] Representative Barr of Georgia warned: "The very foundations of our society are in danger of being burned. The flames of hedonism, the flames of narcissism, the flames of self-centered morality are licking at the very foundations of our society: the family unit."[54] Representative Seastrand from California told her colleagues, "Traditional marriage is a house built on a rock. As shifting sands of public opinion and prevailing winds of compromise damage other institutions, marriage endures, and so must its historically legal definition."[55] The proposal to broaden the definition of marriage to include homosexual couples was linked by Representative Buyer from Indiana with a more general "humanism" that adheres to the principle "that the human being can do whatever they [sic] want, as long as it feels good and does not hurt others," and the Representative took his stand against this radical principle, calling for a return to traditional "religious principles."[56] Representative Hyde argued, "Now two men loving each other does not hurt anybody else's marriage, but it demeans, it lowers the concept of marriage by making it something that it should not be and is not, celebrating conduct that is not approved by the majority of the people."[57] In each of these cases, the argument is essentially that we should not change tradition because doing so would be a change from tradition; none of the above statements offers reasons for why it is

[52] *CR,* H4791.
[53] *Washington Post,* May 21, 1996; in *CR* H7495.
[54] *CR,* H4782.
[55] *CR,* H7485.
[56] *CR,* H7486.
[57] *CR,* H7499.

good to adhere to traditions, or to this particular tradition, built as it is on religious principles. Bennett comes close when he says the tradition reflects "the accumulated wisdom of millennia," but never explains why what is old is wise.

That an institution is old is not itself a reason not to change it, a point made by Representative Studds, an opponent of the act:

> It is a mistake sometimes to say this is the way things have always been, and therefore, that is good and they should always be that way. When this country was founded our revered Constitution was written in part by men who owned slaves. Women themselves were, in most of these States of ours, were virtually chattel. They did not have the right to own property. People of color were property for many years after this country was founded.[58]

Some representatives defending the act argued not simply that we must adhere to tradition for its own sake but that changing our traditional institution of marriage would have harmful consequences—they asserted that legal recognition of homosexual marriages would bring "social deterioration," the "ruin of families," and confusion, especially among young people, about sexual identities. Representative DeLay of Texas argued, "Children do best in a family with a mom and a dad. We need to protect our social and moral foundations. We should not be forced to send a message to our children that undermines the definition of marriage as the union between one man and one woman. Such attacks on the institution of marriage will only take us further down the road of social deterioration."[59] Representative Stearns made a similar point: "You threaten the future of families which have traditional marriage at their very heart. If traditional marriage is thrown by the wayside, brought down by your manipulation of the definition that has been accepted since the beginning of civilized society, children will suffer because family will lose its very essence. Instead of trying to ruin families we should be preserving them for future generations."[60] Representative Funderburk alluded to a conclusion of the Family Research Council: "Homosexuality has been discouraged in all cultures because it is inherently wrong and harmful to individuals, families, and societies."[61] Representative Smith of Texas also warned of the adverse consequences of radically revising the definition of marriage. Traditional marriage has served across the majority of cultures as a foundation for a stable society. Undermining traditional marriage by forcing States to legalize same-sex "marriages" will have far-reaching social consequences.[62] William J. Bennett also suggested an argument that changing this tradition would be harmful, in his editorial entered into the *Congressional Record*: same-sex marriage, he claims, would send "signals," particularly to the young: "Societal indifference about het-

---

[58] *CR*, H7491.
[59] *CR*, H7487.
[60] *CR*, H7488.
[61] *CR*, H7487.
[62] *CR*, H7494.

erosexuality and homosexuality would cause a lot of confusion."[63] And Representative Lipinski argued that "homosexual marriages would destroy thousands of
years of tradition which has upheld our society."[64]

None of their assertions were supported by any convincing evidence and seem
especially weak in light of arguments made by opponents of the act.[65] But at least
those making these assertions made an effort to provide reasons for maintaining
traditional practice. Once we see the tremendous difference between arguing that
we should maintain heterosexual marriage simply because it is what we have
always practiced, and providing reasons for why it is good to maintain the practice, then more energy could be more effectively spent focusing on whether ex-
tending marriage to include homosexual couples really would harm society. That
would be a more convincing reason for defending the act than the argument that
we should have things this way because this is how they always have been; or
even that the majority's values reflect tradition and changing tradition would
therefore be inconsistent with the majority's values.

The Defense of Marriage Act presents us with an example of how we need to
subject traditions to critical scrutiny and not simply accept them because they are
our traditions. A sizable number of people in the United States want to change
accepted practice, a much larger group is opposed to this change, and this leads
us naturally to consider whether practice as it is is as it should or must be. But
that we can and on many occasions should subject our traditions to critical scrutiny rather than simply accept them because they are so entrenched, does not
mean that in thinking about every issue with ethical or legal implications it is
appropriate to question all of the practices associated with the issue, to employ
principled criticism "all the way down." That has been the argument of the book.
In the final sections I consider some of the implications of the argument for
contemporary debates in political theory between liberals and communitarians,
and between cultural relativists and universalists.

---

[63] *CR*, H7494–95.

[64] *CR*, H7496. The clause "which has upheld our society" is important: Representative Lipinski
implies with it not simply that it is inherently wrong to change a long-standing tradition, but that
doing so would have harmful consequences—if we change what has held our society up, then,
presumably, that society may crumble. Of course if all Lipinski means in implying our society would
no longer be "upheld" is that certain traditions would no longer survive, then his argument belongs
more properly to the sort that holds we must adhere to tradition for its own sake.

[65] Representative Barney Frank responded to the claim that allowing homosexual marriages would
undermine traditional marriages: "People talk about their marriages being threatened. I find it implau-
sible that two men deciding to commit themselves to each other threatens the marriage of people a
couple of blocks away. I find it bizarre, even by the standards that my Republican colleagues are using
for this political argument here, to tell me that two women falling in love in Hawaii, as far away as you
can get and still be within the United States, threatens the marriage of people in other States" (*CR*,
H7483–84). Representative Gunderson added: "This legislation will do nothing to defend marriage.
May I suggest that no gay man is after your wives, and no lesbian is after your husbands. If marriage is
at risk in this country, and it may be—there are other more real factors at the heart of this problem.
May I suggest that alcohol abuse, spousal abuse, and even Sunday football are far more likely to
destroy marriage" (*CR*, H7493).

PRACTICES, PRINCIPLES, AND THE LIBERAL-COMMUNITARIAN DEBATE

Communitarianism has been described as "an amorphous and complex topic that has as yet no theoretical statement."[66] Communitarianism is an elusive theory, its proponents hard to pin down. MacIntyre, widely regarded as a leading communitarian, has recently disassociated himself from the label.[67] Much of the language of communitarian thinkers, in its emphasis on civic virtue, republicanism, and strong fellow feelings, suggests that the theory supposes a homogeneous group of people who interact face to face and care deeply about each other.[68] Some communitarians, though, deny that this is a requirement of genuine community. One recent critic of communitarianism declares that leading communitarians insist only that there be "widespread opportunities for everyone to participate in the important affairs of the community."[69] Yet neither MacIntyre nor Hegel, who is often pointed to as a "classical" source of communitarian thought, emphasize the importance of participation; Hegel, quite the contrary, wields some of his harshest criticism against adherents of participatory democracy. The intention of some communitarians seems less to assert truth claims about political life, more to instill an attitude in citizens that would contribute to the quality of our public life.[70] In this section I shall consider how this book's argument that social practices play an essential role in ethical and legal judgment bears on the elusive liberal-communitarian debate, and on one aspect of the debate in particular—what Stephen Gardbaum has referred to as a "metaethical debate" about the importance of social practice as a source of value.[71]

Efforts to characterize liberalism or communitarianism will probably fail to capture some of the subtleties of the theories bearing those labels. Nevertheless it is useful to consider some important differences one tends to find in the two sorts of theories. One difference concerns their accounts of the basis of legitimate political authority. According to classical liberal thought, the state's authority is legiti-

[66] Daley, ed. *Communitarianism*, ix. Cf. Susan Okin, *Justice, Gender, and the Family* (New York: Basic Books, 1989), 42, on communitarians lacking "any kind of developed theory."

[67] Daly, in her preface, thanks MacIntyre, "who allowed me to reprint his Lindley Lecture even though he denies that his philosophy is communitarian" (*Communitarianism*, xi).

[68] See Derek Phillips, *Looking Backward* (Princeton: Princeton University Press, 1993), 164: "It is in the nature of the communitarian ideal that membership is restricted to those having certain things in common: place of habitation, ancestors, language, tradition, religion, cultural patterns, and the like"; and Daly, ed., *Communitarianism*, xv: "The relationships [in a community] are personal and unmediated, usually face-to-face; friendship or a sense of obligation, rather than self-interest, holds the members together."

[69] Phillips, *Looking Backward*, 16; cf. Sullivan, in *Communitarianism*, ed. Daly, 199–200.

[70] See William Sullivan, *Reconstructing Public Philosophy* (Berkeley: University of California Press, 1982); Philip Selznick, *The Moral Community: Social Theory and the Promise of Community* (Berkeley: University of California Press, 1992); and Sheldon Wolin, "Contract and Birthright," *Political Theory* 14, no. 2 (May 1986): 179–93.

[71] Stephen A. Gardbaum, "Law, Politics, and the Claims of Community," *Michigan Law Review* 90, no. 4 (February 1992): 693.

mate insofar as it derives from the consent of the governed. On the classical liberal view, a state is a voluntary group of members with rights and obligations based on consent. The state is something we join for the sake of convenience, and specifically to protect our life and property. The state cannot legitimately ask us to do anything to which we would not reasonably have consented—both Hobbes and Beccaria infer that capital punishment is illegitimate because no one would have rationally agreed to join the state at all if that would entail the loss of his life.[72] To the communitarian, in contrast, the locus of political authority lies not in the preferences or wills of individuals but in customs, traditions, and practices shared by members of a community, which no individual ever explicitly chooses.[73] For Hegel (who has been called the "original mouthpiece of modern communitarianism,"[74] perhaps misleadingly), we do not choose to live in a state—we must. The question "Who is to frame the constitution?" is, Hegel says, nonsensical, "for it presupposes that there is no constitution there, but only an agglomeration of atomic individuals."[75]

While there is a tendency for liberals to be consent theorists or social-contract theorists, and for communitarians to reject this theory of political obligation, it would be misleading to characterize the liberal-communitarian debate as *essentially* about the role of consent in a theory of political obligation. One needn't be a communitarian to oppose liberal social-contract theory or the idea that authority is legitimate because it is consented to, views to which not all contemporary political theorists who would regard themselves as liberal would assent. I have argued that some ethical and legal judgments necessarily make reference to social practices that are never consented to, and insofar as these judgments establish obligations, such as an obligation to keep a promise upon which someone has reasonably relied, or to avoid interfering with a reasonable expectation of privacy, then the content of these particular obligations are not voluntarily undertaken or consented to, even if the general obligation conferring institution (be it the practice of promising or the civil law concerning the tort of invasion of privacy) is consented to. But this point has little bearing on the debate about why we should obey laws or otherwise comply with the demands of the state. There are more effective criticisms of consent theories of political obligation than the criticism that we don't always consent to all of the conditions that shape the content of our obligations.

Sometimes liberals are characterized as pluralists who defend the diversity and ultimate subjectivity of values and insist that a state must respect this diversity,

[72] Cesare Bonesana Beccaria, *An Essay on Crimes and Punishments* (Philadelphia: William P. Farrand, 1809); Thomas Hobbes, *Leviathan* (New York: Collier Books, 1962), chap. 21. For discussion, see Tunick, *Punishment: Theory and Practice,* 77–78.

[73] Cf. Christina Hoff Sommers, "Filial Morality," *Journal of Philosophy* 8 (1986): 439–56, on how we never voluntarily undertake or consent to many of our obligations.

[74] Sibyl A. Schwarzenbach, "Rawls, Hegel, and Communitarianism," *Political Theory* 19, no. 4 (November 1991): 562.

[75] G. W. F. Hegel, *Philosophy of Right,* trans. T. M. Knox (Oxford: Oxford University Press, 1952), par. 273 Remark, p. 178.

while communitarians are seen as insisting that values are objective, defined not by individuals' subjective preferences but by objective standards of a given community that are shared by all its members. Isaiah Berlin writes:

> Most modern liberals, at their most consistent, want a situation in which as many individuals as possible can realize as many of their ends as possible, without assessment of the value of these ends as such, save in so far as they may frustrate the purposes of others. They wish the frontiers between individuals or groups of men to be drawn solely with a view to preventing collisions between human purposes, all of which must be considered to be equally ultimate, uncriticizable ends in themselves.[76]

Faced with a world created and recreated by human beings, with no design or blueprint to be followed, the liberal is said to celebrate the right of self-creation, the freedom from preordained constraints, and insists the space that we have come to see as our space to fill remains accessible to different voices of different creators. We need stability and order but only enough to provide us with the opportunities to pursue our own conception of the good life. The liberal, wanting a safe space in which each of us can pursue our own conception of the good, advocates either a minimalist state that secures individual rights and would constrain individual liberty only to prevent an individual from harming another (the harm principle) or, on some versions, a moderately interventionist state that promotes our capacity to realize our own good.[77] But communitarians worry about all this space being filled up with self-styled personal philosophies that flout tradition. Hegel worried about this most of all, castigating those who think that the ethical world "should be given over—as in fact of course it is not—to the subjective accident of opinion and caprice."[78]

This characterization of the debate is also misleading, for not all liberals believe that values are ultimately subjective and not all communitarians would suggest that individuals should pursue the same ends, or share the same preferences. Hegel in particular believes that the modern state necessarily gives voice to individual "particularity," allowing people to pursue their own preferences in the realm of civil society. The argument of this book implies that ethical or legal judgments are not a matter of personal preference or taste, and rather are subject to societal standards of reasonableness, but it does not imply that members of the same community should have the same values or pursue the same ends. The book's argument points to a communitarian truth far more modest and plausible than the overblown claim sometimes attributed to communitarians that political societies consist of homogeneous members who share the same values and conception of the good. By understanding some of the ways in which local understandings of reasonableness shape ethical and legal judgments, we can see that communitarianism need not imply that political communities consist of like-

[76] Isaiah Berlin, "Two Concepts of Liberty," in *Four Essays on Liberty* (Oxford: Oxford University Press, 1969), 153, n. 1.

[77] For one defense of liberalism that is consistent with some degree of paternalism, see Cass Sunstein, "Preferences and Politics," *Philosophy and Public Affairs* 20 (1991): 3–34.

[78] Hegel, *Philosophy of Right*, preface, 6.

thinking people, or that it is proper for the state to legislate conformity by restricting individuals from leading diverse lifestyles. Agreeing to the proposition that local understandings shape ethical and legal judgments does not entail commitment to the politically conservative position that justifies state restrictions of individual liberty for the sake of promoting a common good.[79] But it does cast doubt on the position some liberals take that individuals are free to roam unconstrained in pursuing their own self-conceived conception of a good life so long as they don't violate certain basic and universal rights, or that we should always be able to subject our practices and laws to critical scrutiny. For example, a community may regard evacuation as private, haggling as an accepted means of market exchange, hugging as a sexual advance, or it may have a particular conception of what respect is due to the dead. These understandings, expressed in their practices and laws, may provide the basis for objectively justified constraints on liberty, constraints that are not up for grabs in this community but which would be illegitimate in other communities with different understandings. But it would be quite odd to declare from this fact that communities share some strong sense of a common good.

It is more accurate to regard liberalism as entailing a commitment to a harm principle, and communitarianism as allowing for greater restraints upon individual liberty than what the harm principle allows. The argument of this book implies neither acceptance nor rejection of the harm principle. But it *does* imply that *whatever* liberty-limiting principle we do apply is constrained in its application by social practices and shared understandings.

We can see some of the implications for the liberal- communitarian debate of the argument that social practices play an essential role in ethical and legal judgment by focusing on what Gardbaum has called the metaethical debate. Communitarians turn to social practices for standards of ethical conduct, challenging a rationalist premise, shared by many liberals, that ethical standards are given not by the existence of practices, but by reason and reflection alone. For example, MacIntyre argues that "what I learn as a guide to my actions and as a standard for evaluating them is never morality as such, but always the highly specific morality of some highly specific social order."[80] MacIntyre contrasts this view with liberalism, which, he says, sees morality as constituted by rules or principles "to which any rational person would under certain ideal conditions give assent" from a standpoint that "is independent of all social particularity." MacIntyre says that liberalism judges all social structures "from a standpoint independent of all of [these structures]."

> According to the liberal account of morality *where* and *from whom* I learn the principles and precepts of morality are and must be irrelevant both to the question of what the

---

[79] Gardbaum argues that there are three distinct communitarian claims: a metaethical claim, a claim about agency, and a political claim; and he argues that metaethical communitarianism does not entail a political position of "strong communitarianism." See Gardbaum, "Law, Politics, and the Claims of Community," 689, 719.

[80] MacIntyre, in *Communitarianism,* ed. Daly, 311.

content of morality is and to that of the nature of my commitment to it, as irrelevant as *where* and *from whom* I learn the principles and precepts of mathematics are to the content of mathematics and the nature of my commitment to mathematical truths.[81]

William Sullivan contrasts the moral ideal of liberalism, which he says is discerned by appeal to abstract principles, with the communitarian moral ideal, which "is understood not through a deduction of abstract concepts but within the kind of interpretive circle that describes all moral life." For communitarians, "discernment of the general good is the guiding norm for discussions of justice," and this discernment, says Sullivan, "always depends on shared understandings derived from a tradition of cultivated experience."[82]

Borrowing Gardbaum's terminology, we can call the position that social practices and shared understandings play an essential role in ethical and legal judgment "metaethical communitarianism."[83] Metaethical communitarianism has not won out, insofar as some leading liberal theorists at times explicitly deny any role for social practice in determining what is right, or insist that even if currently moral or legal judgments refer to social practices we can always explain the judgments by referring to principles that do not presume the existence of any shared social practices. I have argued that they are wrong and that we should be committed to metaethical communitarianism. Of course many liberal theorists would agree that social practice plays some role in ethical and legal judgment. Such recognition is of little use unless it is made clear precisely what role practice plays and what significance this role has. There *is* disagreement about the role of social practice in ethical and legal judgment among liberals and communitarians, but the basis of disagreement is elusive and will remain so unless we are attentive to the complicated ways in which practices and principles interact. The implications of metaethical communitarianism need to be spelled out if commitment to it is to have any real meaning.

I have argued that social practice plays an essential role even in a principled account of ethics or law. One implication of the argument has been that sometimes ethical or legal judgments presuppose practices that themselves are not subject to critical scrutiny, that deference to practice is sometimes appropriate and even justified. Some leading liberal theorists are critical of such deference. Instead of using community standards to evaluate people's preferences, they argue, we should adjust these standards to the pattern of people's preferences.[84]

---

[81] MacIntyre, in *Communitarianism*, ed. Daly, 310–11. Cf. Daly: for the liberal, "the moral value of an action is determined by a body of universally applicable principles" (*Communitarianism*, xvi).

[82] William Sullivan, in *Communitarianism*, ed. Daly, 198, 200.

[83] I borrow Gardbaum's term and share his view that commitment to metaethical communitarianism does not entail commitment to other communitarian claims, a position earlier advanced by Charles Taylor in his "Cross-Purposes: The Liberal-Communitarian Debate," in *Liberalism and the Moral Life*, ed., Nancy Rosenblum (Cambridge: Harvard University Press, 1989), 159–82. However, I do not follow Gardbaum's particular account of the metaethical debate. In particular, he characterizes this debate as about the "source of value, not the content" (Gardbaum, "Law, Politics, and the Claims of Community," 706), whereas in my view social practices, in being a source of ethical and legal judgments, determine the content of these judgements.

[84] Will Kymlicka, *Contemporary Political Philosophy* (Oxford: Oxford University Press, 1990), 206.

Metaethical communitarianism, it is argued, insists that we conform with existing social customs and practices, and is unable to apply any standards to those practices to see whether they are right.[85] Liberals, in contrast, "insist that we have an ability to detach ourselves from any particular social practice," that nothing is "set for us," and that we can always question and replace the practices given to us rather than necessarily accept them as the community's values. Where the communitarian points us to how we are already born into a community with social practices, to how we cannot "start from scratch" as liberal contractarian thinkers seem to imply, the liberal replies that "we do indeed find ourselves in various relationships, but we do not always like what we find. . . . we feel capable of questioning" whether our practices are valuable.[86] Some liberals accuse communitarians of being blindly committed to existing practices. This commitment strikes the liberal not only as irrational—for surely there should be good reasons for being committed to our practices apart from their happening to be our practices; it is relativistic as well, implying that if a different community believes that social practices that we regard as egregiously cruel and barbaric are part of that community's common good, this is sufficient to justify these practices, while for the liberal, it is not.[87]

Such liberal criticisms of metaethical communitarianism miss the mark because they mistakenly equate metaethical communitarianism with the rejection of principled criticism or with a theory of political obligation that sees no place for justified disobedience. Hegel, for example, is a metaethical communitarian, but he insists that the practices to which we appeal in determining what is right are rational and he does leave open the possibility for justified disobedience.[88] However, if metaethical communitarianism is not to collapse into a liberal theory that recognizes how practices shape preferences but which nevertheless insists that we can always subject our practices to the critical scrutiny of reason, or to the vote of a majority or supermajority at an actual or hypothetical constitutional convention, then it must see practice as somehow constraining our application of principles. In the previous chapters I have shown some of the complex ways in which practices and principles interact, and in doing so I have argued that social practices can play precisely this role. The liberal is sometimes right to insist that we not simply defer blindly to customs and traditions; yet that doesn't mean that we are never warranted in deferring to social practices, even those to which we never, or would not hypothetically, consent. The liberal is sometimes right to refuse unquestioningly to obey whatever practices we happen to find, and to detach herself

---

[85] Jeremy Waldron, "Particular Values and Critical Morality," *California Law Review* 77, no. 3 (May 1989): 561–90; Kymlicka, *Contemporary Political Philosophy,* 207. Cf. Joseph Tussman, *Obligation and the Body Politic* (New York: Oxford University Press, 1960), 6: "moral shrinks to 'mores'"; and Derek Phillips, *Looking Backward,* 183–84.

[86] Kymlicka, *Contemporary Political Philosophy,* 210–11, 213; cf. 215, 222. Cf. Phillips, *Looking Backward,* 183–84, on communitarian thinking being "unreflective."

[87] See Okin, *Justice, Gender, and the Family,* 62–68.

[88] See Mark Tunick, "Hegel on Justified Disobedience," forthcoming in *Political Theory,* and chapter two, above.

from particular practices and ask whether they should be accepted, to ask whether they accord with valid principles; yet that doesn't mean that in ethical and legal judging we should, or can, subject practices to principled criticism "all the way down"; it does not mean that all of our conventions are always up for grabs. Sometimes it is appropriate simply to accept the fact that we have certain norms. Sometimes it is not. Rather than adhere to a theoretical position that insists that morality is nothing but convention, and is based on nothing but the shared understandings and practices of a community; or to the position that morality ultimately involves reflection and application of valid principles only, and that these principles are natural principles that do not refer to the existence of a social practice, we need to recognize the complexity of ethical and legal judgment, its contextual nature, and how in some contexts it is reasonable to defer to culturally variant social practices, while in other contexts it is necessary to "step outside the city" and subject practices to critical scrutiny. Application of principles sometimes necessarily involves appeal to social practices that are justified perhaps for no other reason than that they have created expectations upon which people rely.

Liberal accusations that communitarians are antirationalists blindly deferring to inherited traditions regardless of whether these traditions are justified often miss the mark, just as do communitarian accusations that liberals completely ignore the role of social practices. (A few do, but most do not.) But it would be wrong to conclude that the liberal-communitarian debate simply collapses because no good liberal theorist would deny that practices are important, and no good communitarian would advocate blind deference to traditions. The point of this book has been to go beyond the proclaimed sensitivity of some liberal, rationalist, enlightenment, and universalist thinkers to the role of culturally variant practices, and to insist that we specify precisely how practice is important, and in what sense we should or must recognize the claims of those who defend practices and traditions against the piercing light of reason. When we understand some of the complex ways in which practices and principles interact, we will be able to show to the unbounded rationalists for whom everything is subject to principled scrutiny that *sometimes* uncritical deference to practice is appropriate and justified, that everything is not always up for grabs. This book specifies a theory of metaethical communitarianism by clarifying precisely how, in a variety of particular contexts, social practices are an important constraint on our selection and application of principles.

One important implication of this account of metaethical communitarianism is that one's political identity shapes one's ethical and legal obligations. Talk of a shared political identity may strike the liberal at best as a comfortable metaphysical blanket, at worst as a dangerous moral and political immaturity.[89] To be sure, fellow citizens all pay taxes to the same government, all carry the same sort of social security card, and are all obligated to obey many of the same laws—but to say that they share in one identity seems to hearken back to the hackneyed and

---

[89] Berlin, "Two Concepts of Liberty," 172.

mystical medieval metaphor of the state as an organism and individuals as its parts. To draw political implications about the proper role of the state from this metaphor is, to the liberal, to turn wishful thinking into an illiberal and potentially dangerous political agenda. In some liberal views, there are no special ties that bind. A body politic, in the classical liberal account, is a voluntary group of members and agents. Individuals create obligations by contracts and promises. They can do this with anyone, the argument goes, since all human beings of sound mind can promise or contract. What leads particular people to form bonds is contingent on with whom they happen to interact. Throughout history these have been people who live in the same territory and who encounter each other repeatedly. But in principle we can be bound to any other human being. For example, in Kant's account, what unites individuals is not the fact that they share traditions, language, or ideals, but that they "can come into practical relations with one another." Eventually, Kant argues, since the earth's surface is closed, we will come to interact with all human beings and the right of nations will lead "inevitably" to a cosmopolitan Right.[90]

In pointing to some of the ways shared social practices and understandings shape ethical and legal judgments, I have implied that Hegel is more accurate than Kant about the nature of political identity. But it is important to see precisely what this means. People within a community may share social practices that create expectations upon which they rely. But acknowledging this is a far cry from asserting some of the claims about homogeneity and shared political identity often attributed to communitarian thinkers. For Michael Walzer, in thinking about questions of distributive justice we ask "what choices have we already made in the course of our common life: What understandings do we (really share)?" Walzer believes there are shared understandings, of what he calls "the political community," which "is probably the closest we can come to a world of common meaning." Its members share a "collective consciousness" and "sensibilities and intuitions." The members have "some special commitment to one another," sharing in a "common life." But, Walzer rightly acknowledges, these communities may not be coextensive with "a growing number of states in the world today where sensibilities and intuitions aren't readily shared."[91]

Even Hegel does not think that members of a modern state are homogeneous:

In our day the tie between members of a state in respect of manners [*Sitten*], education [*Bildung*], language may be rather loose or even non-existent. Identity in these matters, once the foundation of a people's union, is now to be reckoned amongst the accidents whose character does not hinder a mass from constituting a public authority. Rome or Athens, like any small modern state, could not have subsisted if the numerous languages current in the Russian Empire had been spoken within their borders, or if amongst their citizens manners [*Sitten*] had been as different as they are in Russia, or for that matter, as manners and education are now in every big city in a large country. Difference in language and dialect (the latter exacerbates separation even more than

---

[90] *MM*, 311.
[91] Walzer, *Spheres of Justice,* 5, 28–29, 62; cf. 26, 103, 228.

complete unintelligibility does), and difference in manners and education in the separate estates, which makes men known to one another in hardly anything but outward
appearance—such heterogeneous and at the same time most powerful factors the pre-
ponderating weight of the Roman Empire's power (once it had become great) was able
to hold together, just as in modern states the same result is produced by the spirit and
art of political institutions. Thus dissimilarity in culture and manners is a necessary
product as well as a necessary condition of the stability of modern states. . . . [I]n
religion at least an identity might have been thought necessary, but this identity too is
something which modern states have found that they can do without.[92]

In this passage from The German Constitution, perhaps more revealing than any
other of his views on political identity, Hegel, often said to be a leading communitarian, emphasizes the diversity among members of a modern state.

So in siding with Hegel against Kant on this point, I am not asserting that
members of a political community are all alike or always in agreement. In the
previous chapters I have indicated several ways in which a community, or even a
nation, may share certain understandings or norms that affect, for example, what
is regarded as a reasonable expectation of privacy. The basis for this commonality
may be as mundane as the fact that their houses all lack heating; or it may be that
they share rituals, or norms for bargaining, technology, conceptions of the body,
or a political ideology. There are dominant norms that shape judgments within a
community of what is reasonable. Of course within the United States there are
peoples with different customs and therefore with different expectations about
when it is reasonable to rely on one's word, or with different understandings of
when it is reasonable to expect privacy. But that dominant understandings may
not be shared by all, or may not exist at all, is no reason to ignore the role social
practice nevertheless plays; we might rather conclude from the fact of difference
that we need to practice tolerance, for if practices do give rise to expectations
upon which people rely, and it is reasonable to respect these expectations, we
should want to give attention when thinking about the reasonableness of an
action in a particular context to whether practices which we think are shared by
all members of the community did indeed come into play in the particular
context.[93]

PRACTICES, PRINCIPLES, AND THE RELATIVISM-UNIVERSALISM DEBATE

One objection made to communitarian political theory is that in asserting that
judgments are based on local conceptions of right and wrong rather than on
standards that we might use to determine whether these conceptions are correct,
the communitarian implies that judgments are relative to these local conceptions.

[92] Hegel, German Constitution, in Hegel's Political Writings, 158. In a paper in progress I discuss this
passage in greater detail; see Tunick, "Political Identity and the Ties that Bind."

[93] This is a topic that I am pursuing further in research devoted to the "cultural defense" in U.S.
criminal law. Here the issue is how U.S. criminal law should be applied to people from different
cultures living in the United States; see chapter 1.

This is objectionable, first, because it surely is possible to criticize community standards;[94] second, because members of society often do not agree on what is right—local conceptions are sometimes contested;[95] and third, because even when there is a dominant understanding, it may be dominant only because a group with power is able to shape understandings through coercive means.[96] These objections assume that there are standards for determining right and wrong that are not relative to local understanding. The liberal-communitarian debate, then, leads naturally to another debate, about whether ethics are relative or whether there are universal standards of right and wrong, and in this final section I want briefly to consider the implications my argument has for this debate.

To some, relativism is the position that "every belief is as good as every other." But few if any philosophers who adhere to a version of relativism would agree with this position.[97] A more common and reputable version of relativism, the one on which I shall focus, is what Hanna Pitkin has usefully called "practice relativism." It holds

> that cultures and societies are divided into distinct practices or activities or spheres (Wittgenstein says "language games"), each with its own norms and standards of excellence embedded in the practice, into which you get initiated as you learn the practice. . . . It is okay to judge by those agreed, shared standards *within* a practice or sphere [on this view], but not across boundaries, for there are no trans-practice standards.[98]

This relativism, a version of what is often called cultural relativism, does not hold that each man's opinion is the measure of truth—it does not contend that truth is subjective. There are objective standards for truth, on this view, standards found by turning to social practices and conventions.[99] (One can believe that there are objectively correct answers to moral questions without thinking that these answers must be universally valid.)[100] It denies the existence not of objective stan-

---

[94] Ronald Dworkin, in *Communitarianism*, ed. Daly, 114: "In the end . . . political theory can make no contribution to how we govern ourselves except by struggling, against all the impulses that drag us back into our own culture, toward generality and some reflective basis for deciding which of our traditional distinctions and discriminations are genuine and which spurious, which contribute to the flourishing of the ideals we want, after reflection, to embrace and which serve only to protect us from the personal costs of that demanding process. We cannot leave justice to convention and anecdote."

[95] Cf. Susan Okin, in *Communitarianism*, ed. Daly, 130–33; and Amy Gutmann, "The Challenge of Multiculturalism in Political Ethics," *Philosophy and Public Affairs* 22 (summer 1993): 175.

[96] Gutmann, "Multiculturalism," 176.

[97] Richard Rorty, for example, distinguishes his brand of relativism from this crude version; he holds not that every belief is as good as every other, but that "there is nothing to be said about either truth or rationality apart from descriptions of the familiar procedures of justification which a given society—ours—uses in one or another area of inquiry" (Richard Rorty, "Solidarity or Objectivity?" 37).

[98] Hanna Pitkin, "Relativism: A Lecture," *Journal of Social Philosophy*, 25th anniversary volume (1994): 179–80.

[99] See Phillips and Mounce, *Moral Practices*, 62; they add that on this nonsubjective relativism, "man remains the measure of all things, for these conventions are nothing but a reflection of what the majority of men have decided to call bad or false."

[100] Cf. Richard Bernstein, *Beyond Objectivism and Relativism: Science, Hermeneutics, and Praxis*

dards but of "any transcultural norms, justifiable by reference to reasons of universal human validity" with which we could criticize "local conceptions of the good."[101] In this view, if according to a culture's social understandings polygamy is just, then it is just for that culture.[102] Universalists oppose relativism. For them certain practices, such as slavery, infanticide, perhaps polygamy, are unjust, regardless of whether they are regarded as just by a particular society.[103]

The implication of my argument is that it is a mistake to think morality is *either* universal *or* relative. Sometimes a judgment that a person has acted badly is appropriate only if that person shares particular social practices. Conduct that is reasonable in one society can be unreasonable in another because different social practices engender different norms of reasonableness. Sometimes to decide whether someone has acted reasonably, morally or legally, requires taking into account that person's cultural upbringing and political identity. It may be unreasonable to chastise a Tongan for failing to keep a promise, or to mete out to Fumiko Kimura the sentence we normally reserve for those who commit voluntary manslaughter, or to criticize a Mehinaku tribesman for overstepping our boundaries of privacy, or to allow a police officer to search through garbage without a warrant if doing so violates societal expectations of privacy.

But this does not mean we can't criticize a society's practices or judgments. My argument holds that there are standards for ethical and legal judgment that can be critical of social consensus; but it denies that these standards come from nowhere, or make no reference to social practice broadly understood. At times it is appropriate to criticize practices regardless of their being recognized as valid, and in doing so we may appeal to principles shared by members of that society or to arguments that a society's members never have accepted but which we feel they

---

(Philadelphia: University of Pennsylvania Press, 1983), 11: "A relativist need not be a subjectivist, and a subjectivist is not necessarily a relativist."

101 Martha Nussbaum, "Non-Relative Virtues: An Aristotelian Approach," in *The Quality of Life*, ed. Martha Nussbaum and Amartya Sen (Oxford: Oxford University Press, 1993), 243.

102 Gutmann, "Multiculturalism," 172–73. Cf. Gilbert Harman, "Moral Relativism Defended," *Philosophical Review* 84 (1975): 3–22, discussed in chapter three; and Richard Bernstein, *Beyond Objectivism and Relativism*, 8: relativism is the view that what's right is relative to a specific form of life, society, or culture.

103 Amy Gutmann provides one important account of this position. Gutmann begins by making what she says is a modest claim of universalism: there are standards of "reasonableness with regard to social justice" that are relative to available understandings but which are not tied to a particular community or placed beyond critical scrutiny. "Some basic human goods span the considerable diversity of modern cultures and support a set of ethical standards that are universal at least for the world as we know it and human beings as we know them"(Gutmann, "Multiculturalism," 191, 193— Gutmann gives as examples of universal wrongs arbitrary arrests and systematic deception, 193). While holding to some version of universalism, Gutmann rejects what she calls "comprehensive universalism," which is an extreme ethical absolutism that ignores the fact of moral disagreement; but at the same time she does not rule out the "possibility of singularly correct resolutions of these conflicts that are not now known"(195). Gutmann's resolution to the relativism-universalism debate is a position she calls "deliberative universalism," which "relies partly upon a core of universal principles and partly upon publicly accountable deliberation to address fundamental conflicts . . . that reason has yet to resolve"(193).

ought to accept. But at other times it is appropriate to defer to existing practices or to invoke principles that are not detached from those practices. Rather than decide whether we should call this position relativist or not, I think it is more useful to reject the dichotomy that sees judgments as *either* appealing to cultural norms and standards that "depend on" social practice, *or* appealing to transcultural standards that are "independent" of the existence of social practices.

Some theorists who have recently addressed the relativism-universalism debate similarly suggest a compromise position; some of these are the same theorists who, in an earlier section, we saw recognize a role for both principle and practice. In addition, there is Richard Bernstein, who refuses to take sides in this debate, which he defines as a debate between relativism and "objectivism," or the view that there is a "permanent, ahistorical matrix or framework to which we can ultimately appeal" to make judgments. He seeks, rather, to overcome the dichotomy by recognizing that there are standards of rationality, that there is reason, but seeing reason as historical or situated reason.[104] In one passage foreshadowing the argument of Nussbaum, Bernstein appeals to a type of reasoning "in which there is a mediation between general principles and a concrete particular situation that requires choice and decision."[105] Charles Taylor also recognizes the role of reason, but also that its application will depend on our background differences. While he leaves room for relativism in situations involving "very different cultures," he insists that "we should not give up on reason too early." We might, for example, "successfully challenge the cosmology or semi-articulate beliefs about the way things have to be" that undergird a culture's judgments about what is just.[106] Alasdair MacIntyre, like Bernstein, does not deny there are standards of rationality, and insists, "No one at any stage can ever rule out the future possibility of their present beliefs and judgments being shown to be inadequate in a variety of ways." But MacIntyre seems to give particular weight to the relativist position for he rejects the view that standards of rationality are "equally available, at least in principle, to all persons, whatever tradition they may happen to find themselves in." Rather, "we, whoever we are, can only begin enquiry from the vantage point afforded by our relationship to some specific social and intellectual past."[107] It isn't entirely clear what this means; it might mean that while we can employ what Walzer calls thin principles that are universally shared, ultimately these thin principles derive from a thick, particular, historically situated morality, which is of course Walzer's position. But in saying there are no standards equally available to all, MacIntyre might mean that there are no thin, universal principles, and that position, I think, tips too much toward an uncompromising relativism. What I think we should say here is that there are some principles that may be universally shared, and they may be shared because certain practices or values

104 Bernstein, *Beyond Objectivism and Relativism*, 37, 172.

105 Ibid., 54.

106 Charles Taylor, "Explanation and Practical Reason," in *The Quality of Life*, ed. Martha Nussbaum and Amartya Sen, 226–27.

107 Alasdair MacIntyre, *Whose Justice? Which Rationality?* (Notre Dame: University of Notre Dame Press, 1988), 361, 393, 401.

have been adapted by all human societies;[108] but precisely what these principles imply in particular situations will often depend on how they are interpreted, and that is something that we can expect to vary among societies. Walzer gives the example of how in the medieval world there was socialized distribution of the "cure of souls" but not of health care, since the former was a highly valued good not the latter. This distribution, which may in some sense reflect a universal principle of just distribution, was nevertheless rooted in a "maximalist morality, a thick understanding of life and death, a human culture"; and, adds Walzer, "it makes no moral sense" to insist they "should have had our understanding of life and death."[109]

By using the case studies presented in this book, I have tried to provide a concrete account of precisely how principles and social practice interact when making ethical and legal judgments. When we turn to particular instances of ethical and legal judging, we find that it is appropriate sometimes to appeal to principles that seem foreign to a culture to criticize aspects of that culture, sometimes to appeal to principles immanent in a culture and its practices, sometimes to defer to expectations arising from practices without subjecting the practices to critical scrutiny. Sometimes we apply principles that transcend any particular culture, such as MacCormick's principle of reliance, Scanlon's principle of fidelity, the principle of utility, the mischance principle, or the harm principle; but practices and local understandings relative to particular cultures or subcultures may determine how the principle is to be applied. Those who want an easy answer to the issues I have presented—practice or principle, which is it? relativism or universalism, which is it?—may be disappointed with an answer that refuses to choose and that insists there is no single answer that covers all of the ethical and legal issues that arise and that we must be attentive to the particular situation in which these issues arise to see what role practices and principles play. But seeing how ethical and legal dilemmas often do not lend themselves to easy answers, it really should not be surprising at all that a theory about how we go about resolving such dilemmas resists either/or approaches.

---

[108] Walzer notes that it may empirically be the case that "certain internal principles, certain conceptions of social goods, are reiterated in many, perhaps in all, human societies" (*Spheres of Justice*, 314 n.).

[109] Walzer, *Thick and Thin*, 28–30.

Amsterdam, Anthony. "Perspectives on the Fourth Amendment." *Minnesota Law Review* 58 (1974): 349–477.

Anscombe, G. E. M. "On Promising and its Justice." In *Ethics, Religion and Politics*. Vol. 3 of *Collected Papers*. Minneapolis: University of Minnesota Press, 1981.

———. "Rules, Rights and Promises." In *Ethics, Religion and Politics*, vol. 3 of *Collected Papers*. Minneapolis: University of Minnesota Press, 1981.

Ardal, Páll S. "And That's a Promise." *Philosophy Quarterly* 18, no. 72 (July 1968): 225–37.

Ariès, Philippe. *Centuries of Childhood: A Social History of Family Life*, translated by Robert Baldick. New York: Random House, 1962.

Ariès, Philippe, and Georges Duby, eds. *A History of Private Life*. 5 vols. Cambridge: Belknap Press of Harvard University, 1987–.

Arndt, H. W. *Australian Quarterly* 21, no. 3 (September 1949): 68–71.

Atiyah, P. S. *Promises, Morals, and Law*. Oxford: Oxford University Press, 1981.

———. Review of Charles Fried's *Contract as Promise*. *Harvard Law Review* 95 (1981): 509–28.

Austin, J. L. *Philosophical Papers*. Oxford: Oxford University Press, 1961.

Avineri, Shlomo. *Hegel's Theory of the Modern State*. Cambridge: Cambridge University Press, 1972.

Barber, Benjamin. *Strong Democracy*. Berkeley: University of California Press, 1984.

Barnett, Randy E. "A Consent Theory of Contract." *Columbia Law Review* 86 (1986): 269–321.

Bedau, Hugo, ed. *Civil Disobedience: Theory and Practice*. New York: Pegasus, 1969.

Benhabib, Seyla. "Obligation, Contract and Exchange: On the Significance of Hegel's Abstract Right." In *State and Civil Society*, edited by Pelczynski.

Benn, Stanley I. "Privacy, Freedom and Respect for Persons." In *Philosophical Dimensions of Privacy*, edited by Schoeman.

Bentham, Jeremy. "Defence of Usury." In *Works*, edited by Bowring, vol. 9.

———. "Of the Influence of Time and Place in Matters of Legislation," in *Works*, edited by Bowring, vol. 1.

———. *Works*, ed. John Bowring, 11 vols. Edinburgh: William Tait, 1838.

Beran, Harry. *The Consent Theory of Political Obligation*. London: Croom Helm, 1987.

———. "In Defense of the Consent Theory of Political Obligation and Authority." *Ethics* 87, no. 3 (April 1977): 260–71.

Berlin, Isaiah. "Two Concepts of Liberty." In *Four Essays on Liberty*. Oxford: Oxford University Press, 1969.

Bernstein, Richard. *Beyond Objectivism and Relativism: Science, Hermeneutics, and Praxis*. Philadelphia: University of Pennsylvania Press, 1983.

Bettelheim, Bruno. "The Right of Privacy Is a Myth." *Saturday Evening Post,* July 27, 1968.

Bloustein, Edward. "Privacy as an Aspect of Human Dignity." *New York University Law Review* 39 (1964): 962–1007. Reprinted in *Philosophical Dimensions of Privacy*, edited by Schoeman.

Brandt, Richard B. "Blameworthiness and Obligation." In *Essays in Moral Philosophy*, edited by A. I. Melden. Seattle: University of Washington Press, 1958.

Brandt, Richard B. "The Concepts of Obligation and Duty." *Mind* 73 (1964): 374–93.

————. "Utility and the Obligation to Obey the Law." In *Law and Philosophy*, edited by Sidney Hook. New York: New York University Press, 1964.

Burke, Edmund. *Reflections on the Revolution in France.* Garden City, N.Y.: Doubleday, 1989.

James A. Bush and Rece Bly. "Expectations of Privacy Analysis and Warrantless Trash Reconnaissance after Katz." *Arizona Law Review* 23 (1981): 283–322.

Cameron, J. R. "The Nature of Institutional Obligation." *Philosophical Quarterly* 22, no. 89 (October 1972): 318–32.

————. "Ought and Institutional Obligation." *Philosophy* 46, no. 178 (October 1971): 309–23.

Carter, W. R. "On Promising the Unwanted." *Analysis* 33, no. 3 (January 1973): 88–92.

Casper, Gerhard, and Philip B. Kurland, eds. *Landmark Briefs and Arguments of the Supreme Court of the United States.* Washington, D.C. University Publications of America, 1990.

Cavell, Stanley. *Must We Mean What We Say.* New York: Charles Scribner's Sons, 1969.

Collins, Hugh. Review of Atiyah, *Promises, Morals, and Law.* In *Modern Law Review* 45 (March 1982): 225–30.

"Comment: A Place for Consideration of Culture in the American Criminal Justice System: Japanese Law and the Kimura Case." *Detroit College of Law Journal of International Law and Practice* 4 (1995): 507–38.

"Comment: Privacy and the Growing Plight of the Homeless: Reconsidering the Values Underlying the Fourth Amendment." *Ohio State Law Journal* 53 (Summer 1992): 869–89.

Corbin, Arthur. "Offer and Acceptance." *Yale Law Journal* 26 (1917): 169–206.

Craswell, Richard. "Contract Law, Default Rules, and the Philosophy of Promising." 88 *Michigan Law Review* 489 (1989): 489–529.

Craswell, Richard, and Alan Schwartz, eds. *Foundations of Contract Law.* New York: Oxford University Press, 1994.

Dagger, Richard K. "What Is Political Obligation." *American Political Science Review* 71, no. 1 (1977): 86–94.

Daly, Markate, ed. *Communitarianism: A New Public Ethics.* Belmont, Calif.: Wadsworth, 1994.

Dawson, John P. *Gifts and Promises: Continental and American Law Compared.* New Haven: Yale University Press, 1980.

"Debate on Sec. 88 (Later Sec. 90) of the Restatement of Contracts." *American Law Institute Proceedings* 4 (1926): 85–114 (appendix).

Downie, R. S. "Three Accounts of Promising." *Philosophical Quarterly* 35, no. 140 (July 1985): 259–71.

Durrant, R. G. "Promising." *Australasian Journal of Philosophy* 41 (1963): 44–56.

Dworkin, Ronald. *Law's Empire.* Cambridge: Harvard University Press, 1986.

————. Review of Walzer, *Spheres of Justice. New York Review of Books,* 14 Apr. 1983, 406; and 21 July 1983, 65–68.

————. *Taking Rights Seriously.* Cambridge: Harvard University Press, 1977.

Eisenberg, Melvin. "The Bargain Principle and Its Limits." *Harvard Law Review* 95, no. 4 (February 1982): 741–801.

————. "Donative Promises." *University of Chicago Law Review* 47, no. 1 (fall 1979): 1–33.

————. "The Principles of Consideration." *Cornell Law Review* 67 (1982): 640–65.

Engelmann, Bernt. *In Hitler's Germany.* New York: Schocken Books, 1986.

Epstein, Richard. "Unconscionability: A Critical Reappraisal." *Journal of Law and Economics* 18 (1973): 293–315.

Farber, Daniel A., and John Matheson. "Beyond Promissory Estoppel: Contract Law and the 'Invisible Handshake.'" *University of Chicago Law Review* 52 (1985): 903–47.

Farnsworth, E. Allan. "The Past of Promise: An Historical Introduction to 'Contract.'" *Columbia Law Review* 69 (1969): 576–607.

———. "Precontractual Liability and Preliminary Agreements: Fair Dealing and Failed Negotiations." *Columbia Law Review* 87 (1987): 217–94.

Farnsworth, E. Allan, and William F. Young. *Contracts: Cases and Materials.* 4th ed. Westbury, N.Y.: Foundation Press, 1988.

Feinman, Jay. "Critical Approaches to Contract Law." *UCLA Law Review* 30 (1983): 829–60.

Flaherty, David H. *Privacy in Colonial New England.* Charlottesville: University Press of Virginia, 1967.

Flathman, Richard E. *Political Obligation.* New York: Atheneum, 1972.

Flechtheim, Ossip. *Hegels Strafrechtstheorie.* Berlin: Duncker und Humblot, 1975.

Fried, Charles. *Contract as Promise.* Cambridge: Harvard University Press, 1981.

———. "Privacy." *Yale Law Journal* 77 (1968): 475–93. Reprinted in *Philosophical Dimensions of Privacy,* edited by Schoeman.

———. Review of Atiyah, *The Rise and Fall of Freedom of Contract. Harvard Law Review* 93 (1980): 1858–68.

Friedman, Lawrence M. *Contract Law in America.* Madison and Milwaukee: University of Wisconsin Press, 1965.

———. *Crime and Punishment in American History.* New York: Basic Books, 1993.

Galante, Mary Ann. "Asian Refugee Who Shot Wife Receives 8-year Prison Term." *National Law Journal,* Dec. 16, 1984.

Gardbaum, Stephen A. "Law, Politics, and the Claims of Community." *Michigan Law Review* 90 (1992): 685–760.

Garfinkel, Simson. "Op-ed." *New York Times,* May 3, 1995.

Gavison, Ruth. "Privacy and the Limits of Law." *Yale Law Journal* 89 (1980): 421–71. Reprinted in *Philosophical Dimensions of Privacy,* edited by Schoeman.

Gellhorn, Walter. "Contracts and Public Policy." *Columbia Law Review* 35 (1935): 679–96.

Gerstein, Robert S. "Privacy and Self-Incrimination." *Ethics* 80 (1970): 87–101. In *Philosophical Dimensions of Privacy,* edited by Schoeman.

Gilliam, John. *Surveillance, Privacy, and the Law: Employee Drug Testing and the Politics of Social Control.* Ann Arbor: University of Michigan Press, 1994.

Gilmore, Grant. *The Death of Contract.* Columbus: Ohio State University Press, 1974.

Godwin, William. *An Enquiry Concerning Political Justice.* Vol. 1. New York: Alfred Knopf, 1926.

Goetz, Charles J., and Robert E. Scott. "Enforcing Promises: An Examination of the Basis of Contract." *Yale Law Journal* 89 (June 1980): 1261–1322.

———. "Principles of Relational Contracts." *Virginia Law Review* 67 (1981): 1089–1150.

Goffman, Erving. *Behavior in Public Places.* New York: Free Press, 1963.

Grant, C. K. "Promises." *Mind* 58, no. 231 (July 1949): 359–66.

Gregor, Thomas. "Exposure and Seclusion: A Study of Institutionalized Isolation among the Mehinaku Indians of Brazil." In *Secrecy,* edited by Tefft.

Gross, Hyman. "Privacy and Autonomy." In *Privacy,* edited by Pennock and Chapman.

Grotius, Hugo. *The Rights of War and Peace,* translated by A. C. Campbell. Washington, D.C.: M. Walter Dunne, 1901.

Gutmann, Amy. "The Challenge of Multiculturalism in Political Ethics." *Philosophy and Public Affairs* 22 (summer 1993): 171–206.

————. "Communitarian Critics of Liberalism." *Philosophy and Public Affairs* 14 (1985): 308–22. Reprinted in Daly, ed., *Communitarianism,* pp. 89–98.

Hale, Robert. "Bargaining, Duress, and Economic Liberty." *Columbia Law Review* 43 (1943): 603–28.

Hall, John Wesley, Jr. *Search and Seizure.* 2d ed. 2 vols. New York: Clark Boardman Callaghan, 1991.

Hamlyn, D. W. "The Obligation to Keep a Promise." *Proceedings of the Aristotelian Society* (1961–1962): 179–94.

Hanfling, Oswald. "Promises, Games and Institutions." *Proceedings of the Aristotelian Society* 75 (1974–1975): 13–31.

Hardimon, Michael. "The Project of Reconciliation: Hegel's Social Philosophy." *Philosophy and Public Affairs* 21, no. 2 (spring 1992): 165–95.

Hardin, Russell. *Morality within the Limits of Reason.* Chicago: University of Chicago Press, 1988.

Hare, R. M. "Ethical Theory and Utilitarianism." In *Utilitarianism and Beyond,* edited by Sen and Williams.

————. "The Lawful Government." In *Philosophy, Politics and Society,* 3d series, edited by Peter Laslett and W. G. Runciman, 157–72. New York: Barnes and Noble, 1967.

————. *Moral Thinking: Its Levels, Method and Point.* Oxford: Oxford University Press, 1981.

————. "The Promising Game." In *The Is-Ought Question,* edited by Hudson.

Harman, Gilbert. "Moral Relativism Defended." *Philosophical Review* 84 (1975): 3–22.

Hart, H. L. A. "Are There Any Natural Rights?" *Philosophical Review* 64, no. 2 (April 1955): 175–91. Reprinted in *Theories of Rights,* edited by Jeremy Waldron. Oxford: Oxford University Press, 1984.

————. "Legal and Moral Obligation." In *Essays in Moral Philosophy,* edited by A. I. Melden. Seattle: University of Washington Press, 1958.

Hegel, G. W. F. *Elements of the Philosophy of Right,* edited by Allen Wood, translated by H. B. Nisbet. Cambridge: Cambridge University Press, 1991. Cited as *PR,* with reference to paragraph numbers, remarks (R), and additions (Z).

————. *Encyclopaedia of the Philosophical Sciences (1830),* translated by William Wallace. 3 vols. Oxford: Oxford University Press, 1971.

————. *German Constitution.* In *Hegel's Political Writings,* translated by T. M. Knox. London: Oxford University Press, 1964.

————. *Grundlinien der Philosophie des Rechts.* Frankfurt am Main: Suhrkamp, 1976.

————. *Lectures on the History of Philosophy,* translated by E. S. Haldane. London: Kegan Paul, 1892.

————. *Lectures on the Philosophy of Religion,* edited by Peter C. Hodgson. Berkeley: University of California Press, 1988.

————. *Natural Law: The Scientific Way of Treating Natural Law, Its Place in Moral Philosophy, and Its Relation to the Positive Sciences of Law,* translated by T. M. Knox. Philadelphia: University of Pennsylvania Press, 1975.

————. *Phenomenology of Spirit,* translated by A. V. Miller. Oxford: Oxford University Press, 1977.

————. *Philosophie des Rechts: Die Vorlesung von 1819/20,* edited by Dieter Henrich. Frankfurt am Main: Suhrkamp, 1983.

————. *Philosophische Propädeutik.* In his *Werke,* edited by Moldenhauer and Michel, vol. 4.

————. *Philosophy of Right,* translated by T. M. Knox. Oxford: Oxford University Press, 1952.

————. *Reason in History,* translated by Robert Hartman. Indianapolis: Bobbs-Merrill, 1953.

————. "System der Sittlichkeit." In *Jenaer Schriften,* edited by Gerd Irrlitz. Berlin: Akademie-Verlag, 1972.

————. *Vorlesungen über Naturrecht und Staatswissenschaft,* edited by Claudia Becker et al. and introduced by Otto Pöggeler. Hamburg: Felix Meiner Verlag, 1983.

————. *Vorlesungen über Rechtsphilosophie (1818–1831),* edited by Karl-Heinz Ilting. 4 vols. Stuttgart-Bad-Canstatt: Friedrich Fromann, 1973.

————. *Werke in zwanzig Bänden,* edited by Eva Moldenhauer and Karl Michel. 20 vols. Frankfurt am Main: Suhrkamp Verlag, 1986.

Helmholz, R. H. "Assumpsit and Fidei Laesio." *Law Quarterly Review* 91 (July 1975): 406–32.

Holmes, Oliver Wendell. "The Path of the Law." *Harvard Law Review* 10 (1897): 457–78.

Hook, Sidney. "Hegel Rehabilitated?" In *Encounter* 24 (January 1965): 53–58.

Horwitz, Morton. *The Transformation of American Law, 1780–1860.* Cambridge: Harvard University Press, 1977.

Hudson, W. D., ed. *The Is-Ought Question.* New York: St. Martin's Press, 1969.

Hume, David. *A Treatise of Human Nature,* edited by L. A. Selby-Bigge, 477–534. 2d ed. Oxford: Oxford Univesity Press, 1978.

Kagehiro et al. "Reasonable Expectations of Privacy and Third-party Consent Searches." 15 *Law and Human Behavior* (1991): 122.

Kant, Immanuel. *Groundwork of the Metaphysic of Morals,* translated by H. J. Paton. New York: Harper and Row, 1964.

————. *The Metaphysics of Morals,* translated by Mary Gregor. Cambridge: Cambridge University Press, 1991.

————. *On a Supposed Right to Lie,* translated by James Ellington. Indianapolis: Hackett, 1993.

"Katz and the 4th Amendment." *Cleveland State Law Review* 23 (1971): 63–81.

Kemmis, Daniel. *Community and the Politics of Place.* Norman: University of Oklahoma Press, 1990.

Kemp, J. "Kant's Examples of the Categorical Imperative." In *Kant,* edited by Wolff.

Klosko, George. "Political Obligation and Gratitude." *Philosophy and Public Affairs* 18, no. 4 (fall 1989): 352–58.

————. "Presumptive Benefit, Fairness, and Political Obligation." *Philosophy and Public Affairs* 16, no. 3 (summer 1987): 241–59.

————. *The Principle of Fairness and Political Obligation.* Lanham, Md.: Rowman and Littlefield, 1992.

Knapp, Charles, "Enforcing the Contract to Bargain." *New York University Law Review* 44 (1969): 673–728.

Korn, Fred, and Shulamit R. Decktor Korn. "Where People Don't Promise." *Ethics* 93, no. 3 (April 1983): 445–50.

Korrgaard, Christine. "Kant's Analysis of Obligation: The Argument of *Foundations I.*" *Monist* 72, no. 3 (July 1989): 311–40.

Krausz, Michael, ed. *Relativism: Interpretation and Confrontation.* Notre Dame, Ind.: Univ of Notre Dame, 1989.

Kronman, Anthony. "Contract Law and Distributive Justice." *Yale Law Journal* 89 (1980): 472–511.

Kull, Andrew, "Reconsidering Gratuitous Promises." *Journal of Legal Studies* 21 (January 1992): 39–65.

Kymlicka, Will. *Contemporary Political Philosophy: An Introduction.* Oxford: Oxford University Press, 1990.

Linzer, Peter, ed. *A Contracts Anthology.* Cincinnati: Anderson, 1989.

———. "Uncontracts: Contexts, Contorts and the Relational Approach." *Annual Survey of American Law* 1988, 137–220.

Locke, Don. "The Object of Morality, and the Obligation to Keep a Promise." *Canadian Journal of Philosophy* 2, no. 1 (September 1972): 135–43.

Loewy, Arnold, "The Fourth Amendment as a Device for Protecting the Innocent." *Michigan Law Review* 81 (1983): 1229–72.

Macaulay, Stuart. "An Empirical View of Contract." *Wisconsin Law Review* (1985): 465–82.

MacCormick, Neil. "Voluntary Obligations and Normative Powers I." *Proceedings of the Aristotelian Society* 46 (1972): supp., 59–78.

MacIntyre, Alasdair. "Is Patriotism a Virtue?" In *The Lindley Lecture.* Lawrence: Kansas University Press, 1984. Also in Daly, ed., *Communitarianism.*

———. *Whose Justice? Which Rationality?* Notre Dame, Ind.: University of Notre Dame Press, 1988.

Macneil, Ian. "The Many Futures of Contract." *Southern California Law Review* 47 (1974): 691–816.

———. "Relational Contract: What We Do and Do Not Know." *Wisconsin Law Review* (1985): 483–525.

Mackie, J. L. *Ethics: Inventing Right and Wrong.* London: Penguin, 1977.

McCloskey, H. J. "An Examination of Restricted Utilitarianism." *Philosophical Review* 66 (1957): 466–85. Also in *Contemporary Utilitarianism,* edited by Michael Bayles. Gloucester, Mass: Peter Smith, 1978.

———. "'Two Concepts of Rules'—A Note." *Philosophical Quarterly* 22, no. 89 (October 1972): 344–48.

McGinn, Colin. *Moral Literacy or How to Do the Right Thing.* Indianapolis: Hackett, 1992.

McNeilly, F. S. "Promises De-Moralized." *Philosophical Review* 81 (1972): 63–81.

Maguigan, Holly. "Cultural Evidence and Male Violence: Are Feminist and Multiculturalist Reformers on a Collision Course in Criminal Courts?" *New York University Law Review* 70 (1995): 36–99.

Melden, A. I. "On Promising." *Mind* 65, no. 257 (June 1956): 49–66.

Melton, Gary B. "Minors and Privacy: Are Legal and Psychological Concepts Compatible?" *Nebraska Law Review* 62 (1983): 455–94.

Midgley, Mary. "The Promising Game." *Philosophy* 49, no. 189 (July 1974): 231–53.

Mish'alani, James. "'Duty,' 'Obligation' and 'Ought.'" *Analysis* 30, no. 2 (December 1969): 33–40.

MM. See Kant, *Metaphysics of Morals.*

Mulholland, Leslie. *Kant's System of Rights.* New York: Columbia University Press, 1990.

Murphy, Robert. "Social Distance and the Veil." In *Philosophical Dimensions of Privacy,* edited by Schoeman.

Narveson, Jan. "The Desert-Island Problem." *Analysis* 23, no. 3 (January 1963): 63–67.

———. "Promising, Expecting, and Utility." *Canadian Journal of Philosophy* 1, no. 2 (December 1971): 207–33.

Nussbaum, Martha. *Love's Knowledge: Essays on Philosophy and Literature.* New York: Oxford University Press, 1990.

———. "Non-Relative Virtues: An Aristotelian Approach." In *The Quality of Life,* edited by Nussbaum and Sen.

———. *Poetic Justice.* Boston: Beacon Press, 1995.

Nussbaum, Martha, and Amartya Sen. "Internal Criticism and Indian Rationalist Traditions." In *Relativism,* edited by Krausz.

———, eds. *The Quality of Life.* Oxford: Oxford University Press, 1993.

Oakeshott, Michael. *Rationalism in Politics and Other Essays.* Indianapolis: Liberty Press, 1991.

O'Hagan, Timothy. "On Hegel's Critique of Kant's Moral and Political Philosophy." In *Hegel's Critique of Kant,* edited by Priest.

Okin, Susan. *Justice, Gender, and the Family.* New York: Basic Books, 1989.

O'Neill, Onora. "Reason and Politics in the Kantian Enterprise." In *Kant's Political Philosophy,* edited by Howard Williams. Chicago: University of Chicago Press, 1992.

———. "Universal Laws and Ends-in-Themselves." *Monist* 72, no. 3 (July 1989): 341–62.

Paine, Thomas. *The Rights of Man.* New York: Doubleday, 1989.

Pateman, Carole. *The Disorder of Women: Democracy, Feminism, and Political Theory.* Stanford: Stanford University Press, 1989.

———. *The Problem of Political Obligation: A Critique of Liberal Theory.* 1979; Berkeley: University of California Press, 1985.

Peetz, Vera. "Promises and Threats." *Mind* 86 (1977): 578–81.

Pelczynski, Z. A., ed. *The State and Civil Society: Studies in Hegel's Political Philosophy.* Cambridge: Cambridge University Press, 1984.

Pennock, J. Roland, and John W. Chapman, eds. *Privacy.* NOMOS, vol. 13. New York: Atherton Press, 1971.

Phillips, Derek L. *Looking Backward: A Critical Appraisal of Communitarian Thought.* Princeton: Princeton University Press, 1993.

Phillips, D. Z., and H. O. Mounce. *Moral Practices.* New York: Shocken Books, 1970.

Pitkin, Hanna. "Obligation and Consent I and II." *American Political Science Review* 59 (December 1965): 990–99; and 60 (March 1966): 39–52.

———. "Relativism: A Lecture." *Journal of Social Philosophy,* 25th anniversary volume (1994): 176–87.

———. *Wittgenstein and Justice.* Berkeley: University of California Press, 1972.

Plamenatz, John. *Consent, Freedom and Political Obligation.* 2d ed. Oxford: Oxford University Press, 1968.

Posner, Richard. *Economic Analysis of Law.* 4th ed. Boston: Little, Brown, 1992.

———. "An Economic Theory of Privacy." *Regulation,* May–June 1978. Reprinted in *Philosophical Dimensions of Privacy,* edited by Schoeman.

———. "Gratuitous Promises in Economics and Law." *Journal of Legal Studies* 6 (1977): 411–26.

Power, Robert C. "Technology and the 4th Amendment: A Proposed Formulation for Visual Searches." *Journal of Criminal Law* 1 (spring 1989): 1–113.

PR. See Hegel, *Elements.*

Prichard, H. A. "The Obligation to Keep a Promise." In his *Moral Obligation.* Oxford: Oxford University Press, 1949.

Priest, Stephen, ed. *Hegel's Critique of Kant.* Oxford: Clarendon Press, 1987.

"Private Places." *New York University Law Review* 43 (1968): 968–87.

Prosser, William. "Privacy: A Legal Analysis." *California Law Review* 48 (1960): 338–423. Reprinted in *Philosophical Dimensions of Privacy,* edited by Schoeman.

Rachels, James, "Why Privacy Is Important." *Philosophy and Public Affairs* 4, no. 4 (summer 1975): 323–33. Reprinted in *Philosophical Dimensions of Privacy,* edited by Schoeman.

Rawls, John. "Legal Obligation and the Duty of Fair Play." In *Law and Philosophy,* edited by Sidney Hook. New York: NYU Press, 1964.

————. *Political Liberalism*. New York: Columbia University Press, 1993.

————. *A Theory of Justice*. Cambridge: Harvard University Press, 1971.

————. "Two Concepts of Rules." *Philosophical Review* 64 (1955): 1–22.

Raz, Joseph. "The Obligation to Obey: Revision and Tradition." *Notre Dame Journal of Law, Ethics and Public Policy* 1 (1984): 139–55.

————, ed. *Practical Reasoning*. Oxford: Oxford University Press, 1978.

————. "Promises and Obligations." In *Law, Morality, and Society*, edited by P. M. S. Hacker and J. Raz. Oxford: Oxford University Press, 1977.

————. "Promises in Morality and Law" (review of Atiyah, *Promises, Morals, and Law*). *Harvard Law Review* 95 (1982): 916–38.

————. "Reasons for Action, Decisions and Norms." In *Practical Reasoning*, edited by Raz.

————. "Voluntary Obligations and Normative Powers II." *Proceedings of the Aristotelian Society* 46 (1972): 79–102.

Rehnquist, William H. "Is an Expanded Right to Privacy Consistent with Fair and Effective Law Enforcement?" 23 *Kansas Law Review* 1 (1974): 1–22.

"Review of Atiyah." *Michigan Law Review* 81 (March 1983): 889–903.

Riley, Patrick. "On Kant as the Most Adequate of the Social Contract Theorists." *Political Theory* 1 (1973): 450–71.

————. *Will and Political Legitimacy*. Cambridge: Harvard University Press, 1982.

Ripstein, Arthur. "Foundationalism in Political Theory." *Philosophy and Public Affairs* 16, no. 2 (spring 1987): 115–37.

Robins, Michael H. "The Primacy of Promising." *Mind* 85 (1976): 321–40.

————. *Promising, Intending, and Moral Autonomy*. Cambridge: Cambridge University Press, 1984.

Rorty, Richard. *Objectivity, Relativism, and Truth: Philosophical Papers*. Vol. 1. Cambridge: Cambridge University Press, 1991.

————. "Solidarity or Objectivity?" In *Relativism*, edited by Krausz.

Ross, David. *The Right and the Good*. Oxford: Oxford University Press, 1930.

Ruben, David Hillel. "Tacit Promising." *Ethics* 83, no. 1 (October 1972): 71–79.

Rubenfeld, Jed. "The Right to Privacy." *Harvard Law Review* 104, no. 4 (February 1989): 737–807.

Rudinow, Joel. "Quitting the Promising Game." *Philosophical Quarterly* 22, no. 89 (October 1972): 355–56.

Sandel, Michael. *Liberalism and the Limits of Justice*. Cambridge: Cambridge University Press, 1982.

Sayers, Sean. "The Actual Is the Rational." In *Hegel and Modern Philosophy*, edited by David Lamb. London: Croom Helm, 1987.

Scanlon, Thomas. "Contractualism and Utilitarianism." In *Utilitarianism and Beyond*, edited by Sen and Williams.

————. "Promises and Practices." *Philosophy and Public Affairs* 19, no. 3 (summer 1990): 199–226.

Schaber, Gordon, and Claude Rohwer. *Contracts in a Nutshell*. 3d ed. St. Paul: West, 1990.

Schneewind, Jerome. "A Note on Promising." *Philosophical Studies* 17, no. 3 (April 1966): 33–35.

Schneider, Carl D. *Shame, Exposure and Privacy*. Boston: Beacon Press, 1977.

Schoeman, Ferdinand D., ed. *Philosophical Dimensions of Privacy: An Anthology*. Cambridge: Cambridge University Press, 1984.

————. "Privacy and Intimate Information." In *Philosophical Dimensions of Privacy*, edited by Schoeman.

————. *Privacy and Social Freedom.* Cambridge: Cambridge University Press, 1992.

————. "Privacy: Philosophical Dimensions of the Literature." In *Philosophical Dimensions of Privacy,* edited by Schoeman.

Searle, John, "How to Derive 'Ought' from 'Is.'" In *The Is-Ought Question,* edited by Hudson.

————. "Prima Facie Obligations." In *Practical Reasoning,* edited by Raz, 81–90.

————. *Speech Acts.* Cambridge: Cambridge University Press, 1969.

Selznick, Philip. *The Moral Commonwealth: Social Theory and the Promise of Community.* Berkeley: University of California Press, 1992.

Sen, Amartya, and Bernard Williams, eds. *Utilitarianism and Beyond.* Cambridge: Cambridge University Press, 1982.

Shell, Susan Meld. *The Rights of Reason: A Study of Kant's Philosophy and Politics.* Toronto: University of Toronto Press, 1980.

Sherman, Rorie. "'Cultural' Defenses Draw Fire; Double Standard." *National Law Journal,* Apr. 17, 1989.

Sherman, Spencer. "Legal Clash of Cultures." *National Law Journal,* Aug. 5, 1985.

Shlapentokh, Vladimir. *Public and Private Life of the Soviet People.* New York: Oxford University Press, 1989.

Sidgwick, Henry. *The Methods of Ethics.* 7th ed. Indianapolis: Hackett, 1981.

Simmons, A. John. "The Anarchist Position: A Reply to Klosko and Senor." *Philosophy and Public Affairs* 16, no. 3 (summer 1987): 269–79.

Simmons, A. J. *Moral Principles and Political Obligation.* Princeton: Princeton University Press, 1979.

Slobogin, Christopher, and Joseph E. Schumacher. "Reasonable Expectations of Privacy and Autonomy in Fourth Amendment Cases: An Empirical Look at 'Understandings Recognized and Permitted by Society.'" *Duke Law Journal* 42 (February 1993): 727–75.

Smiley, Marion. *Moral Responsibility and the Boundaries of Community.* Chicago: University of Chicago Press, 1992.

Smith, J. C. *Legal Obligation.* London: Athlone Press, 1976.

Smith, Steven. *Hegel's Critique of Liberalism.* Chicago: University of Chicago Press, 1989.

Sommers, Christina Hoff. "Philosophers Against the Family." In *Person to Person,* edited by George Graham and Hugh LaFollette. Philadelphia: Temple University Press, 1989. Also in Daly, ed., *Communitarianism.*

Spiro, Herbert J. "Privacy in Comparative Perspective." In *Privacy,* edited by Pennock and Chapman.

Stanlis, Peter J. *Selected Writings and Speeches of Edmund Burke.* Gloucester, Mass.: Peter Smith, 1968.

Steele, Lisa J. "Waste Heat and Garbage: The Legalization of Warrantless Infrared Searches." *Criminal Law Bulletin* 19 (1993): 19–39.

Steinberger, Peter. *The Concept of Political Judgment.* Chicago: University of Chicago Press, 1993.

Sullivan, William. *Reconstructing Public Philosophy.* Berkeley: University of California Press, 1982.

Summers, Robert. "The General Duty of Good Faith—Its Recognition and Conceptualization." *Cornell Law Review* 67 (1982).

Sunstein, Cass. "Preferences and Politics." *Philosophy and Public Affairs* 20 (1991):3–34. Reprinted in Daly, ed., *Communitarianism.*

Taylor, Charles. "Alternative Futures: Legitimacy, Identity, and Alienation in Late Twentieth Century Canada." In *Constitutionalism, Citizenship, and Society in Canada,* edited by

Alan Cairns and Cynthia Williams. Toronto: University of Toronto Press, 1985. Reprinted in Daly, ed., *Communitarianism*.

———. "Explanation and Practical Reason." In *The Quality of Life*, edited by Nussbaum and Sen.

———. *Hegel*. Cambridge: Cambridge University Press, 1975.

Tefft, Stanton K., ed. *Secrecy: A Cross-Cultural Perspective*. New York: Human Sciences Press, 1980.

Thomson, Judith Jarvis. "The Right to Privacy." *Philosophy and Public Affairs* 4, no. 4 (summer 1975): 295–314. Reprinted in *Philosophical Dimensions of Privacy*, edited by Schoeman.

Tunick, Mark. "Are There Natural Rights?—Hegel's Break with Kant." In *Hegel on the Modern World*, edited by Ardis B. Collins. Albany: SUNY Press, 1994.

———. "Hegel's Justification of Hereditary Monarchy." *History of Political Thought* 12 (1991): 481–96 (1991).

———. "Hegel's Nonfoundationalism: A Phenomenological Account of the Structure of *Philosophy of Right*." *History of Philosophy Quarterly* 11 (1994): 317–38.

———. "Hegel on Justified Disobedience." Forthcoming in *Political Theory*.

———. *Hegel's Political Philosophy*. Princeton: Princeton University Press, 1992.

———. "Is Kant a Retributivist?" *History of Political Thought* 17, no. 1 (spring 1996): 60–78.

———. *Punishment: Theory and Practice*. Berkeley: University of California Press, 1992.

Tussman, Joseph. *Obligation and the Body Politic*. New York: Oxford University Press, 1960.

Van den Haag, Ernest. "On Privacy." In *Privacy*, edited by Pennock and Chapman.

Wade, A. John. "Restitution for Benefits Conferred without Request." *Vanderbilt Law Review* 19 (1966): 1183–1214.

Waldron, Jeremy. "Particular Values and Critical Morality." *California Law Review* 77, no. 3 (May 1989): 561–90.

———. "Special Ties and Natural Duties." *Philosophy and Public Affairs* 22, no. 1 (winter 1993): 3–30.

Walker, A. D. M. "Obligations of Gratitude and Political Obligation." *Philosophy and Public Affairs* 18, no. 4 (fall 1989): 359–64.

Walker, A. D. M. "Political Obligation and the Argument from Gratitude." *Philosophy and Public Affairs* 17, no. 3 (summer 1988): 191–211.

Walzer, Michael. "The Communitarian Critique of Liberalism." *Political Theory* 18, no. 1 (February 1990): 6–23.

———. *Obligations: Essays on Disobedience, War, and Citizenship*. Cambridge: Harvard University Press, 1970.

———. Rejoinder to Dworkin. *New York Review of Books*, 21 July 1983, 65–68.

———. *Spheres of Justice*. New York: Basic Books, 1983.

———. *Thick and Thin*. Notre Dame, Ind.: University of Notre Dame Press, 1994.

Warnock, G. J. *The Object of Morality*. London: Methuen, 1971.

Warren, Samuel, and Louis Brandeis. "The Right to Privacy." *Harvard Law Review* 4 (1890): 193–220. Reprinted in *Philosophical Dimensions of Privacy*, edited by Schoeman.

Wasserstrom, Richard. "Privacy: Some Arguments and Assumptions." In *Philosophical Dimensions of Privacy*, edited by Schoeman.

Welch, Cheryl B., and Murray Milgate. "Implicit Contracts: Social Norms as Rational Choice." Paper presented at Western Political Science Association Conference, Pasadena, Calif., 1993.

Westin, Alan F. *Privacy and Freedom*. New York: Atheneum, 1967.

Wilkins, Richard G. "Defining the 'Reasonable Expectation of Privacy': An Emerging Tripartite Analysis." *Vanderbilt Law Review* 40 (1987): 1077–1129.

Williams, Howard. "Politics and Philosophy in Kant and Hegel." In *Hegel's Critique of Kant*, edited by Priest.

Wittgenstein, Ludwig. *On Certainty*, translated by Denis Paul and G. E. M. Anscombe. New York: Harper & Row, 1969.

Wolff, Robert Paul. *Kant: A Collection of Critical Essays.* Garden City, N.Y.: Doubleday, 1967.

Wolin, Sheldon. "Contract and Birthright." *Political Theory* 14, no. 2 (May 1986): 179–93. Reprinted in Daly, ed., *Communitarianism.*

Wood, Allen. "The Emptiness of the Moral Will." *Monist* 72, no. 3 (July 1989): 454–83.

———. *Hegel's Ethical Thought.* Cambridge; Cambridge University Press, 1990.

Yeager, Daniel B. "Criminal Law: Search, Seizure and the Positive Law: Expectations of Privacy Outside the Fourth Amendment." *Journal of Criminal Law* 84 (1993): 249–309.

Zemach, E. M. "Ought, Is, and a Game Called 'Promise.'" *Philosophical Quarterly* 21, no. 82 (January 1971): 61–63.

About the Author

MARK TUNICK is Assistant Professor of Political Science at Stanford University. He is the author of *Punishment: Theory and Practice* and *Hegel's Political Philosophy: Interpreting the Practice of Legal Punishment* (Princeton).